EXTERNAL DEBT

STATISTICS

GUIDE FOR COMPILERS AND USERS

 Bank for International Settlements

 Commonwealth Secretariat

 Eurostat

 International Monetary Fund

 Organisation for Economic Co-operation and Development

 Paris Club Secretariat

 United Nations Conference on Trade and Development

 World Bank

INTERNATIONAL MONETARY FUND

2003

Cataloging-in-Publication Data

External debt statistics : guide for compilers and users. — Washington, D.C. :
International Monetary Fund, 2003.
     p.   cm.

   Includes bibliographical references.
   ISBN 1-58906-060-1

   1. Debts, External — Statistics. 2. Debts, External — Statistical methods.
I. International Monetary Fund.
HJ8011.E75 2003

Price: $60.00

Please send orders to:
International Monetary Fund, Publication Services
700 19th Street, N.W., Washington, D.C. 20431, U.S.A.
Tel.: (202) 623-7430   Telefax: (202) 623-7201
E-mail: publications@imf.org
Internet: http://www.imf.org

recycled paper

Contents

PART I: CONCEPTUAL FRAMEWORK

Figures

Foreword

This volume, *External Debt Statistics: Guide for Compilers and Users* (the *Guide*), has been prepared under the joint responsibility of our eight organizations, through the mechanism of the Inter-Agency Task Force on Finance Statistics. The preparation of the *Guide*, under way since mid-1999, was based on the broad range of experience of our institutions in close consultation with national compilers of external debt and balance of payments statistics.

International financial crises in the late 1990s underscored the importance of reliable and timely statistics on external debt as a critical element for the early detection of countries' external vulnerability. Against this background, improving the quality and timeliness of key external debt data and promoting convergence of recording practices have been the focus in the preparation of the *Guide*. The *Guide* is a useful source of reference both for national compilers and users of external debt statistics.

The *Guide* updates the previous international guidelines on external debt statistics, *External Debt: Definition, Statistical Coverage and Methodology*, published by four of our organizations in 1988. During the 1990s, new statistical guidelines for national accounts and balance of payments statistics were established, and a substantial growth in financial flows between private sector institutions occurred, including the use of debt instruments and financial derivatives to manage and redistribute risk. The concepts set out in the *Guide* are harmonized with those of the *System of National Accounts 1993* and the fifth edition of the IMF's *Balance of Payments Manual*, also published in 1993.

We recommend that countries adopt the *Guide* as the basis for compiling and disseminating external debt statistics.

Andrew Crockett
General Manager
Bank for International Settlements

Donald C. McKinnon
Commonwealth Secretary-General
The Commonwealth Secretariat

Yves Franchet
Director-General
Statistical Office of the European Communities
  (Eurostat)

Horst Köhler
Managing Director
International Monetary Fund

Donald J. Johnston
Secretary-General
Organisation for Economic Co-operation and
  Development

Delphine d'Amarzit
Secretary-General
The Paris Club Secretariat

Rubens Ricupero
Secretary-General
The United Nations Conference on Trade
  and Development

James D. Wolfensohn
President
The World Bank Group

Preface

The need for comprehensive, comparable, and reliable information on external debt to inform policymakers, financial markets, and other users of statistics has long been recognized. This was once again reinforced by the international financial crises in the 1990s. Because they carry obligations to make future payments, external debt liabilities have the potential to create circumstances that render an economy vulnerable to solvency and liquidity problems. Moreover, as experience has shown, external vulnerability can have widespread economic costs, and not just for the initially affected economy. It is clear, therefore, that external debt needs to be measured and monitored. To this end, *External Debt Statistics: Guide for Compilers and Users* (the *Guide*) provides guidance on (1) the concepts, definitions, and classifications of external debt data, (2) the sources and techniques for compiling these data, and (3) the analytical uses of these data. The *Guide* is intended to be of use to both compilers and users of external debt statistics.

Evolution of This *Guide*

The previous international guidance on external debt statistics, *External Debt: Definition, Statistical Coverage and Methodology* (the "Grey Book"), was published in 1988 by the Bank for International Settlements (BIS), International Monetary Fund (IMF), Organisation for Economic Co-operation and Development (OECD), and World Bank. This publication provided a common definition of external debt. However, since its publication there have been new international statistical guidelines for national accounts and balance of payments statistics—the *System of National Accounts 1993* (*1993 SNA*) and the fifth edition of the IMF's *Balance of Payments Manual (BPM5)*; a tremendous growth in private sector financial flows, especially to private sector debtors; and, associated with these financial flows, an increased use of instruments such as debt securities and financial derivatives to manage and redistribute risk.

Against this background, the *Guide* provides a comprehensive conceptual framework, derived from the *1993 SNA* and *BPM5*, for the measurement of gross external debt of the public and private sectors. It draws on many of the concepts introduced in the Grey Book and is intended to provide clear guidance that can be applied consistently across the different sectors of an economy and across the different debt instruments used for borrowing. Thereafter, the *Guide* provides a scheme for classifying external debt by instruments and sectors that is developed into a presentation table for the gross external debt position. Data disseminated using this presentation table, and employing the concepts outlined earlier in the *Guide*, are essential for providing a comprehensive and informed picture of the gross external debt position for the whole economy. For countries in which there is a particular interest in public sector debt, the sector information can be rearranged to give focus to public and publicly guaranteed debt, consistent with the approach used by the World Bank's Debtor Reporting System. Such a presentation may be of central importance where public sector external debt is dominant, although vigilance in monitoring private sector debt liabilities is necessary because experience has shown that these can grow rapidly.

Further, from the evidence of the international financial crises of the 1990s, and from the experience of many countries, additional data series may be vital to assist in identifying potential vulnerability to solvency and liquidity problems arising from the gross external debt position. The important need for data on debt-maturity profiles and currency breakdowns has been highlighted in international forums and, together with improving coverage of private sector debt liabilities, has helped to motivate preparation of the *Guide*.

So, the *Guide* provides additional conceptual guidance, and presentation tables, for data series such as the debt-service schedule (especially relevant for liquidity analysis), the currency composition of debt, and other series known from experience to be of analytical use. The *Guide* also explains the concept of net external debt—that is, a comparison of the stock of external debt with holdings of external financial assets of similar instrument type—and incorporates financial derivative positions into external debt analysis.

Drawing on the broad range of experience in the international agencies involved in its production, the *Guide* provides advice on the compilation of external debt statistics, and the analytical use of such data. This advice is not intended to be comprehensive, but rather provides an overview of the issues. The work of international agencies in the field of external debt is outlined. Because the *Guide* is primarily intended to be a source of reference for both compilers and users of external debt statistics, certain sections will be more relevant for some audiences than others. For instance, the first section discusses complex conceptual measurement issues and provides detailed advice as a source of reference—this guidance is intended particularly for the compiler. In contrast, the section on the use of external debt data is directed toward both users and compilers. It is hoped that by this approach the *Guide* will contribute to better external debt statistics and an improved understanding of the complex issues involved in both compiling and analyzing them.

Acknowledgments

The production of the *Guide* has been jointly undertaken by the international agencies that participate in the Inter-Agency Task Force on Finance Statistics (TFFS), in close consultation with national compilers of external debt and balance of payments statistics. The TFFS is one of the interagency task forces formed under the aegis of the United Nations Statistical Commission and the Administrative Committee on Coordination—Sub-Committee on Statistical Activities, and was set up in 1992. It was reconvened in 1998 to coordinate work among the participating agencies to improve the methodological soundness, transparency, timeliness, and availability of data on external debt and international reserve assets. The TFFS was chaired by the IMF, and the work on the *Guide* involved representatives from the BIS, the Commonwealth Secretariat, the European Central Bank (ECB), Eurostat, the IMF, the OECD, the Paris Club Secretariat, the United Nations Conference on Trade and Development (UNCTAD), and the World Bank. The core participants in the TFFS's work on the *Guide* are listed below (affiliations are those in effect at the time of preparation of the *Guide*). Their expert contributions and comments made possible the production of the *Guide*.

Chair	Mrs. Carol S. Carson (IMF)
BIS	Mr. Karsten von Kleist
Commonwealth Secretariat	Dr. Raj Kumar
ECB	Mr. Remigio Echeverría
	Mr. Jean Galand
	Mr. Reimund Mink
Eurostat	Mr. Eduardo Barredo-Capelot
IMF	Mr. Neil Patterson
	Mr. Roger Pownall
	Mr. Robert Heath
	Mr. John Motala
	Mr. Christian Mulder
	Mr. Eduardo Valdivia-Velarde
OECD	Mr. Brian Hammond
	Ms. Deborah Guz
	Mrs. Jane Saint-Sernin
Paris Club Secretariat	Mr. Jérôme Walter
UNCTAD	Mr. Enrique Cosio-Pascal
World Bank	Ms. Punam Chuhan

The preparation of the *Guide* was primarily undertaken in the IMF. Mr. Robert Heath (Senior Economist, Balance of Payments and External Debt Division II, Statistics Department) was the primary drafter and also coordinated and edited the contributions of TFFS participants, national agencies, and other experts. The work was supervised by Mr. Neil Patterson (Assistant Director, Balance of Payments and External Debt Division I, Statistics Department) and Mr. Roger Pownall (Chief, Balance of Payments and External Debt Division II, Statistics Department).

The *Guide* benefited from the written contributions of other experts in the participating agencies; in particular, Mr. Jean Kertudo (BIS); Mr. Dev Useree, Mr. Andrew Kitili, and Mr. Jose Maurel (all Commonwealth Secretariat); Ms. Silvia von Ledebur (ECB); Mr. Marco Committeri, Mr. Richard Harmsen, Mr. Damoni Kitabire, Mr. René Piché, Mr. Sukhwinder Singh, and Ms. Beatrice Timmermann (all IMF); Mr. Steve Cutts (OECD); Mr. Pal Borresen (UNCTAD); and Mr. Paul Beckerman, Mr. Misha V. Belkindas, Mr. Anthony Richard Howe Bottrill, Ms. Hana Polackova Brixi, Ms. Nevin Fahmy, Mr. Sundarshan Gooptu, Mr. Frederick Henry Jensen, Ms. Marie-Helene Le Manchec, Mr. Deepak K. Mishra, and Ms. Gloria R. Moreno (all World Bank). Mr. Eduardo Valdivia-Velarde (Senior Economist, Balance of Payments and External Debt Division II, Statistics Department, IMF) was responsible for overseeing the preparation of the *Guide* in its final stages through publication, coordinating final comments, and refining the text. Ms. Elva Harris and Ms. Marlene Pollard (Statistics Department, IMF) provided administrative support in preparing the manuscript, and Mr. James McEuen (External Relations Department, IMF) copyedited the final manuscript and coordinated publication of the *Guide*.

Also, the TFFS acknowledges, with gratitude, the contributions of many compilers and users of external debt statistics in member countries. Responses to requests for comments on the draft *Guide* posted on the Internet in March 2001 came from many official agencies and others in countries across the world, and the text benefited enormously from these views. In addition, the following agencies, listed alphabetically by country, provided the case studies of country experience in various aspects of the compilation and use of external debt data. These case studies are set out in Chapter 14.

Australia	Australian Bureau of Statistics
Austria	Oesterreichische Nationalbank
Canada	Statistics Canada
Chile	Central Bank of Chile
India	Ministry of Finance and Reserve Bank of India
Israel	Bank of Israel
Mexico	Department of Public Credit
New Zealand	Statistics New Zealand
Philippines	Bangko Sentral ng Pilipinas
Turkey	Central Bank of Turkey
Uganda	Bank of Uganda

Carol S. Carson
Director
Statistics Department
International Monetary Fund

Abbreviations and Acronyms

ADB	Asian Development Bank
AfDB	African Development Bank
BIS	Bank for International Settlements
BOP	Balance of payments
BOPSY	*Balance of Payments Statistics Yearbook* (IMF)
BPM5	*Balance of Payments Manual*, fifth edition (IMF)
CBDMS	Computer-based debt-management system
CIRR	Commercial Interest Reference Rate (OECD)
CMFB	Committee on Monetary, Financial and Balance of Payments Statistics (EU)
CPIS	Coordinated Portfolio Investment Survey (IMF)
CRS	Creditor Reporting System (OECD)
CS-DRMS	Commonwealth Secretariat's Debt Recording and Management System
DAC	Development Assistance Committee (OECD)
DMFAS	Debt Management and Financial Analysis System (UNCTAD)
DOD	Disbursed and outstanding debt
DRS	Debtor Reporting System (World Bank)
DSM Plus	Debt Sustainability Module Plus (World Bank)
ECB	European Central Bank
ESA95	*European System of Accounts, ESA 1995*
EU	European Union
GDDS	General Data Dissemination System
GDP	Gross domestic product
GNF	Global note facility
Grey Book	*External Debt: Definition, Statistical Coverage and Methodology* (Bank for International Settlements, International Monetary Fund, Organisation for Economic Co-operation and Development, and World Bank, 1988)
HIPC Initiative	Initiative for heavily indebted poor countries
IADB	Inter-American Development Bank
IBRD	International Bank for Reconstruction and Development
IBS	International Banking Statistics (BIS)
IDA	International Development Association
IFMS	Integrated Financial Management System
IFS	*International Financial Statistics* (IMF)
IIP	International investment position
IMF	International Monetary Fund
ISIN	International security identification number
LIBOR	London interbank offered rate
MEFMI	Macroeconomic and Financial Management Institute for Eastern and Southern Africa
MOF	Multiple options facility
NIF	Note issuance facility

NNA	National numbering agency
NPISH	Nonprofit institutions serving households
ODA	Official development assistance
OECD	Organisation for Economic Co-operation and Development
OTC	Over-the-counter [markets]
Repo	Repurchase agreement
RUF	Revolving underwriting facility
SDDS	Special Data Dissemination Standard
SDR	Special drawing rights (IMF)
1993 SNA	*System of National Accounts 1993*
SPE	Special purpose entity
TFFS	Inter-Agency Task Force on Finance Statistics
UNCTAD	United Nations Conference on Trade and Development

1. Overview

1.1 The purpose of the *External Debt Statistics: Guide for Compilers and Users* (the *Guide*) is to provide comprehensive guidance for the measurement and presentation of external debt statistics. It also provides advice on the compilation of these data and on their analytical use. The intention is to contribute to both an improvement in, and a greater understanding of, external debt statistics. In doing so, the *Guide* is responding to the concerns of markets and policymakers for better external debt statistics to help assess external vulnerabilities at a time when increasing international capital flows are resulting in greater market interdependence.

The Grey Book

1.2 Previous guidance on the measurement of gross external debt was provided in *External Debt: Definition, Statistical Coverage and Methodology* (the "Grey Book"), published jointly in 1988 by the Bank for International Settlements (BIS), International Monetary Fund (IMF), the Organisation for Economic Co-operation and Development (OECD), and the World Bank. The Grey Book provided an agreed definition of what constituted external debt, with the intention of encouraging a greater consistency of approach in the measurement of external debt:

> Gross external debt is the amount, at any given time, of disbursed and outstanding contractual liabilities of residents of a country to nonresidents to repay principal, with or without interest, or to pay interest, with or without principal.

1.3 The measure of external debt using this definition is commonly known as disbursed and outstanding debt (DOD) and is valued on a nominal-value basis. Under this definition, there must be a contractual liability to make principal or interest payments, or both. The contractual liability—used in the wide sense of entailing a legal obligation—must be a claim of a nonresident on a resident to qualify as external debt, and only that part of the liability that is outstanding and disbursed qualifies as debt.

1.4 The DOD approach is a basic cornerstone of external debt statistics and provides the conceptual basis for the majority of the existing external debt compilation systems, including those of countries using the Commonwealth Secretariat and United Nations Conference on Trade and Development (UNCTAD) debt-management systems, and those of the OECD and World Bank. It has facilitated vulnerability, debt-sustainability, and creditworthiness analyses and can provide a transparent standard for comparable statistics across countries. For instance, the World Bank's *Global Development Finance* and the OECD's *External Debt Statistics* present and analyze data on a DOD basis.

1.5 To a considerable extent, the Grey Book reflects the traditional focus of external debt statistics, which is on borrowing from banks and government sources, often by the public sector. For the purposes of public debt management, a DOD measure of external debt allows a debt manager to determine how much is owed, to make budgetary projections, and to inform policymakers of the borrowing position in relation to any authorized limits. Also, DOD can serve as a baseline for debt managers to analyze the impact of exchange rate movements and indexation of principal on the stock of debt outstanding. In a number of countries, DOD is typically a measure derived from a debt-management system that records contractual obligations on existing debt, which are essential for cash-flow management and for implementing payments.

Conceptual Approach in the *Guide*

1.6 Depending on the stage of economic development, borrowing by the public sector from banks and government sources may still remain the focus of external debt analysis for a number of countries. But for many countries, the growth during the 1990s of cross-border private sector capital flows, the exposure of the private sector to foreign borrowing, the widespread issuance of debt securities, and the use of financial derivatives and similar instruments, have necessitated a wider scope of external debt analysis. In other words, in addition to the traditional focus, a need has increasingly arisen to monitor the cross-border financial borrowing activities of the nonbank private sector, including external borrowing by all sectors of the economy in the form of debt securities.

1.7 In responding to these developments, the *Guide* introduces a comprehensive conceptual framework that is derived from that contained in the *System of National Accounts 1993 (1993 SNA)*[1] and the IMF's *Balance of Payments Manual,* fifth edition *(BPM5)*[2] for measuring the gross external debt position. This approach facilitates consistency and comparability among external debt statistics and other macroeconomic statistics, such as balance of payments, the international investment position (IIP), and national accounts. Under this conceptual framework, external debt includes all liabilities as defined in the *1993 SNA* (excluding equity liabilities and financial derivatives) that are owed to nonresidents, and the total amount of such liabilities is presented as the gross external debt position.

1.8 This new conceptual framework draws on many of the concepts introduced in the Grey Book. For instance, external debt continues to include those instruments that are owed to nonresidents, require payments of interest and/or principal, and are out-standing. Thus, compilation systems developed to produce data on the basis of the Grey Book, particularly for the public sector, can be a statistical building block for the measurement of the gross external debt position outlined ahead. But the new framework also discusses and clarifies many items not discussed or decided in the Grey Book, particularly in respect to the range of instruments that are classified as external debt.

1.9 Tables are provided for the presentation of the gross external debt position, and related data, both for the whole economy and by sector of debtor. Using the concepts provided in Chapters 2 and 3, data compiled and presented in the format of the table in Chapter 4 provide a comprehensive and informed picture of the gross external debt position for the whole economy. Subsequently in Chapter 5, the gross external debt position is presented in a table that highlights the role of the public sector, a table particularly relevant for countries where the public sector is centrally involved in external debt borrowing activity, as a borrower and/or guarantor.

1.10 Further, the *Guide* provides additional accounting principles to assist in compiling data series of analytical use in understanding the gross external debt position. The priority that individual countries give to compiling each of these data series will vary depending on circumstances. But such data series as the debt-service schedule—that is, a schedule that provides information on the expected amounts and timing of future payments—and the foreign currency composition of external debt—one indication of the exposure of the economy to movements in the exchange rate—can reveal essential information on potential external vulnerabilities facing an economy. Similarly, the *Guide* advises on the measurement and presentation of the net external debt position—gross external debt less external assets in the form of debt instruments. For economies whose private sector is active in international financial markets, this concept, and indeed, that of the net asset position of the IIP,[3] is particularly relevant in assessing sustainability of the external position.

---

[1]The *1993 SNA* was published jointly by the Commission of the European Communities (Eurostat), IMF, OECD, United Nations, and World Bank. The *1993 SNA* is a comprehensive, consistent, and flexible set of macroeconomic accounts intended to meet the needs of government and private sector analysts, policymakers, and decision takers. Also, it is the point of reference in establishing standards for related statistics, such as government finance and monetary and financial statistics.

[2]*BPM5* was published by the IMF in 1993 and provides international guidelines for the compilation of data for an articulated set of international accounts encompassing the measurement of external transactions (balance of payments), on the one hand, and the stock of financial assets and liabilities (the international investment position, or IIP), on the other. There is harmonization to the maximum extent possible with the national accounts as articulated in the *1993 SNA*.

[3]The IIP of an economy is the balance sheet of the stock of external financial assets and liabilities, with the difference being the net asset (or liability) position. The IIP is described in Chapter 17 and its standard components are set out in Chapter 3.

Structure of the *Guide*

1.11 The *Guide* is presented in four parts:
  (I) Conceptual Framework—covering Chapters 2–9;
  (II) Compilation: Principles and Practice—Chapters 10–14;
  (III) Use of External Debt Statistics—Chapters 15 and 16; and
  (IV) Work of International Agencies—Chapters 17–19.

There are also several appendices.

Conceptual Framework

1.12 The structure of Part I is as follows:
- Chapter 2 provides a definition for gross external debt and explains in detail the accounting principles required for the measurement of the gross external debt position. Chapter 3 discusses the identification of institutional sectors and financial instruments.
- Chapter 4 sets out a table for the presentation of the gross external debt position. Highest priority is given to institutional sectors, followed by maturity and then type of instrument. Chapter 5 provides a table for the presentation of data on public and publicly guaranteed external debt.
- Chapter 6 provides further accounting principles for compiling additional data series of analytical use in understanding the gross external debt position. Chapter 7 provides further presentation tables (for example, a debt-service payment schedule and foreign currency debt tables).
- Chapter 8 discusses the dissemination of appropriate information on the impact of debt reorganization on external debt. Chapter 9 considers contingent liabilities and provides a table for the presentation of external debt on an ultimate-risk basis.

Compilation: Principles and Practice

1.13 Chapter 10 provides an overview of compilation methods, and Chapters 11, 12, and 13 cover compilation methods for government and public sector data; banks and "other sectors" data; and data on traded securities, respectively. Chapter 14 contains case studies of country experience in the compilation of external debt statistics.

Use of External Debt Statistics

1.14 Chapters 15 and 16 cover the analytical use of external debt data. These chapters are included to help compilers place their work in context and to assist users in interpreting the range of information that can be available. Chapter 15 briefly describes debt-sustainability analysis and explains some of the most commonly used debt ratios. Chapter 16 highlights the need to analyze external debt data in a broad context.

Work of International Agencies

1.15 Chapter 17 sets out the external debt data available from the BIS, IMF, OECD, and the World Bank, all of which have been developed to meet specific analytical needs. Chapter 18 covers the debt-monitoring systems of the Commonwealth Secretariat and UNCTAD. Chapter 19 discusses technical assistance activities in external debt statistics, and related macroeconomic statistics, of the international agencies involved in production of the *Guide*.

Appendices

1.16 Appendix I provides detailed definitions and classifications of debt instruments, and specific transactions. Appendix II discusses reverse security transactions and how they should be recorded in the gross external debt position. Appendix III provides a glossary of external debt terms. Appendix IV describes the relationship between the national accounts and the IIP. Finally, Appendix V explains the Initiative for Heavily Indebted Poor Countries (the HIPC Initiative).

PART I

Conceptual Framework

2. The Measurement of External Debt: Definition and Core Accounting Principles

Introduction

2.1 This chapter begins by updating the definition of external debt so that it is consistent with the concepts of *1993 SNA* and *BPM5*. The definition of external debt remains based on the notion that if a resident has a current liability to a nonresident that requires payments of principal and/or interest in the future, this liability represents a future claim on the resources of the economy of the resident, and so is external debt of that economy. Such an approach provides a comprehensive measure of external debt that is consistent across the range of debt instruments regardless of how they may be structured. The focus of the definition remains on gross liabilities—that is, excluding any assets.

2.2 A common theme throughout the *Guide* is that analysis of the gross external debt position of an economy requires information that, as far as possible, is compatible with related data series both within and among countries. Compatibility enhances the analytical usefulness and the reliability of data by allowing interrelationships with other related macroeconomic data series to be examined and comparisons across countries to be undertaken on a clear and consistent basis. Also, compatibility encourages the rationalization of collection procedures, through the integration of domestic and external debt data (thus lowering of the costs of data production). For these reasons, this chapter introduces accounting concepts for the measurement of external debt that are drawn from the *1993 SNA* and *BPM5*.

Definition of External Debt

2.3 The *Guide* defines gross external debt as follows: *Gross external debt, at any given time, is the outstanding amount of those actual current, and not contingent, liabilities that require payment(s) of principal and/or interest by the debtor at some point(s) in the future and that are owed to nonresidents by residents of an economy.*

Outstanding and Actual Current Liabilities

2.4 For a liability to be included in external debt it must exist and be outstanding. The decisive consideration is whether a creditor owns a claim on the debtor. Debt liabilities are typically established through the provision of economic value—that is, assets (financial or nonfinancial including goods), services, and/or income—by one institutional unit, the creditor, to another, the debtor, normally under a contractual arrangement.[1] Debt liabilities can also be created by the force of law,[2] and by events that require future transfer payments.[3] Debt liabilities include arrears of principal and interest. Commitments to provide economic value in the future cannot establish debt liabilities until items change ownership, services are rendered, or income accrues; for instance, amounts yet to be disbursed under a loan or export credit commitment are not to be included in the gross external debt position.

Principal and Interest

2.5 The provision of economic value by the creditor, or the creation of debt liabilities through other means, establishes a principal liability for the debtor, which, until extinguished, may change in value over time. For debt instruments alone, for the use of the

---

[1]In many instances, such as cash purchases by households in shops, economic value is provided against immediate payment, in which instance no debt liability is created.

[2]These liabilities could include those arising from taxes, penalties (including penalties arising from commercial contracts), and judicial awards at the time they are imposed. However, in some instances an issue will arise about whether a government has jurisdiction to impose such charges on nonresidents.

[3]These include claims on nonlife insurance companies, claims for damages not involving nonlife insurance companies, and claims arising from lottery and gambling activity.

principal, interest can (and usually does) accrue on the principal amount, resulting in an interest cost for the debtor. When this cost is paid periodically, as commonly occurs, it is known in the *Guide* as an interest payment. All other payments of economic value by the debtor to the creditor that reduce the principal amount outstanding are known as principal payments.

2.6 For long-term debt instruments, interest costs paid periodically are defined as those to be paid by the debtor to the creditor annually or more frequently; for short-term instruments (that is, with an original maturity of one year or less), interest costs paid periodically are defined as those to be paid by the debtor to the creditor before the redemption date of the instrument.

2.7 The definition of external debt does not distinguish between whether the payments that are required are principal or interest, or both. For instance, interest-free loans are debt instruments although no interest is paid, while perpetual bonds are debt instruments although no principal is to be repaid. In addition, while it may normally be expected that payments will be made in the form of financial assets, such as currency and deposits, the definition does not specify the form in which payments need to be made. For instance, payments could be made in the form of goods and services. It is the future requirement to make payments, not the form of those payments, that determines whether a liability is a debt instrument or not.

2.8 Also, the definition does not specify that the timing of the future payments of principal and/or interest need be known for a liability to be classified as debt. In many instances, the schedule of payments is known, such as on debt securities and loans. However, in other instances the exact schedule of payments may not be known. For example, the timing of payment might be at the demand of the creditor, such as non-interest-bearing demand deposits; the debtor may be in arrears, and it is not known when the arrears will actually be paid; or the timing of a payment may depend on certain events, such as the exercise of an embedded put (right to sell) or call (right to buy) option. Once again, it is the requirement to make the payment that determines whether the liability is debt, rather than the timing of the payment. So, the liabilities of pension funds and life insurance companies to their nonresident participants

and policyholders are regarded as debt of those institutions because at some point in time a payment is due, even though the timing of that payment may be unknown.

Residence

2.9 To qualify as external debt, the debt liabilities must be owed by a resident to a nonresident. Residence is determined by where the debtor and creditor have their centers of economic interest—typically, where they are ordinarily located—and not by their nationality. The definition of residence is explained in more detail later in this chapter and is the same as in *BPM5* and the *1993 SNA*. Clarification of the determination of residence for entities legally incorporated or domiciled in "offshore centers" is provided.

Current and Not Contingent

2.10 Contingent liabilities are not included in the definition of external debt. These are defined as arrangements under which one or more conditions must be fulfilled before a financial transaction takes place.[4] However, from the viewpoint of understanding vulnerability, there is analytical interest in the potential impact of contingent liabilities on an economy and on particular institutional sectors, such as government. For instance, the amount of external debt liabilities that an economy potentially faces may be greater than is evident from the published external debt data if cross-border guarantees have been given. Indeed, the *Guide* encourages countries to set up systems to monitor and disseminate data on contingent liabilities, as is discussed in more detail in Chapter 9.

Relationship with Instruments in the *1993 SNA*

2.11 From the viewpoint of the national accounts, the definition of external debt is such that it includes all financial liabilities recognized by the *1993 SNA* as financial instruments—except for shares and other equity, and financial derivatives—that are owed to nonresidents. Shares and other equity are excluded because they do not require the payment of

---

[4]The exclusion of contingent liabilities does not mean that guaranteed debt is excluded, but rather that the guaranteed debt is attributed to the debtor not the guarantor (unless and until the guarantee is called).

principal or interest. For the same reason, financial derivatives, both forwards and options, are excluded—no principal amount is advanced that is required to be repaid, and no interest accrues on any financial derivative instrument. Both forwards and options are described in more detail in Chapter 3. Nonetheless, an overdue obligation to settle a financial derivatives contract would, like any arrears, be a debt liability because a payment is required. Monetary gold and IMF special drawing rights (SDRs) are financial assets included in the *1993 SNA* but are not debt instruments because they are, by convention, assets without a corresponding liability.

Core Accounting Principles

2.12 This section considers the concepts of residence, time of recording, valuation, the unit of account and exchange rate conversion, and maturity. Unless otherwise specified, these concepts are applicable throughout the *Guide*.

Residence[5]

2.13 Debt liabilities of residents that are owed to nonresidents are to be included in the presentation of an economy's gross external debt position. Debt liabilities owed to residents are excluded. Hence the definition of residence is central to the definition of external debt. In the *Guide*, as in the *BPM5* and the *1993 SNA*, an institutional unit—that is, an entity such as a household, corporation, government agency, etc., that is capable, in its own right, of owning assets, incurring liabilities, and engaging in economic activities and in transactions with other entities—is a resident of an economy when it has its center of economic interest in the economic territory of that country.

2.14 To determine residence, the terms "economic territory" and "center of economic interest" also require definition. A country's economic territory consists of a geographic territory administered by a government; within this geographic territory, persons, goods, and capital circulate freely. Economic territory may not be identical with boundaries recognized for political purposes, although there is usually a close correspondence. For maritime countries, geographic territory includes any islands subject to the same fiscal and monetary authorities as the mainland. International (multilateral) organizations have their own territorial enclave(s) over which they have jurisdiction and are not considered residents of any national economy in which the organizations are located or conduct affairs; although employees of these bodies are residents of the national economy—specifically, of the economies in which they are expected to maintain their abodes for one year or more.

2.15 An institutional unit has a center of economic interest and is a resident unit of a country when, from some location (dwelling, place of production, or other premises) within the economic territory of the country, the unit engages and intends to continue engaging (indefinitely or for a finite but long period of time) in economic activities and transactions on a significant scale. The location need not be fixed as long as it remains within the economic territory. For statistical purposes, the conduct or intention to conduct economic activities for a year or more in an economic territory normally implies residence of that economy. But the one-year period is suggested only as a guideline and not as an inflexible rule.

2.16 In essence, an institutional unit is a resident of the economy in which it is ordinarily located. For instance, a branch or subsidiary is resident in the economy in which it is ordinarily located, because it engages in economic activity and transactions from that location, rather than necessarily the economy in which its parent corporation is located. Unincorporated site offices of major construction and similar projects, such as oil and gas exploration, that take over a year to complete and are carried out and managed by nonresident enterprises will, in most instances, meet the criteria of resident entities in the economy in which they are located, and so can have external debt (although the claims on the office by the parent might well represent an equity investment).[6]

2.17 The residence of offshore enterprises—including those engaged in the assembly of components manufactured elsewhere, those engaged in trade and financial operations, and those located in special zones—is attributed to the economies in which they are located. For instance, in some countries, banks, including branches of foreign banks, that are licensed to take deposits from and lend primarily, or

---

[5]See also *BPM5*, Chapter IV.

[6]The classification of parent claims on unincorporated branches is discussed in more detail in Chapter 3, in the section on direct investment.

even only, to residents of other economies are treated as "offshore banks" under exchange control and/or other regulations. These banks usually face different supervisory requirements and may not be required to provide the same amount of information to supervisors as "onshore" banks. Nonetheless, the liabilities of the offshore banks should be included in the external debt statistics of the economy in which they are located, provided that the liabilities meet the definition of external debt.

2.18 Similar issues can arise with "brass plate companies," "shell companies," or "special purpose entities" (SPEs). These entities may have little physical presence in the economy in which they are legally incorporated or legally domiciled (for example, registered or licensed), and any substantive work of the entity may be conducted in another economy. In such circumstances, there might be debate about where the center of economic interest for such entities lies. The *Guide* attributes external debt to the economy in which the entity, which has the liabilities on its balance sheet, and so on whom the creditor has a claim, is legally incorporated, or in the absence of legal incorporation, is legally domiciled. So, debt issues on the balance sheet of entities legally incorporated or domiciled in an offshore center are to be classified as external debt of the economy in which the offshore center is located. Any subsequent on-lending of the funds raised through such debt issues to a nonresident, such as to a parent or subsidiary corporation, is classified as an external asset of the offshore entity and external debt of the borrowing entity.

2.19 In some economies, separate identification of the gross external debt (and external assets) of resident "offshore banks" and other "offshore entities" is necessary because of the potential size of their liabilities relative to the rest of the economy.

2.20 In contrast, a nonresident may set up an agency in the resident economy usually to generate business in that economy. So, for instance, a resident agent may arrange for its parent foreign bank to lend funds to a fellow resident (the borrower). Unless the agent takes the transactions between the borrower and the creditor bank onto its own balance sheet, the borrower records external debt and not the agent. This is because the debtor/creditor relationship is between the lending bank and the borrowing entity, with the agent merely facilitating the transaction by bringing the borrower and lender together. If the agent does

take the transactions onto its balance sheet then it, not the final borrower, should record external debt from its parent foreign bank.

2.21 A regional central bank is an international financial organization that acts as a common central bank for a group of member countries. Such a bank has its headquarters in one country and usually maintains national offices in each of the member countries. Each national office acts as central bank for that country and is treated as a resident institutional unit in that country. The headquarters, however, is an international organization, and thus a nonresident from the perspective of the national central banks. However, for statistics relating to the economic territory of the whole group of member countries, the regional central bank is a resident institutional unit of this territory

Time of Recording[7]

2.22 The guiding principle for whether claims and liabilities exist and are outstanding is determined at any moment in time by the principle of ownership. The creditor owns a claim on the debtor, and the debtor has an obligation to the creditor.[8] Transactions are recorded when economic value is created, transformed, exchanged, transferred, or extinguished.

2.23 When a transaction occurs in assets, both financial and nonfinancial, the date of the change of ownership (the value date), and so the day the position is recorded, is when both creditor and debtor have entered the claim and liability, respectively, in their books. This date may actually be specified to ensure matching entries in the books of both parties. If no precise date can be fixed, the date on which the creditor receives payment or some other financial claim is decisive. For example, loan drawings are entered in the accounts when actual disbursements are made, and so when financial claims are established, and not necessarily when an agreement is signed.

2.24 For other transactions, when a service is rendered, interest accrues, or an event occurs that creates a transfer claim (such as under nonlife insurance), a debt liability is created and exists until payment is made or forgiven. Although not usual, like interest, service charges can accrue continu-

---

[7]See also *BPM5*, Chapter VI.
[8]Thus, the *Guide* does not recognize any unilateral repudiation of debt by the debtor.

ously. Although equity securities are not debt instruments, dividends once they are declared payable are recorded in *other debt liabilities* until paid.

2.25 The *Guide* recommends that interest costs accrue continuously on debt instruments, thus matching the cost of capital with the provision of capital. This recommendation is consistent with the approach taken in related international statistical manuals and in commercial accounting standards (see Box 2.1). For interest costs that accrue in a recording period, there are three measurement possibilities: (1) they are paid within the reporting period, in which instance there is no impact on the gross external debt position; (2) they are not paid because they are not yet payable (referred to hereafter as "interest costs that have accrued and are not yet payable")— for example, interest is paid each six months on a loan or security, and the gross external debt position is measured after the first three months of this period—in which instance the gross external debt position increases by the amount of interest that has accrued during the three-month period; and (3) they are not paid when due, in which instance the gross external debt position increases by the amount of interest costs that have accrued during the period and are in arrears at the end of the period.

Interest costs that have accrued and are not yet payable

2.26 Traditionally, external debt-recording systems have not recorded as external debt interest costs that have accrued and are not yet payable. At the time of publication of this *Guide*, the preference of many debt compilers remains to continue to exclude such interest costs from the gross external debt position. This is for two reasons. First, for countries with a few large external loans, borrowed at irregular periods, that have annual or semiannual interest payments, significant variation over time in the debt stock could arise from the inclusion of interest costs that have accrued and are not yet payable. Second, from a practical viewpoint, for some countries the inclusion of such interest costs in the gross external debt position could take some time to implement because it could involve a significant change to their present compilation system.

2.27 It is thus recognized that the recording of interest costs accruing on deposits and loans may have to follow national practices and be classified under *other debt liabilities*. Nonetheless, for those countries that can do so, the *Guide* recommends including interest costs that have accrued and are not yet payable as part of the value of the underlying instruments. That is, the accrual of interest costs not yet payable continuously increases the principal amount outstanding of the debt instrument until these interest costs are paid. This is consistent with the approach in the *1993 SNA* and *BPM5*. However, in order to maintain comparability of external debt statistics across time and across countries and to identify the variation introduced by the timing of recording of interest costs that have accrued and are not yet payable, the *Guide* requires that countries recording such interest costs complete the memorandum item identifying the sectoral and maturity breakdown of the item (as described in Chapter 4, paragraphs 4.8 and 4.9).

2.28 When bond securities (including deep-discount and zero-coupon bonds), bills, and similar short-term securities are issued at a discount (or at a premium), the difference between the issue price and its face or redemption value at maturity is treated, on an accrual basis, as interest (negative interest) over the life of the bond. When issued at a discount, the interest costs that accrue each period are recorded as being reinvested in the bond, increasing the principal amount outstanding. This approach can be described as the capitalization of interest; it is not a holding gain for the security owner. When issued at a premium, the amount accruing each period reduces the value of the bond.

Arrears

2.29 When principal or interest payments are not made when due, such as on a loan, arrears are created (a short-term liability that is included under *other debt liabilities*). But to ensure that the debt is not counted twice, there is a corresponding reduction in the appropriate debt instrument (for example, a loan). So, the nonpayment, when due, of principal and/or interest results in a reduction in the amount outstanding of the appropriate instrument, such as a loan, and an increase in arrears, leaving the external debt position unchanged. *Arrears* should continue to be reported from their creation—that is, when payments are not made[9]—until they are extinguished, such as when they are repaid, rescheduled, or forgiven by the creditor.

---

[9]In some instances arrears arise for operational reasons rather than from a reluctance or inability to pay. Nonetheless, in principle such arrears, when outstanding at the reference date, should be recorded as arrears.

Box 2.1. The Choice of a Recording Basis: The Case for Accrual Accounting[1]

Meaning of the Term "Recording Basis"

In the context of a macroeconomic statistical system, recording bases are defined mainly according to the time at which transactions are recorded in that system. Alternative recording bases are possible because for many transactions there can be a time lag between the change of ownership of the underlying item, the due date for payment, and the actual date for payment. Also, given the nature of the different recording bases the transactions and positions captured by them will also differ. Thus, an important consideration in choosing a recording basis is the information intended to be conveyed in the statistical system. For external debt statistics, the intention is to provide users of these data with a comprehensive measure of external debt liabilities at the end of the reporting period, and to allow them to identify the types of flows during the reporting period that affect the size and composition of these liabilities. Consequently, the *Guide* introduces the use of the accrual recording basis, for reasons explained below.

Main Types of Recording Bases

Three types of recording bases have most commonly been used in macroeconomic statistical systems: cash recording; due-for-payment recording; and accrual recording. In practice, variations on each of these main bases are often found.

With *cash recording*, transactions are recorded when a payment is made or received, irrespective of when the assets involved change ownership. In its strictest form, only those flows that involve cash as the medium of exchange are included (that is, cash inflows and outflows). The stocks recorded at the end of the reporting period in such a system are restricted to cash balances. But in practice, cash reporting basis is often modified to include other balances such as debt balances. In other words, when cash is disbursed on a debt instrument, an outstanding debt stock is recorded, and subsequent repayments of principal, in cash, reduce that outstanding debt.

A *due-for-payment recording* basis records transactions when receipts or payments arising from the transaction fall due, rather than when the cash is actually received or paid. The due-for-payment basis can be considered as a modification of the cash basis. In addition to cash balances, the due-for-payment basis

takes into account amounts due or overdue for payment. Typically, a due-for-payment basis of recording will record debt stocks on the basis of the redemption amount of the outstanding liability—the amount due for payment at maturity.[2] This amount may differ from the amount originally disbursed for a variety of reasons, including discounts and premiums between the issue and redemption price, repayment of principal, and revaluation of the debt due to indexation. Also, this recording basis will capture debt arising from some noncash transactions, such as arrears and the assumption of debt from one entity to another (for example, to the government).

On an *accrual recording* basis, transactions are recorded when economic value is created, transformed, exchanged, transferred, or extinguished. Claims and liabilities arise when there is a change of ownership. The accrual reporting basis thus recognizes transactions in the reporting period in which they occur, regardless of when cash is received or paid, or when payments are due. Gross external debt positions at the end of a reporting period depend on the stock of gross external debt at the beginning of the period, and transactions and any other flows that have taken place during the period.[3] The accrual recording basis records what an entity owes from the perspective of economic, not payment, considerations.

The different approaches of the three recording bases can be illustrated by the example of a loan, on which interest costs are paid periodically until the loan is repaid at maturity. The initial loan disbursement would be recorded in all three recording bases at the same time—that is, when the disbursement is made. All three systems would record a debt liability.[4] However, on an accrual reporting basis, interest costs are recorded as accruing continuously, reflecting the cost of the use of capital, and increasing the outstanding amount of the debt liability during the life of the loan, until the interest costs become payable. But on a cash or due-for-payment basis, no such increase would arise.

Interest payments on the loan and repayment of principal at maturity are recognized at the same time in all three systems, pro-

---

[1]This box draws on Efford (1996), which was prepared in the context of the development of the *Government Finance Statistics Manual*, IMF (2001).

[2]This is the approach taken in the IMF's *A Manual on Government Finance Statistics* (1986); see p. 217.

[3]In the *1993 SNA*, economic flows in financial assets and liabilities are limited to those financial assets and liabilities for which economic value can be demonstrated or observed.

[4]On the basis of the descriptions above of the cash, due-for-payment, and accrual reporting bases. For each reporting basis, there can be modifications of approach.

---

records an arrear until the creditor invokes the contract conditions permitting the guarantee to be called. Once the guarantee is called, the debt payment is attributed to the guarantor, and the arrear of the original debtor is extinguished, as though repaid.

classified as arrears of the guarantor but instead is classified as a short-term *other debt liability* until any grace period for payment ends.

Box 2.1 *(concluded)*

---

vided that these payments are made in the reporting period in which they are due. But if payments are not made when due, arrears would be recorded on the due-for-payment and accrual recording bases, but not on the cash basis (although in practice, a cash-based system might well be modified to include arrears). In the due-for-payment and accrual recording bases, a debt payment would be recorded as though made by the debtor, with an associated increase in (short-term) liabilities (arrears). Arrears are reduced when the payment is actually made. On a cash basis, no transactions would be recorded until the (overdue) payment is actually made; no arrears are recorded.

Thus, from the above example it can be seen that the accrual recording basis will record transactions at the same time as or before the cash and due-for-payment bases, and the due-for-payment basis would record transactions at the same time as or before the cash basis. For positions, on a cash basis, only amounts disbursed in cash and repaid in cash are taken into account; on a due-for-payment basis, amounts disbursed and repaid in cash are recognized along with any outstanding liabilities arising from noncash transactions—such as arrears; the accrual recording basis, in contrast, recognizes all existing liabilities regardless of whether cash has been disbursed or repaid, or payment is due or not.

Measuring External Debt Positions

Disadvantages of Cash and Due-for-Payment Bases

Both the cash and the due-for-payment bases have deficiencies in providing a comprehensive measure of gross external debt positions.

The cash recording basis contains information "only" on debt arising from cash flows; noncash transactions are not covered (for example, the provision of goods and services on which payment is delayed, and liabilities not met are not recognized, such as arrears). Thus, it provides insufficient coverage of external debt. Though the due-for-payment approach, as an extension of the cash basis, includes noncash transactions such as arrears and indexation, it still provides an incomplete measure of external debt. For instance, on a due-for-payment recording basis, payments not yet due for goods and services already delivered are not considered debt (unless, for example, there is a contractual agreement to extend trade credit). Also, interest is not recorded until due for payment, regardless of whether interest is in the form of a discount to the face value on issuance or in the form of interest payments (that is, paid periodically).

Advantage of an Accrual Basis

The accrual recording basis, which has long been used as the basis for commercial accounting, provides the most comprehensive information of the bases described, because it measures external debt on the basis of whether a creditor has ownership of a financial claim on a debtor. The accrual basis provides the most consistent measure of external debt, both in terms of coverage and size, in that it is indifferent (1) to the form of payment—debt can be created or extinguished through cash and/or noncash payments (that is through the provision of value); (2) to the time of payment—debt is created or extinguished dependent on the time at which ownership of a claim is established or relinquished; and (3) to whether the future payments required on existing liabilities are in the form of principal or interest.[5] As financial markets continue to innovate, this consistency of approach helps to ensure that the size and coverage of external debt is determined foremost by economic, and not payment, considerations.[6]

Finally, recording external debt on an accrual basis has the advantage of being consistent with other macroeconomic statistical systems, such as the *1993 SNA* and the *BPM5*, both of which employ an accrual basis of recording. These systems provide information on the types of economic flows during the reporting period that affect the size and composition of external debt. The *Government Finance Statistics Manual* (IMF, 2001) and the *Monetary and Financial Statistics Manual* (IMF, 2000d) are also on an accrual recording basis. Besides enhancing comparability of information across different sets of macroeconomic statistics for data users, the adoption of a common recording basis would also contribute to a reduction in compilation costs through the ability to use common data series in related statistical systems.

---

[5]In principle, under an accrual reporting basis the stock of external debt at any one moment in time reflects past transactions and other economic flows, and, provided that the same valuation method is employed, equals the discounted value of future payments of interest and principal. For instance, if financial markets convert interest into principal, such as through stripped securities, the process of conversion has no impact on the measured stock of external debt because no new debt is created (although on a market value basis there could be valuation consequences arising from such a conversion).

[6]Although information on payment arrangements might well be valuable in its own right.

Valuation[10]

2.31 The *Guide* recommends that debt instruments are valued at the reference date at nominal value,

---

[10]See also *BPM5*, Chapter V.

and, for traded debt instruments, at market value as well. The nominal value of a debt instrument is a measure of value from the viewpoint of the debtor because at any moment in time it is the amount that the debtor owes to the creditor. This value is typically established by reference to the terms of a contract between the debtor and creditor, and it is frequently used to construct debt ratios, such as those described in Chapter 15. The market value of a traded debt instrument is determined by its prevailing market price, which, as the best indication of the value that economic agents currently attribute to specific financial claims, provides a measure of the opportunity cost to both the debtor and the creditor.[11] It is the valuation principle adopted in the *1993 SNA* and *BPM5*.

2.32 The nominal value of a debt instrument reflects the value of the debt at creation; any subsequent economic flows, such as transactions (for example, repayment of principal); valuation changes (including exchange rate and other valuation changes other than market price changes); and any other changes. Conceptually, the nominal value of a debt instrument can be calculated by discounting future interest and principal payments at the existing contractual interest rate(s) [12] on the instrument; these interest rates may be fixed rate or variable rate. For fixed-rate instruments and instruments with contractually predetermined interest rates, this principle is straightforward to apply because the future payment schedule and the rate(s) to apply are known,[13] but it is less straightforward to apply to debt liabilities with variable rates that change with market conditions. The appendix at the end of this chapter provides examples of calculating the nominal value of a debt instrument by discounting future payments of interest and principal.

2.33 Face value has been used to define nominal value in some instances, since face value is the undiscounted amount of principal to be repaid. While of interest in showing amounts contractually due to be paid at a future date, the use of face value as nominal

value in measuring the gross external debt position can result in an inconsistent approach across all instruments and is not recommended. For instance, the face value of deep-discount bonds and zero-coupon bonds includes interest costs that have not yet accrued, which is counter to the accrual principle.

2.34 The market value of a traded debt instrument should be determined by the market price for that instrument prevailing on the reference date to which the position relates. The ideal source of a market price for a traded debt instrument is an organized or other financial market in which the instrument is traded in considerable volume and the market price is listed at regular intervals. In the absence of such a source, market value can be estimated by discounting future payment(s) at an appropriate market rate of interest. If the financial markets are closed on the reference date, the market price that should be used is that prevailing on the closest preceding date when the market was open. In some markets the market price quoted for traded debt securities does not take account of interest costs that have accrued but are not yet payable, but in determining market value these interest costs need to be included.

Nontraded debt instruments

2.35 As does *BPM5*, the *Guide* recommends that debt instruments that are not traded (or tradable) in organized or other financial markets—such as loans, currency and deposits, and trade credit—be valued at nominal value only.[14] The nominal value of a debt instrument could be less than originally advanced if there have been repayments of principal, debt forgiveness, or other economic flows, such as arising from indexation, that affect the value of the amount outstanding. The nominal value of a debt instrument could be more than originally advanced because, for example, of the accrual of interest costs, or other economic flows.

2.36 For debt instruments that accrue no interest—for example, liabilities arising because dividends are

---

[11]In the HIPC Initiative (see Appendix V), a representative market rate is used to discount future payments. This provides another measure of opportunity cost and is specific to countries in that program.

[12]A single rate is usually used to discount payments due in all future periods. In some circumstances, using different rates for the various future payments may be warranted. Even if a single rate of discount is used, dependent on the time until due, a different discount factor applies to each payment. For example, at a rate of discount of 10 percent, the discount factor for payments one year hence is 0.909 (or $1/(1 + 0.1)$) and for payments two years hence is 0.826 (or $1/(1 + 0.1)^2$) and so on. See also the example in Table 2.1.

[13]For a debt liability on which the interest rate steps up or down by contractually predetermined amounts over its life, the time profile of the discount factors to be applied to future payments would be nonlinear, reflecting these step changes.

[14]International statistical manuals consider that for nontraded instruments, nominal value is an appropriate proxy for market value. Nonetheless, the development of markets, such as for credit derivatives linked to the credit risk of individual entities, is increasing the likelihood that market prices can be estimated even for nontraded instruments. As these markets extend, consideration might be given to compiling additional information on market values of nontraded debt.

declared but not yet payable—the nominal value is the amount owed. If there is an unusually long time[15] before payment is due on an outstanding debt liability on which no interest costs accrue, then the value of the principal should be reduced by an amount that reflects the time to maturity and an appropriate existing contractual rate, and interest costs should accrue until actual payment is made.

2.37 For some debt, such as a loan, repayment may be specified in a contract in terms of quantities of commodities or other goods to be paid in installments over a period of time. At inception the value of the debt is equal to the principal advanced. The rate of interest, which will accrue on the principal, is that which equates the present value of the required future provision of the commodity or other good, given its current market price, to the principal outstanding. Conceptually, this type of contract is equivalent to the indexation of a loan, and so the initial rate of interest that accrues will change as the market price of the specified item changes, subject to any contractual arrangement (for example, limits in monetary terms on the maximum and minimum value that is to be paid by the debtor). When payments are made in the form of the good or commodity, the value of the principal outstanding will be reduced by the market value of the good or commodity at the time the payment is made.

2.38 In contrast, the value of the commodities, other goods, or services to be provided to extinguish a trade credit liability, including under barter arrangements, is that established at the creation of the debt; that is, when the exchange of value occurred. However, as noted above, if there is an unusually long time before payment, the value of the principal should be reduced by an amount that reflects the time to maturity and an appropriate existing contractual rate, and interest costs should accrue until actual payment is made.

2.39 The *Guide* recognizes the debt liabilities of pension funds and insurance companies to their nonresident participants and policyholders. The debt liability for a defined-benefit pension scheme is the present value of the promised benefits to nonresi-

dents; while for a defined-contribution scheme the debt liability is the current market value of the fund's assets prorated for the share of nonresidents' claims vis-à-vis total claims.[16] For life insurance, the debt liability is the value of the reserves held against the outstanding life insurance policies issued to nonresidents. The debt liability to nonresidents of nonlife insurance companies is the value of any prepayments of premiums by nonresidents, and the present value of amounts expected to be paid out to nonresidents in settlements of claims, including disputed, but valid, claims.

2.40 For arrears, the nominal value is equal to the value of the payments—interest and principal—missed, and any subsequent economic flows, such as the accrual of additional interest costs.

2.41 For nontraded debt instruments where the nominal value is uncertain, the nominal value can be calculated by discounting future interest and principal payments at an appropriate existing contractual rate of interest.

Traded debt instruments

2.42 The *Guide* recommends that debt instruments traded (or tradable) in organized and other financial markets be valued at both nominal and market value.[17] For a traded debt instrument, both nominal and market value can be determined from the value of the debt at creation and subsequent economic flows, except that market valuation takes account of any changes in the market price of the instrument, whereas nominal value does not.

2.43 For debt securities that are usually tradable but for which the market price is not readily observable, by using a market rate of interest the present value of the expected stream of future payments associated with the security can be used to estimate market value. This and other methods of estimating market value are explained in Box 2.2. For unlisted securities, the price reported for accounting or regulatory

---

[15]What constitutes an unusually long time in this context will depend on the circumstances. For instance, for any given time period, the higher the level of interest rates, the greater is the opportunity cost of delayed payment.

[16]In a defined-benefit scheme, the level of pension benefits promised by the employer to participating employees is guaranteed and usually determined by a formula based on participants' length of service and salary. In a defined-contribution scheme, the level of contributions to the fund by the employer is guaranteed, but the benefits that will be paid depend on the assets of the fund.

[17]This includes debt securities acquired under reverse transactions (see Table 4.5 in Chapter 4).

Box 2.2. General Methods for Estimating Market Value

When market-price data are unavailable for tradable instruments, there are two general methods for estimating market value or, as it is sometimes called, fair value:

- Discounting future cash flows to the present value using a market rate of interest; and
- Using market prices of financial assets and liabilities that are similar.

The first general method is to value financial assets and liabilities by *basing market value on the present, or time-discounted, value of future cash flows*. This is a well-established approach to valuation in both theory and practice. It calculates the market value of a financial asset or liability as the sum of the present values of all future cash flows. Market value is given by the following equation:

$$\text{Discounted present value} = \sum_{t=1}^{n} \frac{(Cash\ flow)_t}{(1 + i)^t}$$

where $(Cash\ flow)t$ denotes the cash flow in a future period (t), n denotes the number of future periods for which cash flows are expected, and i denotes the interest rate that is applied to discount the future cash flow in period t.

The method is relatively easy to apply in valuing any financial asset or liability if the future cash flows are known with certainty or can be estimated, and if a market interest rate (or series of market interest rates) is observable.

Directly basing market value on the market price of a similar financial instrument is a well-used technique when a market price is not directly observable. For example, the market price of a bond with five-year remaining maturity might be given by the market price of a publicly traded five-year bond having comparable default risk. In other cases, it may be appropriate to use the market price of a similar financial instrument, but with some adjustment in the market value to account for differences in liquidity and/or risk level between the instruments.

In some cases, the financial asset or liability may possess some characteristics of each of several other financial instruments, even though its characteristics are not generally similar to any one of these instruments. In such cases, information on the market prices and other characteristics (for example, type of instrument, issuing sector, maturity, credit rating, etc.) of the traded instruments can be used in estimating the market value of the instrument.

purposes might be used, although this method is less preferable than those mentioned above. Similarly, for deep-discount or zero-coupon bonds, the issue price plus amortization of the discount could be used in the absence of a market price.

2.44 If arrears are traded on secondary markets, as sometimes occurs, then a separate market value could be established.

Nondebt instruments

2.45 Positions in financial derivatives, equity securities, and equity capital and reinvested earnings on foreign direct investment are not included in the gross external debt position because they are not debt instruments, but they are recognized by the *Guide* as memorandum items to the position. These instruments are to be valued at market value.

2.46 The market value of a forward financial derivatives contract is derived from the difference between the agreed-upon contract price of an underlying item and the prevailing market price (or market price expected to prevail) of that item, times the notional amount, appropriately discounted. The notional amount—sometimes described as the nominal amount—is the amount underlying a financial derivatives contract that is necessary for calculating payments or receipts on the contract. This amount may or may not be exchanged. In the specific case of a swap contract, the market value is derived from the difference between the expected gross receipts and gross payments, appropriately discounted; that is, its net present value. The market value for a forward contract can therefore be calculated using available information—market and contract prices for the underlying item, time to maturity of the contract, the notional value, and market interest rates. From the viewpoint of the counterparties, the value of a forward contract may become negative (liability) or positive (asset) and may change both in magnitude and direction over time, depending on the movement in the market price for the underlying item. Forward contracts settled on a daily basis, such as those traded on organized exchanges—and known as futures—have a market value, but because of daily settlement it is likely to be zero value at each end-period.

2.47 The price of an option depends on the potential price volatility of the price of the underlying item, the time to maturity, interest rates, and the difference between the contract price and the market price of the underlying item. For traded options, whether they are traded on an exchange or not, the valuation should be based on the observable price. At inception the market value of a nontraded option is the amount of the premium paid or received. Subsequently nontraded options can be valued with the use of mathematical models, such as the Black-Scholes formulas, that take account of the factors mentioned above that determine option prices. In the absence of a pricing model, the price reported for accounting or regulatory purposes might be used. Unlike forwards, options cannot switch from negative to positive value, or vice versa, but they remain an asset for the owner and a liability for the writer of the option.

2.48 For equity securities that are listed in organized markets or are readily tradable, the value of outstanding stocks should be based on market prices. The value of equity securities not quoted on stock exchanges or not traded regularly should be estimated by using prices of comparable quoted shares as regards past, current, and prospective attributes such as earnings and dividends. Alternatively, the net asset values of enterprises to which the equities relate could be used to estimate market values if the balance sheets of the enterprises are available on a current-value basis, but this is not a preferred method given the possibly large difference between balance sheet and equity market valuations.

2.49 For equity capital and reinvested earnings related to foreign direct investment, it is recognized that, in practice, balance sheet values of direct investment enterprises or direct investors are generally utilized to determine their value. If these balance sheet values are on a current market value basis, this valuation would be in accordance with the market value principle, but if these values are based on historical cost and not current revaluation, they would not conform to the principle. If historical cost from the balance sheets of direct investment enterprises (or investors) is used to determine the value of equity capital and reinvested earnings, compilers are also encouraged to collect data from enterprises on a current market value basis. In instances where the shares of direct investment enterprises are listed on stock exchanges, the listed prices should be used to calculate the market value of shares in those enterprises.

Unit of Account and Exchange Rate Conversion

2.50 The compilation of the gross external debt position statement is complicated by the fact that the liabilities may be expressed initially in a variety of currencies or in other standards of value, such as SDRs. The conversion of these liabilities into a reference unit of account is a requisite for the construction of consistent and analytically meaningful gross external debt statistics.

2.51 From the perspective of the national compiler, the domestic currency unit is the obvious choice for measuring the gross external debt position. Such a position so denominated is compatible with the national accounts and most of the economy's other economic and monetary statistics expressed in that unit. However, if the currency is subject to significant fluctuation relative to other currencies, a statement denominated in domestic currency could be of diminished analytical value because valuation changes could dominate interperiod comparisons.

2.52 The most appropriate exchange rate to be used for conversion of external debt (and assets) denominated in foreign currencies into the unit of account is the market (spot) rate prevailing on the reference date to which the position relates. The midpoint between buying and selling rates should be used. For conversion of debt in a multiple rate system,[18] the rate on the reference date for the actual exchange rate applicable to specific liabilities (and assets) should be used.

Maturity

2.53 For debt liabilities, it is recommended that the traditional distinction between long- and short-term maturity, based on the formal criterion of original maturity, be retained. Long-term debt is defined as debt with an original maturity of more than one year or with no stated maturity. Short-term debt, which includes currency, is defined as debt repayable on demand or with an original maturity of one year or less. If an instrument has an original maturity of one year or less it should be classified as short-term, even if the instrument is issued under an arrangement that is long-term in nature.

Appendix: Accrual of Interest Costs— How Should This Be Implemented?

2.54 The *Guide* introduces the idea of including interest costs that have accrued and are not yet

---

[18]A multiple exchange rate system is a scheme for which there are schedules of exchange rates, set by the authorities, used to apply separate exchange rates to various categories of transactions or transactors.

payable in the gross external debt position. This annex presents the theoretical framework for the accrual of interest costs, and a more detailed discussion on how to apply the accrual principle, by type of instrument.

2.55 Because the focus of the *Guide* is on position statistics, the debate about whether the rate at which interest should accrue on market-traded instruments should be based on the current market value of the debt (the so-called creditor approach) or as stipulated in the original contract (the so-called debtor approach) is not relevant. This is because the market value position to be reported is based on the market price of the instrument, and that value should include any interest costs that have accrued and are not yet payable.[19] Given this, unless otherwise stated, this annex focuses on nominal value.

2.56 At the outset, it is worth noting some key principles for applying the accrual of interest costs principle in both the nominal and market value presentations of external debt:

• All financial instruments bearing interest are included;
• The accrual of interest costs can be calculated by the straightline or compound interest method;
• All instruments issued at a discount are treated in a similar manner; and
• The accrual of interest costs also applies to variable-rate and index-linked instruments.

Theoretical Framework for the Accrual of Interest Costs

2.57 Three examples, drawn from work undertaken by Statistics Canada (see Laliberté and Tremblay, 1996), are provided to illustrate the theoretical framework for the accrual of interest costs. These examples, and the discussion on accruing interest costs on a straightline or compound basis that immediately follows, provide an explanation of the basic principles.

2.58 The first example is that of a simple instrument that is issued and redeemed at the same price

and pays fixed annual interest at the end of each year; the second example is of an instrument issued at a price that is at a discount to the redemption price, and that also makes annual interest payments; and the third example is of an instrument issued at a discount that has no interest payments. These examples have general applicability throughout the *Guide*, in that they explain how future payments can be discounted to produce the stock of external debt at any moment in time.

Example 1: Present Value and the Accrual of Interest Costs—Simple Case

2.59 In this simple example, a debt instrument is issued with a five-year maturity, a principal amount of $100, and annual payments of $10 each year as interest. That is, the interest rate on the instrument is fixed at 10 percent a year. Given this, as seen in Table 2.1, in present value terms the payment of $10 in a year's time is worth $10/(1+0.1)$, or 9.09; the payment of $10 in two years' time is worth $10/(1+0.1)^2$, or 8.26; and so on. In present value terms, the principal amount advanced to be repaid at maturity is worth $100/(1+0.1)^5$, or 62.09. The present value for each payment is provided in the left-hand column, and it can be seen that the present value of all future payments equals the issue price of $100.

2.60 Because interest costs accrue at 10 percent a year on a continuous basis, and are added to the principal amount, after six months of the first year the principal amount has increased. It equals the $100 principal amount due to be paid at maturity, plus half of the year's interest payment, $5 (calculated on a straightline basis), or plus just under half, $4.88 (calculated on a compound basis). Any payments of interest, or principal, would reduce the amount outstanding.

2.61 Alternatively, the principal amount outstanding after six months could be calculated by discounting all future payments. The present value of each payment after six months is presented in parentheses in the left-hand column. After six months, each of the values in the left-hand column has increased because the payments are closer to being made, and time is being discounted at a rate of 10 percent a year. The discounted value of each payment after six months can be seen to sum to $104.88, the same amount outstanding as with

---

[19]If an economy was disseminating a debt-service ratio with future interest and principal payments calculated using the current yield on debt, then if the market value of external debt rises, part of the future interest payments could become principal payments.

Table 2.1. Present Value and the Accrual of Interest Costs: Example 1 (Simple Case)

Present Value in 2001		2002	2003	2004	2005	2006
9.09	(9.54)*	$10/(1+0.1)$				
8.26	(8.66)		$10/(1+0.1)^2$			
7.52	(7.89)			$10/(1+0.1)^3$		
6.83	(7.16)				$10/(1+0.1)^4$	
6.21	(6.51)					$10/(1+0.1)^5$
37.91	(39.76)	$10/(1+0.1)$	$10/(1+0.1)^2$	$10/(1+0.1)^3$	$10/(1+0.1)^4$	$10/(1+0.1)^5$
+62.09	(65.12)					$100/(1+0.1)^5$
=100.00	(104.88)					

*(9.54) = The present value of the payment six months after issuance of the debt instrument.

the compound approach to accruing interest costs. One practical advantage of maintaining a system that discounts each payment to its present value is that if the instrument is stripped (see below)—that is, all payments traded separately—the compilation system will already be prepared for such a situation.

2.62 Unless there are early repayments that reduce the amount of principal outstanding—for instance, with certain types of asset-backed securities, partial repayments of principal could occur at any time—the amounts described above would be recorded in the gross external debt position; that is, after six months with a contractual interest rate of ten percent per annum, the amount outstanding would be $104.88 (or $105 on a straightline basis).

2.63 The rate relevant for discounting all the payments to a market value would be implicit in the market price, or to put it another way, the market value amount would equal future payments discounted at the current market rate of interest for that debt instrument. The market value of external debt should include any interest costs that have accrued and are not yet payable.

Example 2: Present Value and the Accrual of Interest Costs—Discounted Principal

2.64 The second example concerns the more complex case of instruments issued at a discount to the redemption value. These instruments will include securities, and any other instruments where the issue price is less than the redemption

price.[20] In this instance, both the coupon payments and the difference between the issue price and the redemption price determine the rate at which interest costs accrue. Table 2.2 presents the calculations involving an instrument similar to that in the first example above—that is, issued with the same 10 percent yield, but "only" having annual interest payments of $8. The difference between the 10 percent yield and the yield implied by coupon payments is reflected in the discount between the issue price and redemption price. Once again, from the left-hand column of the table it can be seen that discounting all the future payments by 10 percent, including the principal amount, provides the issue price of $92.40.

2.65 How is the accrual of interest costs calculated? Simply, interest costs accrue at a yield of 10 percent each year, of which $8 is paid out in interest payments and the rest is reinvested (or capitalized) into the original principal amount. The principal amount grows from year to year, due to the continued reinvestment of interest costs that have accrued, and as a consequence, so does the absolute amount of interest costs that accrue each year. As with the first example, the present value of each payment

---

[20]For instruments issued at a discount, issue price is a generic term that means the value of principal at inception of the debt; redemption price is similarly a generic term that means the amount of principal to be paid at maturity. This is because some instruments are "issued" without a price as such (for instance, trade credit). In such instances, the issue price equals the economic value provided (that is, of goods or services provided) and the redemption price equals the amount owed when the debt liability is due to be paid.

Table 2.2. Present Value and the Accrual of Interest Costs: Example 2 (Discounted Principal)

Present Value in 2001		2002	2003	2004	2005	2006
7.27	(7.62)*	$8/(1+0.1)$				
6.61	(6.93)		$8/(1+0.1)^2$			
6.01	(6.30)			$8/(1+0.1)^3$		
5.46	(5.73)				$8/(1+0.1)^4$	
4.97	(5.21)					$8/(1+0.1)^5$
30.31	(31.79)	$8/(1+0.1)$	$8/(1+0.1)^2$	$8/(1+0.1)^3$	$8/(1+0.1)^4$	$8/(1+0.1)^5$
+62.09	(65.12)					$100/(1+0.1)^5$
=92.40	(96.91)					

*(7.62) = The present value of the payment six months after issuance of the debt instrument.

after six months is presented in parentheses in the left-hand column. In the position data, the amount outstanding can be seen to be $96.91 after six months.

Example 3: Present Value and the Accrual of Interest—Zero-Coupon Instrument

2.66 The third example covers zero-coupon instruments. If the instrument is issued at discount and has no coupon, then the principal amount increases in value over time by the implicit yield on the security at issuance, derived from the difference between the issue price and the redemption price. In the example below, the zero-coupon instrument is issued at $62.09 and is to be redeemed at $100; the difference implies a 10 percent yield. As can be seen in Table 2.3, the principal amount grows each year because of the continued reinvestment of interest costs that accrue, and so after the first year the amount outstanding has increased by 10 percent to $68.30, by a further 10 percent in year two to $75.13, and so on until redemption at $100 at the end of year five.[21]

Straightline or compound interest

2.67 In calculating the accrual of interest costs by a straightline approach, an equal amount of the interest costs to be paid is attributed to each period—for example, $5 for the first six months in the first

example above. For bonds with interest payments (that is, annual or more frequent), on secondary markets the buyer of the bond pays to the seller the amount accrued since the last payment, according to a very simple arithmetic proportionality. For many international loans, debt-monitoring systems record the accrual of interest costs on a straightline basis.

2.68 However, the accrual of interest costs can also be calculated on a compound basis—that is, continuously adding the accrued interest costs not yet payable to the principal amount each period, and applying to that amount the interest yield on the debt in order to calculate the interest costs for the next period. This method is the theoretically preferred approach because it relates the cost to the provision of capital and allows reconciliation between amounts accrued and the discounted value of future payments. Such an approach is commonly used when information on individual instruments owned by nonresidents is unknown, and so to calculate the accrual of interest costs an average yield is applied to positions. Of course, in such instances the theoretical benefit of using a yield is offset by the approximation of applying an average yield to a range of instruments.

2.69 Differences in methods may well have a small effect on the gross external debt position. However, as is evident from the first example, for each instrument the straightline approach will overestimate the position in the short term. For fixed-rate instruments, this will be gradually "unwound" as the time of the interest payment approaches.

---

[21]A worked example of accruing interest on a zero-coupon bond in the balance of payments is given in the IMF's *Balance of Payments Textbook* (1996), paragraphs 400 and 401, p. 83.

Table 2.3. Present Value and the Accrual of Interest Costs: Example 3 (Zero-Coupon Instrument)

Present Value in 2001	2002	2003	2004	2005	2006
$100/(1 + 0.1)$ $= 62.09$	$62.09\,(1 + 0.1)$ $= 68.30$	$62.09\,(1 + 0.1)^2$ $= 75.13$	$62.09\,(1 + 0.1)^3$ $= 82.64$	$62.09\,(1 + 0.1)^4$ $= 90.90$	$62.09\,(1 + 0.1)^5$ $= 100$

Specific Instruments[22]

Fixed-rate instruments

Loans

2.70 For loans (except interest-free loans) interest costs are recorded as accruing continuously, increasing the value of the loan outstanding, until paid. When loans have been rescheduled and a new (moratorium) interest rate agreed between the debtor and creditor, interest costs should accrue on the rescheduled debt at the new moratorium interest rate. It is recognized that interest costs that accrue on loans may have to follow national practices and be classified under *other debt liabilities*.

Deposits

2.71 For deposits, interest may be credited to the account (reinvested) at certain times, such as the end of a given period. In the *Guide*, interest costs accrue continuously and become part of principal on a continuous basis. It is recognized that interest costs that accrue on deposits may have to follow national practices and be classified under *other debt liabilities*.

2.72 For some deposits, such as time or savings deposits, a given rate of interest may be paid only under the condition of a minimum holding period. An early liquidation, if contractually allowed, is balanced by a reduction in the rate of interest paid to the holder. For recording the accrual of interest costs, the rate of interest to use is the maximum rate that the depositor could receive in the normal course of the contract (that is, respecting the arrangements about maturity or notice). In the event, if the arrangements are not fully respected, the amount of interest costs that accrued previously are corrected in line with the rate the depositor actually received. As the revised amount is in all likelihood globally very small compared with the total interest costs for deposits, for practical reasons the correction could be included in the last period of compilation (as opposed to revising back data).

Securities

2.73 For securities for which the issue and redemption prices are the same, interest costs accrue in the same manner as for loans.

Instruments issued at a discount

2.74 Instruments for which the issue price is less than the redemption price are all treated in the same way. This includes nontraded instruments where the amount to be paid is greater than the economic value provided at inception of the debt. The method of accrual for instruments issued at a discount or premium was described in paragraph 2.28 above.

2.75 For short-term negotiable instruments,[23] issuance at a discount is very frequent. Generally these instruments are akin to zero-coupon bonds (example 3 above), and so the treatment of such instruments is the same. Without information on individual securities, one practical approach is to base estimates of the accrual of interest costs on average maturities and average rates of interest at issuance.

2.76 External debt, particularly general government debt, could be issued in the form of fungible bonds (also named linear bonds). In this case, secu-

---

[22]This text has drawn upon that in Eurostat (2000), the *ESA95 Manual on Government Deficit and Debt*.

[23]A negotiable financial instrument is one whose legal ownership is capable of being transferred from one unit to another unit by delivery or endorsement.

rities are issued under one similar "line" (in terms of coupon amounts and payment dates, and final redemption price and maturity date) in tranches, generally issued during a rather short period but sometimes over a longer one. Each tranche is issued at a specific issue price according to the prevailing market conditions. Fungible bonds may be seen as a good example of instruments with two interest components: the coupon (representing the interest payment), and the difference between the issue price and redemption price. Thus, in principle each tranche should be identified separately because the nominal interest rate might well differ from tranche to tranche given the different market conditions that existed when they were issued. Once issued, however, the tranches may mix and so may not trade separately on secondary markets, nor be identified separately in portfolios. If so, it is necessary to estimate a weighted-average interest rate resulting from issuing different tranches, updated at each new issue, and apply this to the amount owed to nonresidents.[24]

Stripped securities

2.77 Stripped securities are securities that have been transformed from a principal amount with interest payments into a series of zero-coupon bonds, with a range of maturities matching the interest payment dates and the redemption date of the principal amount. The essence of stripping was described in the first example above: the coupon payment amounts are separately traded. In itself, the act of stripping does not affect the nominal value of the debt outstanding for the issuer of the securities that have been stripped.

2.78 There are two types of stripping. First, if the stripped securities are issued by a third party, who has acquired the original securities and is using them to "back" the issue of the stripped securities, then new funds have been raised by the third party, with the interest rate determined at the time of issuance.

2.79 On the other hand, if the owner of the original security has asked the settlement house or clearing house in which the security is registered to "issue" strips from the original security, the strips replace the original security and remain the direct obligation of the issuer of the original security. In the gross external debt position on a nominal value basis, it is unrealistic from a practical point of view to take into account the rate prevailing at the issuance of each strip. Rather, since stripping provides no additional funding to the issuer and there is no impact on the original cost of borrowing, fully determined at the issuance time (in the case of fixed-rate) or following rules that cannot be changed (in the case of variable-rate), it is assumed that stripping does not change the cost of borrowing. So, unlike other zero-coupon bonds, the interest rate used for calculating the accrual of interest costs for strips is not the rate prevailing at the time of stripping, but rather the original cost of borrowing—that is, on the underlying security.

2.80 In some countries, strips of interest payments may refer to coupons of several bonds, with different nominal amounts but paid at the same date. In this case, best efforts should be made to use the weighted-average nominal interest rate of the different underlying bonds to calculate the accrual of interest costs on the stripped securities.

Arrears

2.81 Interest that accrues on arrears (both principal and interest arrears) is known as late interest. For arrears arising from a debt contract, interest costs should accrue at the same interest rate as on the original debt, unless the interest rate for arrears was stipulated in the original debt contract, in which case this stipulated interest rate should be used. The stipulated rate may include a penalty rate in addition to the interest rate on the original debt. For other arrears, in the absence of other information, interest costs accrue on these arrears at the market rate of interest for overnight borrowing. Also, any additional charges relating to past arrears, agreed by the debtor and creditor at the time the arrears are rescheduled, and to be paid by the debtor to the creditor, should be regarded as an interest cost of the debtor at the time the agreement is implemented. If an item is purchased on credit and the debtor fails to pay within the period stated at the time the purchase was made, any extra charges incurred should be regarded as an interest cost and accrue until the debt is extinguished.

---

[24]A creditor might focus on the prevailing market interest rate, or the rate prevailing when they purchased the security, and hence might record the claim at a value different from that recorded by the debtor.

Variable-rate instruments

Interest-rate-linked instruments

2.82 For loans, deposits, and securities, the same principles as with fixed-rate instruments apply, except that in the absence of firm information, the accrual of interest costs should be estimated and added to the gross external debt position, using the most recent relevant observation(s) of the reference index. Revisions to back data should be undertaken when the amount of interest costs that have accrued is known with certainty.

2.83 In addition, if the interest rate can vary only under the condition of a minimum change in the index and/or within specific upward limits, any estimate of the accrual of interest costs should take account of any such conditions. If there is a link between the nature of the rate index and the frequency of interest payments—for example, interest is indexed on a quarterly basis and is normally paid every quarter with a delay of one quarter—then the exact amount paid to the owners of the securities may well be known in advance, and so can be accrued with certainty. This is known as interest being "predetermined."

Index-linked instruments

2.84 External debt might be indexed to indices other than interest rate indices. Examples include indexing to the price of a commodity, an exchange rate index, a stock exchange index, or the price of a specific security, and so on. Principal as well as interest payments may be indexed. The index can apply continuously over all or part of the life of the instrument. Any change in value related to indexation is recorded as an interest cost, and so affects the principal amount outstanding until paid. The impact of the indexation on the principal amount is recorded on a continuous basis for the period during which the indexing is operative.

2.85 The method of calculation is the same as that for variable-rate interest discussed above; that is, the accrued amount should be estimated using the most recent relevant observation(s) of the reference index and added to the gross external debt position. For instance, if in the first example above interest payments were indexed, and movement in the index after six months suggested that interest payments would increase to $12 a year, then the interest costs accrued to date would be $6 on a straightline basis (or $5.80 on a compound basis), and the amount outstanding $106 ($105.80). Revisions to back data are undertaken when the amount of interest costs that have accrued is known with certainty.

2.86 As mentioned above, a loan that is repayable in commodities or other goods in installments over a period of time (see paragraph 2.37) is conceptually equivalent to an indexed loan. At inception the principal amount outstanding is the value of principal advanced; as with other debt instruments, interest costs will accrue on this amount, increasing its value. At any moment in time, the interest rate that accrues is that which equates the market value of the commodities or other goods to be paid with the principal amount then outstanding; as the market price of the commodity or other good changes, so will the implicit interest rate.

2.87 Index-linked instruments may include a clause for a minimum guaranteed redemption value. Any estimate of the accrual of interest costs should take account of such conditions. For instance, if strict application of the index had the effect of reducing the amount outstanding to less than the minimum, it would not be relevant to record any reduction below the minimum guaranteed redemption value. Normally, the current market price of debt instruments takes into account such a clause.

Instruments with grace periods

2.88 Some debt instruments may have a grace period during which no interest payments are to be made. Provided that the debtor can repay, without penalty, the same amount of principal at the end of the grace period as at the beginning, no interest costs accrue during the grace period. This remains true even if the rate of interest applied in a second and/or subsequent time period is adjusted (for example, there is a step up), so that the final yield is roughly similar to normal conditions over the total life of the instrument.

Instruments with embedded derivatives

2.89 Some instruments may have embedded derivatives that could, if exercised, affect the rate of interest. For such instruments, interest costs should accrue, and be included in the gross external debt position, as "normal." If the financial derivative is exercised and so affects the interest rate, this should be reflected in the rate at which interest accrues—for example, in a structured note with a maximum interest rate, when, and as long as, the maximum is reached and so the financial derivative is "exercised," interest costs should accrue at the maximum rate and no more. The market price of debt instruments should reflect the likelihood of the financial derivative being exercised.

Foreign currency instruments

2.90 Interest costs should accrue (or not) in foreign currency on an instrument denominated in foreign currency, adding to the outstanding principal amount, until paid or in arrears. The principal amount in foreign currency should be converted into the unit of account at the midpoint between the buying and selling market (spot) rates on the reference date to which the position relates.

3. Identification of Institutional Sectors and Financial Instruments

Introduction

3.1 In the *Guide*, as in the *1993 SNA* and *BPM5*, institutional units, and the instruments in which they transact, are grouped into categories so as to enhance the analytical usefulness of the data. Institutional units are grouped into institutional sectors, and financial instruments are classified by their nature into instrument categories. However, the classifications of institutional sectors and financial instruments are determined by the analytical needs of external debt statistics and so can differ from other macroeconomic datasets. For instance, the central bank, an institutional unit, is an institutional subsector in the *1993 SNA* but may not necessarily undertake all monetary authority activities (such as currency issuance or international reserve management) in an economy. In the *Guide*, all the monetary authority-type activities are included together in the monetary authorities sector regardless of whether they are actually undertaken in the central bank or not. Given the importance of ensuring compatibility and consistency across related macroeconomic datasets, the institutional sectors defined in the *Guide* can be reconciled with those in the *BPM5*.

3.2 The institutional sector breakdown groups institutional units with common economic objectives and functions: general government, monetary authorities, banks, and *other sectors*. These sectors are defined in this chapter, as are the subsectors of *other sectors*: nonbank financial corporations, nonfinancial corporations, and households and nonprofit institutions serving households. *BPM5* does not provide definitions of the subsectors of *other sectors*.

3.3 On the classification of financial instruments, the *Guide* gives prominence to four categories of instruments in particular: debt securities, trade credit, loans, and currency and deposits. There is also an *other debt liabilities* category; this would include items such as accounts payable. This chapter explains the nature of these types of financial instruments in the context of the *BPM5* functional categories from which they are drawn. Further, Appendix I defines specific financial instruments and transactions and provides classification guidance; it therefore should be consulted in conjunction with this chapter.

Institutional Sectors

3.4 The institutional sector presentations below are consistent with the *1993 SNA* except that, in line with *BPM5*, the *Guide* has a slightly different definition for the general government and central bank sectors.[1]

3.5 The *monetary authorities* sector is a functional concept used in the balance of payments that covers the central bank (or currency board, monetary agency, etc.) and any other operations that are usually attributable to the central bank but are carried out by other government institutions or commercial banks. Such operations include the issuance of currency; maintenance and management of international reserves, including those resulting from transactions with the IMF; and the operation of exchange stabilization funds.

3.6 The *general government* sector, with the exception noted in the previous paragraph, is defined consistently with the definition of that sector in the *1993 SNA*. The government of a country consists of the public authorities and their agencies, which are entities established through political processes that exercise legislative, judicial, and executive authority within a territorial area. The principal economic functions of a government are (1) to assume respon-

---

[1]Institutional sectors are also described in detail in Chapter IV of the *1993 SNA*.

sibility for the provision of goods and services to the community on a nonmarket basis, either for collective or individual consumption, and (2) to redistribute income and wealth by means of transfer payments. An additional characteristic of government is that these activities must be financed primarily by taxation or other compulsory transfers. General government consists of (i) government units that exist at each level—central, state, or local—of government within the national economy; (ii) all social security funds operated at each level of government; and (iii) all nonmarket nonprofit institutions that are controlled and mainly financed by government units. Public corporations, and unincorporated enterprises that function as if they were corporations (so-called quasi-corporations) are explicitly excluded from the general government sector and are allocated to the financial or nonfinancial corporate sectors, as appropriate. A quasi-corporation can be owned by a resident or nonresident entity but typically will keep a separate set of accounts from its parent and/or, if owned by a nonresident, be engaged in a significant amount of production in the resident economy over a long or indefinite period of time.

3.7 The *banking* sector is identical with the "other (than the central bank) depository corporations" subsector of the financial corporate sector in the *1993 SNA*.[2] Included are all resident units engaging in financial intermediation as a principal activity and having liabilities in the form of deposits payable on demand, transferable by check, or otherwise used for making payments, or having liabilities in the form of deposits that may not be readily transferable, such as short-term certificates of deposit, but that are close substitutes for deposits and are included in measures of money broadly defined. Thus, in addition to commercial banks, the banking sector encompasses institutions such as savings banks, savings and loan associations, credit unions

or cooperatives, and building societies. Post office savings banks or other government-controlled savings banks are also included if they are institutional units separate from the government.

3.8 The *other sectors* category comprises nonbank financial corporations, nonfinancial corporations, and households and nonprofit institutions serving households subsectors.

3.9 The *nonbank financial corporations* subsector comprises insurance corporations and pension funds, other nonbank financial intermediaries, and financial auxiliaries. These types of institutions are all resident subsectors in the *1993 SNA*. Insurance corporations consist of incorporated, mutual, and other entities whose principal function is to provide life, accident, sickness, fire, and other types of insurance to individual units or groups of units through the pooling of risk. Pension funds are those that are constituted in such a way that they are separate institutional units from the units that create them and are established for purposes of providing benefits on retirement for specific groups of employees (and, perhaps, their dependents). These funds have their own assets and liabilities and engage in financial transactions on the market on their own account. Other financial intermediaries consist of all resident corporations or quasi-corporations primarily engaged in financial intermediation, except for banks, insurance corporations, and pension funds. The types of corporations included under this heading are security dealers, investment corporations, and corporations engaged in personal finance and/or consumer credit. Financial auxiliaries consist of those resident corporations and quasi-corporations that engage primarily in activities closely related to financial intermediation but that do not themselves perform an intermediation role, such as security brokers, loan brokers, and insurance brokers.

3.10 The *nonfinancial corporations* subsector consists of resident entities whose principal activity is the production of market goods or nonfinancial services. This sector is defined consistently with the definition in the *1993 SNA*. The sector includes all resident nonfinancial corporations; all resident nonfinancial quasi-corporations, including the branches or agencies of foreign-owned nonfinancial enterprises that are engaged in significant amounts of production on the economic territory on a long-term basis; and all resident nonprofit institutions

---

[2]Covering both the deposit money corporations (S.1221) and other (S.1222) subsectors of the *1993 SNA*. In the IMF's *Monetary and Financial Statistics Manual* (2000d), other depository corporations are defined to include only those financial intermediaries issuing deposits and close substitutes that are included in the national definition of broad money, which may exclude (include) institutional units that are included (excluded) within the *1993 SNA* definition. Rather than as banks, these excluded institutional units would be classified as nonbank financial corporations (or vice versa). While it is recommended in the *Guide* that the definition of banks be consistent with the *1993 SNA* and *BPM5*, it is recognized that countries may rely on data from monetary surveys to compile external debt statistics for the banking sector.

Table 3.1. Standard Components of the IIP: Direct Investment

Assets	Liabilities
Direct investment abroad	*Direct investment in reporting economy*
Equity capital and reinvested earnings	Equity capital and reinvested earnings
Claims on affiliated enterprises	Claims on direct investors
Liabilities to affiliated enterprises	Liabilities to direct investors
Other capital	Other capital
Claims on affiliated enterprises	Claims on direct investors
Liabilities to affiliated enterprises[1]	Liabilities to direct investors[1]

[1]Instruments in these categories are debt liabilities to be included in external debt.

---

that are market producers of goods or nonfinancial services.

3.11 The *households and nonprofit institutions serving households (households and NPISH)* subsector comprises the household sector, consisting of resident households, and the nonprofit institutions serving households sector, consisting of such entities as professional societies, political parties, trade unions, charities, etc.

3.12 In the presentation of the gross external debt position (see below), *intercompany lending* liabilities under a direct investment relationship are separately identified. Equity liabilities arising from a direct investment, like all equity liabilities, are excluded from external debt. These instruments are described in more detail in paragraph 3.16.

Instrument Classification

3.13 This section defines the types of financial instruments to be included in the presentation of the gross external debt position. They are defined in the context of the *BPM5* functional categories—direct investment, portfolio investment, financial derivatives, other investment, and reserve assets—from which they are drawn. This allows the compiler, if necessary, to derive the gross external debt position data from the IIP statement.

3.14 *Direct investment* (Table 3.1) refers to a lasting interest of an entity resident in one economy (the direct investor) in an entity resident in another economy (the direct investment enterprise), defined in *BPM5* as ownership of 10 percent or more of the or-

dinary shares or voting power (for an incorporated enterprise) or the equivalent (for an unincorporated enterprise).[3] Once established, all financial claims of the investor on the enterprise, and vice and versa, and all financial claims on, or liabilities to, related (affiliated) enterprises, are included under direct investment (with two exceptions: financial derivatives and certain intercompany assets and liabilities between two affiliated financial intermediaries—see paragraph 3.18). Of the direct investment components, *other capital*, when owed to nonresident direct investors or affiliates, is included in the gross external debt position; but the other components are not.

3.15 *Other capital* covers borrowing and lending of funds—including debt securities and suppliers' credits (for example, trade credits)—among direct investors and related subsidiaries, branches, and associates. In the gross external debt position tables, other capital is presented as *direct investment: intercompany lending*.

3.16 *Equity capital and reinvested earnings* (comprising equity in branches, subsidiaries, and associates—except nonparticipating, preferred shares, which are classified as debt instruments—and other capital contributions, such as the provision of machinery) is not a debt instrument.

3.17 In practice, it is sometimes difficult to distinguish whether the claims of a direct investor on a di-

---

[3]Further information on the methodology for measuring direct investment is available in *BPM5*, Chapter XVIII, and its related publications, and in the *OECD Benchmark Definition of Foreign Direct Investment, Third Edition* (OECD, 1996).

Table 3.2. Standard Components of the IIP: Portfolio Investment

Assets	Liabilities
Equity securities	*Equity securities*
Monetary authorities	Banks
General government	Other sectors
Banks	*Debt securities*
Other sectors	Bonds and notes[1]
Debt securities	Monetary authorities
Bonds and notes	General government
Monetary authorities	Banks
General government	Other sectors
Banks	Money market instruments[1]
Other sectors	Monetary authorities
Money market instruments	General government
Monetary authorities	Banks
General government	Other sectors
Banks	
Other sectors	

[1]Instruments in these categories are debt liabilities to be included in external debt.

rect investment enterprise are other capital, which is classified as external debt, or equity capital, which is not. Differentiation is particularly difficult when an enterprise is 100 percent owned by a direct investor, such as when the direct investment enterprise is a branch or unincorporated enterprise. In these situations, the classification of capital could be the same as used in the direct investment enterprise's accounting records. That is, when a claim of the direct investor on the direct investment enterprise is considered to be equity capital or shareholder funds in the accounting records of the direct investment enterprise, this claim is also considered equity capital for external debt purposes. Subject to this condition: if liabilities are only to be repaid in the event that a profit is made by the direct investment enterprise, then the liabilities are classified as equity capital. Similarly, in some instances the direct investor might fund local expenses directly and also receive directly the income arising from the output of the direct investment enterprise. The *Guide* regards such payments and receipts as the provision and withdrawal of equity capital, respectively, in the direct investment enterprise by the direct investor.

3.18 The stocks of intercompany assets and liabilities between two affiliated financial intermediaries, including special purpose entities (SPEs) principally engaged in financial intermediation, that

are recorded under direct investment are limited to permanent debt (loan capital representing a permanent interest)—classified as direct investment: intercompany lending—and equity capital and reinvested earnings. Other intercompany debt liabilities between affiliated financial intermediaries are classified by type of instrument, such as loans, debt security, etc., and are attributed to the institutional sector of the debtor entity. For this purpose, financial intermediaries are defined as enterprises principally engaged in providing financial intermediation services or services auxiliary to financial intermediation and comprise those corporations and quasi-corporations that are grouped, in the *1993 SNA*, into the following subsectors: (1) other depository corporations (other than the central bank); (2) other financial intermediaries, except insurance corporations and pension funds; and (3) financial auxiliaries.

3.19 *Portfolio investment* (Table 3.2) includes traded securities (other than those included in direct investment and reserve assets). These instruments are usually traded (or tradable) in organized and other financial markets, including over-the-counter (OTC) markets. When they are owed to nonresidents, of the portfolio investment components, debt securities—that is, *bonds and notes*, and *money market instruments*—are included in the gross external debt position. *Equity securities,* including share investments in mutual funds and investment trusts,[4] are not included in the gross external debt position.

3.20 Debt securities issued with an original maturity of more than one year are classified as *bonds and notes*, even though their remaining maturity at the time of the investment may be less than one year. Bonds and notes usually give the holder the unconditional right to a fixed money income or contractually determined variable money income (payment of interest being independent of the earnings of the debtor). With the exception of perpetual bonds, bonds and notes also provide the unconditional right to a fixed sum in repayment of principal on a specified date or dates. Included among bonds and notes

---

[4]A mutual fund or investment trust liability that requires payment(s) of principal and/or interest by the mutual fund or investment trust to the creditor at some point(s) in the future is to be recorded as a debt instrument and, if owed to nonresidents, included in the gross external debt position. The instrument classification would be dependent on the characteristics of the liability—for example, as a deposit (see paragraph 3.34).

are so-called asset-backed securities and collateralized debt obligations; that is, securities on which payments to creditors are explicitly dependent on a specific stream of income—for example, future lottery receipts or a pool of nontraded instruments (say, loans or export receivables); see Appendix I for more details.

3.21 Debt securities issued with an original maturity of one year or less are classified as *money market instruments*. These instruments generally give the holder the unconditional right to receive a stated, fixed sum of money on a specified date. These short-term instruments are usually traded, at a discount, in organized markets; the discount is dependent on the interest rate and the time remaining to maturity. Examples of money market instruments include treasury bills, commercial and financial paper, and banker's acceptances. Like bonds and notes, money market instruments can be "backed" by a specific stream of income or pool of nontraded instruments.

3.22 Further, where an instrument is provided by an importer to an exporter with such characteristics that it is tradable in organized and other financial markets, such as a promissory note, it should be classified as a debt security—either *bonds and notes*, or *money market instruments* depending on its original maturity—in the gross external debt position. Separate identification of the outstanding value of such instruments is also encouraged because of their role in financing trade. (See also the description of trade-related credit in Chapter 6.)

3.23 *Equity securities* cover all instruments and records acknowledging, after the claims of all creditors have been met, claims to the residual value of incorporated enterprises. These securities are not debt instruments and so are not external debt liabilities. Shares, stocks, preferred stock or shares, participation, or similar documents—such as American Depository Receipts—usually denote ownership of equity. Shares of collective investment institutions, e.g., mutual funds and investment trusts, are also included.

3.24 *Financial derivatives*[5] (Table 3.3) are financial instruments that are linked to a specific financial in-

---

[5]The treatment of financial derivatives in the balance of payments and IIP is described in *Financial Derivatives: A Supplement to the Fifth Edition (1993) of the Balance of Payments Manual* (IMF, 2000c).

Table 3.3. Standard Components of the IIP: Financial Derivatives

Assets	Liabilities
Financial derivatives	*Financial derivatives*
Monetary authorities	Monetary authorities
General government	General government
Banks	Banks
Other sectors	Other sectors

strument, indicator, or commodity and through which specific financial risks can be traded in financial markets in their own right. As explained in Chapter 2 (see paragraph 2.11), financial derivatives are not debt instruments, but information on them can be relevant for external debt analysis.

3.25 Under a *forward-type contract*, the two counterparties agree to exchange an underlying item— real or financial—in a specified quantity, on a specified date, at an agreed contract (strike) price or, in the specific instance of a swap contract, the two counterparties agree to exchange cash flows, determined with reference to the price(s) of, say, currencies or interest rates, according to prearranged rules. The typical requirement under a foreign exchange forward contract to deliver or receive foreign currency in the future can have important implications for foreign currency liquidity analysis and is captured in the table in Table 7.7 in Chapter 7. Under an *option contract*, the purchaser of the option, in return for an option premium, acquires from the writer of the option the right but not the obligation to buy (call option) or sell (put option) a specified underlying item—real or financial—at an agreed contract (strike) price on or before a specified date. Throughout the life of the contract the writer of the option has a liability and the buyer an asset, although the option can expire worthless; the option will be exercised only if settling the contract is advantageous for the purchaser. Typical derivatives instruments include *futures* (exchange traded forward contract), *interest and cross-currency swaps, forward rate agreements, forward foreign exchange contracts, credit derivatives*, and various types of options.

3.26 *Other investment* (Table 3.4) covers all financial instruments other than those classified as direct

Table 3.4. Standard Components of the IIP: Other Investment

Assets	Liabilities
Trade credits	*Trade credits*[1]
General government	General government
Long-term	Long-term
Short-term	Short-term
Other sectors	Other sectors
Long-term	Long-term
Short-term	Short-term
Loans	*Loans*[1]
Monetary authorities	Monetary authorities
Long-term	Use of IMF credit and loans
Short-term	from the IMF
General government	Other long-term
Long-term	Short-term
Short-term	General government
Banks	Long-term
Long-term	Short-term
Short-term	Banks
Other sectors	Long-term
Long-term	Short-term
Short-term	Other sectors
	Long-term
Currency and deposits	Short-term
Monetary authorities	
General government	*Currency and deposits*[1]
Banks	Monetary authorities
Other sectors	Banks
Other assets	*Other liabilities*[1]
Monetary authorities	Monetary authorities
Long-term	Long-term
Short-term	Short-term
General government	General government
Long-term	Long-term
Short-term	Short-term
Banks	Banks
Long-term	Long-term
Short-term	Short-term
Other sectors	Other sectors
Long-term	Long-term
Short-term	Short-term

[1]Instruments in these categories are debt liabilities to be included in external debt.

investment, portfolio investment, financial derivatives, or reserve assets. When owed to nonresidents, all the components of other investment—*trade credit*, *loans*, *currency and deposits*, and *other debt liabilities*—are included in the gross external debt position.

3.27 *Trade credits* consist of claims or liabilities arising from the direct extension of credit by suppliers for transactions in goods and services, and advance payments by buyers for goods and services

and for work in progress (or to be undertaken). Long- and short–term trade credits are shown separately. Trade-related loans provided by a third party, such as a bank, to an exporter or importer are not included in this category but under *loans*, below (see also the description of trade-related credit in Chapter 6).

3.28 *Loans* include those financial assets created through the direct lending of funds by a creditor (lender) to a debtor (borrower) through an arrangement in which the lender either receives no security evidencing the transactions or receives a nonnegotiable document or instrument. Collateral, in the form of either a financial asset (such as a security) or nonfinancial asset (such as land or a building) may be provided under a loan transaction, although it is not an essential feature. In the gross external debt position, loans include *Use of IMF credit* and *loans from the IMF*.

3.29 If a loan becomes tradable and is, or has been, traded in the secondary market, the loan should be reclassified as a debt security. Given the significance of reclassification, there needs to be evidence of secondary market trading before a debt instrument is reclassified from a loan to a security. Evidence of trading on secondary markets would include the existence of market makers and bid-offer spreads for the debt instrument. The *Guide* encourages the separate identification of the outstanding value of any such loans reclassified.

3.30 Reverse security transactions and financial leases are two types of arrangements for which the change of ownership principle is not strictly adhered to.

3.31 A *reverse securities transaction* is defined to include all arrangements whereby one party legally acquires securities and agrees, under a legal agreement at inception, to return the same or equivalent securities on or by an agreed date to the same party from whom they acquired the securities initially. If the security taker under such a transaction provides cash funds, and there is agreement to reacquire the same or equivalent securities at a predetermined price at the contract's maturity, a loan transaction is recorded. This is the so-called collateralized loan approach to a *reverse securities transaction*, with the securities representing the collateral. These transactions include security repurchase agreements (repos), securities lending involving cash, and sale/buy backs. The security provider under a reverse security transaction acquires a repo loan liability and the security taker a repo loan asset. If no cash is provided, no loan transaction is reported. Under the collateralized loan approach, the security is assumed not to have changed ownership and remains on the balance sheet of the security provider. A similar recording procedure is adopted for transactions where gold rather than securities is provided as collateral for cash (so-called gold swaps).

3.32 If the security taker sells the security acquired under a reverse security transaction, they record a negative position in that security. This treatment reflects economic reality in that the holder of the negative position is exposed to the risks and benefits of ownership in an equal and opposite way to the party who now owns the security (see also Appendix II). On-selling of gold by the gold taker, similarly reported as a negative holding, does not affect the gross external debt position because gold is an asset without any corresponding liability.

3.33 A *financial lease* is a contract under which a lessee contracts to pay rentals for the use of a good for most or all of its expected economic life. The rentals enable the lessor over the period of the contract to recover most or all of the costs of goods and the carrying charges. While there is not a legal change of ownership of the good, under a financial lease the risks and rewards of ownership are, de facto, transferred from the legal owner of the good, the lessor, to the user of the good, the lessee. For this reason, under statistical convention, the total value of the good is imputed to have changed ownership. So, the debt liability at the inception of the lease is defined as the value of the good and is financed by a loan of the same value, a liability of the lessee. The loan is repaid through the payment of rentals (which comprise both interest and principal payment elements) and any residual payment at the end of the contract (or alternatively, by the return of the good to the lessor).

3.34 *Currency and deposits* consists of notes and coin and both transferable and other deposits.[6] Notes and coin represent claims of a fixed nominal value usually on a central bank or government; commemorative coins are excluded. Transferable deposits consist of deposits that are (1) exchangeable on demand at par and without penalty or restriction, and (2) directly usable for making payments by check, giro order, direct debit/credit, or other direct payment facility. Other deposits comprise all claims represented by evidence of deposit—for example, savings and fixed-term deposits; sight deposits that permit immediate cash withdrawals but not direct third-party transfers; and shares that are legally (or practically) redeemable on demand or on short notice in savings and loan associations, credit unions, building societies, etc. Depending on national practice, gold that is borrowed (without cash being provided in exchange) from a nonresident could be classified by the borrower as a foreign currency deposit.

3.35 *Other assets/other liabilities* covers items other than trade credit, loans, and currency and deposits. Such assets and liabilities include liabilities of pension funds and life insurance companies to their nonresident participants and policyholders, claims on nonlife companies; capital subscriptions to international nonmonetary organizations; arrears (see below); and accounts receivable and payable, such as in respect of taxes, dividends declared payable but not yet paid, purchases and sales of securities, and wages and salaries. Short- and long-term other liabilities are shown separately as *other debt liabilities* in the gross external debt presentation.

3.36 *Arrears* are defined as amounts that are past due-for-payment and unpaid. Arrears can arise both through the late payment of principal and interest on debt instruments as well as through late payments for other instruments and transactions. For instance, a financial derivatives contract is not a debt instrument for reasons explained above, but if a financial derivatives contract comes to maturity and a payment is required but not made, arrears are created. Similarly, if goods are supplied and not paid for on the contract payment date or a payment for goods is made but the goods are not delivered on time, then arrears are created. These new debt liabilities should be recorded in the gross external debt position as *arrears*.

3.37 Payments may be missed for a variety of reasons beyond simply the inability or unwillingness of the debtor to meet its payment obligations. Some-

---

[6]Because the IIP does not provide a short-term/long-term attribution, it is recommended that all currency and deposits are included in the short-term category unless detailed information is available to make the short-term/long-term attribution.

Table 3.5. Standard Components of the IIP: Reserve Assets

Assets
Gold
Special drawing rights
Reserve position in the IMF
Foreign exchange
Currency and deposits
With monetary authorities
With banks
Securities
Equities
Bonds and notes
Money market instruments
Financial derivatives (net)
Other claims

falling due—but the agreement has yet to be signed and implemented. In the meantime, payments due under the existing agreement are not made, and arrears arise—so-called *technical arrears*.[7] Such arrears might typically arise in the context of Paris Club agreements between the time of the Paris Club rescheduling session and the time when the bilateral agreements are signed and implemented. If the agreement in principle lapses before the agreement is signed, then any accumulated arrears are no longer *technical arrears*.

3.38 *Reserve assets* (Table 3.5) consist of those external assets that are readily available to and controlled by the monetary authorities for direct financing of payments imbalances, for indirectly regulating the magnitude of such balances through intervention in exchange markets to affect the currency exchange rate, and/or for other purposes.[8] By definition, reserve assets are not included in the gross external debt position.

times arrears arise not from the ability of the original debtor to provide national currency but from the inability of the monetary authorities to provide foreign exchange to a domestic entity, so preventing that entity from servicing its foreign currency debt. These so-called *transfer arrears* remain those of the original debtor sector. Another circumstance may be when the creditor has agreed in principle to reschedule debt—that is, reorganize payments that are

---

[7]If the creditor bills and the debtor pays on the basis of the new agreement, even though it is not signed, no arrears arise.

[8]In addition to *BPM5*, Chapter XXI, see *International Reserves and Foreign Currency Liquidity: Guidelines for a Data Template* (Kester, 2001), which also provides guidance on the measurement of official reserve assets.

4. Presentation of the Gross External Debt Position

Introduction

4.1 This chapter provides a table for the presentation of the gross external debt position and related memorandum tables. Data compiled using the concepts outlined in the previous chapters and presented in the format of this table are essential to providing a comprehensive and informed picture of the gross external debt position for the whole economy, and so

their dissemination on a frequent basis is encouraged (see also Box 4.1).

4.2 In disseminating data on the gross external debt position, compilers are encouraged to provide methodological notes explaining the concepts and methods used in compiling the data. For any presentation of gross external debt position it is particularly important for the compiler to indicate whether

---

Box 4.1 SDDS and GDDS Specifications Regarding Dissemination of External Debt Statistics

In the aftermath of the 1994–95 international financial crisis, the Interim Committee (now called the International Monetary and Financial Committee) of the IMF's Board of Governors endorsed the establishment of a two-tier standard to guide member countries in the provision of economic and financial data to the public. The first tier, named the Special Data Dissemination Standard (SDDS), was approved by the IMF's Executive Board on March 29, 1996. The other tier, named the General Data Dissemination System (GDDS), was approved on December 19, 1997.[1]

The purpose of the SDDS is to guide IMF member countries in the provision to the public of comprehensive, timely, accessible, and reliable economic and financial statistics in a world of increasing economic and financial integration. The SDDS is geared to those countries that have, or might seek, access to international capital markets. Subscription to the SDDS is voluntary. By subscribing to the SDDS, members undertake to provide the supporting information to the IMF and to observe the various elements of the SDDS.

With respect to the external debt data category, the SDDS prescribes the dissemination of quarterly data with a one-quarter lag, covering four sectors (general government, monetary authorities, the banking sector, and other). Furthermore, the data are to

be disaggregated by maturity—short- and long-term—and provided on an original maturity basis and by instrument, as set out in *BPM5*. The SDDS encourages countries to disseminate supplementary information on future debt-service payments, in which the principal and interest components are separately identified, twice yearly for the first four quarters and the following two semesters ahead, with a lag of one quarter. The data should also be broken down into sector—general government, monetary authorities, the banking sector, and other sectors. The dissemination of a domestic/foreign currency breakdown of external debt with quarterly periodicity and timeliness is also encouraged.

The GDDS is a structured process focused on data quality that assists countries in adapting their statistical systems to meet the evolving requirements of the user community in the areas of economic management and development. Participating countries voluntarily commit to adhering to sound statistical practices in developing their statistical systems.

The core data category for external debt in the GDDS includes public and publicly guaranteed debt, and the associated debt-service schedule. Recommended good practice would be that the stock data, broken down by maturity, be disseminated with quarterly periodicity and timeliness of one or two quarters after the reference date. In addition, the associated debt-service schedules should be disseminated twice yearly, within three to six months after the reference period, and with data for four quarters and two semesters ahead. Data on nonguaranteed private debt and debt-servicing schedules, with annual periodicity, are encouraged data categories to be disseminated within six to nine months after the reference period.

---

[1]On March 29, 2000, the IMF's Executive Board made a number of amendments to the SDDS, which included the introduction of a separate data category for external debt. At the same time, the Board amended the GDDS to include public and publicly guaranteed external debt and a debt-service schedule as a core data category.

traded instruments are valued at nominal or market value,[1] and whether interest costs that have accrued but are not yet payable are included, or not.

Presentation Table

4.3 The presentation of the gross external debt position is set out in Table 4.1.

- The first level of disaggregation is by institutional sector. The primary disaggregation is by the four sectors of the compiling economy described in the previous chapter—*general government, monetary authorities, banks,* and *other sectors.* A disaggregation of the other sectors into *nonbank financial corporations, nonfinancial corporations,* and *other sectors (households and nonprofit institutions serving households)* is provided.

  Intercompany lending between entities in a direct investment relationship is separately presented because the nature of the relationship between debtor and creditor is different from that for other debt, and this affects economic behavior. Whereas a creditor principally assesses claims on an unrelated entity in terms of the latter's ability to repay, claims on a related entity may be additionally assessed in terms of the overall profitability and economic objectives of the multinational operation.

- The second level of disaggregation is by the maturity of external debt—short-term and long-term on an original maturity basis. A maturity attribution is not provided for intercompany lending, but in separately identifying arrears (see below), which by definition are short-term liabilities, a partial short-term attribution is provided.[2]

- The third level of disaggregation is by type of debt instrument. The debt instruments are described in Chapter 3.

4.4 *Other debt liabilities (other liabilities* in the IIP), and *intercompany lending* are explicitly subdivided between *arrears* and *other. Arrears* are separately identified because such information is of particular analytical interest to those involved in external debt analysis, since the existence of arrears

---

[1]A table reconciling nominal and market valuation of traded debt instruments is provided in Chapter 7 (Table 7.13).

[2]If a short-/long-term maturity attribution of intercompany lending data is available to the compiler on an original maturity basis, the *Guide* encourages dissemination of these data.

Table 4.1. Gross External Debt Position: By Sector

	End-Period
General Government	
Short-term	
Money market instruments	
Loans	
Trade credits	
Other debt liabilities[1]	
Arrears	
Other	
Long-term	
Bonds and notes	
Loans	
Trade credits	
Other debt liabilities[1]	
Monetary Authorities	
Short-term	
Money market instruments	
Loans	
Currency and deposits[2]	
Other debt liabilities[1]	
Arrears	
Other	
Long-term	
Bonds and notes	
Loans	
Currency and deposits[2]	
Other debt liabilities[1]	
Banks	
Short-term	
Money market instruments	
Loans	
Currency and deposits[2]	
Other debt liabilities[1]	
Arrears	
Other	
Long-term	
Bonds and notes	
Loans	
Currency and deposits[2]	
Other debt liabilities[1]	
Other Sectors	
Short-term	
Money market instruments	
Loans	
Currency and deposits[2]	
Trade credits	
Other debt liabilities[1]	
Arrears	
Other	
Long-term	
Bonds and notes	
Loans	
Currency and deposits[2]	
Trade credits	
Other debt liabilities[1]	

Table 4.1 (concluded)

	End-Period
Other Sectors (continued)	
Nonbank financial corporations	
Short-term	
Money market instruments	
Loans	
Currency and deposits[2]	
Other debt liabilities[1]	
Arrears	
Other	
Long-term	
Bonds and notes	
Loans	
Currency and deposits[2]	
Other debt liabilities[1]	
Nonfinancial corporations	
Short-term	
Money market instruments	
Loans	
Trade credits	
Other debt liabilities[1]	
Arrears	
Other	
Long-term	
Bonds and notes	
Loans	
Trade credits	
Other debt liabilities[1]	
Households and nonprofit institutions serving households (NPISH)	
Short-term	
Money market instruments	
Loans	
Trade credits	
Other debt liabilities[1]	
Arrears	
Other	
Long-term	
Bonds and notes	
Loans	
Trade credits	
Other debt liabilities[1]	
Direct Investment: Intercompany Lending	
Debt liabilities to affiliated enterprises	
Arrears	
Other	
Debt liabilities to direct investors	
Arrears	
Other	
Gross External Debt	

[1]*Other debt liabilities* are *other liabilities* in the IIP statement.
[2]It is recommended that all currency and deposits be included in the short-term category unless detailed information is available to make the short-term/long-term attribution.

indicates the extent to which an economy has been unable to meet its external obligations. All *other debt liabilities* and *intercompany lending* that are not *arrears* are classified as *other*.

4.5 For some economies arrears are very significant. For such economies, a further disaggregation of arrears into arrears of principal, arrears of interest, interest on arrears of principal, and interest by institutional sector is encouraged. Also, if the amounts of technical and/or transfer arrears are significant, it is encouraged that data on these amounts be separately identified and disseminated by the compiling economy.

4.6 The chapter also presents tables for memorandum items, data on which, depending on an economy's circumstances, can enhance the analytical usefulness of the data presented in the gross external debt position.

Memorandum Items

4.7 To enhance analytical usefulness, various memoranda data series might be presented along with the presentation of the gross external debt position. The first memorandum item discussed below covers outstanding liabilities arising from periodic interest costs that have accrued and are not yet payable. The other three memorandum items—financial derivatives, equity liabilities, and debt securities issued by residents that are involved in reverse security transactions between residents and nonresidents—provide information on instruments that are not captured in the gross external debt position but that potentially could render an economy vulnerable to solvency and, particularly, liquidity risks.

Periodic Interest Costs That Have Accrued and Are Not Yet Payable: Outstanding Liabilities

4.8 A memorandum table is set out in Table 4.2 for the presentation of data on outstanding liabilities arising from periodic interest costs that have accrued and are not yet payable. Periodic interest costs are those interest costs that result in an interest payment, as defined in Chapter 2. In attributing these liabilities by sector and maturity in this table, compilers should be consistent with their approach in compiling gross external debt position data. For example,

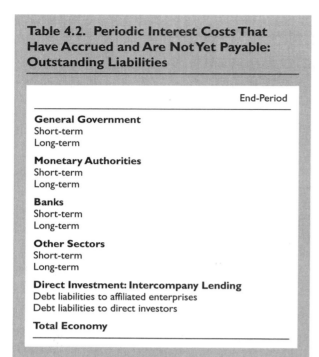

Table 4.2. Periodic Interest Costs That Have Accrued and Are Not Yet Payable: Outstanding Liabilities

	End-Period
General Government	
Short-term	
Long-term	
Monetary Authorities	
Short-term	
Long-term	
Banks	
Short-term	
Long-term	
Other Sectors	
Short-term	
Long-term	
Direct Investment: Intercompany Lending	
Debt liabilities to affiliated enterprises	
Debt liabilities to direct investors	
Total Economy	

Table 4.3. Financial Derivatives Position

	End-Period
Liabilities	
General government	
Monetary authorities	
Banks	
Other sectors	
Nonbank financial corporations	
Nonfinancial corporations	
Households and nonprofit institutions serving households (NPISH)	
Total	
Assets[1]	
General government	
Monetary authorities	
Banks	
Other sectors	
Nonbank financial corporations	
Nonfinancial corporations	
Households and nonprofit institutions serving households (NPISH)	
Total	
Total Economy	

[1]Excludes financial derivatives that pertain to reserve asset management and are included in reserve assets data.

interest costs attributed to short-term government debt in the gross external debt position should be attributed to general government, short-term in this table. A more detailed disaggregation of these interest cost liabilities by type of instrument could be provided, if necessary.

4.9 Separate data on outstanding liabilities arising from periodic interest costs that have accrued and are not yet payable allow for the calculation of the gross external debt position excluding these liabilities, which in turn facilitates comparisons both across countries and across time—that is, allows comparisons with gross external debt position data that might exclude such liabilities produced either by other countries, or by the same country in earlier time periods. Information on such liabilities also provides a broad indication of the scale of short-term interest payments to be made (the more frequent these data are disseminated, the more relevant this information), and can help clarify national practice on the treatment of accrual of interest costs.

Financial Derivatives

4.10 A memorandum table for the presentation of position data on financial derivatives is provided in

Table 4.3. Because of the use of financial derivatives to hedge financial positions as well as to take open positions, these contracts can add to an economy's liabilities and, if used inappropriately, cause significant losses. However, in comparing financial derivatives data with external debt, the user should be aware that financial derivatives might be hedging asset positions, or a whole portfolio of assets and liabilities. In this regard, the net external debt position presentation in Chapter 7 is also relevant.

4.11 The table includes gross assets as well as gross liabilities because of the market practice of creating offsetting contracts, and the possibility of forward-type instruments to switch from asset to liability positions, and vice versa, from one period to the next. For instance, a borrower hedging a foreign currency borrowing with a forward contract might find that the value of the hedge switches from asset to liability position from period to period depending on the movement in exchange rates. To present only the liability position in financial derivatives along with gross external debt would imply that the foreign currency borrowing was only

---

Table 4.4. Equity Liability Position

	End-Period
Banks	
Other sectors	
Nonbank financial corporations	
Nonfinancial corporations	
Total	
Direct investment in reporting economy: Equity capital and reinvested earnings	
Total Economy	

Table 4.5. Debt Securities Acquired Under Reverse Security Transactions:[1] Positions

	End-Period
Debt securities issued by residents and acquired by nonresidents from residents (+)	
Debt securities issued by residents and acquired by residents from nonresidents (−)	

[1]Reverse security transactions include all arrangements whereby one party acquires securities and agrees, under a legal agreement at inception, to return the same or similar securities on or by an agreed date to the same party from whom they acquired the securities initially. The acquiring party must have full title to the securities such that they can be sold to a third party. These arrangements can include those known as repurchase agreements (repos), security loans, and sell/buy backs.

---

hedged when the forward contract was in a liability position, so creating a misleading impression. Thus, financial derivatives liability positions should be considered alongside financial derivatives asset positions. If an economy includes financial derivatives in its reserve assets data, because they pertain to reserve asset management, these financial derivatives should be excluded from this memorandum item.

Equity Liabilities

4.12 Table 4.4 shows a memorandum table for the presentation of position data on equity liabilities—that is, both equity securities, and equity capital and reinvested earnings of direct investment enterprises. Similar to financial derivatives positions, equity securities can add to an economy's liabilities and so could potentially be a source of vulnerability. Also, equity capital in direct investment enterprises, particularly branches/unincorporated enterprises, could be withdrawn.

4.13 In some instances, resident mutual funds are used as a vehicle by nonresident investors to acquire positions in domestic debt securities. If the nonresidents decide to sell these investments, the sales can have a direct impact on the domestic debt securities market. As explained in Chapter 3, such investments by nonresidents are classified as equity liabilities of the resident economy. Nonetheless, identifying equity investment in mutual funds, under *nonbank financial corporations* in the table, might be considered. Further, if the amounts are significant and concentrated in mutual funds that are entirely or almost entirely owned by nonresidents, memoranda data on

the investments of these mutual funds might also be disseminated.

Resident-Issued Debt Securities Involved in Reverse Security Transactions

4.14 In financial markets, activity in reverse security transactions is commonplace. It is one method of providing an investor with financial leverage in the debt markets—that is, greater exposure to market price movements than the value of own funds invested. To understand the dynamics of this leverage activity, and to track developments and hence potential vulnerability, a memorandum table is provided in Table 4.5 for the presentation of position data on debt securities issued by residents that are acquired from or provided to nonresidents under reverse security transactions. Such data would also help to interpret external debt, in particular security debt data when reverse security activity is significant, and could be affecting the recorded position. For debt securities to be included in this memorandum table, the acquiring party must have full title to the securities such that they can be sold to a third party.

4.15 In the table, the total value of debt securities issued by residents that have been acquired by nonresidents from residents under outstanding reverse security transactions, even if subsequently on-sold, are included with a positive sign. The total value of debt securities issued by residents that have been acquired by residents from nonresidents under outstanding reverse security transactions, even if subsequently on-sold, are included with a negative sign. This sign convention tracks the change of ownership of debt securities. Other things being equal, if nonresidents acquire these securities under reverse security transactions, the security claims on the resident economy are greater than recorded in the gross external debt position, whereas if residents acquire these securities from nonresidents under reverse security transactions, the debt security claims on the resident economy are less than recorded in the gross external debt position. Appendix II provides more information on reverse security transactions and explains how different types of reverse security transactions should be recorded in the gross external debt position and in this memorandum table.

5. Public and Publicly Guaranteed External Debt

Introduction

5.1 For countries in which there is a particular interest in public sector debt, this chapter provides a table for the presentation of the gross external debt position in which the role of the public sector is highlighted. The data for this table should be compiled using the concepts outlined in Chapters 2 and 3, except the debt of resident entities should be attributed according to whether the debtor is publicly owned or not, and if not, by whether the debt instrument is guaranteed or not by a public sector entity. For convenience, this presentation is described as being a "public-sector-based approach" and is consistent with the framework of the World Bank's Debtor Reporting System.

5.2 In economies where public sector external debt is dominant, the presentation table provided in this chapter could be the primary one used for disseminating data. Indeed, in circumstances where the public sector is centrally involved in external debt borrowing activity, both as a borrower or guarantor, it is essential. As private sector debt becomes more important in the economy, more detailed breakdowns of private sector debt are required, such as provided in the previous chapter, but the presentation set out in this chapter would remain relevant for monitoring external debt liabilities of the public sector.

5.3 Because the concepts for its measurement remain consistent throughout the *Guide*, the gross external debt position for the whole economy—depending on whether traded debt instruments are valued at nominal or market value—should be the same regardless of whether the presentation table in this or the previous chapter is used to disseminate such data.

5.4 In disseminating data, compilers are encouraged to provide methodological notes explaining the concepts and methods used in compiling the data. For any presentation of gross external debt position, it is particularly important for the compiler to indicate whether traded instruments are valued at nominal or market value, and whether interest costs that have accrued but are not yet payable are included, or not.

Definitions

5.5 For the presentation of the external debt position in a public-sector-based approach, the first determination is whether or not a resident entity is in the public sector.[1] In comparison with the institutional sector approach outlined in Chapter 3, the *public sector* includes the general government, monetary authorities, and those entities in the banking and other sectors that are public corporations. A *public corporation* is defined as a nonfinancial or financial corporation that is subject to control by government units, with control over a corporation defined as the ability to determine general corporate policy by choosing appropriate directors, if necessary. Control can be established through government ownership of more than half of the voting shares or otherwise controlling more than half of the shareholder voting power (including through ownership of a second public corporation that in turn has a majority of the voting shares).[2] In addition, it may be possible to exercise control through special legislation, decree, or regulation that empowers the government to determine corporate

---

[1]For more details, please refer to the World Bank's *Debtor Reporting System Manual* (World Bank, 2000), available on the Internet at *http://www.worldbank.org/data/working/DRS/drs_manual.doc*.

[2]This definition is derived from the *1993 SNA* and the IMF's *Government Finance Statistics Manual* (IMF, 2001). It is consistent with *ESA95* (Eurostat, 1996) and *ESA95 Manual on Government Deficit and Debt* (Eurostat, 2000), which also provide additional guidance on recognizing such corporations.

policy or to appoint directors. Any domestic institutional unit not meeting the definition of public sector is to be classified as *private sector*. In terms of institutional sector attribution, the classification of a public corporation as a monetary authority (central bank), bank, nonbank financial corporation, or nonfinancial corporation depends on the nature of the activity it undertakes.

5.6 *Publicly guaranteed private sector external debt* is defined as the external debt liabilities of the private sector, the servicing of which is contractually guaranteed by a public entity resident in the same economy as the debtor.[3] The private sector can include resident entities in the banks and other sectors. External debt of the private sector that is not contractually guaranteed by the public sector resident in the same economy is classified as *nonguaranteed private sector external debt*. If external debt of the private sector is partially guaranteed by the public sector resident in the same economy, such as if principal payments or interest payments alone are guaranteed, then only the present value of the payments guaranteed should be included within *publicly guaranteed private sector external debt*, with the nonguaranteed amount included within *nonguaranteed private sector external debt*.

Presentation of Public and Publicly Guaranteed External Debt Position

5.7 The presentation of the gross external debt position on the basis of a public-sector-based approach is set out in Table 5.1.
- The first level of disaggregation is by sector. The primary disaggregation is between public and publicly guaranteed debt, and nonguaranteed private sector external debt. Because of the nature of the relationship between debtor and creditor, intercompany lending between entities in a direct investment relationship is separately identified under each category, but when combined equals

[3]External debt for which guarantees are provided to the creditor by a public sector entity resident in a different economy from that of the debtor is not covered under this definition.

Table 5.1. Gross External Debt Position: Public and Publicly Guaranteed Debt and Nonguaranteed Private Sector Debt

End-Period

Public and Publicly Guaranteed Debt
Short-term
Money market instruments
Loans
Currency and deposits[1]
Trade credits
Other debt liabilities[2]
  Arrears
  Other

Long-term
Bonds and notes
Loans
Currency and deposits[1]
Trade credits
Other debt liabilities[2]

Direct investment: Intercompany lending
Debt liabilities to affiliated enterprises
  Arrears
  Other
Debt liabilities to direct investors
  Arrears
  Other

Nonguaranteed Private Sector External Debt
Short-term
Money market instruments
Loans
Currency and deposits[1]
Trade credits
Other debt liabilities[2]
  Arrears
  Other

Long-term
Bonds and notes
Loans
Currency and deposits[1]
Trade credits
Other debt liabilities[2]

Direct investment: Intercompany lending
Debt liabilities to affiliated enterprises
  Arrears
  Other
Debt liabilities to direct investors
  Arrears
  Other

Gross External Debt

[1]It is recommended that all currency and deposits be included in the short-term category unless detailed information is available to make the short-term/long-term attribution.
[2]*Other debt liabilities* are *other liabilities* in the IIP statement.

Table 5.2. Gross External Debt Position: Public Sector Debt and Publicly Guaranteed Private Sector Debt

	End-Period
Public Sector External Debt	
Short-term	
Money market instruments	
Loans	
Currency and deposits[1]	
Trade credits	
Other debt liabilities[2]	
Arrears	
Other	
Long-term	
Bonds and notes	
Loans	
Currency and deposits[1]	
Trade credits	
Other debt liabilities[2]	
Direct investment: Intercompany lending	
Debt liabilities to affiliated enterprises	
Arrears	
Other	
Debt liabilities to direct investors	
Arrears	
Other	
Total	
Publicly Guaranteed Private Sector External Debt	
Short-term	
Money market instruments	
Loans	
Currency and deposits[1]	
Trade credits	
Other debt liabilities[2]	
Arrears	
Other	
Long-term	
Bonds and notes	
Loans	
Currency and deposits[1]	
Trade credits	
Other debt liabilities[2]	
Direct investment: Intercompany lending	
Debt liabilities to affiliated enterprises	
Arrears	
Other	
Debt liabilities to direct investors	
Arrears	
Other	
Total	

[1]It is recommended that all currency and deposits be included in the short-term category unless detailed information is available to make the short-term/long-term attribution.

[2]_Other debt liabilities_ are _other liabilities_ in the IIP statement.

direct investment: intercompany lending for the total economy as presented in the previous chapter.

- The second level of disaggregation is by the maturity of external debt—short-term and long-term on the basis of original maturity. A maturity attribution is not provided for intercompany lending, but in separately identifying arrears (see below), which by definition are short-term liabilities, a partial short-term attribution is provided.[4]

- The third level of disaggregation is by type of debt instrument, as described in Chapter 3. Arrears are separately identified, because such information is of particular analytical interest.

5.8 Memoranda data, on a public sector basis, on outstanding liabilities arising from periodic interest costs that have accrued and are not yet payable, financial derivatives, equity liabilities, and reverse security transactions could be provided along with Table 5.1. These memorandum items are described in Chapter 4.

5.9 Table 5.2 separates public sector external debt and publicly guaranteed private sector external debt. Such a separation allows identification of external debt owed by the public sector and, combined with the information in Table 5.1, external debt of the private sector.

5.10 Further, as defined in paragraphs 5.5 and 5.6 above, public sector data can be attributed to general government, monetary authorities, banks, and other sectors, while private sector information can be attributed to banks and other sectors. In this regard, it is recommended that if detailed records are kept, the institutional sector of the debtor be identified, so as to allow an economy that is presenting data on a public sector basis to also compile data on an institutional sector basis.

[4]If a short-/long-term maturity attribution of intercompany lending data is available to the compiler on an original maturity basis, the _Guide_ encourages dissemination of these data.

6. Further External Debt Accounting Principles

Introduction

6.1 Data compiled and presented using the concepts described in the previous chapters provide comprehensive coverage and an informed picture of the gross external debt position for the whole economy and/or the public sector. However, such data do not provide a complete picture of emerging vulnerabilities to solvency and liquidity risk. For instance, the currency and interest rate composition of external debt liabilities, and the pattern of future payments, might all be potential sources of vulnerability. To assist in compiling additional data series of analytical use in understanding the gross external debt position, this chapter provides further accounting principles. These principles, as well as those described in earlier chapters, are drawn upon to provide illustrative presentation tables in the next chapter.

6.2 This chapter discusses further accounting principles under three broad headings:
- Sectors, maturity, and instruments;
- Specific characteristics of external debt; and
- Principles for the compilation of debt-service and other payment schedules.

Sectors, Maturity, and Instruments

Creditor Sectors

6.3 Information on the nonresident creditor sector that owns external debt is disseminated by many economies. The sectors defined in Chapter 3—general government, monetary authorities, banks, and other sectors—and in Chapter 5—public and private sectors—are creditor as well as debtor sectors. Other commonly identified creditor sectors are *multilateral (international) organizations* and *official creditors.*

6.4 *Multilateral organizations* are established by political agreements among member countries that have the status of international treaties. Multilateral

organizations are accorded appropriate privileges and immunities and are not subject to the laws and regulations of the economies in which the organizations are located. Typically these organizations provide nonmarket services of a collective nature for the benefit of members and/or financial intermediation, or the channeling of funds between lenders and borrowers in different economies. As creditors, multilateral organizations are sometimes also referred to as *official multilateral creditors.*

6.5 *Official creditors* are public sector creditors, including multilateral organizations. External debt owed to official creditors might also include debt that was originally owed to private creditors but that was guaranteed by a public entity in the same economy as the creditor (for example, an export credit agency). *Official bilateral creditors* are official creditors in individual countries. This category of creditor is particularly relevant in the context of Paris Club discussions. The Paris Club is an umbrella arrangement under which creditors and debtors meet, discuss, and arrange debt-relief packages and is not an institutional unit in its own right (see Box 8.2 in Chapter 8).

Remaining Maturity

6.6 While it is recommended that in the gross external debt position the short-term/long-term maturity attribution be made on the basis of original maturity, there is also analytical interest in attribution on the basis of remaining maturity. Remaining-maturity measures (sometimes referred to as residual maturity measures) provide an indication of when payments will fall due, and so of potential liquidity risks facing the economy. Particularly important is information on payments coming due in the near term.

6.7 The *Guide* recommends that short-term remaining maturity be measured by adding the value of outstanding short-term external debt (original maturity) to the value of outstanding long-term external debt (original maturity) due to be paid in one year or less. Conceptually, at the reference date the value of outstanding long-term external debt (original maturity) due to be paid in one year or less is the discounted value of payments to be made in the coming year, both interest and principal.[1] The value of outstanding long-term (original maturity) debt due to be paid over one-year ahead is classified as long-term debt on a remaining-maturity basis.

6.8 The information content provided is one reason for recommending such an approach. Short-term debt on an original maturity basis is identifiable from the gross external debt position. Measuring the value of outstanding long-term external debt (original maturity) falling due in one year or less may raise practical difficulties, in which instance, one proxy measure that might be used is the undiscounted value of principal payments on long-term external debt obligations (original maturity basis) due to mature in one year or less. This proxy measure is incomplete in its coverage of interest payments falling due in the coming year but can be compiled using the principles for projecting payments in a debt-service schedule (see below).[2]

Trade-Related Credit

6.9 In the *Guide*, trade credit as presented in the gross external debt position is defined in Chapter 3—the direct extension of credit by suppliers for transactions in goods and services, and advance payments by buyers for goods and services, and for work in progress (or to be undertaken)—consistent with the *1993 SNA* and *BPM5*. To assist in compiling additional data series, this chapter introduces a wider con-

cept of trade-related credit, which also captures other credits provided to finance trade activity, including through banks. It is defined as including trade credit, trade-related bills (see below), and credit provided by third parties to finance trade, such as loans from a foreign financial or export credit institution to the buyer. A table for presenting data on trade-related credit is provided in the next chapter.

6.10 A particularly difficult issue of classification arises from bills drawn on the importer and provided to the exporter, which are subsequently discounted by the exporter with a financial institution. These instruments might be regarded by the importer as the direct extension of credit by the exporter but once discounted become a claim by a third party on the importer. Where an instrument is provided to th exporter with such characteristics that it is tradable in organized and other financial markets, such as a promissory note, it should be classified as a security in the gross external debt position and included in the concept of trade-related credit.

6.11 If the importer's bill has been endorsed (or "accepted") by a bank in the importer's own economy in order to make the bill acceptable to the exporter, it is known as a banker's acceptance, classified as a security in the gross external debt position, and included in the concept of trade-related credit. Banker's acceptances are to be classified as a financial liability of the bank (or, if not a bank, the financial institution that has endorsed the bill) because they represent an unconditional claim on the part of the holder and an unconditional claim on the bank. However, national practices and variations in the nature of these acceptances may suggest flexibility in the application of this guideline.

Specific Characteristics of External Debt

Currency Composition

6.12 Domestic currency is that which is legal tender in the economy and issued by the monetary authority for that economy or for the common currency area to which the economy belongs.[3] Under this definition,

---

[1]For those economies that do not wish to include interest costs that have accrued but are not yet payable in the gross external debt position for all instruments, the nominal value of outstanding long-term external debt at the reference date that is due to be paid in one year or less is the sum of principal payments on this debt to be made in the coming year, except where the debt is in the form of securities issued at a discount, in which instance the principal amount to be paid will exceed the nominal amount outstanding at the reference date.

[2]Some countries that have debt primarily in the form of instruments on which principal is paid only at maturity attribute the full value of each long-term (original maturity) debt instrument on a remaining basis by when the instrument is due to mature. However, from the viewpoint of liquidity risk analysis, this method is imperfect because payments coming due in the near term, such as interest and partial payments of principal, are not captured within short-term remaining-maturity debt if the debt instrument has a maturity date further than a year ahead.

[3]In this context, a common currency area is one in which more than one economy belongs and has a regional central bank with the legal authority to issue the same currency within the area. To belong to this area, the economy must be a member of the regional central bank.

an economy that uses as its legal tender a currency issued by a monetary authority of another economy—such as U.S. dollars—or of a common currency area to which it does not belong should classify the currency as a foreign currency, although domestic transactions are settled in this currency.

6.13 The attribution of external debt by currency is primarily determined by characteristics of the future payment(s). Foreign currency debt is defined as debt that is payable in a currency other than the domestic currency; a subcategory of foreign currency debt is debt that is payable in a foreign currency but with the amounts to be paid linked to a domestic currency (domestic-currency-linked debt). Foreign-currency-linked debt is debt that is payable in domestic currency but with the amounts to be paid linked to a foreign currency. Domestic currency debt is debt that is payable in the domestic currency, and not linked to a foreign currency. In the unusual instance of interest payments to be paid in a foreign currency but principal payments to be paid in a domestic currency, or vice versa, only the present value of the payments to be paid in a foreign currency need be classified as foreign currency debt (and similarly for foreign-currency-linked debt).

6.14 In attributing external debt by type of foreign currency—U.S. dollar, euro, Japanese yen, etc.—the currency to which payments are linked is the determining criterion. Some types of foreign currency borrowing are denominated in more than one currency. However, if the amounts to be paid on such borrowing are linked to one specific currency, the borrowing should be attributed to that currency. Otherwise, compilers are encouraged to disaggregate such multicurrency borrowing by the component currencies. If, for any reason at the time the data are compiled for a particular reference date, the amounts attributable to each currency at that date are not known with precision, the borrowing should be attributed to each type of currency using the latest firm information available to the compiler—such as the currency attribution at the previous reference date together with any known payments in specific currencies made during the subsequent period—and revised once firm information for the new reference date are known.[4]

Interest Rates

Variable- and fixed-rate external debt

6.15 Variable-rate external debt instruments are those on which interest costs are linked to a reference index—for example, LIBOR (London interbank offered rate), or the price of a specific commodity, or the price of a specific financial instrument that normally changes over time in a continuous manner in response to market pressures. All other debt instruments should be classified as fixed-rate. Interest on external debt that is linked to the credit rating of another borrower should be classified as fixed-rate because credit ratings do not change in a continuous manner in response to market pressures, whereas interest on external debt that is linked to a reference price index should be classified as variable-rate, provided that the price(s) that are the basis for the reference index are primarily market-determined.

6.16 The classification of an instrument can change over time, if, say, it switches from fixed to variable rate. For instance, interest may be fixed for a certain number of years and then becomes variable. While a fixed rate is paid, the instrument is to be classified as fixed-rate debt, and when it switches to variable rate it is classified as variable-rate debt. If interest is linked to a reference index or commodity price or financial instrument price but is fixed unless the reference index or price passes a particular threshold, it should be regarded as fixed-rate. But if thereafter interest becomes variable, then it should be reclassified as a variable-rate instrument. Alternatively, if interest is variable-rate until it reaches a predetermined ceiling or floor, it becomes fixed-rate debt when it reaches that ceiling or floor.

6.17 As in *BPM5*, when the value of the principal is indexed, the change in value resulting from indexation—periodically and at maturity—is classified as interest. So, if principal only is indexed, such debt is to be classified as variable-rate regardless of whether interest is fixed or variable, provided that the reference index meets the criterion above: it normally changes over time in a continuous manner in response to market pressures.

---

[4]For World Bank currency pool loans, while the composition of the currency pool changes on a daily basis, the currency ratios have been maintained within narrow limits since 1991. In the absence of other information, debtors may wish to report the currency compo-

sition of currency pool loans as 30 percent U.S. dollar, 30 percent euro, 30 percent Japanese yen, and 10 percent other currencies (until or unless the World Bank changes its ratio limits).

Average interest rates

6.18 The average interest rate is the weighted-average level of interest rates on the outstanding gross external debt as at the reference date. The weights to be used are determined by the value in the unit of account of each borrowing as a percentage of the total. For example, for the general government sector the weight given to the interest rate on each external debt instrument equals the value in the unit of account of that debt as a percentage of total external debt for the general government sector. Similarly, the weight given to the average level of interest rates for the general government sector when calculating the average interest rate for the whole economy is equal to the total value in the unit of account of general government external debt as a percentage of total economy-wide external debt.

6.19 The relevant interest rate level for each debt instrument is affected by whether it has a fixed- or variable-linked interest rate. If the interest rate is contractually fixed, then this rate should be used, taking account of any discount and premium at issuance. If the rate of interest had been variable in the past but is now fixed, the current fixed-rate should be used. For variable-rate instruments, the rate of interest on each instrument should be the rate accruing on the reference day. In other words, usually variable rates of interest are reset on a periodic basis, and it is the level of the interest rate applicable on the reference day that should be used. If the interest rate is reset on the reference date, that rate should be reported and not the previous interest rate. If for any reason the variable rate is not observable, then the level of the reference index or appropriate price on the reference date, or, if the link is to a change in the reference index, the recorded change for the relevant period up to the reference date, or the closest relevant time period available, together with any existing additional margin the borrower needs to pay, should be used to calculate the interest rate level.

6.20 For calculating the weighted average of interest rates agreed on new borrowing during the period, the interest rates recorded would be those established at the time of the borrowing. If the interest rate is contractually fixed, then this rate should be used. For variable-rate borrowing, the rate of interest on each instrument should be that which is accruing on the day the claim is established. The weights to be used in compiling average interest rate data are determined by the value in the unit of account of each borrowing, on the date the claim was established, as a percentage of the total borrowed during the period.

Location of Securities Issuance

6.21 Debt securities issued by a resident of the same economy in which the security is issued are to be classified as domestically issued, regardless of the currency of issue. All other issues are to be classified as foreign issued. If there is uncertainty over the location of issue, then the following criteria should be taken into account in descending order of preference to determine whether a resident of the economy has issued a domestic or a foreign debt security:

- The debt security is listed on a recognized exchange in the domestic economy (domestic issue) or in a foreign economy (foreign security).
- The debt security has an International Security Identification Number (ISIN) with a country code the same as the legal domicile of the issuer, and/or is allocated a domestic security code by the domestic national numbering agency (domestic security). Or the debt security has an ISIN code with a country code different from that where the issuer is legally domiciled and/or has a foreign security code issued by a foreign national numbering agency (foreign security).
- The security is issued in a domestic currency (domestic issue), as defined in paragraph 6.12 above, or in a foreign currency (foreign issue).

Concessional Debt

6.22 There is no unique definition of concessionality, and the *Guide* does not provide nor recommend one. Nonetheless, the definition of the OECD's Development Assistance Committee (DAC)[5] is commonly used. Under the DAC definition, concessional lending (that is, lending extended on terms that are substantially more generous than market terms) includes (1) official credits with an original grant element of 25 percent or more using a 10 percent rate of discount (that is, where the excess of the face value of a loan from the official sector over the sum of the discounted future debt-service payments to be

---

[5]The Development Assistance Committee of the OECD was created in 1960. Its membership at mid-2001 comprised 22 countries and the Commission of the European Union.

made by the debtor is 25 percent or more using a 10 percent rate of discount); and (2) lending by the major regional development banks (African Development Bank, Asian Development Bank, and the Inter-American Development Bank) and from the IMF and World Bank, with concessionality determined on the basis of each institution's own classification of concessional lending. All external debt not classified as concessional should be classified as nonconcessional.

Debt-Service and Other Payment Schedules

6.23 A payment schedule provides a projection of future payments, at a reference date, based on a certain set of assumptions that are likely to change over time. A debt-service payment schedule projects payments on the outstanding gross external debt position at the reference date and helps in the assessment of liquidity risk by allowing the data user, and debtor, to monitor whether a bunching of payments is developing regardless of the original maturity of the debt instrument. For the debtor, early warning of such bunching might allow countervailing action to be taken.

6.24 Because the projection of a payment schedule requires assumptions to be made, to assist compilers, some guidance is provided below on the assumptions to apply. In compiling payment schedules, the *Guide* encourages the compiler to make best efforts in projecting payments. Consistent with the definitions in Chapter 2 (paragraph 2.5), in the debt-service payment schedule, interest payments are periodic payments of interest costs, while principal payments are all other payments that reduce the principal amount outstanding.

Projected Payments of Foreign Currency External Debt

6.25 External debt payments may be required in a currency different from the unit of account used for presenting data in the debt-service payment schedule. For such external debt payments, projected payments should be converted to the unit of account using the market exchange rate (that is, the midpoint between the buying and the selling spot rates) prevailing on the reference date (that is, the last day before the start of the forward-looking period). In

other words, if a debt-service payment schedule is drawn up for external debt outstanding on an end-calendar-year reference date, then the exchange rate prevailing at the end of the calendar year (on the last day of that year) should be used.[6]

6.26 For borrowing in multicurrencies, payments should be projected with reference to the component currencies of the borrowing and to the market exchange rates (the midpoint between the buying and the selling spot rates) prevailing on the reference date. For World Bank currency pool loans, future payments should be projected in U.S. dollar equivalent terms on the basis of the pool units to be "paid" on each due date and the pool unit value at the reference date, and then converted into the unit of account, if this is not the U.S. dollar,[7] at the market exchange rate (the midpoint between the buying and the selling spot rates) prevailing on the reference date.

Receiving or Paying Foreign Currency Under a Financial Derivative Contract

6.27 Consistent with the foreign-currency-conversion approach adopted throughout the *Guide*, the amounts of foreign currency contracted to be paid and received under a financial derivatives contract that is current and outstanding at the reference date should

---

[6]From a theoretical viewpoint, and given that the debt-service payment schedule is making projections, forward rates may be considered the best estimate of exchange rates for specific dates in the future. However, while such an approach might well be readily applied in many instances for shorter-term debt in major currencies, there may be a lack of readily observable forward rates for longer-term borrowing and for "smaller" currencies, thus leading to possible inconsistent approaches between economies and different maturity periods. Also, there always remains uncertainty about the future course of interest and currency rates. The *Guide* takes the view that projections of future payments of external debt linked to currency and interest rate movements should be based on end-period spot rates, rather than, say, forward rates, because this approach is more transparent, easier to compile, and more readily understandable to users than projections based on rates in forward markets—even though it is recognized that the use of a single day's exchange rate to convert payments to be made over a forward period could be misleading if temporary factors affect the exchange rate for that day.

[7]Currency pool loans are loans that are committed in U.S. dollar equivalent terms and converted into pool units, the base unit the borrower owes, through a conversion rate—pool unit value—that is calculated on the basis of the relationship between the U.S. dollar and the component currencies in the pool. When pool units are to be repaid, they are converted back into the dollar-equivalent amount using the prevailing pool unit value. Currency pool loans are described in more detail in Appendix I.

be converted to the unit of account using the market exchange rate (the midpoint between the buying and the selling spot rates) prevailing on the reference date (the last day before the start of the forward looking period).

Projected Interest Payments on Deposits

6.28 Interest on deposits that is payable once a year or more frequently is projected as a future interest payment. Interest payments on deposits should be projected on the basis of those deposits that are outstanding on the reference date, using interest rates current on the reference date, unless there are contractual reasons to assume otherwise.

6.29 Interest on deposits that are withdrawable on demand or subject to a notice of withdrawal, and not subject to a maturity date, should be projected into the future,[8] whereas those interest payments on those deposits with a maturity date should be projected only to that maturity date. Payments on deposits for which notice of withdrawal has been given should be projected on the assumption that these deposits will be withdrawn on the due date, and no assumption of reinvestment should be made unless there are explicit instructions from the depositor that indicate otherwise.

Projected Payments of Index-Linked External Debt, Including Variable-Rate Interest

6.30 Interest and principal payments on external debt may be linked to a reference index that changes over time—for instance, a variable reference interest rate index, a commodity price, or another specified price index. For such payments, projected payments should be estimated using the level of the reference index on the last day before the start of the forward-looking period or, if the link is to a change in the reference index, the recorded change for the relevant period up to the last day before the start of the forward-looking period, or the closest relevant time period available. If the margin over the reference index is subject to change, then the margin on the last day before the start of the forward-looking period should be used. For debt payable in commodities or

other goods, future payments are valued using the market price of a commodity or good as at the reference date, with the split between principal and interest payments based on the implicit interest rate at the reference date (see also Chapter 2, paragraph 2.37).

Projected Payments on Loans Not Fully Disbursed

6.31 No payments should be projected for loans that are not yet disbursed. If loans have been partially disbursed, payments should be projected only for those funds that have been disbursed. If the payment schedule in the loan contract is based on the assumption that all funds are disbursed, but only partial disbursement has occurred by the reference date, then, in the absence of any other information that clearly specifies the payment schedule arising from funds that have been disbursed, it is recommended that the payment schedule in the loan contract should be prorated by the percentage of the loan that has been disbursed—for example, if half of the loan has been disbursed, then half of each payment in the loan schedule should be reported in the debt-service schedule.[9]

Projected Payments of Service-Related Debts

6.32 In the *Guide*, if a payment to a nonresident for a service that has been provided is outstanding at the reference date, it is classified as an external debt liability. Given this, any future payments for services—such as fees, charges, and commissions that have already been provided by the reference date—are classified as principal payments, within *other debt liabilities* (unless they are classified as debt liabilities to affiliated enterprises/direct investors). Any projection of fees that depend on moving reference amounts, such as undrawn commitments, should be based on the reference amount at the reference date. While not encouraged, it is recognized that national practice might be to classify service charges related to a loan along with interest in the debt-service schedule.

---

[8]In principle, the future could be indefinite, but compilers are encouraged to make some commonsense assumptions about the average maturity of deposits with no stated maturity.

[9]For prudent debt-management purposes, in some national practices, even if only partially disbursed, the full amounts foreseen in the payment schedule of the loan are projected for each period until the external debt outstanding at the reference date is fully repaid. Under this "truncated" approach, if half the amount is disbursed on the reference date, the loan is "repaid" in half the time that is expected in the loan schedule, thus "front-loading" the debt-service schedule.

Projected Payments of External Debt with the Provision for Early Repayment

6.33 An external debt liability may include a provision that allows the creditor to request early repayment. For instance, the creditor may have an option to redeem the debt early through a put (sell) option. In principle, projected payments can be estimated both without and with reference to this embedded put option. For instance, a ten-year bond with a put option after five years can be assumed at inception to have a repayment date of ten years, and payments recorded up until that date. Alternatively, for this bond the earliest possible date for repayment of five years could be assumed, with projected payments finishing at that time. The preference in the *Guide* is to project debt-service payments on the basis of the original maturity (ten years in the example), but to provide additional information on payments based on the earliest repayment date (five years in the example). But it is recognized that national practice may be to estimate projected payments on bonds wit embedded put options only until the option date (five years in the example), with additional information on the projected payments on the bond up until the original maturity date (ten years in the example).[10]

Projected Payments of Credit-Linked External Debt

6.34 Payments of interest and/or principal may be linked to the credit rating of another borrower(s),

such as in a credit-linked note. In these instances the credit rating of the other borrower(s) on the last day before the start of the forward-looking period should be used to project payments.

Projected Payments Arising from Reverse Transactions

6.35 Under the recording approach for reverse transactions—the collateralized loan approach—a security provider records a loan liability. In the debt-service payment schedule, the security provider records the full amount of the loan to be paid at maturity under principal. If the reverse transaction has an "open" maturity,[11] the loan should be recorded as on-demand, under the immediate time category in the presentation of the debt-service payment schedule, unless there is clear evidence to suggest otherwise.

Projected Payments on Financial Leases

6.36 Projected payments on financial leases must be divided into interest and principal payments. The amount of interest payments can be calculated using the implicit rate of interest on the loan, with all other payments recorded as principal payments. Conceptually, at inception, the implicit rate of interest on the loan is that which equates the value of the good provided—the value of the loan—with the discounted value of future payments, including any residual value of the good to be returned (or purchased) at the maturity of the lease.

---

[10]The debtor might have an option to call (buy back) external debt early, which would also result in a drain on liquidity. But unlike the put option for the creditor, this drain is unlikely to be exercised except at a convenient time for the debtor. Consequently, in assessing vulnerability, information on external debt containing put options is more significant.

---

[11]"Open" maturity is where both parties agree daily to renew or terminate the agreement. Such an arrangement avoids settlement costs if both parties wish to renew the reverse transaction on a continuing basis.

7. Further Presentation Tables of External Debt

Introduction

7.1 This chapter introduces presentation tables that facilitate a more detailed examination of the potential liquidity and solvency risks to the economy that might arise from the acquisition of external liabilities. These tables provide information that supplements that included in the gross external debt position presented earlier in the *Guide*. More specifically, this chapter provides presentation tables on:

- External debt by short-term remaining maturity (Tables 7.1 and 7.2);
- Debt-service payment schedule (Tables 7.3 and 7.4);
- Foreign and domestic currency external debt (Tables 7.5–7.7);
- Interest rates and external debt (Tables 7.8–7.9);
- External debt by creditor sector (Table 7.10);
- Net external debt position (Table 7.11);
- Reconciliation of external debt positions and flows (Table 7.12);
- Traded debt instruments (Tables 7.13 and 7.14); and
- Cross-border trade-related credit (Table 7.15).

7.2 For any individual economy, the relevance of any table in this chapter will depend upon the circumstances facing it, and so the *Guide* does not provide a list of priorities for compiling the tables ahead. Indeed, the tables are provided as flexible frameworks to be used by countries in the long-term development of their external debt statistics. But experience suggests that data on debt-maturity profiles and currency breakdowns are essential to a comprehensive analysis of external vulnerability for countries with substantial but uncertain access to international capital markets. For the IMF's data dissemination standards, the tables for the debt-service payment schedule—Table 7.3 (Special Data Dissemination Standard, SDDS) and Table 7.4 (General Data Dissemination System, GDDS)—are relevant,

as is the table on foreign currency and domestic currency debt, Table 7.5 (SDDS).[1]

7.3 Because the concepts for its measurement remain consistent throughout the *Guide*, the gross external debt position for each institutional sector and for the total economy should be the same regardless of the presentation table employed, provided that the same approach to valuing traded debt instruments is adopted throughout. Also, because the concepts remain consistent, if necessary, compilers can combine different characteristics of external debt in presentations other than those set out below. In disseminating data, compilers are encouraged to provide methodological notes explaining the concepts and methods used in compiling the data.

7.4 Throughout this chapter, except where stated otherwise, the first level of disaggregation by row is by debtor sector, followed (where relevant) by maturity on an original maturity basis. In the tables, the institutional sector presentation is provided, but in principle the presentations can also be provided on a public sector basis, as set out in Chapter 5. Because of the particular importance of both measures, the debt-service payment schedule is presented on both institutional (Table 7.3) and a public sector basis (Table 7.4).

External Debt by Short-Term Remaining Maturity

7.5 Tables are provided for presenting gross external debt position data by short-term remaining maturity for the total economy (Table 7.1), and then by institutional sector (Table 7.2). Information on the total short-term debt of the total economy, both on

---

[1]Box 4.1 in Chapter 4 provides the precise requirements for the external debt category of the IMF's data dissemination standards.

**Table 7.1. Gross External Debt Position:
Short-Term Remaining Maturity—Total Economy**

End-Period

Short-term debt on an original maturity basis
Money market instruments
Loans
Currency and deposits[1]
Trade credits
Other debt liabilities[2]
  Arrears
  Other

Total

*Long-term debt obligations due for payment
  within one year or less*
Bonds and notes
Loans
Currency and deposits[1]
Trade credits
Other debt liabilities[2]

Total

Total Economy

[1]It is recommended that all currency and deposits be included in the short-term category unless detailed information is available to make the short-term/long-term attribution.
[2]*Other debt liabilities* are *other liabilities* in the IIP statement.

**Table 7.2. Gross External Debt Position:
Short-Term Remaining Maturity—By Sector**

End-Period

General Government
*Short-term debt on an original
  maturity basis*
Money market instruments
Loans
Trade credits
Other debt liabilities[1]
  Arrears
  Other
Total
*Long-term debt obligations due for
  payment within one year or less*
Bonds and notes
Loans
Trade credits
Other debt liabilities[1]
Total
Monetary Authorities
*Short-term debt on an original
  maturity basis*
Money market instruments
Loans
Currency and deposits[2]
Other debt liabilities[1]
  Arrears
  Other
Total
*Long-term debt obligations due for
  payment within one year or less*
Bonds and notes
Loans
Currency and deposits[2]
Other debt liabilities[1]
Total
Banks
*Short-term debt on an original
  maturity basis*
Money market instruments
Loans
Currency and deposits[2]
Other debt liabilities[1]
  Arrears
  Other
Total
*Long-term debt obligations due for
  payment within one year or less*
Bonds and notes
Loans
Currency and deposits[2]
Other debt liabilities[1]
Total

---

an original and remaining maturity basis, as well as by sector, is of analytical interest (see Box 7.1). For compiling the data for these tables, *direct investment: intercompany lending* should be attributed to long-term maturity unless detailed information is available to provide data on a short-term remaining maturity basis.

7.6 Compiling such information helps in the assessment of liquidity risk by indicating that part of the gross external debt position that is expected to fall due in the coming year. Also, by separately indicating short-term debt on an original maturity basis from debt on a long-term basis falling due in the coming year, the presentation provides additional information content, such as the extent to which high short-term remaining maturity data is due (or not) to significant debt payments expected on long-term debt (original maturity basis).

7.7 The concept of short-term remaining maturity can also be applied to other tables in this chapter, such as those relating to foreign-currency external debt.

Debt-Service Payment Schedule

7.8 Like the short-term remaining maturity presentation table, as mentioned in the previous chapter, a debt-service payment schedule supports the assessment of liquidity risk.

Table 7.2 (concluded)

	End-Period
Other Sectors	
Short-term debt on an original maturity basis	
Money market instruments	
Loans	
Currency and deposits[2]	
Trade credits	
Other debt liabilities[1]	
Arrears	
Other	
Total	
Long-term debt obligations due for payment within one year or less	
Bonds and notes	
Loans	
Currency and deposits[2]	
Trade credits	
Other debt liabilities[1]	
Total	
Total	
Direct Investment: Intercompany Lending[3]	
Short-term debt on an original maturity basis	
Debt liabilities to affiliated enterprises	
Arrears	
Other	
Debt liabilities to direct investors	
Arrears	
Other	
Long-term debt obligations due for payment within one year or less	
Debt liabilities to affiliated enterprises	
Debt liabilities to direct investors	
Total Short-Term External Debt (remaining maturity basis)	

[1]*Other debt liabilities* are *other liabilities* in the IIP statement.

[2]It is recommended that all currency and deposits be included in the short-term category unless detailed information is available to make the short-term/long-term attribution.

[3]If data on intercompany lending on a short-term remaining maturity basis are available.

7.9 Table 7.3 gives a presentation of a debt-service payment schedule. The data to be presented in this table are projected future payments of interest and principal on gross external debt outstanding on the reference date.[2] The data should not cover projected

---

[2]Debt-service payments can also be projected on the basis not only of outstanding debt on the reference date but additionally on debt not yet, but expected to be, outstanding—for example, loans that have been agreed but not disbursed and short-term debt that might be assumed to be renewed. This *Guide* does not provide guidance for projecting payments on expected disbursements because its focus is on outstanding, and not projected, debt.

Box 7.1. High-Frequency Debt-Monitoring Systems

To enable authorities to monitor developments in short-term capital flows as a source of external vulnerability, a number of countries, with the help of IMF staff, have developed monitoring systems that generate timely high-frequency data on the liabilities of domestic banks to foreign banks. This box briefly sets out the rationale for such systems, their coverage, the institutional considerations, and the use of these data.

Rationale and Design Objective

High-frequency debt-monitoring systems are intended to monitor developments in short-term financial flows, which are a major source of external vulnerability and an important factor in crisis prevention and/or resolution. Such systems are designed to obtain high-quality data within very short time intervals (typically, a day).

Coverage

Given these objectives, high-frequency debt-monitoring systems are typically limited to cover consolidated interbank transactions of domestic banks, including their offshore branches and subsidiaries, vis-à-vis foreign banks. The core set of instruments that are typically covered include short-term interbank credits, trade credit lines, payments falling due on medium- and long-term loans, and receipts and payments related to financial derivatives. Reporting institutions usually provide data on amounts due and paid in the reporting period, new lines extended, interest spreads over LIBOR, and maturities. As regards country classification, individual banks are attributed to the country in which their headquarters is located.

Institutional Considerations

Monitoring systems have been tailored to the specific circumstances of individual countries. However, there are certain minimum requirements—in general, a capacity to collect, process, and communicate high-quality data with short lags. Key factors in the success of such systems include close coordination between the authorities and banks, which may be facilitated by preexisting reporting requirements, and the proportion of external financial flows being channeled through the domestic banking system (and, if relevant, other reporting institutions). Although a capacity must be developed to respond promptly to questions, and to identify and approach banks about emerging problems, the authorities need to be sensitive to concerns that private sector participants might misinterpret requests for information.

Use and Interpretation of Data

The information provided permits the tracking of rollover rates, changes in exposure and the terms of external obligations, which help to assess changes in international capital market conditions and creditors' assessments of the borrowing country. (It may also reveal differing assessments of different institutions within the country.) Interpretation of the data involves considerable judgment, requiring analysis of supply- and demand-side factors in order to shed more light on the agents' motivations behind the monitored transactions and thus the soundness of a country's external position. Supply-side considerations include factors such as shifts in creditor bank strategies, banking sector or country risk, and institutional/regulatory changes in the source country. Demand for interbank lines may be affected, for example, by fluctuations of imports or an increase/decrease in the reliance on local financing sources, such as foreign currency time deposits.

Table 7.3. Debt-Service Payment Schedule: By Sector

| | For Outstanding External Debt as at End-Period | | | | | | | |
| | One year or less (months) | | | | | Over one year to two years (months) | | Over two years |
	Immediate[1]	0–3	4–6	7–9	10–12	13–18	19–24	
General Government								
Debt securities								
Principal								
Interest								
Loans								
Principal								
Interest								
Trade credits								
Principal								
Interest								
Other debt liabilities[2]								
Principal								
Interest								
Monetary Authorities								
Debt securities								
Principal								
Interest								
Loans								
Principal								
Interest								
Currency and deposits								
Principal								
Interest								
Other debt liabilities[2]								
Principal								
Interest								
Banks								
Debt securities								
Principal								
Interest								
Loans								
Principal								
Interest								
Currency and deposits								
Principal								
Interest								
Other debt liabilities[2]								
Principal								
Interest								
Other Sectors								
Debt securities								
Principal								
Interest								
Loans								
Principal								
Interest								
Currency and deposits								
Principal								
Interest								
Trade credits								
Principal								
Interest								

Table 7.3 *(continued)*

	For Outstanding External Debt as at End-Period							
	One year or less (months)				Over one year to two years (months)		Over two years
	Immediate[1]	0–3	4–6	7–9	10–12	13–18	19–24	

Other Sectors *(concluded)*
  Other debt liabilities
  Principal
  Interest

    Nonbank financial corporations
      Debt securities
      Principal
      Interest

      Loans
      Principal
      Interest

      Currency and deposits
      Principal
      Interest

      Other debt liabilities[2]
      Principal
      Interest

    Nonfinancial corporations
      Debt securities
      Principal
      Interest

      Loans
      Principal
      Interest

      Trade credits
      Principal
      Interest

      Other debt liabilities[2]
      Principal
      Interest

    Households and nonprofit institutions serving households (NPISH)
      Debt securities
      Principal
      Interest

      Loans
      Principal
      Interest

      Trade credits
      Principal
      Interest

      Other debt liabilities[2]
      Principal
      Interest

Direct Investment: Intercompany Lending

  Debt liabilities to affiliated enterprises
  Principal
  Interest

  Debt liabilities to direct investors
  Principal
  Interest

Table 7.3 (concluded)

	For Outstanding External Debt as at End-Period							
		One year or less (months)				Over one year to two years (months)		Over two years
	Immediate[1]	0–3	4–6	7–9	10–12	13–18	19–24	
Gross External Debt Payments								
Of which: Principal								
Interest								
Memorandum item								
Securities with Embedded Options[3]								
General Government								
Principal								
Interest								
Monetary Authorities								
Principal								
Interest								
Banks								
Principal								
Interest								
Other Sectors								
Principal								
Interest								

[1]Immediately available on demand or immediately due.
[2]*Other debt liabilities* are *other liabilities* in the IIP statement.
[3]Include only those securities that contain an embedded option with a date on which or after which the debt can be sold back to the debtor.

future payments on external debt not yet outstanding. *Direct investment: intercompany lending* is separately identified, although it is recognized that sometimes the payments schedule on debt liabilities between related enterprises might not always be known with precision.

7.10 In the table, the columns are time periods of one year and less, over one year to two years, and over two years. The time frame in the table could be extended. Annual payment data for each year from two years up to five years ahead would help to identify potential significant payment amounts well in advance. Some countries provide annual data for each year out to 10 or 15 years.

7.11 Subperiods are presented within the time periods of one year or less, and over one year to two years: in the one year or less period, quarterly subperiods are presented together with an "immediate" category (see below); in the over one year to two years time period, semiannual (semester) subperiods are presented. The column "0–3" months covers

payments of up to three months (excluding those payments falling under "immediate"); the column "4–6" months covers payments due in more than three months up to six months; the column "7–9" months covers payments due in more than six months up to nine months; the column "10–12" months covers payments due in more than nine months up to 12 months; the column "13–18" months covers payments due in more than 12 months up to 18 months; the column "19–24" months covers payments due in more than 18 months up to 24 months.

7.12 The time period of one year or less includes a subperiod of "immediate" that covers all debt that is payable on demand—for example, certain types of bank deposits, as well as debt that is past due (arrears, including interest on arrears). Debt that is technically due immediately is different in nature from debt due in one year or less because the actual timing of payment on debt due immediately is uncertain. Without an "immediate" time period specified, there is a possibility that an analytically misleading impression could be given by the data for short-term debt—some of this debt might not be repaid for some time.

7.13 When securities contain an embedded option with a date on which or after which the debt can be put (sold) back to the debtor by the creditor, as explained in the previous chapter the preference of the *Guide* is that projected payments in Tables 7.3 and 7.4 be estimated without reference to these embedded put options, but that memorandum items on projected payments be provided assuming early repayment at the option date.

7.14 If national practice is to estimate projected payments on bonds with embedded put options only until the option date, additional memorandum information could be provided on the projected payments on the bond up until the original maturity date.

7.15 Other embedded options might not include a set date, but their exercise may be dependent on certain conditions occurring, such as a credit rating downgrade, or in the instance of a convertible bond, the price of equity reaching a certain level. While no memorandum item is provided for these instruments, where significant, additional data could be compiled on the value and type of this external debt. In particular, and if significant, credit-linked note instruments should be separately identified in a memorandum item. In some economies, there may be interest in historical debt-service data—that is, past payments of principal and interest on longterm borrowings including prepayments of debt.

7.16 For public debt managers, the monitoring of the debt-service payment schedule for public and publicly guaranteed debt is essential for debt management strategy and to ensure that payments are made on a timely basis. Table 7.4 provides a debt-service payment schedule that presents debt-service payments on a public sector basis but is otherwise identical to Table 7.3.

Foreign Currency and Domestic Currency External Debt

7.17 Experience suggests that information on the currency composition of the gross external debt position is necessary for monitoring an economy's potential vulnerability to solvency and liquidity risk. For instance, a depreciation of the exchange rate can

increase the burden of foreign currency debt liabilities in domestic currency terms for the resident debtor (although there may be beneficial effects such as an improvement in the competitiveness of an economy's exports of goods and services), while payments on foreign currency debt can cause downward pressure on the domestic exchange rate and/or outflows of foreign currency from the economy. Some of the impact can be offset through the use of financial derivatives, and natural hedges such as foreign currency assets and income, but, unlike the domestic currency, the domestic monetary authority cannot create additional foreign currency.

7.18 Three tables are provided to help users understand the risks to the economy of foreign currency external debt. Table 7.5 is a simple foreign currency/domestic currency split of the gross external debt position; Table 7.6 provides more information on the foreign currency external debt position; and Table 7.7 provides information on foreign currency payments.

Domestic Currency/Foreign Currency Split of the Gross External Debt Position

7.19 Table 7.5 provides information on the foreign currency and domestic currency split of the gross external debt position for the total economy. The definition of foreign currency debt in this table includes both foreign currency[3] and foreign-currency-linked debt. Foreign-currency-linked debt is included with foreign currency debt because a depreciation of the exchange rate can increase the burden of foreign-currency-linked debt liabilities in domestic currency terms for the resident debtor.

7.20 A special case arises where an economy uses as its legal tender a currency issued by a monetary authority of another economy—such as U.S. dollars—or of a common currency area to which the economy does not belong. While this currency is to be classified as a foreign currency, it has some of the attributes of a domestic currency because domestic transactions are settled in this currency. With this in mind, information could be separately provided on external debt payable in and/or linked to a foreign currency used as legal tender in the domestic economy, and other foreign currency external debt.

---

[3]Including external debt payable in a foreign currency but with the amounts to be paid linked to a domestic currency.

Table 7.4. Debt-Service Payment Schedule: Public and Publicly Guaranteed Debt and Nonguaranteed Private Sector Debt

	For Outstanding External Debt as at End-Period							
		One year or less (months)				Over one year to two years (months)		Over two years
	Immediate[1]	0–3	4–6	7–9	10–12	13–18	19–24	
Public and Publicly Guaranteed Debt								
Debt securities								
Principal								
Interest								
Loans								
Principal								
Interest								
Currency and deposits								
Principal								
Interest								
Trade credits								
Principal								
Interest								
Other debt liabilities[2]								
Principal								
Interest								
Direct investment: Intercompany lending								
Debt liabilities to affiliated enterprises								
Principal								
Interest								
Debt liabilities to direct investors								
Principal								
Interest								
Nonguaranteed Private Sector Debt								
Debt securities								
Principal								
Interest								
Loans								
Principal								
Interest								
Currency and deposits								
Principal								
Interest								
Trade credit								
Principal								
Interest								
Other debt liabilities[2]								
Principal								
Interest								
Direct investment: Intercompany lending								
Debt liabilities to affiliated enterprises								
Principal								
Interest								
Debt liabilities to direct investors								
Principal								
Interest								
Gross External Debt Payments								
Of which: Principal								
Interest								
Memorandum item **Securities with Embedded Options**[3]								
Public and Publicly Guaranteed Debt								
Principal								
Interest								
Nonguaranteed Private Sector Debt								
Principal								
Interest								

[1]Immediately available on demand or immediately due.
[2]*Other debt liabilities* are *other liabilities* in the IIP statement.
[3]Include only those securities that contain an embedded option with a date on which or after which the debt can be sold back to the debtor.

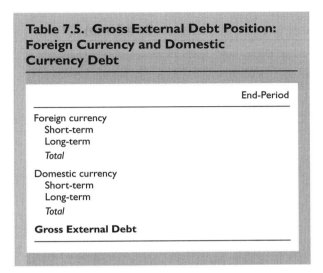

Table 7.5. Gross External Debt Position: Foreign Currency and Domestic Currency Debt

	End-Period
Foreign currency	
Short-term	
Long-term	
Total	
Domestic currency	
Short-term	
Long-term	
Total	
Gross External Debt	

7.21 While Table 7.5 is based on the original maturity concept, data could also be compiled on a remaining-maturity basis. Also, further disaggregation of the table into institutional sectors and instruments is possible. If significant, the foreign currency data could be disaggregated into external debt that is payable in foreign currency and external debt that is payable in domestic currency but with the amounts to be paid linked to a foreign currency (foreign-currency-linked debt).

Gross Foreign Currency External Debt

7.22 For those economies with significant gross foreign currency external debt, Table 7.6 presents more detailed information on the position. This table provides an attribution of foreign currency and foreign-currency-linked external debt by major foreign currency—U.S. dollars, euros, and Japanese yen. Further individual currencies could be added. Dissemination of this detailed information is encouraged because it provides further information on the exposure to exchange rate movements to that set out in Table 7.5.

7.23 The table could be extended to also include foreign currency and foreign-currency-linked debt owed by each resident sector to each other resident institutional sector. While such debt is beyond the definition of external debt, it can result in cross-institutional sector transfers of income when there are movements in the domestic exchange rate vis-à-vis foreign currencies, thus affecting eco-

nomic activity and financial stability. However, if such data are added to the data on nonresident claims, it should be remembered that if, for example, a resident bank funds a foreign currency loan to a resident corporation by borrowing from a nonresident, the foreign currency liabilities would appear in both the resident/resident and resident/nonresident data.

7.24 In the special case where an economy uses as its legal tender a foreign currency, borrowing in this currency from nonresidents could be separately identified in the table.

7.25 A memorandum item is provided in Table 7.6 for the notional value—the amount underlying a financial derivatives contract that is necessary for calculating payments or receipts on the contract—of foreign currency and foreign-currency-linked financial derivatives contracts with nonresidents both to receive and pay foreign currency, and by type of currency.[4] A financial derivatives contract to purchase foreign currency with domestic currency is classified as a financial derivative to receive foreign currency. If instead the contract is to purchase domestic currency with foreign currency at a future date, this is a financial derivative to pay foreign currency. Similarly, an option to buy foreign currency (sell domestic currency) is classified as a financial derivative to receive foreign currency, and vice versa. The decisive factor in determining whether the financial derivative is to be classified as receiving or paying foreign currency is the exposure to currency movements, so if payment of a financial derivatives contract is linked to a foreign currency even though payment is required in domestic currency, the financial derivative is to be classified as a contract to pay foreign currency, and vice versa.

7.26 Through the use of financial derivatives, the economy could become more, or less, exposed to exchange rate risk than is evidenced in the gross foreign currency external debt data; in this context, the notional value data—by providing a broad indication of the potential transfer of price risk underlying the financial derivatives contract—are analytically useful.

---

[4]For those economies that use a foreign currency—such as the U.S. dollar—as legal tender, information on the notional value of foreign currency derivatives to receive and pay this foreign currency—such as U.S. dollars—could be presented.

Table 7.6. Gross External Foreign Currency and Foreign-Currency-Linked Debt Position

	End-Period				
	Total	U.S. dollar	Euro	Yen	Other
General Government					
Short-term					
Long-term					
Monetary Authorities					
Short-term[1]					
Long-term					
Banks					
Short-term[1]					
Long-term					
Other Sectors					
Short-term					
Long-term					
Nonbank financial corporations					
Short-term					
Long-term					
Nonfinancial corporations					
Short-term					
Long-term					
Households and nonprofit institutions serving households (NPISH)					
Short-term					
Long-term					
Direct Investment: Intercompany Lending					
Debt liabilities to affiliated enterprises					
Debt liabilities to direct investors					
Gross External Foreign Currency and Foreign-Currency-Linked Debt					
Memorandum item					
Financial Derivatives: Notional Value of Foreign Currency and Foreign-Currency-Linked Contracts with Nonresidents[2]					
To Receive Foreign Currency					
General Government					
Forwards					
Options					
Monetary Authorities					
Forwards					
Options					
Banks					
Forwards					
Options					
Other Sectors					
Forwards					
Options					
Nonbank financial corporations					
Forwards					
Options					
Nonfinancial corporations					
Forwards					
Options					
Households and NPISH					
Forwards					
Options					
Total					

Table 7.6 (concluded)

		End-Period			
	Total	U.S. dollar	Euro	Yen	Other
To Pay Foreign Currency					
General Government					
Forwards					
Options					
Monetary Authorities					
Forwards					
Options					
Banks					
Forwards					
Options					
Other Sectors					
Forwards					
Options					
Nonbank financial corporations					
Forwards					
Options					
Nonfinancial corporations					
Forwards					
Options					
Households and NPISH					
Forwards					
Options					
Total					

[1]It is recommended that all currency and deposits be included in the short-term category unless detailed information is available to make the short-term/long-term attribution.

[2]Excludes financial derivatives that are included in reserve assets data; that is, financial derivatives that pertain to the management of reserve assets, are integral to the valuation of such assets, are settled in foreign currency, and are under the effective control of the monetary authorities.

7.27 The notional amount is comparable with the values for debt instruments; for instance, if a foreign currency debt instrument is issued and the proceeds sold for domestic currency with an agreement to repurchase the foreign currency with domestic currency at a future date—known as a currency or forex swap—the notional amount of the financial derivative is equal to the amount swapped. So, these amounts provide an indication of the scale of activity by institutional sectors in foreign currency financial derivatives; the extent to which institutional sectors might be covering the foreign currency risk of their borrowing; and/or the extent to which institutional sectors may be exposed to foreign currency risk through financial derivative contracts.

7.28 A breakdown of positions by institutional sector into forwards (including swaps) and options is provided because of their different characteristics. Notably, forwards are likely to involve the delivery or receipt of the notional amount of foreign currency underlying the contract, whereas the settlement of an option is likely to involve only a net settlement of the market value.[5]

7.29 If a single financial derivatives contract both pays and receives foreign currency, the notional amount should be included under both pay and receive foreign currency. Not only does this ensure completeness of reporting, it also allows for the possibility of attributing financial derivatives contracts by type of currency. If a financial derivatives contract requires the payment or receipt of foreign currency in return for something other than a currency (for example, a commodity), the notional amount should be included under either the receipt or payment of the foreign currency, as appropriate. If these contracts are significant, they could be separately identified.

---

[5]According to data published semiannually by the Bank for International Settlements (BIS), market values of foreign currency options are typically around 3–5 percent of the notional amount.

Projected Payments in Foreign Currencies Vis-à-Vis Nonresidents

7.30 Table 7.7 sets out a foreign currency payment schedule, and a memorandum item of selected foreign currency and foreign-currency-linked external assets. It provides an idea of the future potential drains of foreign currency resources from the economy to nonresidents, along with the external foreign currency assets that may be available to meet such drains in the short-term. While there is always difficulty in ascertaining the extent to which it might be possible to use assets to meet outstanding debt obligations as they come due, the memorandum item provides a broad approximation of the concept of foreign currency liquidity by listing selected asset types that would most likely be available in the short term. Only obligations to and claims on nonresidents are to be included in this table.

7.31 The bank, nonbank financial, and nonfinancial corporate sectors are presented in the table, but not the general government and monetary authority sectors because a framework for the dissemination of similar, but not identical, data for the monetary authorities and the central government is provided by the Data Template on International Reserves and Foreign Currency Liquidity.[6] However, the table could be extended to cover these sectors.

7.32 The rows in the table present types of foreign currency payments (and receipts); the time period columns are defined identically to those in the debt-service schedule (Table 7.3).[7] Because the focus is on foreign currency drains, all payments in domestic currency, even if linked to a foreign currency, are excluded. Foreign currency external debt payments are those payments that are included in the debt service payment schedule and are required in foreign currency. The requirements to deliver and receive foreign currency from nonresidents under forward contracts include only contractual agreements to deliver and receive the nominal (notional) amounts of foreign currency underlying forward contracts, such as forward foreign exchange contracts, and cross-currency swaps, on contracts current and outstanding at the reference date.

7.33 This item is not intended to include projected net settlements of financial derivative contract involving foreign currency, because such amounts are not required under the contract and are not known until the time of settlement.[8] Consequently, contracts such as options and nondeliverable forwards that require only net settlement are not covered by this table. However, such contracts contribute relatively little to the value of foreign currency delivered under financial derivatives because the settlement amounts are much smaller than the notional amount and because these types of contracts have a relatively small share of the market. Table 7.6 distinguishes between forwards and options and so can be used to indicate their relative shares of total foreign currency financial derivatives.

7.34 The memorandum item in Table 7.7 covers positions in (and not payments of) foreign currency and foreign-currency-linked debt instruments that represent claims on nonresidents—a subcategory of the debt assets presented in the net external debt table (see Table 7.11)—plus foreign currency and foreign-currency-linked equity securities. The instruments in the table are selected on the assumption that they represent assets that might be available to meet a sudden drain of foreign exchange; that is, as mentioned above, they provide an approximation of the concept of foreign currency liquid assets. All short-term instruments (defined on an original maturity basis) are included along with those long-term instruments (original maturity basis) that are traded or tradable (bonds and notes, and equity). Foreign-currency-

---

[6]This is a template on international reserves and foreign currency liquidity that was introduced as a prescribed component of the SDDS in March 1999 by the IMF's Executive Board. The template provides a considerably greater degree of transparency on international reserves and foreign currency borrowing by the authorities than hitherto. Details are provided in the *International Reserves and Foreign Currency Liquidity: Guidelines for a Data Template* (Kester, 2001).

[7]This table could be extended to also include foreign currency payments and receipts to each other resident institutional sector. However, as mentioned in paragraph 7.23, combining resident/nonresident and resident/resident foreign currency data could result in double counting (for example, payments on a foreign currency loan by a resident corporation that was funded by a domestic bank from abroad).

---

[8]As set out in Chapter 6, paragraph 6.27, future requirements to pay/receive foreign currency under forward derivatives contracts are to be converted into the unit of account at the market (spot) rate on the reference date; that is, consistent with the foreign-currency-conversion approach adopted throughout the *Guide*. Consequently, any gains or losses in the unit of account on these financial derivative contracts are not reflected in this table, but would be reflected in the market value data to be reported in the financial derivatives memorandum table presented in Chapter 4 (Table 4.3) and in the net external debt position table set out later in this chapter (see Table 7.11).

Table 7.7. Projected Payment Schedule in Foreign Currency Vis-à-Vis Nonresidents: Selected Institutional Sectors

	For External Debt and Derivatives Contracts Outstanding as at End-Period							
		One year or less (months)				Over one year to two years (months)		Over two years
	Immediate[1]	0–3	4–6	7–9	10–12	13–18	19–24	
Banks								
Foreign currency external debt payments								
Requirements under forward financial derivatives contracts								
To deliver foreign currency								
To receive foreign currency								
Nonbank financial corporations								
Foreign currency external debt payments								
Requirements under forward financial derivatives contracts								
To deliver foreign currency								
To receive foreign currency								
Nonfinancial corporations								
Foreign currency external debt payments								
Requirements under forward financial derivatives contracts								
To deliver foreign currency								
To receive foreign currency								
Memorandum item								
Selected Foreign Currency and Foreign-Currency-Linked External Assets								
Banks								
Short-term								
Money market instruments								
Currency and deposits								
Loans								
Other debt liabilities[2]								
Long-term								
Equities								
Bonds and notes								
Nonbank financial corporations								
Short-term								
Money market instruments								
Currency and deposits								
Loans								
Other debt liabilities[2]								
Long-term								
Equities								
Bonds and notes								
Nonfinancial corporations								
Short-term								
Money market instruments								
Currency and deposits								
Loans								
Trade credits								
Other debt liabilities[2]								
Long-term								
Equities								
Bonds and notes								

[1]Immediately available on demand or immediately due.
[2]*Other debt liabilities* are *other liabilities* in the IIP statement.

Table 7.8. Gross External Debt Position: Interest Rate Composition

	End-Period				
	Fixed-rate-linked		Variable-rate-linked		
	Amount	Percent of total	Amount	Percent of total	Total
General Government					
Short-term					
Long-term					
Monetary Authorities					
Short-term[1]					
Long-term					
Banks					
Short-term[1]					
Long-term					
Other Sectors					
Short-term					
Long-term					
Nonbank financial corporations					
Short-term					
Long-term					
Nonfinancial corporations					
Short-term					
Long-term					
Households and nonprofit institutions serving households (NPISH)					
Short-term					
Long-term					
Direct Investment: Intercompany Lending					
Debt liabilities to affiliated enterprises					
Debt liabilities to direct investors					
Gross External Debt					
(percentage of total external debt)					
Memorandum item (to include if significant)					
Notional Value of Financial Derivatives: Single-Currency Interest Rate-Related Contracts[2]					
To receive fixed-rate-linked payment					
General government					
Monetary authorities					
Banks					
Other sectors					
Nonbank financial corporations					
Nonfinancial corporations					
Households and NPISH					
From affiliated enterprises and direct investors					
Total					
To receive variable-rate-linked payment					
General government					
Monetary authorities					
Banks					
Other sectors					
Nonbank financial corporations					
Nonfinancial corporations					
Households and NPISH					
From affiliated enterprises and direct investors					
Total					

[1]It is recommended that all currency and deposits be included in the short-term category unless detailed information is available to make the short-term/long-term attribution.

[2]Excludes financial derivatives that pertain to reserve asset management and are included in reserve assets data.

linked assets are included to ensure consistency with the foreign currency and foreign-currency-linked external debt position data presented in Table 7.6. Indeed, foreign currency liabilities might be hedged by foreign-currency-linked assets, and vice versa. If foreign-currency-linked assets become significant, they could be separately identified.

Interest Rates and External Debt

Interest Rate Composition of External Debt

7.35 As with the currency composition, experience suggests that information on the interest rate composition of the gross external debt position can be necessary for monitoring an economy's potential vulnerability to solvency and liquidity risk. For instance, economies with high amounts of variable-rate debt are vulnerable to a sharp increase in interest rates. Hence, Table 7.8 provides a presentation of the amounts of the gross external debt position, both in relative and absolute terms, on which interest is fixed-rate and variable-rate. Along with the value, for each cell the percentage contribution to external debt is presented. In this table, the purchase of a separate financial derivatives contract, which might alter the effective nature of the interest cash payments, does not affect the classification of the underlying instrument (see also below).

7.36 A memorandum item is provided on the notional (or nominal) value of single-currency financial derivatives contracts with nonresidents for instances where the amounts involved are significant. These are broken down into contracts to receive fixed-rate-related cash payments and receive variable-rate-related cash payments. For instance, if all sectors reported that their external debt was all fixed-rate-linked but they had entered into derivatives contracts with nonresidents to swap all their interest payments into variable-rate-related payments, then the memorandum item would show that despite the apparent exposure of the economy to fixed-rate interest rates, it is actually exposed to variable rates.

7.37 In financial derivatives markets, interest rate contracts are typically referenced to a variable-rate index. To receive variable-rate-linked is to pay fixed-rate-linked, and vice versa. A financial derivative that receives variable-rate-linked is one that would have an increasing positive value, or a decreasing negative

Table 7.9. Gross External Debt Position: Average Interest Rates

	End-Period
General Government	
Monetary Authorities	
Banks	
Other Sectors	
Nonbank financial corporations	
Nonfinancial corporations	
Households and nonprofit institutions serving households (NPISH)	
Direct Investment: Intercompany Lending (from affiliated enterprises and direct investors)	
Total Economy	

value, as the variable rate specified in the contract increases; similarly a financial derivative that receives fixed-rate-linked has an increasing positive value, or a decreasing negative value, as the variable rate specified in the contract decreases.

Average Interest Rates

7.38 There is analytical interest in average interest rates on external debt. While financial derivatives contracts might arguably render these data less relevant than otherwise, these data provide information on the borrowing costs of the economy and can be used to help estimate debt-service interest rate payments, or be used to cross-check those data. Also, concessionality of borrowing can be imputed. Information on average interest rates on direct investment borrowing is of value because, often for tax reasons, average interest rates on this debt can vary widely. Information on average interest rates on short- and long-term original maturity instruments, by institutional sector, could additionally be provided.

7.39 In addition to weighted-average interest rates on outstanding external debt, Table 7.9 could be used to present data on the weighted-average level of interest rates agreed on new borrowing during the period.

External Debt by Creditor Sector

7.40 Table 7.10 provides for the presentation of creditor sector data for five nonresident creditor sec-

---

Table 7.10. Gross External Debt Position: Creditor Sector Information

Debtor Sectors	End-Period					
	Creditor Sectors					
	Multilateral Organizations[1]	General Government[1,2]	Monetary Authorities[1]	Banks	Other Sectors	Total
General Government						
Short-term						
Long-term						
Monetary Authorities						
Short-term[3]						
Long-term						
Banks						
Short-term[3]						
Long-term						
Other Sectors						
Short-term						
Long-term						
Nonbank financial corporations						
Short-term[3]						
Long-term						
Nonfinancial corporations						
Short-term						
Long-term						
Households and nonprofit institutions serving households (NPISH)						
Short-term						
Long-term						
Gross External Debt Excluding Direct Investment						
Of which: Short-term						
Long-term						
Direct Investment: Intercompany Lending						
(Total column only)						
Debt liabilities to affiliated enterprises						
Debt liabilities to direct investors						
Gross External Debt						

[1]For the multilateral organizations, general government, and monetary authorities creditor sectors, short-term lending, on an original maturity basis, may be insignificant—under which circumstances a short-/long-term split may not be necessary.
[2]Excluding multilateral organizations.
[3]It is recommended that all currency and deposits be included in the short-term category unless detailed information is available to make the short-term/long-term attribution.

---

tors: multilateral organizations, general government (excluding multilateral organizations),[9] monetary authorities,[10] banks, and "other sectors." Traditionally, this information has been most readily available for nontraded instruments and has been essential when undertaking debt-reorganization discussions. More broadly, information on creditor sectors has been compiled because different types of creditors may respond to changing circumstances differently, and this can have implications for the economic situation of an economy.

7.41 Most economies may face practical difficulties in identifying owners of traded debt securities. Economies might attribute the value of all traded debt securities to "other sectors" as the creditor sector. If so, this assumption should be clearly identified in any presentation of data because it may be only very broadly reliable: for instance, monetary authorities hold significant quantities of cross-

---

[9]In *BPM5*, multilateral organizations form part of the foreign general government sector.

[10]This category excludes multilateral monetary institutions such as the IMF, which are included under multilateral organizations, but includes regional central banks.

border securities as part of their foreign exchange reserves. An alternative approach would be to have a separate column for traded debt securities and exclude holdings of such securities from all the "sector" columns.

7.42 Table 7.10 can be rearranged and extended as appropriate. One possibility is to divide the creditor sector information between official and other creditors. The official creditors could be further subdivided by *multilateral* and *official bilateral creditors*, and the latter could distinguish between Paris Club member creditors and non–Paris Club creditors. Also, official bilateral debt could be separated between concessional and nonconcessional debt.

7.43 Because direct investment liabilities do not fall naturally into this presentation, totals are drawn before and after *direct investment: intercompany lending*. Also, the "other sectors" as creditor sectors are not subdivided into nonbank financial, nonfinancial corporations, and households and NPISH, since this would create an additional degree of difficulty in obtaining this creditor information. On the other hand, as private sector capital flows increase, and these creditor sectors become more significant, there could be analytical interest in identifying their claims separately.

Net External Debt Position

7.44 As an economy increasingly integrates with the rest of the world, so analysis of the external liability position, and gross external debt position in particular, needs to take into account positions in external assets. Indeed, for risk-management purposes, entities may well manage external liabilities and assets in an integrated manner. On the other hand, there is difficulty in ascertaining the extent to which assets might be usable to meet outstanding debt liabilities. Table 7.11 provides a presentation of net external debt position data, placing gross external debt in the context of claims on nonresidents in the form of debt instruments.

7.45 The rows in the table are structured as in the gross external debt position table (Table 4.1), and the columns present gross external debt, gross external assets in debt instruments, and net debt position. A total of net external debt position plus the net financial derivatives position (this position is valued at

Table 7.11. Net External Debt Position: By Sector

	End-Period		
	Gross External Debt Position (1)	External Assets in Debt Instruments (2)	Net External Debt (3) = (1) – (2)
General Government			
Short-term			
Money market instruments			
Loans			
Currency and deposits[1]			
Trade credits			
Other debt instruments[2]			
Arrears			
Other			
Long-term			
Bonds and notes			
Loans			
Currency and deposits[1]			
Trade credits			
Other debt instruments[2]			
Monetary Authorities			
Short-term			
Money market instruments			
Loans			
Currency and deposits[1]			
Other debt instruments[2]			
Arrears			
Other			
Long-term			
Bonds and notes			
Loans			
Currency and deposits[1]			
Other debt instruments[2]			
Banks			
Short-term			
Money market instruments			
Loans			
Currency and deposits[1]			
Other debt instruments[2]			
Arrears			
Other			
Long-term			
Bonds and notes			
Loans			
Currency and deposits[1]			
Other debt instruments[2]			
Other Sectors			
Short-term			
Money market instruments			
Loans			
Currency and deposits[1]			
Trade credits			
Other debt instruments[2]			
Arrears			
Other			
Long-term			
Bonds and notes			
Loans			
Currency and deposits[1]			
Trade credits			
Other debt instruments[2]			

Table 7.11 (continued)

	End-Period		
	Gross External Debt Position (1)	External Assets in Debt Instruments (2)	Net External Debt (3) = (1) – (2)
Other Sectors (continued)			
Nonbank financial corporations			
Short-term			
Money market instruments			
Loans			
Currency and deposits[1]			
Other debt instruments[2]			
Arrears			
Other			
Long-term			
Bonds and notes			
Loans			
Currency and deposits[1]			
Other debt instruments[2]			
Nonfinancial corporations			
Short-term			
Money market instruments			
Loans			
Currency and deposits[1]			
Trade credits			
Other debt instruments[2]			
Arrears			
Other			
Long-term			
Bonds and notes			
Loans			
Currency and deposits[1]			
Trade credits			
Other debt instruments[2]			
Households and nonprofit institutions serving households (NPISH)			
Short-term			
Money market instruments			
Loans			
Currency and deposits[1]			
Trade credits			
Other debt instruments[2]			
Arrears			
Other			
Long-term			
Bonds and notes			
Loans			
Currency and deposits[1]			
Trade credits			
Other debt instruments[2]			
Direct Investment: Intercompany Lending			
Debt liabilities to affiliated enterprises			
Arrears			
Other			
Debt liabilities to direct investors			
Arrears			
Other			
Net External Debt (3)			

market value and should include the position in financial derivatives held as reserve assets) is drawn at the bottom of the table. Because of their different characteristics, information distinguishing forwards (including futures and swaps) and options within financial derivatives is encouraged.

7.46 The data on external assets in the form of debt instruments to be included in this table are the same as presented in the IIP, with short- and long-term defined on an original maturity basis. The net external debt position is equal to gross external debt less gross external assets in debt instruments.

7.47 Provided that traded debt instruments are valued at market value, net external debt in this table equals the net IIP position excluding all equity assets and liabilities, all financial derivatives assets and liabilities, and holdings of SDRs and monetary gold. This approach facilitates comparability with other statistics. An alternative approach, which is undertaken within the banking industry, is to present traded debt instrument liabilities at nominal value and traded debt instrument assets at market value.

Reconciliation of External Debt Positions and Flows

7.48 Between any two end-periods, the change in the gross external debt position can be disaggregated into component flows. These are financial transactions, valuation changes, and other adjustments. Such a disaggregation helps the compiler to reconcile and verify data, and it provides useful analytical information to the user of data (for example, the extent to which changes in the gross external debt position since the previous period are due to transactions, valuation changes, and/or revisions to the previous period data).

7.49 The reconciliation of gross external debt positions at two different reference dates is set out in Table 7.12. In this table, the first column is the gross external debt position at the beginning of the period, followed by the transactions during the period. Because the conceptual approach taken in the *Guide* is consistent with *BPM5*, the balance of payments transaction data can be used in the transactions column (although the subsector analysis of "other sectors" is not explicitly identified in *BPM5*). The next two columns are price changes[11] and exchange rate changes. These changes assume greater importance with increased volatility of prices in security and exchange rate markets. A nominal-valuation presentation of traded debt instruments would exclude any changes in value arising from market prices. Before the position at the end of the period, a fifth item of "other adjustments" is included. These adjustments include reclassifications of external debt such as when entities switch from one institutional sector to another, and when the nature of a debt instrument changes—an example being of an instrument moving from a specific type (say, a loan) to *direct investment: intercompany lending*, when the relationship between the creditor and debtor becomes that of direct investment.

Traded Debt Instruments

Reconciliation of Nominal and Market Value

7.50 The *Guide* recommends that traded debt instruments be valued in the gross external debt position at nominal and market value. The sole difference between these two valuation measures is that market value takes account of market price changes, whereas nominal value does not. Market prices change over time for a number of reasons, including changes in market interest rates, changes in investor perception of the creditworthiness of the debtor, and changes in market structure (such as might affect market liquidity).

7.51 The divergence in the market and nominal value of traded debt instruments at one moment in time, and over time, is of analytical value. For this reason, Table 7.13 provides a framework for reconciling nominal and market valuation of traded debt instruments included in the gross external debt position. The instruments in the table include money market instruments, bonds and notes, and, if applicable, arrears. It is intended that data be presented in absolute amounts in the same unit of account used to present the gross external debt position.

Location of Debt Securities Issuance

7.52 Information on the location of issuance of debt securities issued by residents and owned by nonresi-

---

[11]In addition to market price changes, this column covers other non-exchange-rate valuation changes—for example, changes in the value of pension fund liabilities to nonresident participants and policyholders arising from revaluations.

Table 7.11 *(concluded)*

Financial Derivatives	Position in Financial Derivatives at End of Period
Liabilities	
General government	
Forwards	
Options	
Monetary authorities	
Forwards	
Options	
Banks	
Forwards	
Options	
Other sectors	
Forwards	
Options	
Nonbank financial corporations	
Forwards	
Options	
Nonfinancial corporations	
Forwards	
Options	
Households and NPISH	
Forwards	
Options	
Total (4)	
Assets	
General government	
Forwards	
Options	
Monetary authorities	
Forwards	
Options	
Banks	
Forwards	
Options	
Other sectors	
Forwards	
Options	
Nonbank financial corporations	
Forwards	
Options	
Nonfinancial corporations	
Forwards	
Options	
Households and NPISH	
Forwards	
Options	
Total (5)	
Net External Debt Position plus Financial Derivatives (6)	
(6) = (3) + (4) − (5)	

[1]It is recommended that all currency and deposits be included in the short-term category unless detailed information is available to make the short-term/long-term attribution.

[2]*Other debt instruments* are other *assets* and other *liabilities* in the IIP statement.

Table 7.12. Gross External Debt Position: Reconciliation of Positions and Flows

	Position at Beginning of Period	Changes in Position Reflecting				Position at End of Period
		Transactions	Price changes	Exchange rate changes	Other adjustments	
General Government						
Short-term						
Money market instruments						
Loans						
Trade credits						
Other debt liabilities[1]						
Arrears						
Other						
Long-term						
Bonds and notes						
Loans						
Trade credits						
Other debt liabilities[1]						
Monetary Authorities						
Short-term						
Money market instruments						
Loans						
Currency and deposits[2]						
Other debt liabilities[1]						
Arrears						
Other						
Long-term						
Bonds and notes						
Loans						
Currency and deposits[2]						
Other debt liabilities[1]						
Banks						
Short-term						
Money market instruments						
Loans						
Currency and deposits[2]						
Other debt liabilities[1]						
Arrears						
Other						
Long-term						
Bonds and notes						
Loans						
Currency and deposits[2]						
Other debt liabilities[1]						
Other Sectors						
Short-term						
Money market instruments						
Loans						
Currency and deposits[2]						
Trade credits						
Other debt liabilities[1]						
Arrears						
Other						
Long-term						
Bonds and notes						
Loans						
Currency and deposits[2]						
Trade credits						
Other debt liabilities[1]						

Table 7.12 (concluded)

	Position at Beginning of Period	Changes in Position Reflecting				Position at End of Period
		Transactions	Price changes	Exchange rate changes	Other adjustments	

Other Sectors *(continued)*
  Nonbank financial corporations
    Short-term
    Money market instruments
    Loans
    Currency and deposits2
    Other debt liabilities1
      Arrears
      Other

    Long-term
    Bonds and notes
    Loans
    Currency and deposits2
    Other debt liabilities1

  Nonfinancial corporations
    Short-term
    Money market instruments
    Loans
    Trade credits
    Other debt liabilities1
      Arrears
      Other

    Long-term
    Bonds and notes
    Loans
    Trade credits
    Other debt liabilities1

  Households and nonprofit institutions
  serving households (NPISH)
    Short-term
    Money market instruments
    Loans
    Trade credits
    Other debt liabilities1
      Arrears
      Other

    Long-term
    Bonds and notes
    Loans
    Trade credits
    Other debt liabilities1

Direct Investment: Intercompany Lending
Debt liabilities to affiliated enterprises
  Arrears
  Other
Debt liabilities to direct investors
  Arrears
  Other

Gross External Debt

1*Other debt liabilities* are *other liabilities* in the IIP statement.

2It is recommended that all currency and deposits be included in the short-term category unless detailed information is available to make the short-term/long-term attribution.

Table 7.13. Gross External Debt Position: Traded Debt Instruments—Reconciliation of Nominal and Market Value

	Nominal Value Position at End of Period	Market Price Change	Market Value Position at End of Period
General Government			
Money market instruments			
Bonds and notes			
Arrears (if applicable)			
Monetary Authorities			
Money market instruments			
Bonds and notes			
Arrears (if applicable)			
Banks			
Money market instruments			
Bonds and notes			
Arrears (if applicable)			
Other Sectors			
Money market instruments			
Bonds and notes			
Arrears (if applicable)			
Nonbank financial corporations			
Money market instruments			
Bonds and notes			
Arrears (if applicable)			
Nonfinancial corporations			
Money market instruments			
Bonds and notes			
Arrears (if applicable)			
Households and nonprofit institutions serving households (NPISH)			
Money market instruments			
Bonds and notes			
Arrears (if applicable)			
Total			
Money market instruments			
Bonds and notes			
Arrears (if applicable)			

dents can also be of analytical value. For instance, such data provide an indication of the motivation of debtors and creditors—whether residents are attracting foreign investors by issuing securities in their markets; and of possible liquidity risk—securities issued in foreign markets may be harder to refinance in the event of an external shock to the economy. Also, in the absence of information on foreign currency debt, these data can provide a broad idea of the foreign currency/domestic currency attribution of debt securities—for instance, foreign-issued debt is likely to be foreign-currency-linked. From a compilation viewpoint, data on securities issued in foreign markets might well be captured in a different manner from that of issues in the domestic market.

7.53 A presentation for these data is provided in Table 7.14. The rows distinguish debt securities issued by general government from those issued by other sectors. The separate identification of government issues reflects the government's important and special role, in most economies, as a borrower. Depending on the extent of security issuance by the other institutional sectors, a further disaggregation of issues, such as for banks, might also be of analytical interest. The maturity attribution is on an original maturity basis, although the table can also be presented on a remaining maturity basis.

7.54 Consistent with the concepts set out in the *Guide*, Table 7.14 only covers information on

Table 7.14. Gross External Debt Position: Resident-Issued Debt Securities Owned by Nonresidents—Location of Issuance

	End-Period
Domestically issued	
Short-term	
General government	
All other sectors	
Long-term	
General government	
All other sectors	
Foreign issued	
Short-term	
General government	
All other sectors	
Long-term	
General government	
All other sectors	

nonresident ownership of resident-issued securities. But there might also be interest in presenting data on resident as well as nonresident ownership of resident-issued securities, both in domestic and foreign markets. By including additional columns for resident- and nonresident-owned

securities, the table can be extended to cover such information.

Cross-Border Trade-Related Credit

7.55 In addition to presenting data by type of instrument, another approach is to present data by the type of use of the borrowing. In this regard, of special interest is information on cross-border trade-related credits by debtor and creditor sector—that is, credits that finance trade. Such credit is directly linked to activity in the real economy. Table 7.15 provides a model for presenting data on borrowing used to finance trade, with the disaggregation by, first, maturity (original basis) and, second, institutional sector. In presenting these data, trade-bills could be separately identified, both because of the analytical interest in such data and to help with reconciliation with creditor-based statistics.

7.56 The debtor sectors are presented in rows, and the creditor sectors in columns. The rows and column for direct investment entities relate only to the provision of trade-related credit between related entities—that is, those transactions classified under direct investment in the balance of payments, and not the provision of trade-related credit by unrelated parties to direct investment entities. The maturity attribution is on an original maturity basis.

Table 7.15. Gross External Debt Position: Cross-Border Trade-Related Credit

	End-Period			
	Creditor Sectors			
Debtor Sectors	General government	Banks[1]	Other sectors	Direct investment entities
Short-term				
General government				
Monetary authorities				
Banks				
Other sectors				
Direct investment entities				
Long-term				
General government				
Monetary authorities				
Banks				
Other sectors				
Direct investment entities				
Total				

[1]It is recommended that any cross-border trade-related debt of monetary authorities be included within the bank category, unless the monetary authorities are significant debtors, in which instance, they should be separately identified.

8. Debt Reorganization

Introduction

8.1 Debt-reorganization transactions are a feature of external debt activity. Economies sometimes face difficulties in meeting their external debt obligations, or debtors may want to change the repayment profile of their external obligations for different reasons, including reducing the risk of future payment difficulties or reducing the cost of borrowing. In this context, they may undertake debt restructuring and debt conversions. This chapter defines debt reorganization, discusses the various types of debt-reorganization operations, and provides guidance on how they affect the measurement of the gross external debt position. Further, this chapter defines debt relief and recommends the measurement and presentation of statistics on debt reduction, which is also defined.

8.2 Reference is made in the chapter to the recording of debt-reorganization transactions in the measured flow data of the balance of payments, the OECD's Development Assistance Committee (DAC) system, and the World Bank's Debtor Reporting System (DRS). Full details of such recording approaches are set out in *BPM5* (IMF, 1993), the OECD's *Handbook for Reporting Debt Reorganization on the DAC Questionnaire* (OECD, 1999), and the *Debtor Reporting System Manual* (World Bank, 2000).[1]

Definitions

8.3 *Debt reorganization* is defined as bilateral arrangements involving both the creditor and the debtor that alter the terms established for the servicing of a debt. Types of debt reorganization include debt rescheduling, refinancing, forgiveness, conversion, and prepayments. A creditor can also reduce

debt through debt write-offs—a unilateral action that arises, for instance, when the creditor regards a claim as unrecoverable, perhaps because of bankruptcy of the debtor, and so no longer carries it on its books. This is not debt reorganization as defined in the *Guide* because it does not involve a bilateral arrangement. Similarly, a failure by a debtor economy to honor its debt obligations (default, moratorium, etc.) is not debt reorganization.

8.4 Generally, debt reorganization is undertaken to provide some *debt relief* to the debtor and can address liquidity and/or sustainability problems arising from future and current payment obligations. *Debt relief* results where there is (1) a reduction in the present value of these debt-service obligations; and/or (2) a deferral of the payments due, thus providing smaller near-term debt-service obligations (this can be measured, in most cases, by an increase in the duration of these obligations; that is, payments become weighted more toward the latter part of the debt instrument's life). However, if debt reorganization results in changes in present value and duration that are countervailing in their impact on the debt burden, then there is no debt relief, unless the net impact is significant, such as could occur if there was a deep reduction in present value (together with small decrease in duration) or a sharp increase in duration (together with a small increase in present value).

8.5 *Debt reduction* is defined as the reduction in the nominal value of external debt arising from a debt-reorganization arrangement, excluding any payments of economic value made by the debtor to the creditor as part of the arrangement. This is the definition to be used for compiling data to be presented in Table 8.1—debt reduction arising from debt reorganization. *Debt reduction in present value terms* is defined as the reduction in the present value of debt-service obligations arising from a debt reorganization, as calculated by discounting the projected future payments of interest and principal both before

---
[1]See also Chapter 17.

Table 8.1. Nominal Value Debt Reduction Arising from Debt Reorganizations

Debtor
Public sector
Of which: Multilateral
       Official bilateral
       Commercial bank[1]
       Bonds and notes

Publicly guaranteed private debt
Of which: Multilateral
       Official bilateral
       Commercial bank[1]
       Bonds and notes

Other private debt
Of which: Multilateral
       Official bilateral
       Commercial bank[1]
       Bonds and notes

Of which:
  Rescheduled and refinanced
    Public and publicly guaranteed debt
    Other private debt
  Forgiven
    Public and publicly guaranteed debt
    Other private debt
  Debt conversions and prepayments
    Public and publicly guaranteed debt
    Other private debt

---

[1]Excluding bonds and notes.

Types of Debt Reorganization

8.7 The three main types of debt reorganization are:
- A change in the terms and conditions of the amount owed, which may result, or not, in a reduction in burden in present-value terms. These transactions are usually described as *debt rescheduling*. They are also sometimes referred to as refinancing or as debt exchanges. Included are transactions that change the type of debt instrument owed—for example, loan for bond swaps—but not debt-forgiveness transactions.
- A reduction in the amount of, or the extinguishing of, a debt obligation by the creditor via a contractual arrangement with the debtor. This is *debt forgiveness* as described in *BPM5* and the DRS and is also classified as debt forgiveness in the DAC system if there is a development/welfare motive.
- The creditor exchanges the debt claim for something of economic value other than another debt claim on the same debtor. This includes *debt conversion*, such as debt-for-equity swaps, debt-for-real-estate swaps, and debt-for-nature swaps,[3] and debt prepayment or buybacks for cash.

8.8 Debt-reorganization packages may involve more than one type; for example, most debt-reorganization packages involving debt forgiveness also result in a rescheduling of the part of the debt that is not forgiven or canceled.

8.9 For clarification purposes, in discussing the statistical treatment of debt reorganization, each of the three types of debt reorganization is considered separately. This has a number of advantages: each type of debt reorganization raises different statistical issues, hence encouraging a type-by-type approach; present international statistical guidelines, on which the guidelines in this chapter are based, are more advanced for some types of debt reorganization than for others; and there is interest in the different types of debt reorganization, and so there is an analytical benefit, where possible, in separately measuring and reporting any debt reduction resulting from their application.

and after the reorganization at a common interest rate and comparing the difference. To illustrate the difference between *debt reduction* and *debt reduction in present value terms,* if the contractual rate of interest is reduced with no impact on the nominal value of external debt, no *debt reduction* is recorded but there is *debt reduction in present-value terms.*

8.6 *Debt swaps* are exchanges of debt, such as loans or securities, for a new debt contract (debt-to-debt swaps), or exchanges of debt-for-equity, debt-for-exports, or debt-for-domestic currency, such as to be used for projects in the debtor country (also known as *debt conversion*).[2] This definition is intended to include debt-for-development swaps where economic value is provided by the debtor to the creditor for use in development projects in the debtor's economy.

---

[2]A debt swap should be distinguished from a financial derivative swap. The financial derivative swap involves two parties agreeing to swap future cash flows, while a debt swap involves the exchange of the debt instrument itself for economic value.

[3]Some agreements described as debt swaps are equivalent to debt forgiveness from the creditor together with a commitment from the debtor country to undertake a number of development, environmental, etc., expenses. These transactions should be considered under the second type of debt reorganization, as counterpart funds are not provided to the creditor.

Debt Rescheduling

8.10 Rescheduling refers to the formal deferment of debt-service payments and the application of new and extended maturities to the deferred amount. This may be conducted: (1) through the exchange of an existing debt instrument for a new one, as in refinancing or debt exchanges; or (2) through a change of the terms and conditions of the existing contracts (this is often simply referred to as rescheduling, as opposed to refinancing). Rescheduling may or may not result in a reduction in the present value of debt, as calculated by discounting the old and new payment schedule by a common interest rate.

8.11 Refinancing of a debt liability involves the replacement of an existing debt instrument or instruments, including arrears, with a new debt instrument or instruments. For instance, the public sector may convert various export credit debt it is owed into a single loan. Refinancing may involve the exchange of one type of debt instrument, such as a loan, for another, such as a bond. Some debt-refinancing arrangements feature new money facilities (see below, paragraph 8.51). Also, refinancing can be said to have taken place when countries with private sector bond creditors exchange existing bonds for new bonds through exchange offers (rather than a change in terms and conditions).

8.12 Rescheduling can be characterized as flow or stock rescheduling. A flow rescheduling typically refers to a rescheduling of specified debt service falling due during a certain period and, in some cases, of specified arrears outstanding at the beginning of that period. A stock rescheduling involves principal payments that are not yet due, and arrears, if any, and like a flow rescheduling, can include both an element of debt forgiveness and a rescheduling of the amounts not reduced.

Recommended treatment

External debt position

8.13 Any agreed change in the terms of a debt instrument is to be recorded as the creation of a new debt instrument, with the original debt extinguished at the time both parties record the change in terms in their books. Whether the gross external debt position increases, decreases, or remains unchanged depends on whether the value of the new instrument(s) is respectively greater than, smaller than, or the same

as the original debts being replaced—this is the case regardless of the valuation method employed to measure external debt instruments.[4] In other words, both before and after a debt rescheduling, the value of the gross external debt position is simply determined by the value of outstanding external debt liabilities of residents owed to nonresidents at the reference date.

8.14 As explained in Chapter 2, and as the examples in that chapter illustrated, the stock of external debt at any moment in time can be calculated by discounting future payments at a specified rate of interest. This interest rate can be the contractual rate (for nominal value), or a market rate for the specific borrower (for market value), or another rate. Using these different rates to discount payments will provide different position data for the same payment schedule. Debt reduction in present-value terms arising from rescheduling might be calculated using any of these rates—in the HIPC Initiative, a market-based rate is used.

8.15 If, as part of official and private debt-reduction packages, loans denominated in foreign currency are swapped for debt securities denominated in the domestic currency, the difference between the value of the loan and the value of the debt security in the domestic currency will be reflected in the gross external debt position. The extinguishment of the old debt liability, the loan, results in a decrease in the value of *short-term* or *long-term loans*, as appropriate, while an increase in *bonds and notes* is recorded.

Flow data

8.16 In the flow data in the balance of payments, both the extinguishment of the old debt liability and the creation of the new debt(s) are recorded. In the DAC system these flows are also recorded, except when the category of debt does not change, in which case only the capitalization of interest is recorded as a flow. The DRS does not record these transactions in flow data (but they are reflected in

---

[4]If external debt is lower or higher because at the time of rescheduling it was agreed between the debtor and creditor that the amount of late interest on arrears was to be more or less than that which accrued, back data of the gross external debt position should not be revised to reflect this agreement, provided that the accrual of interest costs on arrears in past periods was in line with the contract(s) that existed at that time.

Box 8.1. Sovereign Bond Restructuring

The restructuring of a country's sovereign bonded external debt (eurobonds and Brady bonds) began with Pakistan at the end of 1999, following the extension of the "comparability of treatment" principle to bondholders in Pakistan's agreement with the Paris Club in January 1999.

In terms of restructuring debt, bonds have a number of characteristics that distinguish them from other types of debt instruments.

- First, there is usually a wider range of investors than for nontraded external debt instruments, and hence various investor groups all with potentially different investment motivations. For instance, the investment motivations of retail—nonfinancial institution—investors may be different from those of financial institutions.
- Second, market prices are invariably quoted. Thus, those investors that mark-to-market frequently—having borne the market-value loss in the secondary market price of the to-be-exchanged bonds, or having purchased at a low market value—might well compare the present value of the exchange offered (discounting payments at a particular interest rate) with the current market price of the to-be-exchanged bonds. In the simplest case, if the present value of the exchange bond is higher than the market price of the original bond, the holder of the to-be-exchanged bond has an incentive to tender his bonds in the exchange.
- Finally, most eurobonds and Brady bonds have cross-default clauses or cross-acceleration clauses in their covenants, thus perhaps making it impossible for a sovereign debtor to pick and choose which bondholders are repaid and which are not. So, markets debate the issue of whether a restructuring of external bonded debt needs to be comprehensive across other foreign currency debt instruments as well.

The consequence of the above is that successful bond restructuring—mostly bond exchanges—has involved the debtors exchanging securities at a premium to the market price, although well below the face value, or providing other "sweeteners" to encourage bondholders to participate. Bonds with the larger percentage of retail investors have tended to pay a higher premium. But, as with creditors for other types of debt instruments, a key consideration of creditors in any restructuring is whether the sovereign borrower is facing a liquidity or solvency problem, or neither.

Debt reduction

8.17 The *Guide* recommends that debt reduction arising from debt rescheduling and debt refinancing—that is, a reduction in the nominal amount outstanding, excluding any external debt-service payments made by the debtor as part of the arrangement—be measured and presented as in the debt-reduction table provided in this chapter. If the new external debt liability is denominated in a different currency from that of the external debt liability it is replacing, then any debt reduction should be determined using the market exchange rate between the two currencies prevailing on the transaction date (that is, the midpoint between the buying and selling spot rates).

8.18 In many instances of debt rescheduling, the method by which debt relief is provided is more complex than a simple reduction in nominal amount outstanding. For instance, a debt might be rescheduled with the same nominal value but with a lower interest rate or with extended maturities. By simply comparing the nominal amounts outstanding before and after the rescheduling, no debt reduction would be evident, but there may be debt reduction in present value terms, calculated by discounting future debt-service payments, both on the old and new debts, at a common rate. In such circumstances, a key issue is which rate to use: in debt-reorganization operations such as those under the HIPC Initiative and similar arrangements, debt reduction in present-value terms is calculated using an interest rate equal to a market-based so-called risk-neutral rate—such as the OECD's Commercial Interest Reference Rates (CIRRs).[6] In other cases, debt reduction in present value may be based on a rate that includes a risk premium, reflecting the creditor's assessment of the value of the claim (this is generally the case for the restructuring of claims held by private creditors).

8.19 Also, in some debt rescheduling, such as with concessional Paris Club agreements (Box 8.2), credi-

the position data). In the balance of payments, any difference between the value of the old and new debts is treated as a valuation change, such as in the case of exchanges of Brady bonds (see Box 8.1) for new global bonds, except when nonmarketable debt owed to official creditors is involved, in which instance any reduction in the nominal value of debt is recorded as debt forgiveness (see below).[5]

---

[5]See *BPM5*, paragraph 534.

[6]These rates are determined monthly for 13 currencies on the basis of secondary market yields on government bonds with a residual maturity of five years, and additionally three and seven years for the Canadian dollar, the U.S. dollar, and the euro. These data are published monthly on the Internet at: *http://www.oecd.org/ statistics/news-releases*. For the HIPC Initiative, debt denominated in currencies for which no CIRR is available, if the currency is pegged to another currency such as the U.S. dollar, the CIRR for the latter should be used; in the absence of an exchange rate arrangement, as well as for the units of account used by various multilateral institutions, the SDR CIRR should be applied.

Box 8.2. Paris Club and Commercial Bank Debt Relief

The Paris Club has developed procedures for the collective rescheduling of official bilateral debt since the 1950s, when Argentina approached bilateral creditors. The Club is an ad hoc organization of creditor countries (mainly OECD members) that responds to requests for debt relief with respect to guaranteed export credits and intergovernmental loans.

Debts to Paris Club official creditors are now restructured through the Paris Club, especially since Russia became a member of the Club in 1997. Debts to commercial banks are typically restructured through consortia of commercial banks. Noninsured supplier credits and debts to governments that do not participate in the Paris Club are normally restructured through bilateral negotiations.

Paris Club

The Paris Club is an informal group of creditor countries. The French Treasury maintains a permanent secretariat, and a senior official serves as Chairman, to administer the Paris Club on behalf of other creditor countries. There are 19 permanent members; nonmember creditor countries may be invited to take part in meetings for the treatment of the debt of a specific debtor country if they have significant claims on that country. The Club meets virtually every month in Paris, both for discussion of debt issues among the permanent members and for the rescheduling of the debt of a specific debtor country.

Countries facing difficulties in servicing of debt to official bilateral creditors will approach the Chairman of the Paris Club and ask to be considered for relief. The creditors at their monthly meeting will agree to hear that country's application, provided that an IMF-supported adjustment program is in place and that there is a financing need that requires rescheduling. Agreement is normally reached in face-to-face negotiations, or by mail if there are very few creditors. The Paris Club can "treat" debt owed (contracted or guaranteed) by the government and/or the public sector of the debtor country to creditor countries or their appropriate institutions: officially guaranteed export credits and bilateral loans. The representatives of the creditor countries at the Paris Club decide on the period over which debt relief will be given (known as the consolidation period), the debts that will be included (current maturities, possibly arrears, possibly previously rescheduled debt), and the repayment terms on consolidated debt (grace and repayment periods).

Two types of "treatment" may be implemented by the Paris Club:
- A flow treatment of usually both scheduled amortization and interest payments falling due in a given period; and
- A stock treatment of the entire outstanding principal at a given date, for countries with a good track record with the Paris Club if this would ensure an end to the rescheduling process.

Paris Club negotiations result in a multilateral framework agreement (Agreed Minute), which must be followed up with bilateral implementing agreements with each creditor agency. The interest rate on rescheduled debt (known as moratorium interest) is not arranged at the Paris Club but is negotiated bilaterally, reflecting market rates.

At the beginning of the debt-relief process, Paris Club creditor countries will establish a "cutoff date." This means that all loan contracts signed after that date will not be eligible for debt relief by the Paris Club. The aim is to help the debtor country reestablish its creditworthiness by paying new obligations on their original schedules. Even though debt relief may extend over many years through a succession of Paris Club agreements, the cutoff date will remain unchanged.

It was increasingly recognized in the 1980s that some low-income countries with high external debt were facing solvency as well as liquidity problems. Over the years, the Paris Club has provided increasingly concessional rescheduling terms to low-income countries. The level of debt reduction on commercial claims was gradually increased from Toronto terms (1988—33.33 percent debt reduction) to London terms (1991—50 percent debt reduction) to Naples terms (1995—50 percent to 67 percent debt reduction) to Lyon terms (1996—80 percent debt reduction) and to Cologne terms (1999—90 percent reduction or more if needed under the HIPC Initiative). The evolution of Paris Club terms up to Lyon terms is presented in Table 8.2.

In 1996, the debt initiative for heavily indebted poor countries (HIPCs) was established, leading for the first time to multilateral creditors providing debt relief to a country. The Paris Club provides its debt-relief effort in the context of the HIPC Initiative through the use initially of Lyon terms, and now of Cologne terms.

A country benefiting from Paris Club debt relief commits to seek at least similar restructuring terms from its other external creditors (other than multilateral creditors, which only provide debt relief to countries eligible for assistance under the HIPC Initiative). This applies to non–Paris Club bilateral creditors, who generally negotiate with the debtor country on a bilateral basis, as well as private creditors (suppliers, banks, bondholders, etc.).

Paris Club agreements may include a debt-swap provision, within a limit usually set at 20 percent of commercial claims. Paris Club creditors on a bilateral basis conduct debt-swap operations.

Commercial Bank Debt Relief

Multilateral debt relief is much more difficult to organize for commercial banks than for official creditors. While a national export credit insurer can negotiate on behalf of any individual creditor, there is no way to consolidate national commercial bank claims. Rather, each creditor bank must approve the resulting agreement and, for loan syndication, the number is often in the hundreds.

The pattern of negotiations was established in a 1970 agreement between the Philippines and its commercial bank creditors. Creditor banks form a committee (sometimes known as the London Club) of about a dozen people who represent the major creditor banks. The composition of the committee— which can be completely different from case to case—takes into account the nationality of the banks in the consortium so that the negotiations can make provision for the different tax and regulatory systems that affect banks of different countries. The committee negotiates an "agreement in principle" with debtor country representatives. After all creditor banks approve this agreement, it is signed. It takes effect when certain requirements are met, such as payment of fees and of arrears. As with the rescheduling of debts to official creditors, banks provide debt relief normally in the context of a debtor country's adjustment program supported by an IMF arrangement. Unlike with Paris Club creditors, there is no "cutoff" date.

Commercial bank agreements restructure principal; consolidation of original interest costs is rare. Like Paris Club agreements, consolidation of short-term debt is also unusual (but when a major portion of arrears has arisen from short-term debt, there is often no option but to restructure). Among the initiatives for reducing the commercial debt burden was the Brady Plan (1989). This market-based debt-restructuring initiative provided a menu of options to the creditor banks. These included buybacks—the debtor government repurchases debt at a discount that is agreed upon with the creditor banks; an exchange of debt into bonds at a discount but offering a market rate of interest (discount bonds); and an exchange at par into bonds that yielded a below-market interest rate (interest-reduction bonds). The discount bonds and the interest-reduction bonds were fully collateralized by zero-coupon U.S. government securities for principal and partially collateralized for interest payments.

tors are offered a choice between different options, one of them being a partial debt reduction, the other one being a rescheduling at a reduced interest rate (debt reduction in present value terms). Some creditors may forgive part of the claims and reschedule the outstanding part at the appropriate market rate ("debt-reduction" option), whereas other creditors reschedule the whole claim at a lower interest rate ("debt-service-reduction" option), resulting in a debt reduction in present value equivalent to the one granted by creditors that chose the "debt-reduction" option. Table 8.2 shows the variety and evolution of Paris Club debt-rescheduling terms.

8.20 Because of the complexities involved, and the different interest rates that may be employed, international statistical standards have not developed to the point where there is general agreement on how to measure and make comparable the different methods of providing debt reduction in present-value terms.

8.21 Given the above, the *Guide* provides no recommended guidance on measuring and presenting debt reduction in present-value terms. Nonetheless, economies that undergo debt rescheduling and refinancing are encouraged to disseminate (1) the total nominal amounts involved; (2) the amount of debt reduction in present-value terms they have achieved—the difference between the present values (using a common interest rate) of the rescheduled/refinanced debt-service payments before and after rescheduling/refinancing (present-value method);[7] and (3) provide detailed information on how the amount of the present-value reduction was calculated, including the interest rate(s) used.

8.22 Similarly, no guidance is provided for measuring debt relief in terms of an increase in duration because of the difficulty in measuring such relief and presenting it in a manner that is comparable with other forms of debt reorganization.

Debt Forgiveness

8.23 Debt forgiveness is defined as the voluntary cancellation of all or part of a debt obligation within a contractual arrangement between a creditor in one

economy and a debtor in another economy.[8] More specifically, the contractual arrangement cancels or forgives all or part of the principal amount outstanding, including interest arrears (interest that fell due in the past) and any other interest costs that have accrued. Debt forgiveness does not arise from the cancellation of future interest payments that have not yet fallen due and have not yet accrued.

8.24 If the debt reorganization effectively changes the contractual rate of interest—such as by reducing future interest payments but maintaining future principal payments, or vice versa—it is classified as debt rescheduling. However, in the specific instance of zero-coupon securities, a reduction in the principal amount to be paid at redemption to an amount that still exceeds the principal amount outstanding at the time the arrangement becomes effective could be classified as either an effective change in the contractual rate of interest, or as a reduction in principal with the contractual rate unchanged. Unless the bilateral agreement explicitly acknowledges a change in the contractual rate of interest, such a reduction in the principal payment to be made at maturity should be recorded as debt forgiveness.

Recommended treatment

External debt position and debt reduction

8.25 Debt forgiveness reduces the gross external debt position by the value of the outstanding principal that has been forgiven. Any reduction in principal is recorded under the appropriate debt instrument when it is received—that is, when both the debtor and creditor record the forgiveness in their books. Where possible, debt forgiveness in nominal terms should be separately identified and recorded under *debt reduction* in Table 8.1.

8.26 If forgiveness relates to payments on debt obligations that are past due and are yet to be paid—that is, arrears of interest and principal—a reduction in the gross external debt position under *arrears* is recorded. Forgiveness of interest costs that have

---

[7]The payment schedule for both the original and rescheduled debt could also be provided as memorandum information.

[8]This includes forgiveness of some or all of the principal amount of a credit-linked note due to an event affecting the entity on which the embedded credit derivative was written, and forgiveness of principal that arises when a type of event contractually specified in the debt contract occurs—for example, forgiveness in the event of a type of catastrophe.

Table 8.2. Evolution of Paris Club Rescheduling Terms

	Middle-Income Countries	Lower-Middle-Income Countries (Houston terms)[1]	Toronto Terms — DR	Toronto Terms — DSR	Toronto Terms — LM	London Terms[3] — DR	London Terms[3] — DSR	London Terms[3] — CMI	London Terms[3] — LM	Naples Terms[4] — DR	Naples Terms[4] — DSR Maturing flows	Naples Terms[4] — DSR Stocks	Naples Terms[4] — CMI	Naples Terms[4] — LM	Lyon Terms[5] — DR	Lyon Terms[5] — DSR	Lyon Terms[5] — CMI	Lyon Terms[5] — LM
Implemented	Since September 1990		Oct. 1988–Jun. 1991			Dec. 1991–Dec. 1994				Since January 1995					Since December 1996			
Grace (in years)	5–6[1]	Up to 8[1]	8	8	14	6	—	5	16[6]	6	—	3	8	20	6	8	8	20
Maturity (in years)	9[1]	15[1]	14	14	25	23	23	23	25	23	33	33	33	40	23	40	40	40
Repayment schedule	Flat/Graduated	Flat/Graduated	Flat			Graduated				Graduated					Graduated			
Interest rate[7]	M	M	M	R[8]	M	M	R[9]	R[9]	M	M	R[10]	R[10]	R[10]	M	M	R[11]	R[11]	M
Reduction in present value (in percent)	—	—	33	20–30[12]	—	50	50	50	—	67	67	67	67	—	80	80	80	—
Memorandum items																		
ODA credits — Grace (in years)	5–6	Up to 10	14			12				16					16			
ODA credits — Maturity (in years)	10	20	25			30				40					40			

Source: Paris Club.

[1] Since the 1992 agreements with Argentina and Brazil, creditors have made increasing use of graduated payments schedules (up to 15 years' maturity and 2–3 years' grace for middle-income countries; up to 18 years' maturity for lower-middle-income countries).

[2] DR refers to the debt-reduction option; DSR to the debt-service-reduction option; CMI denotes the capitalization of moratorium interest; LM denotes the nonconcessional option providing longer maturities. Under London, Naples, and Lyon terms, there is a provision for a stock-of-debt operation, but no such operation took place under London terms.

[3] These have also been called "Enhanced Toronto" and "Enhanced Concessions" terms.

[4] Most countries are expected to secure a 67 percent level of concessionality; countries with a per capita income of more than $500, and an overall indebtedness ratio on present-value loans of less than 350 percent of exports may receive a 50 percent level of concessionality decided on a case-by-case basis. For a 50 percent level of concessionality, terms are equal to London terms, except for the DSR option under a stock-of-debt operation that includes a three-year grace period.

[5] These terms are to be granted in the context of concerted action by all creditors under the HIPC Initiative. They also include, on a voluntary basis, an official development assistance (ODA) debt-reduction option.

[6] Fourteen years before June 1992.

[7] Interest rates are based on market rates (M) and are determined in the bilateral agreements implementing the Paris Club Agreed Minute. R = reduced rates.

[8] The interest rate was 3.5 percentage points below the market rate or half of the market rate if the market rate was below 7 percent.

[9] Reduced to achieve a 50 percent present-value reduction.

[10] Reduced to achieve a 67 percent present-value reduction; under the DSR option for the stock operation, the interest rate is slightly higher, reflecting the three-year grace period.

[11] Reduced to achieve an 80 percent present-value reduction.

[12] The reduction of present value depends on the reduction in interest rates and therefore varies. See footnote 8.

accrued during the period or amounts disbursed in the current recording period has no impact on the gross external debt position at the end of the period because any increase in the outstanding value of the debt instrument is matched by the debt forgiveness. However, any such forgiveness should be reported under *debt reduction* in Table 8.1.

8.27 A special case of debt forgiveness is where the creditor provides a grant to the debtor that is used to pay the debt-service payments as they fall due. In such instances, the gross external debt position is only affected when debt-service payments are made—that is, the same as for all debt instruments being serviced. Nonetheless, such assistance is recorded in the table as *debt reduction* when the debt-service payments are made.

Flow data

8.28 In flow terms, debt forgiveness is recorded in the balance of payments as a capital transfer, and in the DAC and DRS systems as a debt-forgiveness grant. The counterpart transaction in the balance of payments and DAC is a repayment of the principal owed. When debt forgiveness is in the form of a grant by the creditor to the debtor (as in the previous paragraph), repayment of the principal owed is generally similarly recorded in the DRS.

Debt Conversion and Debt Prepayments

8.29 External debt conversion is an exchange of debt—typically at a discount—for a non-external debt claim, such as equity, or for counterpart funds, such as can be used to finance a particular project or policy. Debt-for-equity, debt-for-nature, and debt-for-development swaps are all examples of debt conversion. A debt buyback is the repurchase, usually at a discount, by a debtor economy (or on its behalf) of all or part of its external debt. It may be undertaken on the secondary market or through negotiations with creditors.

Debt conversion

8.30 Rather than exchanging debt for debt, countries might enter into a debt conversion process—the legal and financial transformation of an economy's liability. Typically, debt conversions involve an exchange of external debt in foreign currency for a nondebt obligation in domestic currency, at a discount. In essence, external debt is prepaid, and the

nature of the claim on the economy is changed. An example is a foreign currency debt-for-equity swap, which results in debt claims on the debtor economy being reduced, and nonresident investments in equity investments increased. Debt-for-equity swaps often involve a third party, usually a nongovernmental organization or a corporation, which buys the claims from the creditor and receives shares in a corporation or local currency (to be used for equity investment) from the debtor. Other types of debt swaps such as external debt obligations for exports (debt for exports), or external debt obligations for counterpart assets that are provided by the debtor to the creditor for a specified purpose such as wildlife protection, health, education, and environmental conservation (debt for sustainable development), are also debt conversions.

Prepayments and buybacks

8.31 Prepayments consist of a repurchase, or early payment, of debt at conditions that are agreed between the debtor and the creditor; that is, debt is extinguished in return for a cash payment agreed between the debtor and the creditor. When a discount is involved relative to the nominal value of the debt, prepayments are referred to as buybacks. Also, debtors may enter the secondary market and repurchase their own debt because market conditions are such that it is advantageous financially to do so.

Recommended treatment

External debt position

8.32 For both debt conversions and debt prepayments, a reduction in the gross external debt position is recorded to the value of the debt instruments that are extinguished, irrespective of the value of the counterpart claim (or assets) being provided. This reduction in gross external debt position should be recorded at the time when the debt instrument is extinguished; more accurately, the gross external debt position no longer includes debt that has ceased to exist.

Flow data

8.33 In the transaction data in the balance of payments, the reduction in the outstanding debt instrument is recorded at the value of the counterpart claim (or assets). Any difference in value is recorded as a valuation change in position data. An exception arises when nonmarketable debt owed to official creditors is involved, and the counterpart claim (assets) has a lower value than the debt, in which instance both the debt instrument and the counterpart claim (or assets) are separately valued, and any difference in value is recorded as debt forgiveness in the balance of payments. The DAC system employs a similar approach, except that all differences in value are classified as transactions and not as valuation changes provided that they are the result of bilateral negotiation and there is a development motive for the operation. The DRS records both the reduction in the nominal value of the debt instrument and the value at which the debt was repurchased, allowing the discount to be measured.

Debt reduction

8.34 Where official debt is exchanged for equity or counterpart funds to be used for development purposes, the difference between the value of the debt being extinguished and the counterpart claim or funds provided is classified as *debt reduction*.[9] This includes cases where the buyback of debt is by a third party, such as a nongovernmental organization or a corporation, which then sells the debt back to the debtor at a discount, under a deal that is arranged under a bilateral arrangement between debtor and government creditor.

8.35 In other cases, replacing a debt instrument with another type of claim may only be the recognition of reality. In other words, and particularly for marketable instruments, the price at which the debtor is willing to repurchase the debt may be greater than the price at which the debt previously traded. So, if the creditor purchased the security at the lower market price, the creditor might be making a holding gain.

8.36 The *Guide* recommends that in measuring and presenting data on debt reduction from such transactions, a distinction is made between (1) collaborative arrangements arising from discussions between the creditor(s) and debtor; and (2) buybacks that are initiated by the debtor through purchases in the secondary market. When buybacks arise from collaborative arrangements, any difference between the value of the counterpart claims (or assets) provided by the debtor and the nominal amount bought back

should be recorded as *debt reduction* in Table 8.1. Debt reduction arising from buybacks in the secondary market initiated by the debtor should not be recorded as *debt reduction* in the table.

8.37 For both public and private sector transactions, if external debt and the counterpart claims (or assets) are denominated in different currencies, any debt reduction should be determined using the market exchange rate between the two currencies prevailing on the transaction date (the midpoint between the buying and selling spot rates).

Presentation of Data on Debt Reduction

8.38 In Table 8.1, as far as possible, economies should present information on *debt reduction* according to the sector of the debtor (public-sector-based approach), and by type of creditor. Additionally, the table captures information on debt reduction arising from debt reorganization of bonds and notes.

8.39 Also, data could be presented by type of debt reorganization under which the debt reduction was given: (1) debt rescheduling; (2) debt forgiveness; and (3) debt conversion and debt prepayments. Where a debt-relief package includes elements of more than one type, separately identifying each type is encouraged. For example, if a part of the debt is to be repaid for cash, a prepayment should be recorded; if part of the debt is cancelled, debt forgiveness should be recorded; if the repayment terms of part of the debt are changed, a debt rescheduling should be recorded. But if it is not possible to provide separate identification, all debt reduction should be included along with the dominant type of reorganization in the package.

8.40 In Table 8.1, debt reduction should be recorded at the time when the external debt is reduced. If all debt reduction occurs at one time, debt reduction should be recorded at that time rather than when the debt-service payments would have fallen due. However, it is recognized that national practices may differ in this regard, and if the latter approach is followed, it should be recorded in a note to the presentation of the debt-reduction data.

8.41 Debt reorganization might also be phased over a period of time, such as under multiphase contracts,

---

[9]In the DAC system it is classified as debt forgiveness, and in the DRS it is classified as debt reduction.

performance-related contracts, and when debt reduction is dependent on contingent events. In such circumstances, debt reduction is recorded when the change in debt-service payment schedule of the debtor takes effect—for instance, if debt reduction occurs when the debt-service payments fall due, then this is the time when the debt reduction is recorded.

8.42 As noted above, the exchange rate used to calculate debt reduction should be the market rate on the transaction date (the midpoint between the buying and selling spot rates).

8.43 It is recommended that methodological notes accompany the presentation of debt-reduction statistics. Inter alia, these notes should cover each type of debt reorganization.

8.44 In Table 8.1, debt reduction is measured only in nominal value terms. This is because the analytical usefulness of presenting debt-reduction data in market-value terms is uncertain. For instance, when an economy faces payment difficulties (which is systematically the case when the country receives debt reduction), its debt is generally valued at a deep discount, since the market is still uncertain about the prospects of payment. In such circumstances, debt reorganization can result in the new debt having a higher value than the old debt. Similarly, in most cases (and in all multilateral agreements, such as those of the Paris Club or the London Club—see Box 8.1—or the HIPC Initiative), debt relief aims to restore the creditworthiness of the debtor country, thus increasing the possibility of repayment of existing debts and hence raising their market value. While there may be analytical interest in measuring the effect of debt reorganization on the value of outstanding debt—that is, the amount by which the market value rises—changes in the nominal amount outstanding rather than the market value is the preferred approach to measuring debt reduction arising from debt reorganization.

Other Transactions Relating to Debt Reorganization

Debt Assumption

8.45 Debt assumption is a trilateral agreement between a creditor, a former debtor, and a new debtor under which the new debtor assumes the for-

mer debtor's outstanding liability to the creditor and is liable for repayment of the debt.

8.46 Debt assumption is recorded—in the transaction and position data—when the creditor invokes the contract conditions permitting a guarantee to be called. If debt assumption arises under other circumstances, it is recorded when the liability is actually removed from the debtor's balance sheet, and the corresponding entries made in the new debtor's balance sheet, and not necessarily the time when agreement was reached to make the debt assumption. The recording by the entity assuming the debt has to be made in one time period: the successive dates of repayment previously foreseen in the context of the former debt are not relevant.

8.47 After it has been assumed, the debt, which was originally a liability of the former debtor, becomes a liability of the new debtor. The debt may carry the same terms as the original debt, or new terms may come into force because the guarantee was invoked. If the original and new debtors are from different institutional sectors, the external debt of the institutional sector of the original debtor is reduced, and the external debt of the institutional sector of the new debtor increased. The amount to be recorded by the new debtor is the full amount of the outstanding debt that is assumed. No debt reduction is recorded, unless there is an agreement with the creditor to reduce the external debt.

8.48 An example of debt assumption could be a government taking over the debts of a corporation. If, in such an example, the government acquires a financial claim on the corporation as a consequence of the debt assumption, the corporation will need to record a new debt liability, which is classified as external debt only if the government and corporation are residents of different economies. Every transfer of liabilities between a quasi-corporation and its owner is reflected in the value of its equity stake.

8.49 Rather than assume the debt, a government may decide to repay a specific borrowing or make a specific payment on behalf of another institutional unit, without the guarantee being called or the debt being taken over. In this case, the debt stays recorded solely in the balance sheet of the other institutional unit, the only legal debtor. If a new liability is created in the form of a government claim on the debtor, this is classified as external debt only if the government and other institutional unit are residents of different economies (and the debtor is not a quasi-corporation of the government).

Borrowing for Balance of Payments Support

8.50 Borrowing for balance of payments support refers to borrowing (including bond issues) by the government or central bank (or by other sectors on behalf of the authorities) to meet balance of payments needs.[10] In the external debt statement, unlike the analytical presentation of the balance of pay-

---

[10]A balance of payments need is defined more fully in paragraphs 451 through 453 of *BPM5*.

ments, no special "below-the-line" recording of these borrowings or their advance repayment is required.

New Money Facilities

8.51 Some debt-reorganization packages feature new money facilities (new loan facilities that may be used for the payment of existing debt-service obligations). In the gross external debt position, outstanding drawings by the debtor on new money facilities are usually recorded under *long-term loans*. If the existing debt liabilities remain outstanding, they should continue to be reported in the gross external debt position, until they are repaid. New money facilities are not to be recorded as debt reduction.

9. Contingent Liabilities

Introduction

9.1 The financial crises of the 1990s highlighted the shortcomings of conventional accounting systems in capturing the full extent of financial exposures arising from traditional "off-balance-sheet" obligations, such as contingent liabilities, and from financial derivatives contracts. The discovery of the magnitude and role of these obligations in these crises reinforced the need to monitor them. This chapter focuses on contingent liabilities.[1] Guidelines for monitoring financial derivatives positions were provided earlier in the *Guide*.

9.2 Contingent liabilities are complex arrangements, and no single measurement approach can fit all situations; rather, comprehensive standards for measuring these liabilities are still evolving. Indeed, experience has shown that contingent liabilities are not always fully covered in accounting systems. Nonetheless, to encourage the monitoring and measurement of contingent liabilities, with a view to enhancing transparency, this chapter provides some measurement approaches, after first defining contingent liabilities and then providing some reasons for their measurement. More specifically, also provided is a table for the dissemination of external debt data on an "ultimate risk" basis; that is, adjusting residence-based external debt data for certain cross-border risk transfers.

Definition

9.3 Contingent liabilities are obligations that arise from a particular, discrete event(s) that may or may not occur. They can be explicit or implicit. A key aspect of such liabilities, which distinguishes them from current financial liabilities (and external debt), is that one or more conditions or events must be fulfilled before a financial transaction takes place.

Explicit Contingent Liabilities

9.4 Explicit contingent liabilities are those defined by the *1993 SNA* as contractual financial arrangements that give rise to conditional requirements—that is, the requirements become effective if one or more stipulated conditions arise—to make payments of economic value.[2] In other words, explicit contingent liabilities arise from a legal or contractual arrangement. The contingent liability may arise from an existing debt—such as an institution guaranteeing payment to a third party; or arise from an obligation to provide funds—such as a line of credit, which once advanced creates a claim; or arise from a commitment to compensate another party for losses—such as exchange rate guarantees. Some of the more common explicit contingent liabilities are set out below.

Loan and other payment guarantees

9.5 Loan and other payment guarantees are commitments by one party to bear the risk of nonpayment by another party. Guarantors are only required to make a payment if the debtor defaults. Some of the common types of risks that are assumed by guarantors are commercial risk or financial performance risk of the borrower; market risk, particularly that arising from the possibility of adverse movements in market variables such as exchange rates and interest rates; political risk, including risk of currency inconvertibility and nontransferability of payments (also called transfer risk), expropriation, and political violence; and regulatory or policy risk, where implementation of certain laws and regulations is critical

---

[1]This chapter draws on work at the World Bank.

[2]The *European System of Accounts: ESA 1995* (Eurostat, 1996) defines contingent liabilities in a similar way.

to the financial performance of the debtor.[3] Loan and other payment guarantees usually increase the initial debtor's access to international credit markets and/or improve the maturity structure of borrowing.

Credit guarantees and similar contingent liabilities

9.6 Lines of credit and loan commitments provide a guarantee that undrawn funds will be available in the future, but no financial liability/asset exists until such funds are actually provided. Undrawn lines of credit and undisbursed loan commitments are contingent liabilities of the issuing institutions— namely, banks. Letters of credit are promises to make payment upon the presentation of prespecified documents.

Contingent "credit availability" guarantees or contingent credit facilities

9.7 Underwritten note issuance facilities (NIFs) provide a guarantee that a borrower will be able to issue short-term notes and that the underwriting institution(s) will take up any unsold portion of the notes. Only when funds are advanced by the underwriting institution(s) will an actual liability/asset be created. The unutilized portion is a contingent liability.

9.8 Other note guarantee facilities providing contingent credit or backup purchase facilities are revolving underwriting facilities (RUFs), multiple options facilities (MOFs), and global note facilities (GNFs). Bank and nonbank financial institutions provide backup purchase facilities. Again, the unutilized amounts of these facilities are contingent liabilities.

Implicit Contingent Liabilities

9.9 Implicit contingent liabilities do not arise from a legal or contractual source but are recognized after a condition or event is realized. For example, ensuring systemic solvency of the banking sector might be viewed as an implicit contingent liability of the central bank.[4] Likewise, covering the obligations of sub-

national (state and local) governments or the central bank in the event of default might be viewed as an implicit contingent liability of the central government. Implicit contingencies may be recognized when the cost of not assuming them is believed to be unacceptably high.[5] Table 9.1 provides a practical way of classifying the types of potential liabilities of the central government.

9.10 Although implicit contingent liabilities are important in macroeconomic assessment, fiscal burden, and policy analysis, implicit contingent liabilities are even more difficult to measure than explicit contingent liabilities. Also, until measurement techniques are developed, there is a danger of creating moral hazard risks in disseminating information on implicit contingent liabilities of the type set out in Table 9.1. Thus, the rest of this chapter focuses only on the measurement of explicit contingent liabilities.

Why Measure Contingent Liabilities?

9.11 By conferring certain rights or obligations that may be exercised in the future, contingent liabilities can have a financial and economic impact on the economic entities involved. When these liabilities relate to cross-border activity, and they are not captured in conventional accounting systems, it can be difficult to accurately assess the financial position of an economy—and the various institutional sectors within the economy—vis-à-vis nonresidents.

9.12 Analysis of the macroeconomic vulnerability of an economy to external shocks requires information on both external debt obligations and contingent liabilities. Experience has shown that contingent liabilities are not always fully covered in accounting systems. Moreover, there is an increasing realization, when assessing macroeconomic conditions, that contingent liabilities of the government and the central bank can be significant. For example, fiscal contingent claims can clearly have an impact on

---

[3]Regulatory or policy-based guarantees are especially relevant in infrastructure financing. For more details and country-specific examples, see Irwin and others (1997).

[4]A case in point is Indonesia, where the government's domestic debt increased from practically nothing, in the period before the crisis (mid-1997), to 500 trillion Indonesian rupiah by the end of

1999, mostly due to the issuance of bonds to recapitalize the banking system. The increase in the government's stock of domestic debt was accompanied by a rise in its assets, which were received in exchange for issuing bank-restructuring bonds. See also Blejer and Shumacher (2000).

[5]See *Guidelines for Public Debt Management* (IMF and World Bank, 2001).

Table 9.1. Fiscal Risk Matrix with Illustrative Examples

Liabilities[1]	Direct (obligation in any event)	Contingent (obligation if a particular event occurs)
Explicit Government liability as recognized by a law or contract	• External and domestic sovereign borrowing (loans contracted and securities issued by central government) • Budgetary expenditures • Budgetary expenditures legally binding in the long term (civil servants' salaries and pensions)	• Central government guarantees for nonsovereign borrowing and obligations issued to subnational governments and public and private sector entities (development banks) • Umbrella central government guarantees for various types of loans (mortgage loans, student loans, agriculture loans, small business loans) • Trade and exchange rate guarantees issued by the central government • Guarantees on borrowing by a foreign sovereign government • Central government guarantees on private investments • Central government insurance schemes (deposit insurance, income from private pension funds, crop insurance, flood insurance, war-risk insurance)
Implicit Obligations that may be recognized when the cost of not assuming them could be unacceptably high	• Future public pensions (as opposed to civil service pensions) • Social security schemes • Future health care financing • Future recurrent cost of public investments	• Default of subnational government, and public entity on nonguaranteed debt and other obligations • Liability cleanup in entities under privatization • Banking failure (support beyond state insurance) • Investment failure of a nonguaranteed pension fund, employment fund, or social security fund (social protection of small investors) • Default of central bank on its obligations (foreign exchange contracts, currency defense, balance of payment stability) • Bailouts following a reversal in private capital flows • Environmental recovery, disaster relief, etc.

Source: Adapted from Polackova Brixi (1999).
[1]The liabilities listed refer to the fiscal authorities, not the central bank.

budget deficits and financing needs, with implications for economic policy. Recognizing the implications of contingent liabilities for policy and analysis, the *1993 SNA* (paragraph 11.26) states:

> Collectively, such contingencies may be important for financial programming, policy, and analysis. Therefore, where contingent positions are important for policy and analysis, it is recommended that supplementary information be collected and presented. . . .

Measuring Contingent Liabilities

9.13 Contingent liabilities give rise to obligations that may be realized in the future, but because of their complexity and variety, establishing a single method for measuring them may not be appropriate. Several alternative ways of measuring contingencies are outlined below. The relevance of each will depend on the type of contingency being measured, and the availability of data.

9.14 A first step in accounting for contingent liabilities is for economic entities to record all such contingent liabilities as they are created, such as with an accrual-based reporting system. But how should such liabilities be valued? One approach is to record these liabilities at full face value or maximum potential loss. Thus, a guarantee covering the full amount of a loan outstanding would be recorded at the full nominal value of the underlying loan. Some governments have adopted this approach. For example, the New Zealand government routinely publishes the maximum potential loss to the government of quantifiable and nonquantifiable contingent liabilities,[6] including guarantees and indemnities, uncalled capital to international institutions, and potential settlements related to legal proceedings and disputes.

---

[6]New Zealand Treasury, *Budget Economic and Fiscal Update* (Wellington, annual). As the name suggests, nonquantifiable contingent liabilities cannot be measured and arise from either institutional guarantees that have been provided through legislation or from agreements and arrangements with organizations.

9.15 Likewise, the Australian government identifies quantifiable and nonquantifiable contingencies.[7] In addition, it identifies "remote" contingent losses (mostly guarantees), including nonquantifiable "remote" contingencies. The Indian government regularly reports the direct guarantees provided by the central government on external borrowings of public sector enterprises, development financial institutions, and nonfinancial private sector corporations.[8] The guarantees are presented by sector and at nominal value.

9.16 The maximum potential loss method has an obvious limitation: there is no information on the likelihood of the contingency occurring. Especially for loan and other payment guarantees, the maximum potential loss is likely to exceed the economic value of the contingent liability because there is no certainty that a default will occur (that is, the expected probability of default is less than unity). Theoretically, a better approach is to measure both the maximum possible loss and the expected loss, but calculating the expected loss requires estimating the likelihood of losses, which can be difficult.

9.17 Several alternative methods of valuing the expected loss exist. These range from relatively simple techniques requiring the use of historical data, to complex options-pricing techniques. The actual approach adopted will depend on the availability of information and the type of contingency. If the expected loss can be calculated, an additional approach is to value this loss(es) in present-value terms—expected present value. In other words, since any payment will be in the future and not immediate, the expected future payment streams could be discounted using a market rate of interest faced by the guarantor; that is, the present value. As with all present-value calculations, the appropriate interest rate to use is crucial; a common practice with government contingent liabilities is to use a risk-free rate like the treasury rate. Under this present-value approach, when a guarantee is issued the present value of the expected cost of the guarantee could be recorded as an outlay or expense (in the operating account) in the current year and included in the position data, such as a balance sheet.

9.18 Exact valuation requires detailed market information, but such information is often unavailable. This is particularly true in situations of market failure or incomplete markets—a financial marketplace is said to be complete when a market exists with an equilibrium price for every asset in every possible state of the world. Other means are then required to value a contingency. One possibility is to use historical data on similar types of contingent operations. For example, if the market price of a loan is not observable, but historical data on a large number of loan guarantees and defaults associated with those guarantees are available, then the probability distribution of the default occurrences can be used to estimate the expected cost of a guarantee on the loan. This procedure is similar to that employed by the insurance industry to calculate insurance premiums. Rating information on like entities is often used to impute default value on loan guarantees as well. The U.S. Export-Import Bank employs this method for valuing loan guarantees that it extends.

9.19 Bank regulatory guidelines established by the Basel Committee on Banking Supervision also draw on historical data to measure risks in banks' off-balance-sheet activities. For traditional off-balance-sheet items like credit contingent liabilities, the guidelines provide "credit conversion factors," which when multiplied with the notional principal amount provide an estimate of the expected "payout" from the contingent liability. The conversion factors are derived from the estimated size and likely occurrence of the credit exposure, as well as the relative degree of credit risk. Thus, stand-by letters of credit have a 100 percent conversion factor; the unused portion of commitments with an original maturity of over one year is 50 percent; and RUFs, NIFs, and similar arrangements are assigned a 50 percent conversion factor as well.

9.20 Market-value measures use market information to value a contingency. This methodology can be applied across a wide range of contingent liabilities, but it is particularly useful for valuing loan and other payment guarantees, on which the following discussion focuses. This methodology assumes that comparable instruments with and without guarantees are observable in the market and that the market has fully assessed the risk covered by the guarantee. Under this method, the value of a guarantee on a financial instrument is derived as the difference between the price of the instrument without a guar-

---

[7]*Aggregate Financial Statement* (Australia, annual).

[8]See the Ministry of Finance's annual publication on external debt, *India's External Debt: A Status Report*.

antee and the price inclusive of the guarantee. In the context of a loan guarantee, the nominal value of the guarantee would be the difference between the contractual interest rate (ip) on the unguaranteed loan and the contractual interest rate (ig) on the guaranteed loan times the nominal value of the loan (L): $(ip - ig)L$. The market value of the guarantee would use market, not contractual, rates.[9]

9.21 Yet another approach to valuing contingent liabilities applies option-pricing techniques from finance theory. With this method, a guarantee can be viewed as an option: a loan guarantee is essentially a put option written on the underlying assets backing the loan.[10] In a loan guarantee, the guarantor sells a put option to a lender. The lender, who is the purchaser of the put option, has the right to "put" (sell) the loan to the guarantor. For example, consider a guarantee on a loan with a nominal value of F and an underlying value of V. If $V - F < 0$, then the put option is exercised and the lender receives the exercise price of F. The value of the put option at exercise is $F - V$. When $V > F$, the option is not exercised. The value of the guarantee is equivalent to the value of the put option. If the value of the credit instrument on which a guarantee is issued is below the value at which it can be sold to the guarantor, then the guarantee will be called.

9.22 Although the option-pricing approach is relatively new and sophisticated, it is being applied in the pricing of guarantees on infrastructure financing and interest and principal payment guarantees.[11] But standard option pricing has its limitations as well. This is because the standard option-pricing model assumes an exogenous stochastic process for underlying asset prices. However, it can be argued that the very presence of a guarantee (especially a government guarantee) can affect asset prices.[12]

Recommended Measures

9.23 The *Guide* encourages the measurement and monitoring of contingent liabilities, especially of guarantees, and has outlined some measurement tech-

niques. However, it is recognized that comprehensive standards for measuring contingent liabilities are still evolving. Consequently, only the recording of a narrow, albeit important, range of contingent liabilities is specified ahead: guarantees of domestic private sector external debt by the public sector, and the cross-border provision of guarantees. In both instances, it is recommended that the contingency should be valued in terms of the maximum exposure loss.

Public sector guarantees

9.24 In Chapter 5 the dissemination of data on publicly guaranteed private sector debt—that is, the value of private sector debt that is owed to nonresidents, and is guaranteed by the public sector—through a contractual arrangement is discussed.

Ultimate risk

9.25 Set out in Table 9.2 is a format that presents external debt according to an "ultimate" risk concept—augmenting residence-based data to take account of the extent to which external debt is guaranteed by residents for nonresidents. Countries could potentially have debt liabilities to nonresidents in excess of those recorded as external debt on a residence basis if their residents provide guarantees to nonresidents that might be called. Also, branches of domestic institutions located abroad could create a drain on the domestic economy if they ran into difficulties and their own head offices needed to provide funds.

9.26 In Table 9.2 residence-based external debt data (column 1) is increased by the amount of debt of nonresidents, not owned by residents, that is guaranteed by a resident entity (inward risk transfer, column 2). Column 3 is the adjusted external debt exposure of the economy. The table is set out in this manner so that external debt on an ultimate-risk basis can be related back to the gross external debt position measured on a residence basis.

9.27 The intention of column 2 is to measure any additional external debt risk exposures of residents arising from contingent liabilities. The definition of contingent liabilities adopted is deliberately narrow. To be included in this definition of contingent liabilities, the debt must exist, so lines of credit and similar potential obligations are not included. The data on the inward transfer of risk covers only the debt of

---

[9]For a further discussion of market-value methods see Towe (1990) and Mody and Patro (1996).

[10]Robert C. Merton (1977) was the first to show this.

[11]See Irwin and others (1997) and Borensztein and Pennacchi (1990).

[12]See Sundaresan (2002) for a detailed exposition on this issue.

Table 9.2. Gross External Debt Position: Ultimate Risk Basis

	End-Period			
	Gross External Debt (1)	Inward risk transfer (+) (2)	External Debt (ultimate-risk basis) (3)	*Memorandum item:* Outward risk transfer (4)
General Government				
Short-term				
Money market instruments				
Loans				
Trade credits				
Other debt liabilities[1]				
Arrears				
Other				
Long-term				
Bonds and notes				
Loans				
Trade credits				
Other debt liabilities[1]				
Monetary Authorities				
Short-term				
Money market instruments				
Loans				
Currency and deposits[2]				
Other debt liabilities[1]				
Arrears				
Other				
Long-term				
Bonds and notes				
Loans				
Currency and deposits[2]				
Other debt liabilities[1]				
Banks				
Short-term				
Money market instruments				
Loans				
Currency and deposits[2]				
Other debt liabilities[1]				
Arrears				
Other				
Long-term				
Bonds and notes				
Loans				
Currency and deposits[2]				
Other debt liabilities[1]				
Other Sectors				
Short-term				
Money market instruments				
Loans				
Currency and deposits[2]				
Trade credits				
Other debt liabilities[1]				
Arrears				
Other				
Long-term				
Bonds and notes				
Loans				
Currency and deposits[2]				
Trade credits				
Other debt liabilities[1]				

Table 9.2 *(concluded)*

	End-Period			
	Gross External Debt (1)	Inward risk transfer (+) (2)	External Debt (ultimate-risk basis) (3)	*Memorandum item:* Outward risk transfer (4)
Other Sectors *(continued)*				
Nonbank financial corporations				
Short-term				
Money market instruments				
Loans				
Currency and deposits[2]				
Other debt liabilities[1]				
Arrears				
Other				
Long-term				
Bonds and notes				
Loans				
Currency and deposits[2]				
Other debt liabilities[1]				
Nonfinancial corporations				
Short-term				
Money market instruments				
Loans				
Trade credits				
Other debt liabilities[1]				
Arrears				
Other				
Long-term				
Bonds and notes				
Loans				
Trade credits				
Other debt liabilities[1]				
Households and nonprofit institutions serving households (NPISH)				
Short-term				
Money market instruments				
Loans				
Trade credits				
Other debt liabilities[1]				
Arrears				
Other				
Long-term				
Bonds and notes				
Loans				
Trade credits				
Other debt liabilities[1]				
Direct Investment: Intercompany Lending				
Debt liabilities to affiliated enterprises				
Arrears				
Other				
Debt liabilities to direct investors				
Arrears				
Other				
Gross External Debt				

[1] *Other debt liabilities* are *other liabilities* in the IIP statement.
[2] It is recommended that all currency and deposits be included in the short-term category unless detailed information is available to make the short-term/long-term attribution.

a nonresident to a nonresident on which, and as part of the agreement between debtor and creditor, payments are guaranteed to the creditor(s) by a resident entity under a legally binding contract—the guarantor will most commonly be an entity that is related to the debtor (for example, the parent of the debtor entity), and debt of a legally dependent nonresident branch of a resident entity that is owed to a nonresident. If debt is partially guaranteed, such as if principal payments or interest payments alone are guaranteed, then only the present value of the amount guaranteed should be included in columns 2 or 4. To avoid double counting the same external debt risk exposure, the following should be excluded from column 2: all debt liabilities of nonresident branches to other nonresident branches of the same parent entity; and any amounts arising from external debt borrowings of nonresidents that were guaranteed by a resident entity and on-lent by the nonresident borrower to that same resident entity or any of its branches. This guidance is not intended to exclude debt exposures of residents from the ultimate risk concept, as defined above, but to ensure that they are counted only once.

9.28 External debt is the liability of the debtor economy. However, as a memorandum item, the amount of external debt of the economy that is guaranteed by nonresidents is also presented (outward risk transfer, column 4). The data on the transfer of risk outward covers only external debt on which, and as part of the agreement between debtor and creditor, payments are guaranteed (or partially guaranteed) to the creditor(s) by a nonresident under a legally binding contract—the guarantor will most commonly be an entity that is related to the debtor (for example, the parent of the debtor entity)—and external debt of a resident entity that is a legally dependent branch of a nonresident entity.

9.29 No reallocation of risk is made because of the provision of collateral by the debtor, or because a debt instrument is "backed" by a pool of instruments or streams of revenue originating from outside of the economy. Because the intention of Table 9.2 is to monitor the potential risk transfer from the debtor side, no reallocation of risk is made if the risk transfer is initiated from the creditor side, without any involvement of the debtor—for example, the creditor has paid a premium to a guarantor, such as an export credit agency unrelated to the debtor, to insure against payment default or has purchased a credit derivative that transfers credit risk exposure.

PART II

Compilation—Principles and Practice

10. Overview of Data Compilation

Introduction

10.1 External debt statistics can be compiled from a variety of sources, using a range of methods. Statistics can be collected from the debtor, from the creditor, or indirectly through information from financial intermediaries in the form of surveys, regulatory reports, and/or from other government administrative records. But a precondition for reliable and timely statistics is that the country has a strong and well-organized institutional setting for the compilation of statistics on public debt—so that all public and publicly guaranteed debt is well monitored and managed (see UNCTAD, 1993)—and private debt, and for the compilation of aggregate external debt statistics.

10.2 This chapter considers some of the important institutional issues that need to be addressed when undertaking the compilation of external debt statistics, and the strategies that need to be considered as the regulatory environment for financial transactions changes. In particular, it emphasizes the need for a coordination of effort among official agencies, with one agency having overall responsibility for compiling and disseminating external debt statistics for the whole economy, and for appropriate legal backing for statistics collection.

10.3 Subsequent chapters provide practical guidance on how external debt statistics might be collected and compiled. They are not intended to be comprehensive. Indeed, some elements of external debt statistics are easier to collect and compile than others. For instance, compiling external debt statistics on, say, a government's foreign currency loan from a group of nonresident banks is more straightforward than, say, collecting information on nonresident ownership of a government's domestic bond issues. But both sets of statistics are required. It is particularly difficult to obtain statistics on nonresident ownership of traded securities, especially

instruments that are not registered—so-called bearer instruments—and so a separate chapter is devoted to this issue. Examples of country practices in compiling and using external debt statistics are provided in Chapter 14.

Coordination Among Official Agencies

10.4 If the responsibility for debt compilation is shared between several agencies, it should be clearly established which agency has the primary responsibility for compiling external debt statistics—the central compiling agency. Responsibility could be assigned through a statistical law or other statutory provision, interagency protocols, executive decrees, etc.

10.5 This chapter does not recommend which institution within an economy should be responsible for compiling and disseminating external debt statistics. This is dependent on the institutional arrangements within the economy. Nonetheless, it is likely that the central compiling agency is either the central bank, the ministry of finance, an independent debt-management office, or a national statistical agency.[1] One approach is to establish the agency in charge of compiling data for the balance of payments and IIP as the central compiling agency for external debt, so promoting consistency among these three related sets of data. Indeed, as noted in Chapter 7, reconciliation of external debt statistics with the financial account of the balance of payments provides a good consistency check, as well as analytically useful information.

10.6 In whatever way the statistics are to be collected and compiled—and invariably a range of

---

[1]A national statistical agency may be a user of the debt data, in the sense that the data are communicated by the ministry of finance and/or the central bank to the national statistical agency for publication.

methods and approaches will be adopted—the process will be resource intensive. Thus, where there is more than one agency involved in the compilation of external debt statistics, there should be a cooperative effort, avoiding duplication of effort and ensuring as far as possible consistency of approach across related data series. With modern computerized techniques, different units can be connected through computer networks facilitating the specialization of the different institutions concerned, without hindering data reporting and compilation. In this regard, procedures to ensure, as far as possible, smooth and timely flows of data between data compiling agencies are essential.

10.7 It is important to ensure that there are well-established contacts between the staff of the different agencies, so that any problems or difficulties can be dealt with in an expeditious manner, and that there is an avoidance of duplication of data coverage in the different institutions. One way of encouraging cooperation, developing contacts, and resolving problems that arise is to hold regular meetings among staff of the various agencies at the working level. Not only could these meetings help resolve problems that might be arising, but there would also be an opportunity to notify each other of upcoming developments and possible future enhancements or changes to collection systems. This type of cooperation helps ideas to spread and improvements to be made, allows institutions to understand each other's position, and helps build important personal contacts.

10.8 Also, if external debt statistics are collected by different agencies, there are a number of considerations that must be borne in mind. First, the concepts used and instruments presented should be consistent, or at least reconcilable. So, in merging together various sources, the central compiling agency must ensure that other contributing agencies are aware of, and supply statistics that are consistent with, core concepts and presentation requirements (such as residence, valuation, etc.) as outlined in the *Guide*. Indeed, the central agency should develop expertise in these standards and, in a sense, act as their guardian within the economy. Also, there are other presentations outlined in the *Guide* that policymakers and other users may encourage compilers to disseminate, or that may need to be compiled to meet international commitments. The data compilers in the central compiling agency will need to ensure that

statistics supplied by the other agencies meet the requirements for these other presentations—both in terms of the coverage as well as the periodicity and timeliness on which these statistics have to be provided.

10.9 Further, it is recommended that, as far as possible, comparison of figures with creditors be carried out on a regular basis, at least once a year, although the compiling agency will need to check whether the creditor data are being compiled on the same basis as the national data. This comparison can be undertaken either on an individual instrument basis (for example, individual government loans) by the agency responsible for compiling these statistics or at an aggregate level using international data sets, such as the Bank for International Settlements (BIS) International Banking Statistics and the *Joint BIS-IMF-OECD-World Bank Statistics on External Debt* (see Chapter 17).

10.10 There should be mechanisms to ensure that the compiled external debt data continue to meet the needs of policymakers and other users. Meetings could be periodically convened with policymakers and other data users to review the comprehensiveness of the external sector statistics and to identify any emerging data requirements. New initiatives could be discussed with policy departments and statistical advisory group(s); such discussions provide scope for seeking additional resources. From these discussions, and in consultation with both users and other compiling agencies, the central compiling agency might devise a strategic plan to improve the quality and coverage of external debt statistics.

Resources

10.11 Resource allocation decisions are the preserve of the authorities in each economy and should be periodically reviewed. Nonetheless, the authorities are encouraged to provide at least adequate resources to perform existing tasks—that is, adequate staff, financial, and computing resources. In particular, key staff should be knowledgeable and well-versed in external debt concepts and compilation methods, and a core contingent of trained external debt statisticians should be retained at any point in time. Instructions for performing existing tasks should be maintained. New compilers could be provided formal and on-the-job training in external debt compilation methods, including international statistical standards and system procedures for handling and processing of data.

Legal Backing for Data Collection

10.12 When the authorities closely regulate foreign borrowing, external debt data may well be a by-product of the regulatory system. But as liberalization of financial flows proceeds, the comprehensiveness of information from regulatory reports may be reduced, and it may become harder to identify entities engaged in external debt transactions. So the need to approach the private sector directly for statistical purposes increases. Without appropriate legal backing, it may be very difficult to acquire the required information from private sector entities.

10.13 Obtaining appropriate legal support for statistics collection could be a complicated and lengthy process that is likely to be undertaken infrequently. Given this, a first step should be to determine whether there is any existing legal support for statistics collection that could be employed to acquire the required information. If not, and it is considered necessary to seek additional legal support, the need may well run wider than "just" the collection of external debt data. Indeed, in an environment of liberalization, a comprehensive review of the sources of statistical information and the legal support needed might be required.

10.14 The terms of legal backing for the collection of statistical information vary from country to country, depending, not least, on the institutional arrangements and the historical development of statistical gathering. Nonetheless, some elements typically covered include:

- The designation of the type of entities that the compiling agency can approach for data (for example, entities in the private business sector) and for what purpose (for example, to monitor economic activity and financial transactions).
- The boundaries of the compiling agency's responsibilities, without being so restrictive that the agency does not have the freedom to adapt as a new development emerges (for example, financial derivatives).
- The possibility of imposing penalties on respondents for nonresponse, which should be accompa-

nied by an appropriate legal mechanism for enforcement.[2]

- A clear statement that information supplied by individual entities would not be separately disclosed and would only be published in the form of statistical aggregates (except, perhaps, where explicit permission is given from an individual entity to disclose information), along with appropriate penalties for the compiling agency and, in particular, individual employees, if such information is disclosed.
- A prohibition on the use by the authorities of information supplied by individual entities for any purpose other than statistics compilation, thus establishing the independence of the statistics compilation function from other government activity (for example, taxation authorities). The prohibition should be supported by penalties and a mechanism for their enforcement.
- A prohibition on other government agencies influencing the content of statistics releases.[3]
- The establishment of an oversight committee of independent experts to help ensure the professionalism and objectivity of the compiling agency.

10.15 With such legal backing, the statistics compiler would have the necessary support for the collection of information from enterprises and commercial banks. Nonetheless, the compiler should not rely solely on legal backing but rather use the legal backing to help and encourage the private sector to report.

Collection Techniques at Different Stages of Liberalization

10.16 As mentioned above, liberalizing financial transactions is likely to affect the information available from statistical reports.[4] Provided that liberalization proceeds on a step-by-step basis, the agency or agencies responsible for external statis-

---

[2]Consideration might also be given to the possibility of imposing penalties on respondents for misreporting (that is, intentionally providing incorrect data).

[3]Data integrity is very important for the statistical function. Where compiling agencies have an operational as well as recording function, consideration might be given to delineating functions so that the statistical function operates at "arm's length" from other functions.

[4]This section draws on Forum for International Development Economics (1998).

tics, including external debt, should develop a strategy to ensure that good-quality statistics continue to be compiled and disseminated. Part of this strategy involves considering whether there is a need to strengthen the statistical infrastructure, as discussed above—the need for legal backing and for improved cooperation and a clear distribution of compilation responsibilities among the various interested compiling agencies. But collection techniques also need to be considered. Figure 10.1 provides a stylized view of the techniques that can be used as the process of economic liberalization proceeds.

10.17 In Figure 10.1, in an environment with strict controls, data are provided primarily from administrative sources, such as foreign investment boards, and from commercial banks, for their own and their domestic clients' transactions. As financial transactions are increasingly liberalized, the information that enterprises need to report directly increases, in terms of the number of enterprises and the information required. The information provided by the public sector and commercial banks on their own debt remains broadly unchanged throughout.

10.18 In a partially liberalized environment, when some enterprises begin to get greater freedom to borrow abroad, the comprehensiveness of the traditional administrative and commercial bank sources of information is reduced. Commercial banks may remain a valuable source of information on their clients' activities, but there could well be a need to supplement this data source by requiring reports from those enterprises given permission to borrow directly abroad—that is, undertaking external transactions without involving the domestic commercial banks. For instance, those borrowing directly abroad could be asked to report on individual borrowings as they are undertaken (that is, to provide information on external debt only) and/or be asked to report periodically on a survey form that covers external assets and liabilities and any associated income flows.

10.19 As liberalization proceeds—and the statistical agency becomes less dependent on administrative and commercial bank sources, and more dependent on obtaining the necessary information from private enterprises—its job becomes more complex. The statistical agency or agencies will need to develop and/or deepen the necessary human skills needed to compile data in a more liberalized environment,

including for a core set of staff.[5] These include developing skills in conducting surveys, in developing and maintaining a register of companies, and in quality control as well as enhancing knowledge of the basic conceptual framework. The partial liberalization phase could provide an opportunity to develop these capabilities in an environment where the traditional sources of information are still relevant, albeit to a lesser extent.

10.20 The idea of a phased approach allows the statistical agency, or agencies, to develop the capabilities required for these changed circumstances over time. Given that there will be difficulties and costs in undertaking the institutional changes required, a phased approach could help minimize these costs for all concerned.

10.21 Whether a country wants to take a phased approach to the implementation of detailed reporting of the foreign activities of private enterprises might depend on a range of factors including the resources and legal backing it has for conducting surveys. But by the time an economy fully liberalizes capital movements, it is important that the statistical agency or agencies have in place the capability to monitor the foreign activities of the private sector. Otherwise, economic policymakers and private sector investors might be misled into underestimating the degree to which private enterprises have accumulated external debt, with consequential negative repercussions for the economy at a later stage.

10.22 Finally, if it is decided that a new system is required both for balance of payments and external debt, perhaps because circumstances have changed such that there is a significant weakening of the reliability of traditional sources of information, it is important that the objectives for the new system are established at the start. For instance, the timeliness and frequency of results need to be determined because these could affect both the types of survey and the resources required. Similarly, the importance of the data to policymakers needs to be ascertained because any collection needs to be considered within

---

[5]One of the potential benefits of compiling external debt statistics in conformity with other macroeconomic data series is that staff mobility can be enhanced. For instance, basic conceptual knowledge and compilation skills developed for a related set of macroeconomic data can also be relevant for external debt statistics, and vice versa.

Figure 10.1. Data Suppliers and Collection Tools in Different Policy Environments

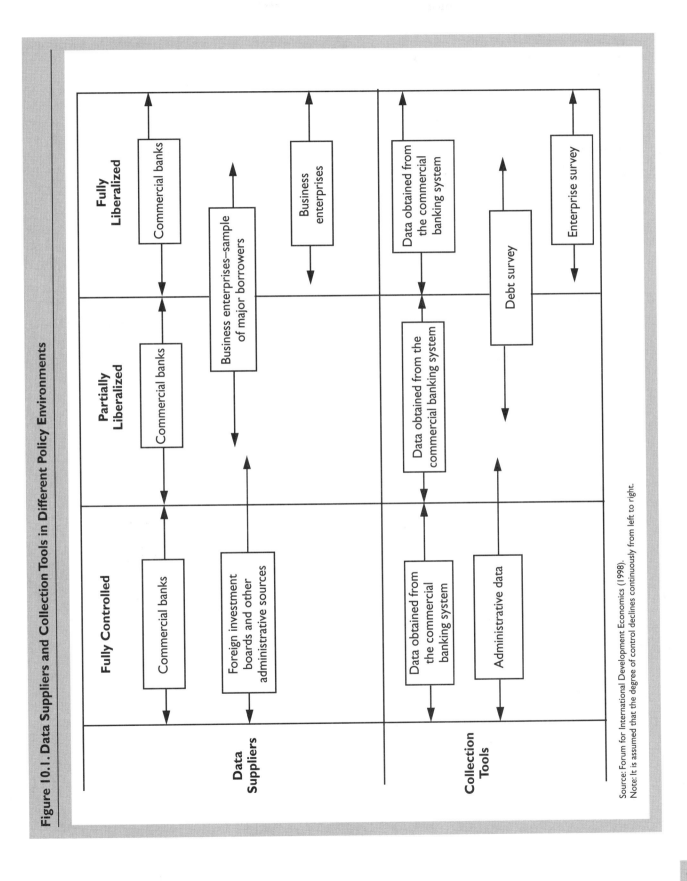

Source: Forum for International Development Economics (1998).
Note: It is assumed that the degree of control declines continuously from left to right.

the context of overall statistical priorities. Inevitably, resources in the compiling agency and among respondents are limited.

Dissemination of External Debt Statistics

10.23 The compilation of external debt statistics is undertaken for the ultimate purpose of making these data available to policymakers and other users. Data should be publicly disseminated on a frequent and timely basis, preferably according to a well-established, preannounced release schedule. The dissemination of data could be in print and/or electronic form. As part of the dissemination process, the concepts, definitions, classifications, and methodology used should be documented and disseminated in publication form at regular intervals. This metadata could also identify any significant deviations from internationally accepted standards, biases in the data, and information about response rates to the main surveys employed in collecting external debt statistics.

10.24 Invariably, to meet the legitimate needs of users, data will be published that could well be subject to later revision. In such instances, users should be alerted that the initially published data are preliminary and may be subject to revision. If revised data are later published, users should be informed of the revisions, with explanations. Also, if major changes to the statistical methodology are to be implemented, it is strongly recommended that users be given advance warning, and sufficient back runs of data provided after the revisions have been published.

10.25 In general, providing the user with such information is likely to engender greater confidence in the statistics and may help encourage a "culture of reporting" to the compiling agency(ies), an issue discussed in Chapter 12, and one that is of universal concern to compilers.

11. Government and Public Sector Debt Statistics

Introduction

11.1 The *Guide* recommends that the collection of data on a government's external debt be linked to the work of those responsible for managing the government's debt position, for the purposes of administrative efficiency and quality control. Those responsible for government debt are invariably a government debt office, either within the ministry of finance or constituted as a separate agency within the government sector, or the central bank, or another government agency. For reasons outlined in the previous chapter, it is also important that the agency responsible for government data cooperate, as appropriate, with any other agencies involved with the compilation of external debt data.

11.2 It is critical to the smooth functioning of a government debt office that the compilation, recording, and dissemination of debt data be undertaken in a timely and comprehensive manner. Proper records of debt are an absolutely essential foundation for effective debt management, and the availability of accurate and up-to-date data indeed determines how effectively the debt office can carry out its other functions—be they operational or analytical. The range of these functions is described in the appendix to this chapter.

11.3 Comprehensive and timely data allow the debt office to monitor the evolution of a country's external liabilities and its debt-service obligations over time; can provide early warning signals of possible debt-servicing problems; and serve as essential inputs for government budget preparation, for approval by parliament, for execution, as well as for compiling balance of payments and IIP statistics and for making projections. The debt office should be adequately resourced to properly carry out the tasks of compiling and recording data on all government borrowings. It is recommended that the compiler of external debt statistics, if outside the debt office, utilize these data rather than develop alternative sources.

How Should Data Be Collected and Compiled by the Debt Office?

11.4 To establish a proper debt record, detailed information about all loans (and other types of borrowing such as bonds, export credits, etc.) and all related transactions needs to be compiled. The debt office should capture data on all public and publicly guaranteed debt. This is why it is very important that the agency collecting information on public and publicly guaranteed debt be the same as the one in charge of servicing or ordering payments.

11.5 For those economies that may not have proper records of debt data, there may be a need to first compile a thorough inventory of existing debt in order to establish the debt stock, including any arrears that have accumulated on principal and interest. Once the debt stock is known, procedures should be put in place to obtain, on a regular basis, information on existing and new borrowing, as well as information on other transactions that affect the debt stock. There may be a need to establish formalized institutional arrangements for the comprehensive and timely flow of information to the debt office. Table 11.1 gives a list of the types of detailed information that should be compiled. This table is explained in more detail below.

11.6 For the purposes of the debt office and its functions, data compilation should be undertaken on an instrument-by-instrument basis, tranche by tranche, and in its original currency. For each borrowing instrument, there are basically three types of information that need to be compiled: (1) the core information on details and terms that will produce the amortization and disbursements tables; (2) data on actual disbursements, as well as the changes in the committed undisbursed amount if, say, there are cancellations and/or increases (for example, with a project loan); and (3) actual debt-service transactions. There are other types of information required, and

Table 11.1. Information To Be Compiled on Each Instrument

Type of Information	Description
I. Details of Borrowing Instrument	
Purpose of borrowing	Descriptive title
Agreement date	Date agreement has been signed
Type of instrument	Type of borrowing instrument
Effective date	Date borrowing becomes effective
Type of borrowing	Whether single currency or multi-currency or multi-tranche
Amount borrowed	Original amount borrowed or revised amount after cancellation or enhancement
Currency of borrowing	Original currency, and currencies of disbursement and repayments
Participants	
• Borrower	Whether government, public enterprises, or private sector
• Implementing agency	Agency in charge of implementing project
• Creditor	Name and type of creditor (multilateral, bilateral, etc.)
• Disbursement agency	Name, if different from lender
• Creditor insurer	Name and country
Guarantee status	Borrowing by public enterprises or the private sector guaranteed by government, and percentage guaranteed
Insured	Whether borrowing is insured by export guarantee agency in creditor country and percentage guaranteed
Economic sector	Economic sector receiving borrowing
Use of funds	Whether to finance a project, etc.
II. Disbursements	
Disbursement period	Period during which disbursement is to take place
Method of disbursement	Such as direct disbursement or reimbursement
Expected disbursement pattern/profile	Forecast of how the borrowing will be disbursed
Actual disbursement	Currencies and amount of each disbursement taking place
III. Borrowing Terms	
Interest	Information on interest charged should include:
	• Interest type: fixed or variable rate
	• For variable rate: specify interest base/reference and margin/spread
	• Interest period: dates of payments
	• Basis for interest calculation (conversion factor: daily/monthly/semiannual/annual, etc.)
	• Months: actual number of days or 30-day month
	• Days in interest year (360/365)
Commitment fee	Rate levied on undisbursed (full or partial) amount
Penalty fees	Charges for late payment of interest and principal
Other fees	Such as agency fee, management fee, front-end fee
Principal	Maturity: repayment period/profile Type of repayment: bullet, equal or annuity-based, etc.
IV. Actual Debt-Service Payments	For each payment (of interest, principal, other charges) made: • Date, currency, and currency of transaction; amount of transaction in original currency, currency of transaction, domestic currency, and perhaps U.S. dollar and SDR For multicurrency borrowing: equivalent amount paid in borrowing currency
V. Exchange Rate	Exchange rates on each transaction date for relevant currency vis-à-vis the local currency Exchange rates for end of period (daily, weekly, month, quarter, year)
VI. Interest Rates	Prevailing variable interest rates of base/reference rate used by the creditor for each interest period
VII. Debt Restructuring	• Changes in terms as a result of debt reorganization, through rescheduling, refinancing (voluntary or involuntary), write-off, etc. • Date required: —Debt concerned; arrears, consolidation period —Debt-relief terms (debt forgiveness, reschedule) —Terms for rescheduled debt (applicable interest rate, repayment profile) —Transactions on actual debt-service payments or for rescheduled debt —Other transactions from buyback or conversion/swap
VIII. Financial Derivatives	• Transactions arising from financial derivatives contracts • Positions measured both in market value and notional amounts in forwards (including swaps) and options

these are described below (under the heading "Additional Data Requirements").

11.7 If the debt instrument is tradable, and nonresidents are allowed by the government to purchase it, additional information will be required in order to attribute ownership by residency. This information may come from a different agency, which is responsible for capturing information on the nonresident ownership of traded securities. Methods of capturing information on nonresident ownership of traded securities are set out in Chapter 13.

Basic Details and Terms of the Borrowing

11.8 Basic information on each debt instrument should normally be available from the loan or credit agreement or related documentation, a copy of which should be deposited—preferably under legal statute—with the debt office for all public or publicly guaranteed debt instruments. As well as compiling data on the amount committed and the currency, where possible, details are also required on the borrower, the creditor and creditor category (government, bank, multilateral institution, etc.), the disbursement agency, the implementing agencies, and the currencies of disbursement and debt service. Data on the purpose or the end use of the amount borrowed (institutional sector and use of funds) are also important for analyzing the sectors that have benefited from the borrowing, while the guarantee status of the debt instrument will help assess the exposure of the government through the extension of guarantees to other borrowing entities.

11.9 In addition to the above, details on the terms of the borrowing should also be compiled, especially any grace period and the maturity date(s), interest rates (variable or fixed) and any fees that are to be paid, and the dates for payments of interest and the type of repayment profile of principal. Information on the terms allows the debt office to forecast the debt-service requirements for each borrowing instrument. In the case of bonds, information such as the issue price and the yield would need to be captured as well.

Disbursements

11.10 The debt office will also need to compile information on disbursements, including actual and expected disbursements. From such information, to the extent possible, accurate projections of debt service can be made. Clearly, actual disbursements affect the total of the undisbursed amounts and, in many cases, the expected future pattern of disbursement. Data on disbursements can usually be obtained from project-implementing agencies and creditors (on an instrument-by-instrument basis or for groups of instruments).

11.11 Because different types of borrowings can be disbursed in various ways, the task of compiling disbursement data can be complex. For instance, in the case of project loans, disbursement can take the form of advances to the borrowing entity, direct payment by the lender to suppliers of goods and services, or on the reimbursement basis after the borrower has already paid the suppliers. The timing of the disbursement under these methods is different. Under the advances approach, it is the periodic payments by the lender to the borrowing government that constitutes disbursement; under the direct payment approach, it is the moment when the lender pays the supplier; and under the reimbursement approach, it is when reimbursements are made to the borrowing government. The debt office must keep track of these transactions and reconcile its records at regular intervals with information maintained by the project-implementing agencies.

Debt-Service Payments

11.12 All data on debt-service payments need to be compiled on a regular and timely basis. Information such as principal repayments, interest payments, commitment fees, service fees, and other fees and charges (including penalty fees) will not only allow the debt office to ensure that payments due are made on time, but also enable it to track those debt instruments that are in arrears. Debt-service data can be obtained from statements sent by creditors. For government loans, information can also be provided by those responsible for making the payments, such as the accountant general or the foreign payment department in the central bank. Debt service on public enterprises' debts can be obtained directly from the borrowing entity or through a unit in the ministry of finance, which monitors this category of debt. Data for private debt that is guaranteed by the government can be obtained through a reporting mechanism agreed upon when guarantees are originally sought.

11.13 Where the debt office is at the center of the government's financial administration and public sector control system, the debt office itself orders the payment for budget execution, triggering at the same time the formal accounting procedures within the government for public debt service. This framework, known as an Integrated Financial Management System (IFMS), is frequently implemented in projects financed by the World Bank, or other regional development banks, through loans for modernization of the public sector. This interface with the budget execution is not only on the expenditure side—that is, debt service—but also on the revenue side; when a deposit in the treasury accounts is made from the proceeds of a debt instrument, the debt office alerts the budget and the treasury of the availability of resources.

Additional Data Requirements

Exchange rates and interest rates

11.14 Given that debts can be contracted in various currencies, it is important that the debt office collects and maintains information on the relevant exchange rates for all currencies in which borrowing has taken place, and those related to financial derivatives contracts in foreign currency. This information should be compiled on a regular basis, including for dates on which transactions have occurred and for end-periods (month, quarter, year, and, for certain short-term instruments, perhaps weekly). This is necessary because the disbursements and the debt-service operations should be recorded in the original currency, the currency of transaction (if different from the original one), and the domestic currency. For those instruments bearing variable interest rates, all relevant base rates should be compiled for each interest period, thus enabling the debt office to project the debt-service requirements with respect to these instruments. If data on exchange and variable interest rates are to be compiled on a daily basis, it is highly convenient to have a specialized computerized service on-line to obtain this information.

Changes in debt instrument amounts and debt restructuring

11.15 Information on any changes to individual debt instruments such as enhancements or cancellation of the amount, or a reorganization of the debt through rescheduling, debt forgiveness, refinancing, or prepayments should also be compiled. Indeed, in this *Guide* a change in the terms of a loan agreement results in a new instrument being created. For instance, for countries that have completed the Paris Club round of discussions, all relevant information on the restructuring provided in the Agreed Minute, the bilateral agreements, and billing statements (with respect to rescheduled debt) should be compiled. Similarly, information on debt reduction given through discounts on debt buybacks should be maintained. Debt office representation at the negotiation processes would help ensure that this kind of information is correctly recorded.

Data on financial derivatives transactions

11.16 Though financial derivatives are not debt per se, they have implications for debt management. For those countries where borrowers use financial derivatives to manage their risk exposures, data on transactions arising from these contracts should be compiled and recorded, as well as positions on outstanding contracts, in both market value and notional amounts. Because financial derivatives can create additional external liabilities, their market value needs to be monitored on an ongoing basis. Any direct increase in debt-service costs arising from hedging using financial derivatives (for example, commission expenses) should be registered.

How Should Information Be Stored?

11.17 A debt office should store information in an efficient and comprehensive computer-based debt-management system (CBDMS) that can undertake a number of tasks and so support both operational and policy functions. Table 11.2 sets out the typical tasks that a CBDMS should be able to undertake. A good CBDMS can also be used to store and retrieve information on private sector external debt.

How Can the Debt Office Validate Data?

11.18 Data validation is essential in ensuring the compilation of reliable, comprehensive, and timely external debt data that are essential for the management and formulation of a country's micro- and macroeconomic policies and strategies. For this reason, the *Guide* recommends that procedures be put in place at various stages of the data compilation and

Table 11.2. What a Computer-Based Debt-Management System (CBDMS) Should Do

Task	Requirements
Debt recording [loan-by-loan]	A CBDMS should be able to maintain a comprehensive inventory of loan information: • Records of loan agreement details—loan title, borrower, creditor, amount, currency, purpose, sector, conditions attached, creditor bank, other parties, etc. • Records of loan terms—effective date, final maturity date, conditions preceding effectiveness, disbursement pattern, commitment fees, interest rate, other fees, repayment profile, prepayment conditions, other loan development details, etc. • Records of actual disbursements—i.e., records of actual loan drawdowns • Records of actual debt-service payments—commitment charges, interest payments, principal payments, agency/management fees, other loan charges • Records of debt-related data—exchange rate, interest rate, and macroeconomic variables • Support day-to-day debt operation functions-ensuring that payments due are paid in time, monitoring arrears, and following up on delays in loans disbursement that can lead to undue payment of commitment fees
Debt reporting [loan-by-loan and on aggregate basis]	A CBDMS should be flexible enough to produce a variety of debt reports that meet the requirements of users both within and outside the country: • Summary reports showing basic details of individual loans or group of loans based on any possible selection criteria • Summary reports on loan utilization rates—for single loans, groups of loans, or entire loan portfolio • Reports on debt stock based on selection criteria such as currency composition, creditor composition, maturity structure, etc. • Reports on debt-service profile (historical and forecast) based on selection criteria—for example, debt service falling due to specific creditors or group of creditors within a given period, debt arrears, etc. • Reports for direct use in the balance of payments statistics, IIP framework, Government Finance Statistics, International Finance Statistics, and Global Development Finance Statistics, etc.
Debt analysis	A CBDMS should be able to perform basic debt analysis: • Portfolio analysis—to carry out sensitivity tests to determine, for example, effect of variation in exchange rates and interest rates on future debt-service profile • Analysis on the impact of new loan offers—test the impact of new loan proposals on the debt-service profile • Analysis of the impact of debt-rescheduling or refinancing proposals on the debt-service profile • Using macroeconomic data to compute standard debt indicators—in both nominal and present-value terms • Compute the grant element of loans as well as the present value of debt • Perform basic economic simulations using macroeconomic data • Allow debt managers to use risk-management techniques
Linkages with other packages	A CBDMS should be flexible enough to interface with other systems: • Export debt data electronically to commonly used applications such as Excel and Lotus spreadsheets • Provide linkages to other systems for specific analysis/reporting—such as the World Bank DSM Plus and Debtor Reporting System • Import data such as exchange rates and interest rates from external sources • Interface with integrated financial management systems (IFMS). This is a paramount utilization of the CBDMS, playing the role of public credit module, in complement to the budget, treasury, public accountancy, and cash-flow for the public sector

recording process to ensure that all data captured are properly validated and reconciled with other data sources. Although data provided to and supplied by the different institutions and departments—both international and domestic—should be checked for mutual consistency, these data may not be identical. But the data validation process should ensure that where differences do exist, the underlying factors for the differences are identified and explained to users of the data.

11.19 Among the various procedures and actions that can be followed are:
• Verification by supervisors of data extracted from debt instrument agreements, other documentation, and statements and recorded in data entry sheets;
• Systems that have built-in validation procedures to check for inconsistencies at the time of the recording of the information in debt recording and management systems;

- Description of procedures for treating different types of debt and their components, including sources of data in a Debt Procedures Manual—a "how-to" manual that accumulates knowledge and passes on experiences;
- Periodic reconciliation of data obtained from one source with other sources of information—for instance, data on debt-service payments can be checked with records kept by the foreign payment department in the central bank; loan balances could also be verified with creditors and debtors on a regular basis;

- An audit mechanism that is consistent with the general rules of public finance control.

Appendix: Functions of the Government Debt Office

11.20 Effective debt management by a government involves seven basic functions (Table 11.3): policy, regulatory, resourcing, recording, analytical, controlling, and operating (including active portfolio management). The policy, regulatory, and resourcing

Table 11.3. Some Recommended Functions of a Debt Office

Functions	Public Debt		Private Debt (depending on economy)
	External	Domestic	
Policy and regulatory	• Institutional arrangements for borrowing, disbursements, and debt service, including laws and regulations as well as policy for public guarantees • Establish debt sustainability standards • Policy Framework for Contingent Liabilities • Determine borrowing needs, desired terms, borrowing sources	• Formulating debt-management objectives and strategy • Decisions on volume, type of instruments, timing, frequency, and selling techniques • Where feasible, development of a benchmark debt structure • Communication linkages within government/cabinet/parliament • Fixing borrowing ceilings according to budgetary and fiscal policy goals	• Determine the policy relating to private borrowing (external) (dependent on nature of exchange regime and capital account liberalization) • Establish sources and institutional arrangements for monitoring private debt, short and long term • Policy Framework for Contingent Liabilities
Recording and operations	• All needed information flows are in place in order to gather the necessary data to cover all information needs for operations and decision making • Ensure appropriate budgetary provisions are made for debt and debt-service contingent liabilities and the planning of reserves for externalization • Checking invoices and ensuring debt service paid on due dates • Managing disbursements including claims for reimbursements • For commercial market borrower, the whole range of activities pertaining to market participation and penetration	*Primary market* • Organize distribution channels and selling procedures • Management of debt operations including auctions, subscriptions, etc. • Institutional arrangements for contacts with market *Secondary market* • Active management of government outstanding portfolio • Development of debt and liquid markets • Institutional arrangements for intervention and contacts with market *Redemption* • For both new and old issues, administration of delivery and redemption of securities *Recording arrangements* • Recording system for debt operations • Management of records of debt holders/stock • Servicing of government debt and its linkage to budgetary execution • Administration of register of government debt instruments	• Where government fully responsible for foreign exchange reserves, perhaps take account of the debt-servicing needs of private sector debt in deciding on the level of foreign reserves

Table 11.3 (concluded)

Functions	Public Debt External	Public Debt Domestic	Private Debt (depending on economy)
Statistical/analytical	• Maintain timely and comprehensive data on loan-by-loan basis (forecast and actual) of commitments, disbursements, debt service, arrears (held for a computerized management system) • Generate periodic reports	• Maintain timely and comprehensive data on all borrowing instruments • Generate periodic reports	• Maintain timely and comprehensive data (including short-term debt) on a loan-by-loan basis, as practicable, from various sectors such as bank, nonbank, etc. (this function might be undertaken by a statistical agency) • Generate periodic reports
Controlling/monitoring	• Monitor debt indicators and other performance criteria to ensure debt sustainability • Undertake analysis of debt portfolio in a macroeconomic framework and IIP framework • Analyze database for debt restructuring including rescheduling • Undertake analysis for the purpose of risk management, especially exchange risks and other market risks	• Projecting government borrowing requirements in context of fiscal and monetary targets and sustainable levels of debt • Evaluate cost of borrowing (yields) of various instruments • Control that the yearly ceilings are respected	• Monitor debt levels, nonperforming loans, and other liabilities bearing systemic risks • Monitor relevant debt indicators and other performance criteria to ensure debt sustainability
Active portfolio management	• Active monitoring of risks (interest rate, exchange rate, and counterparty risks) • Performance measurement using benchmark or other yardsticks • Continuous market analysis • Constant innovation		• Ensure effective risk management is encouraged • Monitor systemic risk through prudent bank supervision • Set standards for transparent and reliable corporate disclosure

functions (known as the executive debt-management functions) are undertaken at a very senior level, i.e., Board of Ministers or a subset of it, and as such might be viewed as establishing the "rules of the game" by the highest levels of government. Hence, direction and organization are given to the whole debt-management system. Once this framework has been decided upon, it is the government debt office that undertakes the other operating functions, implementing and executing the set of agreed "rules of the game" mainly through the controlling/monitoring and the controlling/coordinating functions.

11.21 *Policy, regulatory, and resourcing.* These functions deal with the formulation of debt-management objectives and strategy including the setting up of debt sustainability levels. A strategy may, for instance, impose statutory limits or overall guidelines on how much borrowing can be done by the

public sector and/or by the economy as a whole, which in many cases is approved by the parliament. These functions also cover the institutional arrangements that govern the determination, raising, and disbursement of funds, and the related debt service, as well as the application of laws and regulations that govern debt management at the policy and operational levels. The resourcing function ensures that the recording, analytical, controlling, and operating functions pertaining to public debt management are performed by qualified staff and involves recruiting, hiring, motivating, training, and retaining staff.

11.22 *Recording, analytical, and operations.* The recording function deals with the recording framework for all relevant debt-management information and with those activities related to the raising of loans, the budgetary and reserves provision of debt-

Figure 11.1. Organizational Chart of a Government Debt Office

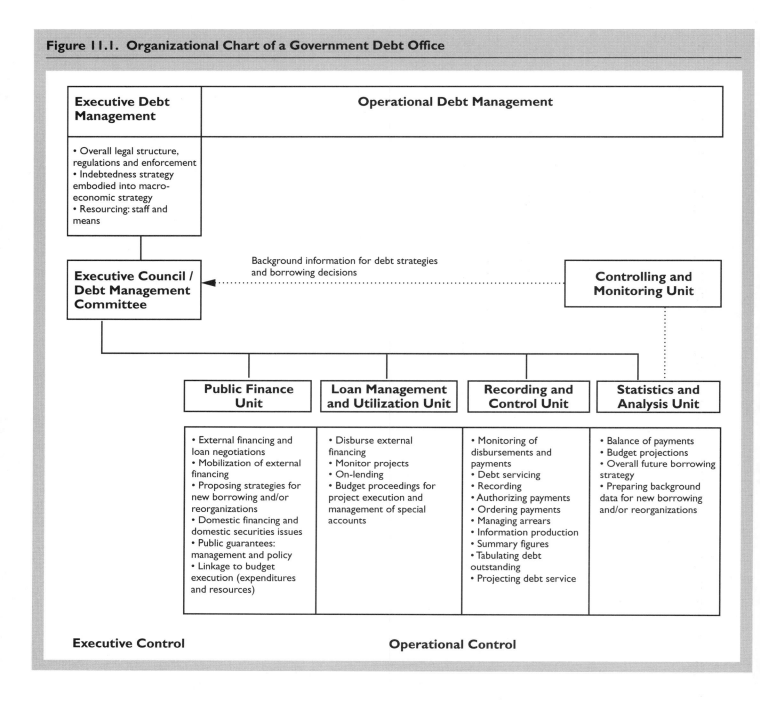

Executive Debt Management	Operational Debt Management
• Overall legal structure, regulations and enforcement • Indebtedness strategy embodied into macro-economic strategy • Resourcing: staff and means	

Background information for debt strategies and borrowing decisions

Executive Council / Debt Management Committee

Controlling and Monitoring Unit

Public Finance Unit	Loan Management and Utilization Unit	Recording and Control Unit	Statistics and Analysis Unit
• External financing and loan negotiations • Mobilization of external financing • Proposing strategies for new borrowing and/or reorganizations • Domestic financing and domestic securities issues • Public guarantees: management and policy • Linkage to budget execution (expenditures and resources)	• Disburse external financing • Monitor projects • On-lending • Budget proceedings for project execution and management of special accounts	• Monitoring of disbursements and payments • Debt servicing • Recording • Authorizing payments • Ordering payments • Managing arrears • Information production • Summary figures • Tabulating debt outstanding • Projecting debt service	• Balance of payments • Budget projections • Overall future borrowing strategy • Preparing background data for new borrowing and/or reorganizations

Executive Control   **Operational Control**

service payments, and the servicing of debt. The analytical, or statistical, function utilizes the information provided by the recording function. At the aggregate level, the analytical function involves macroeconomic analysis to explore the various options available, given economic and market conditions, and determining the future structure of the external debt. The operating function involves nego-

tiation, utilization of loan proceeds, and the servicing of debt.

11.23 *Controlling/monitoring and controlling/coordinating.* The monitoring function covers the entire range of activities involved in the maintenance of debt statistics and their analysis. This function helps ensure that policy objectives are realized and assists in the determination of debt-management policies. The controlling/monitoring function must ensure, among other things, that the terms of new borrowings fall within the guidelines set by the senior level; that funds are being utilized on time and appropriately; and that repayments are made according to schedule. At the aggregate level, the controlling/ coordinating function is essential in ensuring that operational debt management is in accordance with executive debt-management actions (that is, the policy and regulatory functions performed at the most senior level).

11.24 *Active portfolio management.* This function covers the day-to-day active management of the debt portfolio. This function takes into account market developments, such as in interest rates and exchange rates, which affect the portfolio in terms of desired performance and risk. Formally, active portfolio management pertains to the operations function, but given its specificity it is best to consider this work separately.

11.25 The location and organizational structure of a government debt office (typically referred to as a debt-management unit) will vary among countries. The differences between developing and developed countries are due to the differences in sources of financing. That is to say that the organizational structure is different if the country is mainly a borrower of International Development Association

(IDA) funds or if the country is issuing bonds in the international financial market.

11.26 For most developing countries, the debt-management functions are not assumed by a single office but dispersed across several institutions. A schematic representation of these functions can be found in Figure 11.1. A common structure has a debt office in the ministry of finance, focusing on public domestic and external debt, with the central bank overseeing private debt, and often taking on the operational functions related to government debt as its financial agent. Ministries of planning and finance and the central bank each make economic forecasts that provide the framework for debt management. A high-level coordinating committee steered by the ministry of finance (or the prime minister's office or a ministry of economic coordination) takes charge of debt strategy and policy, which should be embodied in the overall macroeconomic targets. In some developed countries, however, an independent government debt office conducts debt operations based on objectives set by the government as part of asset-liability management operations. Ireland, New Zealand, Sweden, and the United Kingdom have set up such structures that delineate separate objectives for debt management and monetary management. No matter what the structure, each country should have a transparent framework for the efficient conduct of all debt office functions.

12. Banks and Other Sectors' External Debt Statistics

Introduction

12.1 In circumstances where controls on foreign borrowing are still in place, it is possible for the central bank to compile information on private sector borrowing from information provided by borrowers for regulatory purposes, such as when they seek approval for foreign borrowing. Also, commercial banks might well be required to report on foreign transactions of their private sector clients. However, as liberalization of financial transactions proceeds, and such information becomes less readily available, there is a need to develop methods of collecting data on private sector debt through other means. This chapter considers the collection of these data from banks and "other sectors" when financial transactions are liberalized. The measurement of external debt in the form of traded securities is covered in the next chapter.

12.2 From the standpoint of compiling external debt data, information collected at the level of the individual debt instrument provides the statistical agency with the greatest flexibility in meeting user requirements. Provided that sufficient detail on the characteristics of the instrument is supplied, potentially varied combinations of characteristics of external debt could be produced as users request (the method by which the compiling agency stores the information supplied could limit the possibilities). Also, instrument-by-instrument detail supports detailed quality checks. However, some compilers may find that it is only realistic to ask respondents to supply aggregate data. If so, the design of the survey form is particularly important because it needs to endeavor to meet all foreseeable data needs—it is unlikely that the form can be changed very frequently, not least because respondents will develop systems to compile the required information—and incorporate quality-control features (for example, cross-checks on the form itself or with related data collections). If the survey form is too complex, there could be a negative

impact on quality as respondents may have difficulty supplying the required information.

12.3 It is recognized that for compilers, compiling comprehensive data for the private sector presents a greater degree of difficulty than for the public sector. Problems can arise from the limitations inherent in the available information sources. For instance, data on arrears may not be readily available from balance sheet reports, nor data for a debt-service schedule. Also, it may be difficult to monitor certain sectors of the economy, such as the household sector. In all such instances, the importance and relevance of the data needs to be weighed against the likely costs of collection, and, where appropriate, alternative sources and methods used to produce data of an acceptable degree of accuracy and reliability (for example, data from creditor sources).

Banks

Reporting of Debt

12.4 An important source of information on external debt is the banking sector. Banks are closely regulated in nearly all countries—and so are usually identifiable to the statistical agency—and have to report balance sheet data to central banks or regulatory agencies both for supervisory and monetary policy purposes. These reports can be a major source of information on the outstanding external debt of banks. External debt includes deposits of nonresident banks with domestic banks, deposits of other nonresidents with domestic banks, and other external liabilities, such as bonds and notes, and other debt securities owned by nonresidents and issued by domestic banks. Domestic banks include resident branches of foreign-owned banks.

12.5 It is essential that the reporting requirements that the central bank agrees with the commercial banks take account of the need for data on external debt. When changes in bank reporting are being considered, a task group could be formed that includes relevant statistical experts on external debt and other external statistics. In particular, attention must be paid to how external liabilities (and assets) are defined, and the external debt, and balance of payments, concept of residence (and not nationality or currency) should be used to determine what is an external liability or asset.

12.6 However, balance sheets typically do not contain sufficient detailed information on the maturity of loans and deposits; and additional information is required to calculate the debt service payment schedule for the banking sector.[1] This is best achieved by obtaining and using information on individual external debt instruments. When these data are not available to the compiling agency, and depending on the type of debt liabilities, the compiler can estimate projected interest costs using position data and appropriate representative interest rates, but some indication of a payment schedule is required for projecting principal payments.

Offshore Banks

12.7 Data on the external debt of "offshore banks" should be collected and included in the gross external debt position. Some compilers argue that banks that are treated as "offshore" under exchange control and other regulations should be excluded from the coverage of external debt statistics because the banks borrow from and lend to nonresidents. In other words, debt of such "offshore banks" does not relate to developments in the domestic economy and should be excluded. However, even if netting is legally binding in the jurisdiction of one country, legal actions by third parties may prevent the local banking institution from enforcing its right of offset. Thus, if the loans of offshore banks become unrecoverable, these banks still need to find the resources to meet their debt obligations. Nonetheless, as noted in Chapter 2, in some economies separate identification of the gross external debt (and external assets) of resident "offshore banks" and other "offshore entities" is necessary because of the

potential size of their liabilities relative to the rest of the economy.

Other Issues

12.8 In addition to their on-balance-sheet liabilities, the compiler could consider collecting data on outstanding guarantees given by banks. Banks do guarantee debts of private nonfinancial sector borrowers, and while not external debt of the banks, but rather the debt of other sectors, there is analytical interest in data on guarantees. Although data on bank guarantees most likely will cover only part of the private sector's external debt, these data may be helpful in cross-checking data provided by other sectors.

12.9 Central government and public enterprises sometimes borrow from resident banks instead of directly from foreign lenders. The loans may be denominated in foreign currency, and the ultimate borrower, not the commercial bank, assumes the exchange risk. There is potential for double counting if the government reports the foreign currency loan as an external liability along with the bank. If the bank borrows externally, it is the bank not the government that has the external debt.

12.10 Also, other private sector entities may borrow foreign currency from resident banks, particularly if the nonbank private sector is not allowed to borrow directly abroad (so that the authorities have close control over capital flows). In these cases, the compiler has two sources of information: the private nonbank entity (perhaps from exchange control forms), and the reports of the bank. The preferred source is the bank because the bank has the external debt, and bank records are normally more comprehensive.

Other Sectors

Enterprise Surveys

12.11 When no comprehensive exchange controls exist, data on loans and other external debt of other sectors are best obtained through a periodic survey of those enterprises (including nonbank financial institutions) that are involved in external transactions.[2]

---

[1]Examples of the type of disaggregated information that could be collected from a balance sheet are set out in IMF (2000d), *Monetary and Financial Statistics Manual* (see, for instance, Box 7.1, p. 76).

[2]IMF (1995), *Balance of Payments Compilation Guide,* provides practical advice on model survey forms for the compilation of balance of payments and IIP data.

The accumulation of transactions data from the balance of payments, together with valuation adjustments, is commonly used to estimate position data between position surveys. The appendix to this chapter provides the methodology for such calculations.

12.12 To ensure good coverage of cross-border activity, it is necessary to develop and maintain a register of nonbank enterprises that have or could have significant cross-border assets and liabilities. Without a good register, serious discrepancies from reality could arise. Enterprises might be identified from customs forms—it seems likely that such entities will be involved in trade credit transactions—and/or from balance of payments reports, such as through a system that relies on bank reporting of individual transactions, and/or by the regulatory authorities, such as information held by foreign investment or monitoring boards. In Chapter 14, the practice of the Australian Bureau of Statistics is described, and this provides more ideas on how to develop a register, including the use of information from industry associations, newspaper articles, etc.

12.13 In developing a register of enterprises to approach, it is vitally important that the work be coordinated with the agency that has the responsbility for the national accounts, as well as the balance of payments compiling agency. Not only will balance of payments and national accounts compilers be interested in information on external liabilities, the national accounts compiling agency may already have developed a centralized national register of reporting entities and be collecting some of the information required. Alternatively, registers may have been developed in different agencies for particular sectors—for example, manufacturing enterprises, banks, etc.—and a register for external debt purposes may be built up by conducting an "exploratory" survey of all these enterprises, in order to identify those that have external positions.

12.14 In determining the reporting population, various approaches are possible:
- *Census*: Including in the survey all members of the population;
- *Partial coverage collection*: Including in the survey all enterprises above a certain threshold measured in terms of their dimensions (for example, nominal capital) or other variable (for example, significant cross-border activity);

- *Random sample*: Including in the survey enterprises that are preferably selected according to rigorous sampling procedures, with the results "grossed" up for the whole population; and
- *Stratified random sample*: A procedure that groups population components according to the size of selected activity so that enterprises within different strata have different probabilities of selection. Usually, this is a combination of the partial coverage and random sample options but is more sophisticated and might produce a high level of coverage while remaining relatively cost-effective.

12.15 It is usually preferable to approach enterprises that engage in a number of activities at the group level because they may have a central organization that handles the external financing transactions of the group. Also, approaching the enterprise at this level reduces the workload for the compiler. However, if external financing transactions are handled by several centers in a group, and/or the group covers more than one type of institutional sector (for example, a bank and a nonbank enterprise), arrangements should be made to collect data from each center, in consultation with the enterprise.

12.16 A survey of nonbank enterprises should cover loans from nonresident banks, securities issued abroad (both long- and short-term), trade credits, and other external liabilities. If the information on debt instruments is provided on an instrument-by-instrument basis, details collected could include name of lender, country and type of lender, currency, amount outstanding, start date of contract, due date of contract, scheduled payments of principal, interest payments, put options, and relationship between borrower and lender. Similar information could be required for securities, although the identity of the lender may be unknown to the borrower. Although this information is detailed, it should be readily available to the entity for its own accounting purposes and, in most instances, should be public knowledge. Also, if possible, it is preferable to collect liability and asset data together on the same survey form, not least because the balance-sheet approach introduces a consistency in its own right, while the development of external debt within an IIP statement, among other things, would focus attention on external assets as well as liabilities.

12.17 When developing survey forms, writing very clear reporting instructions is an essential but not easy task—different respondents must be clear about what types of transactions they should report. The overwhelming evidence from compilers is that report forms and instructions should be kept as simple as possible. Practical experience invariably shows that where compilers complicate the form and the instructions, perhaps to collect that extra bit of detail, the compiler is disappointed with the information received. Reporting instructions must be clear on concepts, on what is to be reported, and on who can be contacted at the statistical agency, together with telephone and fax numbers and e-mail addresses, in the event of the respondent having a question about the reporting requirements.

12.18 The compiler is advised to undertake form testing—that is, finding out from a sample of respondents whether the instructions are clear and workable before they become operational. Also, seminars and workshops explaining the reporting requirements for respondents are of value to both respondents and the compiling agency, and are encouraged by the *Guide*. On an ongoing basis, the maintenance of an electronic register that keeps track of respondents who have called and when, who was the contact person, their phone number, etc., is information that helps ensure a well-run statistical operation. Through such a register, corporate memory at the statistical agency can be developed.

12.19 Even so, private nonbank entities may be more reluctant than banks and the government to report to the compiling agency. How can they be "encouraged?" There are at least three important steps that can be taken.
- As mentioned above, there should be legal backing for the surveys, so that as a last resort the compiler has some means of redress if the respondent proves unwilling to report. However, this legal backing must make clear that any data supplied will be used only for statistical purposes, and this statement must be honored in letter and spirit by the compiling agency. Nonbank respondents may well be reluctant to supply data if they believe the data will be shared among other agencies.
- Other elements of government that have a policy interest in external assets and liabilities should be made aware of the reporting needs and encouraged to promote the need for good reporting whenever possible when dealing with private enterprises. Better data helps promote better-informed policy-making. In other words, the authorities should

build the idea of good reporting into their policy objectives in this field. Often, those with policy responsibilities have access to senior officials in private entities and so can deliver the message of good reporting at a more senior level than might be available to the statistical agency.
- The compiling agency along with other agencies responsible for statistics should encourage a "culture of reporting." This is not easily achieved in a short time period and should not just cover external debt data, or the private nonbank sector. Steps to encourage a culture of reporting include meeting potential respondents and discussing issues of concern; developing report forms that as easily as possible fit in with management reporting systems and are not overly complex; and disseminating and promoting the final output in a transparent manner. If data are captured and compiled in an efficient manner and the output is seen to be important, private sector respondents are more likely to report.

12.20 Even if data are supplied, how can they be confirmed to be reliable? First, if data are supplied in a balance-sheet form this adds a degree of consistency in its own right. Also, if a publicly quoted company supplies data, published accounts from the company are likely to be available against which data can be checked.[3] Second, wherever possible data should be cross-checked with other sources. For instance, transactions data can be compared with changes in position data if different sources are used. Net borrowing data from income and expenditure accounts, or profit and loss accounts of companies, can be compared with the buildup of net financial assets and liabilities because the two are interrelated. Income data could be compared with position data to see whether the implied rates of return on liabilities and assets are realistic. Data on nonbank liabilities to foreign banks could be cross-checked with the international banking statistics from the BIS, although conceptual differences between BIS and national data need to be taken into account.[4] Some economies may make periodic requests to creditors to verify the status of loans that they have extended to organizations in the country, but nonresident creditors may be

---

[3]Because accounting standards do differ in some respects from statistical standards, this approach may provide a broad rather than close check.

[4]See the case study for Chile in Chapter 14 and the BIS report *Comparison of Creditor and Debtor Data on Short-Term External Debt* (2002).

unwilling to provide information to foreign government agencies when private debtors are involved.

Other Approaches

Direct reporting companies

12.21 A variation of the enterprise surveys mentioned above is the establishment of so-called *direct reporting companies* (DRCs). DRCs are intended to constitute a representative sample of companies involved in cross-border activity, and to report on a regular and frequent basis to the compiling agency on transactions and positions with nonresidents. This approach, derived from an exchange-control-type administrative system, could be appropriately developed in a partially liberalized environment. In some countries, DRCs are divided into "general" and "partial" direct reporting companies.

- *General direct reporting companies* (GDRCs) are companies or groups of companies, the volume of whose cross-border transactions exceeds a certain threshold in a given period. For GDRCs, with the exceptions of certain portfolio investment transactions (see below), all cross-border transactions are covered in the reports to the compiling agency, including flows via foreign accounts and netting. There may be no threshold for the items to be reported. The reports may give details of the currency, amount, economic nature, and geographical breakdown of the transactions. The reports of GDRCs may not include flows/positions concerning portfolio investment cash management and investment income when these transactions are conducted through resident commercial banks. Instead, these types of transactions/positions are reported by the domestic commercial banks involved in the particular transactions. However, if these transactions are carried out or held directly via foreign accounts, they remain under the responsibility of the GDRC in question to report, because the GDRC is the only domestic entity aware of these transactions/positions.
- *Partial direct reporting companies* (PDRCs) are companies that hold accounts abroad or participate in an international netting arrangement through which payments are made or received. These companies are subject to direct reporting requirements when the monthly total of incoming and outgoing payments through the accounts exceeds the agreed threshold. The reports of PDRCs are similar to those of the GDRCs, but they cover only flows/

positions via their foreign accounts and changes of position within these accounts. Other transactions/positions between PDRCs and nonresidents are reported by the resident banking sector.

Registers of external loans

12.22 Some external debt compilers use so-called *registers of external loans* to obtain data on loans received by the nonbank sector. These data, usually collected for exchange control purposes, allow monitoring of both loans from nonresidents and nonmarketable securities issued to nonresidents. If the exchange controls are abolished, the administrative accounting documents created for that purpose might be transformed into reporting documents for statistical purposes. The figures obtained from this source usually cover both loans between related (parent companies and affiliates) and nonrelated companies, and financing obtained through international bonds and notes, commercial paper, and other issuance programs.

Monitoring Short-Term Debt and Trade Finance

12.23 Monitoring short-term debt—that is, loans with an original maturity of one year or less—is of great importance because high levels of short-term debt can make an economy particularly vulnerable to shifts in market conditions and, in the case of trade credits, can have an important impact on real economy activity.[5] However, monitoring such liabilities is a complex process, not the least because there are many small transactions and many participants. In particular, if foreign trade is large relative to total production, there are likely to be many enterprises that receive foreign short-term credits.

12.24 Short-term loans and trade finance could be covered by the kind of enterprise surveys, and other approaches, discussed above. While collecting data on a loan-by-loan basis has some advantages, information on private sector short-term debt is likely, for practical reasons, to be compiled only in aggregate. Because of the sheer number of transactions involved and their short maturity, information on

---

[5]As was seen in some Asian economies in 1997–98, a sudden restriction on trade credit finance can depress imports, impacting on the production process and the level of exports when these activities have a high import propensity.

short-term debt may not necessarily be easy to compile on a transaction-by-transaction basis for all categories of short-term debt.

12.25 Also, policymakers may require more up-to-date detailed information so that the short-term financing position of the economy can be closely monitored. For banks, this might include daily or weekly reports covering interbank lines—the amount, the confirming bank, etc.—because these lines are the core of external funding and sensitive to changes in perceived credit worthiness. Also, key borrowers might be asked to prepare monthly position reports on trade finance covering amounts, currency, counterpart country, and sector.

12.26 An alternative approach for those countries with balance of payments compilation systems that rely on banks' reporting of individual transactions is to estimate the stock of trade credit debt by accumulating the transactions to the existing position data, taking account of exchange rate fluctuations. However, the main drawback of this approach is that banks may not identify trade credit accurately, or its coverage may not be comprehensive. For instance, new extensions of trade credit for importers might be better identified by banks than repayments of that credit, leaving trade credit stocks artificially high.[6] Also, the recording of cross-border merchandise trade financed through direct credit between importers and their suppliers might be missed because it involves no payment transactions. Although comparing the level of imports recorded by customs with the import payment figures recorded through bank reports might get around this latter problem, there would be a need to ensure that the customs and the banks are taking a consistent approach to classifying and recording imports.

12.27 In the gross external debt position, trade financed or intermediated—such as through the discounting of bills—by a bank is not classified trade credit but rather as a loan or short-term security. However, Chapter 7 provided a table for the presentation of all trade-related credit because of its importance for the real economy.

---

[6]To counter this problem, some countries have developed their systems such that repayment of trade credit is assumed after a certain period of time (for example, three months). Any such approach should be supported by periodic direct surveys of trade credit positions.

Financial Derivatives

12.28 In the external debt statement, positions in financial derivatives should be recorded on a gross basis and valued at market prices. However, at the time of the preparation of the *Guide,* few countries had a system for measuring financial derivatives position data. Furthermore, in some countries the statistical recording of positions in financial derivatives is hampered by the existing accounting rules for banks and enterprises that do not require financial derivatives positions to be recorded on-balance-sheet and valued at market prices.

12.29 In some countries where information on stocks is available, it is based on regular reports from the largest players, particularly the banking sector. Indeed, available information indicates that derivatives markets are highly concentrated, and so a survey of the major banks and investment houses, which includes information on the counterparties to their derivatives positions, along with the major enterprises that borrow abroad, might cover a considerable amount of resident activity in financial derivative instruments. Given the complexities involved, when developing a financial derivatives survey, it is strongly recommended that it be coordinated with those responsible for other macroeconomic data series that also require information on financial derivatives. Also, it is important that data on market value of positions are collected, since the market value determines the asset or liability position of the financial derivatives contract. Chapter 7 includes tables that present the nominal or notional positions of foreign currency derivatives, and, if significant, interest rate derivatives. These data could also be collected.

12.30 By way of example, in a survey of financial derivatives positions the types of analytical detail that compilers might consider collecting include:
- *Product category*: Forwards (including futures and swaps) and options;
- *Risk category*: Exchange rate, interest rate, and other risk (perhaps, if significant, disaggregated into commodity, credit, and "other"); and
- *Counterparty information*: General government, monetary authorities, banks, other financial institutions, other residents, and nonresidents.

12.31 While the *Guide* does not explicitly recommend the collection of data on the notional or nominal value for all risk types of financial derivatives, such information can be of analytical value. For instance, the nominal or notional amount provides some indication of the size of the risk transfers underlying financial derivatives instruments, while, as a quality check, the ratio of market to nominal value that is reported could be compared with the "normal" ratio derived from the BIS's semiannual statistics on the open positions in the global over-the-counter (OTC) derivatives market.

12.32 The BIS semiannual derivatives data were introduced in June 1998.[7] They cover the notional amounts and gross market values outstanding of the worldwide consolidated OTC derivatives exposure of major banks and dealers in the G-10 countries, with four main categories of market risk reported: foreign exchange, interest rate, equity, and commodities. Because they are not residence-based, the direct usefulness of the BIS data in the compilation of residence-based statistics is limited. Nonetheless, the BIS data do provide a good indication of the relative size and importance of different types of derivatives instruments, and, as mentioned above, of the relationship between market and notional amounts.

Direct Investment

12.33 The external debt statement includes information on liabilities of resident direct investment enterprises to foreign direct investors, and of resident direct investors to their foreign direct investment enterprises. Measuring direct investment activity is an integral element of balance of payments and IIP statistics. Many economies take a particularly close interest in direct investment activities because of the benefits this activity is perceived to bring to the economy. Thus, it is recommended that in compiling external debt, use be made of the information on direct investment in the balance of payments and IIP.[8] Care must be taken to avoid double counting of securities, or other debt, in both direct investment and their instrument category. Direct investment takes precedence; for example, a bond issued by a

resident direct investment enterprise and owned by its foreign direct investor is classified under direct investment rather than under debt securities (that is, equivalent to portfolio investment in the balance of payments).

Household Sector

12.34 Obtaining data on the external debt of the household sector is difficult. In many economies, the household sector will focus its borrowing on resident financial institutions, not least because of familiarity. However, with modern forms of communication and their ability to advertise products across borders, borrowing from abroad might become more prevalent. One method of collecting information might be to include foreign borrowing questions in a household survey of expenditures, income, financial assets, and liabilities.

12.35 For countries that rely on a bank reporting system, specific procedures are sometimes set up to capture data on cross-border asset and liabilities held by residents with nonresident financial institutions, since these positions are not covered by the resident banks' reporting. Under these procedures, all households are obliged to report such positions to the central bank on a regular basis (monthly, quarterly, or annually). Also, transactions settled through these accounts abroad are to be reported by households, with the frequency and detail of individual reporting dependent on the scale of the activity undertaken.

Appendix: Estimating Position Data with Transactions Information

12.36 Changes in positions between end-periods are accounted for by up to four factors: transactions; changes in the price of debt instruments; changes in exchange rates; and other adjustments, such as reclassifications. For all instruments, there can be transactions and other adjustments, but not all instruments are affected by changes in prices or exchange rates. This appendix considers the estimation of position data using transactions data, starting with instruments that are relatively straightforward, and moving on to those that raise more complex issues. Because estimating positions for instruments whose prices change raises the most complex problems, a distinction is made between those instruments that are not traded and those that are.

---

[7]A regular press release on these data is available on the Internet, at the BIS website, *http://www.bis.org/statistics/index.htm*.

[8]In 2001, the IMF and OECD updated a survey of data availability, data sources, compilation practices, and methodology used to compile FDI data. The metadata for 56 individual countries and cross-country comparison tables are available on the IMF's website at *http://www.imf.org/external/np/sta/di/mdb97.htm*.

Nontraded Debt Instruments

12.37 For nontraded instruments, a distinction needs to be made between those whose value is linked to the unit of account and those whose value is not.

Debt instruments with value linked to the unit of account

12.38 For a debt instrument issued in the unit of account, the estimation of position data with transactions data, in principle, is simply a case of adding transactions in the period to the previous position, and taking account of any other adjustments. However, even for such instruments, mismeasurement of position data is possible if the coverage of transactions data is not complete—for instance, due to incomplete population coverage—or if there is misreporting of transactions, including an inability of respondents to report transactions when they occur. Indeed, the compilation of position data through the accumulation of transactions data could lead to a significant mismeasurement over time, in such circumstances. Thus, even for nontraded instruments whose value is linked to the unit of account, there is a need to undertake position surveys from time to time, both to help ensure the quality of position data and also as a check on the reported transactions data.

Debt instruments with value linked to a foreign currency

12.39 For instruments whose value is linked to foreign currencies, not only is there a need to take account of the same factors as mentioned above, but also of the currency composition of transactions and positions.

12.40 It is recommended that if positions are to be calculated for instruments linked to a foreign currency, data best be compiled on a currency-by-currency basis. In other words, in the original currency, transactions in the period are added to positions at the end of the previous period, and after taking account of any other adjustments in the period, the end-period position is converted into the unit of account using the end-period exchange rate.[9]

The positions in all foreign currencies, plus that in the domestic currency, are aggregated into a total position.

12.41 Essential to such calculations is the availability, at some point in the past, of data on the currency composition of position data. For instance, if the currency composition of position data is available on an annual frequency at end-year, then in the absence of information on the currency composition of transactions data, quarterly position data could be estimated on the assumption that the currency composition of transactions is the same as in the observed end-year position data. Before making such an assumption, it would be necessary to check the observed changes in currency composition over a number of years—the less variable over time the proportions for each currency, the more robust the assumption might be. Once further end-year data are available, revisions to back data to reflect the new information are almost certain to be required.

12.42 In the absence of data on the currency composition of position data for the whole economy, one sector (for example, banks) might provide such information. A comparison between the currency composition of bank liabilities and those for other sectors could be made for periods when both are available. Provided that there is some similarity, the data from banks could be drawn upon to estimate the currency proportions for the rest of the economy, until new data for all sectors become available.

12.43 An alternative approach is to ignore the currency composition and, in effect, assume that all foreign currency liabilities are in the same currency. This "currency" could be the trade-weighted exchange rate or the known dominant currency in the country's financial flows, such as the U.S. dollar. Under this approach, positions could be estimated by revaluing both the previous end-period position, the transactions during the period, and any other adjustment:[10]

---

[9]For nontraded instruments, the amount of the change between end-period positions in domestic currency terms attributable to exchange rate variation is equal to the difference between the

opening and closing positions, less transactions over the period in domestic terms less any other adjustments in domestic currency terms. For the calculation to be accurate, the transactions and other adjustments need to be translated into domestic currency at the exchange rate at the time they occurred.

[10]The adjustment could increase or decrease positions.

$$\hat{K}_t = K_{t-1}\left(\frac{x_t}{x_{t-1}}\right) + F_t\left(\frac{x_t}{\overline{x}_t}\right) + A_t\left(\frac{x_t}{x_a}\right), \qquad (12.1)$$

where

$\hat{K}_t$ = estimated end-period position

K_{t-1} = previous end-period position

F_t = transactions in the period in the unit of account

x_t = end-period exchange rate

x_{t-1} = end-previous period exchange rate

$\overline{x}_t$ = average period exchange rate

A_t = adjustment in the period

x_a = exchange rate at the time the adjustment occurred.

In the above calculation, the exchange rate should be entered in terms of the number of units of the unit of account received for one unit of the foreign currency. The example below illustrates the principles involved.

12.44 Assume that country A's gross external debt position was 1,000 in domestic currency terms at t–1, all of which was owed in U.S. dollars, and that there are transactions of 150 in domestic currency terms during the period. There were no other adjustments. The exchange rate was 10 of the domestic currency to 1 U.S. dollar at t–1, and 14 to 1 U.S. dollar at t, with an average rate during the period of 12 to 1 U.S. dollar:

$$\left(1{,}000 \times \frac{14}{10} = 1{,}400\right) + \left(150 \times \frac{14}{12} = 175\right)$$

$$= 1{,}575 \text{ (estimated end-period total)}.$$

12.45 Whichever approach is used to estimate end-period positions, in the absence of full currency information, there will be estimation weaknesses. Where end-period currency compositions are assumed for subsequent periods, clearly the actual currency composition of transactions could be different, and this is also true when using one sector's data. Not making any assumption about currency composition is essentially akin to assuming that all other currencies move in an identical way in relation to the unit of account. In both cases, the more volatile the exchange rate, the greater the likelihood of mismeasurement. Even more so than for nontraded instruments linked to the domestic currency, frequent observations of position data for instruments whose value is linked to a foreign currency are recommended, otherwise significant mismeasurement could arise over time.

Traded Debt Instruments

12.46 Calculating positions with transactions data is particularly difficult for traded debt instruments, whose prices change from period to period. In addition to taking account of other adjustments, and, if need be, movements in exchange rates, as above, there is a need to take account of movements in market prices. One particular difficulty is that there are many traded instruments all with their own price. Also, unlike nontraded instruments, the debtor is unlikely to know the extent to which traded instruments are owned by nonresidents if nonresidents purchase instruments in domestic markets, or the debtor borrows in foreign markets. So, as noted in Chapter 13, the compiler cannot rely on the debtor for detailed information on traded instruments owned by nonresidents.

12.47 To make exact calculations, knowledge is required on the whole sequence of intraperiod prices, exchange rates, and transactions: such information may not be readily available to individual respondents, let alone national compilers. So, some simplifying assumptions or models are therefore needed to produce estimates.

12.48 The data model most widely employed in the field of external statistics is that recommended in various methodological publications prepared by the IMF.[11] For this model, in addition to information on exchange rates, some estimate of market prices of the instruments is needed. As with exchange rates, the more detailed information available to the compiler, the better. For market prices, the simplest approach might be to base estimates on a representative government bond price(s) for domestic instruments, if available, and/or benchmark prices in other markets where domestic residents have issued instruments.

12.49 With the required information, the data model can be used for a variety of purposes: calculating transactions on the basis of position data; calculating positions with transactions data; or "validating" both sets of data. The first two variants are particularly useful when only one of these variables is measured directly; the third when both variables are measured,

---

[11]See the IMF (1995), *Balance of Payments Compilation Guide*, paragraphs 732–43 and 778–83, and the IMF (1996), *Coordinated Portfolio Investment Survey Guide*, Appendix VIII, pp. 155–58. The BIS and the OECD contributed to the latter publication.

using either the same source or different sources or samples (in which case it is necessary to check on whether reported data on positions and transactions are mutually consistent). The model was originally employed to derive transactions data from positions data:

$$\hat{F}_t = K_t \left(\frac{\overline{x}_t}{x_t} \frac{\overline{p}_t}{p_t} \right) - K_{t-1} \left(\frac{\overline{x}_t}{x_{t-1}} \frac{\overline{p}_t}{p_{t-1}} \right), \qquad (12.2)$$

where
$\hat{F}_t$ = estimate of transactions
p_t = end-period prices
$\overline{p}_t$ = average period prices.

12.50 However, it can also be used to derive positions data with transactions data. Indeed, equation (12.3) is similar to equation (12.1), once the adjustment factor is introduced, except that equation (12.3) also includes price effects, based on period averages. If the value of the instrument is linked to the unit of account, then the exchange rate factors are redundant.

$$\hat{K}_t = K_{t-1} \left(\frac{x_t}{x_{t-1}} \frac{p_t}{p_{t-1}} \right) + F_t \left(\frac{x_t}{\overline{x}_t} \frac{p_t}{\overline{p}_t} \right) + A_t \left(\frac{x_t}{x_a} \frac{p_t}{p_a} \right), \quad (12.3)$$

where
p_a = price at which adjustment occurred.

12.51 The example below illustrates the principles involved. Again assume that country A's gross external debt position was 1,000 in domestic currency terms at $t-1$, all of which was owed in U.S. dollars, and there are transactions of 150 in domestic currency terms during the period. There were no other adjustments. The exchange rate was 10 of the domestic currency to 1 U.S. dollar at $t-1$, and 14 to 1 U.S. dollar at t, with an average rate during the period of 12 to 1 U.S. dollar. The securities owed to nonresidents were valued at 1.1 at $t-1$, at 1.045 at t, and at 1.066 during the period:

$$\left[1,000 \times \left(\frac{14}{10} \times \frac{1.045}{1.1} \right) = 1,330 \right]$$

$$+ \left[150 \times \left(\frac{14}{12} \times \frac{1.045}{1.066} \right) = 171.5 \right]$$

$$= 1,501.5 \text{ (estimated end-period total)}.$$

12.52 The accuracy of the model depends on the volatility of financial prices and transactions in the period covered; in particular, the accuracy of estimates is inversely related to the combined amount of intraperiod dispersion in prices and transactions.

Estimated values would approach the "true" values when transactions are spread more uniformly and/or prices (including those of currencies) are less dispersed around their mean. Such conditions are more likely to prevail when the reference period chosen for compiling statistics is short (a month, or a quarter, rather than a year).

12.53 Also, accuracy improves when flows are small compared with the initial stock, in which case intraperiod valuation effects would be of secondary importance. As a consequence, lower-frequency statistics compiled using the model could still be reasonably accurate when transactions are very small, even in periods of highly dispersed prices and exchange rates.

12.54 In addition, research at the IMF (Committeri, 2000) has shown that the availability of more detailed financial information, allowing disaggregated estimates based on homogeneous groupings of instruments and currencies, results in estimates that are closer to the actual values of the relevant variables, irrespective of the intraperiod dispersion of prices and exchange rates. Creating homogeneous groupings might be achieved by collecting data on an instrument-by-instrument basis or on an aggregate basis, where information is collected by currency, maturity, and by type of instrument (such as whether the instrument has a fixed or variable rate of interest).

12.55 Clearly, the more periods over which estimates are carried forward, the greater the possibility that the estimates will diverge from "reality." So, frequent observations of position data for instruments whose price can change are recommended.

12.56 The data model set out in equation (12.3) above also offers manageable formulas for estimating the reconciliation adjustment (equation (12.4)), and its price and exchange rate components:[12]

---

[12]Adding equations (12.4a) and (12.4b) would not necessarily give equation (12.4), even if there were no "other adjustments." The difference represents the compound effect in equation (12.4) of changes in p and x, which cannot be further divided into "price" and "exchange rate" elements. The difference will be zero only when either x or p is constant. See Committeri (2000), pp. 6 and 8. Assuming no "other adjustments," one approach could be to estimate the exchange rate component first, and calculate the price component by residual; that is, subtract equation (12.4b) from equation (12.4).

$$ADJ_t = K_{t-1}\left(\frac{x_t}{x_{t-1}}\frac{p_t}{p_{t-1}} - 1\right) + F_t\left(\frac{x_t}{\overline{x}_t}\frac{p_t}{\overline{p}_t} - 1\right)$$
$$+ A_t\left(\frac{x_t}{x_a}\frac{p_t}{p_a} - 1\right) \qquad (12.4)$$

$$ADJ_t^{price} = K_{t-1}\left(\frac{p_t}{p_{t-1}} - 1\right) + F_t\left(\frac{p_t}{\overline{p}_t} - 1\right) + A_t\left(\frac{p_t}{p_a} - 1\right) \quad (12.4a)$$

$$ADJ_t^{xrate} = K_{t-1}\left(\frac{x_t}{x_{t-1}} - 1\right) + F_t\left(\frac{x_t}{\overline{x}_t} - 1\right) + A_t\left(\frac{x_t}{x_a} - 1\right), \quad (12.4b)$$

where

ADJ_t = total reconciliation adjustment between positions and transactions

ADJ_t^{price} = the price component of the total reconciliation adjustment

ADJ_t^{xrate} = the exchange rate component of the total reconciliation adjustment.

13. Traded Securities

Introduction

13.1 External debt in the form of traded securities corresponds to debt securities in the inward portfolio investment component of the balance of payments and IIP. In recent decades, the relaxation of restrictions on the foreign investment activities of banks and other institutional investors, combined with continued financial innovation, has resulted in a surge of cross-border investment in bonds (and equities). This has increased the interest of policymakers in data on this activity.

13.2 However, ensuring comprehensive coverage of traded securities is among the most difficult in the field of balance of payments and external debt statistics. In particular, the resident issuer is, in many cases, not in a position to identify the beneficial owner of their securities, and so may be unaware of whether the creditor is a resident or nonresident. Thus, almost inevitably, to compile position data, other than by accumulating flows on a previous position, the compiler needs to obtain information on the stock of traded securities of residents, and the owners of those securities, from a variety of sources. While it is relatively straightforward, but not a simple task, to obtain data on nontraded debt liabilities, for the following reasons, it is more difficult to identify the owner of a traded security.

- Liberalization has facilitated the development of new channels through which investment can flow. In other words, compilers can no longer rely solely on traditional domestic data sources, such as banks or security dealers, because investors increasingly use foreign intermediaries, and security issuers may access foreign markets directly.
- Unlike banks, which have a tradition of reporting to the central banks, as noted in the previous chapter, nonbank economic agents may be reluctant to report to the authorities on their ownership of traded securities, because, among others, of concern that data sent to the statistical agency may be passed on to other agencies. This, once again, highlights the need for the promotion of statistical integrity within the country.[1] Noncompliance by respondents leads to gaps in coverage at a time when activity is rising.

- The participation of various financial intermediaries in international transactions and the practice of registering of investment under nominee companies and in trusts can obscure the beneficial owner of the security.
- International markets in certain "new" instruments have grown quickly in the past decade, causing difficulty in determining the "true" owner of the security. An example is the use of securities in reverse security transactions.
- Rarely, if at all, is it possible for a government to have legal powers to require a nonresident investor to report on their ownership of securities issued by domestic residents.

Ways in which these difficulties might be overcome are examined in this chapter.[2]

General Observations

13.3 In looking at ways to capture activity in securities for external debt purposes, countries should take into account any existing system they already have in place for the collection of data on portfolio invest-

---

[1]Integrity of disseminated data is one of the four dimensions of the IMF's Special Data Dissemination Standard (SDDS) and General Data Dissemination System (GDDS). Among the type of actions that the SDDS and GDDS outline to promote integrity is the dissemination of the terms and conditions under which official statistics are produced, including those relating to the confidentiality of individually identifiable information.

[2]Although a practical guide for the measurement of assets, a helpful source of information on compiling position data for traded securities is IMF (1996), *Coordinated Portfolio Investment Survey Guide*, and its second edition (IMF, 2002), is available on the Internet at the IMF's website, *http://www.imf.org/np/sta/pi/cpisgd.htm*.

ment and, more generally, balance of payments data, and also arguably, national accounts data. Respondents will know the existing system, and a considerable amount of human capital will have been invested in it at the compiling agency. Those concerned with external debt statistics should draw on this knowledge and expertise, not least because a detailed system of collecting data on inward and outward security investment can be resource intensive.

13.4 Also, there is a close linkage between cross-border securities activity and other data series such as direct investment. More important, inward, and outward, portfolio investment is directly affected by domestic activity. Whereas direct investment generally involves the establishment of a longer-term relationship between parent companies and their foreign affiliates, securities investment involves securities—both domestic and foreign—that potentially can be traded between residents and nonresidents. Depending on regulations and institutional arrangements, ownership of domestic and foreign securities can change quickly. Indeed, as exchange controls are lifted, inward or outward capital flows can arise from security transactions of both residents and nonresidents. So, while the focus in the *Guide* is on foreign investment in securities issued by residents, when considering how to measure this activity due regard should be given to the measurement of residents' investment in securities—issued by both residents and nonresidents.

13.5 This close relationship between data on traded securities in external debt, the balance of payments, and the national accounts means that it is important for agencies to cooperate. Otherwise potentially useful information may not be utilized, while at worst, respondents could end up reporting essentially the same information to two different statistical agencies. Cooperation need not only involve statistical agencies. In other government agencies there will be potential users of the data collected. For instance, information on nonresident ownership of government securities is likely to be of interest to finance ministries in helping to formulate government debt policy. Policy ministries can help the compiler in devising report forms, encouraging responses, and in evaluating the (aggregate) data.

13.6 Finally, any development of the data system to capture investment in domestic securities by nonresidents will inevitably lead to questions about the computer system on which data are to be stored and manipulated. Computer systems are obviously tools that help facilitate a more efficient statistical operation, but before a computer system is installed, it is necessary to consider the form of the data capture and manipulation; the data output required both in final form and from interrogation of the system; as well as any need to be compatible with data stored in other systems.

Key Considerations

13.7 An important starting point in deciding how to measure positions (and flows) in traded securities is ascertaining how and through which channels security investment flows into and out of the country. This involves talking to market participants and generally gaining an understanding of the domestic security markets. The issues to explore are:

- How do nonresidents invest in domestic securities?
- Through which institutions do they invest?
- Where do nonresidents arrange for the custody of their domestic securities? How are records held?
- Where are trades settled?
- Are security codes used in monitoring security positions?
- Do residents issue securities directly abroad? Do residents invest in these securities?

13.8 The importance of preliminary research cannot be overstated because, once completed, the compiler can decide at which point or points in the "chain" of activity it is most appropriate to collect information. There is no one obvious answer for all compilers. For legal, institutional, and historical reasons, different countries have different market structures and practices, and so what suits one country may not suit another. Nonetheless, the pros and cons of collecting information from different types of market participants can be indicated, and these are set out in Table 13.1. The relevant importance of the various advantages and disadvantages will depend on individual economy circumstances. For different instruments and markets, different collection methods may be appropriate.

13.9 Before discussing the advantages and disadvantages of approaching different types of respondents, the relationship between the collection of transactions and position data needs to be considered. There are various ways transactions and position data can inter-

Table 13.1. Inward Security Investment: Potential Respondents—Advantages and Disadvantages for Positions and Transactions Data

Potential Respondent	Advantages	Disadvantages
Issuer of security	Will know about securities issued.	Unlikely to know beneficial owner of the security either at issue or during secondary market trading.
Financial intermediary *Banks* (receipts/payments)	Transactions in domestic currency require settlement through resident banks. Transactions recorded could be cumulated on a previous position and, with appropriate valuation adjustments, provide new position data.	Nature of transaction may be difficult to establish. May have a problem in identifying direct investment transactions. Although a method for compiling position data in the short term, a more direct measure of the stock position might be required in the medium term, depending on the complexity of the reporting system. Also, only covers investment in securities issued in the domestic market.
Issuing agency (security house/bank)	Will know about securities issued.	May not know beneficial owners at issue and, unless a dealer, will not know about secondary trading.
Dealer (security house/bank)	Will have information on sales and purchases of securities. As with banks, transactions data could be used to compile position data.	May not cover all nonresident purchases of resident securities. May have a problem with nominees and identifying direct investment transactions.
Fund manager	Will have information on beneficial owners.	Unlikely to cover all nonresident purchases and holdings of resident securities.
Organized exchange	Will have a record of transactions on the exchange and perhaps positions. Data on positions might also be available via member firms.	May not cover all nonresident purchases and holdings of resident securities. May have a problem with nominee accounts.
Settlement agency	Will have a record of transactions.	May not cover all nonresident purchases and holdings of resident securities. May have a problem with nominee accounts and identifying direct investment transactions/positions. Records may not be kept in a form appropriate for external debt/balance of payments purposes.
Registrar	Will know who owns which securities.	Use of bearer securities undermines the use of a securities register. May have a problem with nominee accounts. May not cover transactions particularly well.
Custodian	Information on ownership available. Fewer in number than investors. Should know information on the outstanding value of holdings.	Coverage of nonresident purchases and holdings of resident securities is uncertain. May have a problem in identifying nonresidents, although tax status may help, and direct investment transactions. May not know exact details of transactions/may have difficulty extracting data in line with balance of payments methodology. Double counting a potential problem if subcustodians used.

act: (1) transactions data can be compiled separately from position data, and cross-checks introduced to validate both sets of data;[3] or (2) transactions data can be added to a previous position and, with appropriate reevaluations and any other adjustments, a new estimated position calculated (although an independent benchmark position survey at periodic intervals is essential to check and improve the quality of the estimated position data)—see the appendix to Chapter 12; or (3) position data can be compiled on a security-by-security basis, supported by a database with information on individual securities issued by domestic residents (Box 13.1), using individual transactions data to update the individual holdings of securities (although even then periodic verification of the derived position data is recommended using alternative or additional inquiries). Whichever method is used, decisions on whom to approach and what to request in terms of position data are at least influ-

---

[3]See IMF (1996), *Coordinated Portfolio Investment Survey Guide*, Appendix VIII, for an explanation of how to reconcile position and transactions data, and to estimate income from position data.

Box 13.1. Security Databases

In measuring positions in traded securities, information may be collected from respondents at the level of the individual instrument. Such an approach potentially provides great flexibility in meeting requirements for external debt statistics. However, to utilize fully the potential of such information, the compiler is advised to develop or acquire a database that contains detailed information on individual securities—price, country of issuer, industrial sector of issuer, etc.—and that uniquely identifies securities through a security identification code.[1] Through such a database, individual securities that are reported with an identification code can be located in the database, and the associated information can be drawn upon to compile information not only on outstanding positions but, depending on the scope of the associated information contained, statistics on the debt-service payments schedule, the currency composition of external debt, etc. Also, such an approach can enhance data quality by allowing the compiler to check the accuracy of submitted data and to resolve conflicting reports.

Sources of Information

Information on individual securities can be obtained from commercial sources, international organizations, and security numbering agencies.

By far the most comprehensive and complete databases are those available from commercial sources, usually at a commercial price. The best of these commercial sources supply high-quality, timely, comprehensive data to the international financial community to support investment activity. At the time of writing, some of the leading commercial vendors, in alphabetic order, are Bloomberg, Euromoney Bondware, Interactive Data, International Financing Review, International Securities Market Association, Reuters, and Telekurs.[2]

---

[1]More detailed information on securities database is available in the IMF (2002), *Coordinated Portfolio Investment Survey Guide,* second edition, available at *http://www.imf.org/np/sta/pi/cpisgd.htm.*
[2]These names are provided for information purposes only and imply no endorsement of any kind; any compiler who approaches any commercial database vendor will need to make his or her own judgments about whether the product being offered meets the compiler's needs.

The Bank for International Settlements (BIS) maintains a database of international debt securities that is available to member central banks and perhaps other governmental organizations, as described in Chapter 17.

The Association of National Numbering Agencies has a database of individual securities that is commercially available. By linking the databases of national numbering agencies (NNAs)—the entities that assign the international security identification number (ISIN) in their own jurisdiction—this database provides key descriptive information on individual securities. Coverage of individual securities differs in completeness among NNAs, and information on market prices is not included. To understand more about the information available on this database, it is recommended that the compiler approach the NNA that allocates ISIN codes to securities issued within the domestic economy.

Role of the Security Identification Code

As noted above, in a compilation approach that uses a database of individual securities, the security identification code is of central importance—the respondent needs to provide a code so that the database can identify the security. However, different respondents could submit different security identifiers for the same security because any widely traded security could be allocated a domestic as well as an international security identifier. For instance, in the United States, a domestic security code (known as CUSIP) will be allocated to a domestic security. As a result, private investors have adopted a variety of different security identification systems as their primary identifier. National compilers should discuss the use of security identifiers with potential survey respondents. If national compilers can rely on survey respondents to use primarily one coding system—for instance, the ISIN—this enhances the efficiency of the compilation procedure. If not, then the agency is advised to acquire a database(s) that contains all the various identifier codes that a given security has been assigned by the different coding systems. These cross-reference databases may well be available from the same commercial firms mentioned above.

---

enced by the approach taken to collecting transactions data. So, in the discussion below, both transactions and positions data are discussed.

Nonresident Investment in Domestically Issued Securities: Potential Respondents

13.10 An obvious approach for compilers is to collect information on nonresident investment in securities issued domestically by residents from domestic financial intermediaries. This approach assumes that nonresidents will involve these intermediaries when undertaking transactions in the domestic market. For instance, for transactions and positions in government securities, the government might consider making such a reporting requirement a condition of any licensing approval that the domestic financial entity may need in order to have settlement accounts in domestic government securities.

13.11 Typically, banks are approached for data on external transactions and positions because of their role in the payments system; if domestic currency is used to settle transactions, a resident bank is likely to be involved. However, money flows through banks for a variety of reasons, and banks may have difficulty in establishing the specific nature of a transaction as a securities transaction. Also, it is important that transactions involving nonresidents are captured not only when money comes into the country but also whenever nonresidents transact in domestic currency, such as when a nonresident draws down a domestic bank account to purchase a resident security. This is the key issue: can banks identify and report in a comprehensive manner investment by nonresidents in domestic securities? The possible use of data from banks in their role as custodians is examined ahead.

13.12 Another method used is to gather data on securities from investment dealers, including banks, that conduct portfolio investment business on behalf of nonresidents. In other words, those who arrange and execute the deals. Dealers usually keep records of client transactions and may be better able to identify portfolio transactions than banks through their payments system activity. Invariably, the number of financial intermediaries are likely to be fewer in number than investors, and, legal circumstances permitting, should be approachable. This method of approach depends, of course, on nonresidents using domestic intermediaries. Also, these institutions will need to be able to identify residents and nonresidents and keep records in a manner that allows their use in external debt, as well as balance of payments and IIP compilation.

13.13 Canada has adopted a system of capturing foreign investment in securities using dealer reports, and this method is set out in Chapter 14. The dealers report individual transactions involving nonresidents and include the value of the deal and the unique code for the security (developed for settlement purposes).[4] Information kept on a database of individual securities is used to confirm the residence of the issuer of the security and provide additional information. Canada's detailed and complex

statistical system also generates income data on an accrual basis.

13.14 Some countries carry out special surveys that are addressed to resident fund (investment) managers, and request information on own account and client account investments in resident and nonresident securities by resident and nonresident investors, thus providing the necessary data on residents' debt liabilities to nonresidents. Data on the country and institutional sectoral distribution of ownership may also be requested. The information can provide good coverage of the household sector's portfolio assets, provided that they use resident fund managers. However, such a survey will not provide comprehensive coverage of nonresident ownership of resident securities unless nonresidents use domestic fund managers extensively.

13.15 Another method is to capture nonresident investment in domestic securities at the point of the trade or settlement—for instance, using information on transactions from the stock market. At the least, the stock exchange usually has to keep a record of individual transactions, and at best may act in a settlement capacity and see the cash change hands. It may be possible for this information to be supplied to the compiling agency. Sometimes there may be a separate but similar market mechanism for bond trades. Through these markets, nonresident investment transactions and holdings may be obtained. For instance, the exchange might have or can obtain the authority to request that information be reported to it on who owns what securities. This might be undertaken not only for statistical but also for regulatory and policy purposes.

13.16 However, there may be reluctance for the stock exchange or settlement agency to release the information required by the compiling agency, and the prevalence of nominee accounts may lead to misidentification of the true investor (a common problem when "intermediaries" report). Other issues that could arise are whether the records kept can be readily utilized for external debt and balance of payments statistics purposes, and the comprehensiveness of the coverage of nonresident investment in resident securities.

13.17 Close links with the stock exchange may be important for the compiler in other regards. The

---

[4]While national numbering agencies (NNAs) frequently issue their own code for securities issued in their jurisdiction, they also allocate a unique international security identification number (ISIN) code for each security. More information on ISIN codes is available in IMF (2002), Appendix VII, pp. 151–53.

stock exchange will be a source of information on market developments; it may well be the agency that needs to be kept informed by quoted corporations of new securities issues—helpful for information on security issues in foreign markets by residents (and domestic security issues by nonresidents); it may be the agency allocating code numbers to individual securities issued in the domestic market; and individual investors may need to inform the stock exchange of large equity holdings, thus helping the compiler to identify direct investment positions and transactions.

13.18 Another avenue is to approach registrars, who store information on the owners of securities (for example, to make coupon payments). For instance, details of ownership of debt securities issued by the government in domestic markets are frequently held on a computerized book-entry register, with change of ownership being evidenced by an entry on this computerized register, rather than the transfer of a physical certificate. Typically, these registers contain useful information such as, for each security, the outstanding balance for each investor, and the amount of accrued interest. Also, debt securities can be valued both at market as well as nominal value and can be classified by original as well as remaining maturity. However, problems arise in identifying ownership, given the frequent use of nominee accounts, not least for administrative efficiency.

13.19 Yet another method of measuring nonresident investment in securities issued by domestic residents is to collect data from custodians. Many countries use custodian surveys of one type or another, and an approach should be explored for compiling at least some element of the data on nonresident ownership of traded securities. Domestic securities owned by nonresidents may be deposited with local custodians for "safekeeping," and these institutions, primarily banks, could be approached through a survey to report transactions and ownership of domestic securities by nonresidents. Such a survey can provide good coverage of resident securities denominated in the domestic currency and traded in national organized markets.

13.20 However, resident securities denominated in foreign currency, issued and usually traded in foreign organized markets (for example, international bonds, etc.), are unlikely to be captured by such a survey. Also, there are other possible drawbacks that the compiler needs to consider.

13.21 The custodian may have difficulty in distinguishing residents from nonresidents, although a possible different tax treatment from that applied to residents may be one way in which this distinction can be made.

13.22 A local custodian may be acting on the instructions of a "global" custodian, located in another economy, and so may not know the name of the beneficial owner of the security—the security might be registered in the name of a foreign global custodian. Resident custodians are likely to record security holdings in the name of the global custodians as nonresident holdings, but resident investors could subsequently purchase the securities but leave them entrusted with the global custodian, causing a mismeasurement of nonresident ownership. Periodic surveys to confirm the beneficial owner of securities may be warranted.

13.23 Another potential problem, and one that arises with all transactions and positions reported through financial intermediaries, is the difficulty in distinguishing securities related to direct investment activity from other cross-border security activity, leading to the possibility of double counting of investment activity if direct investment data are separately collected, which is usually the case.

13.24 Securities data from custodians can be reported on an individual or aggregate basis. As mentioned above, data reported on an individual basis is best supported by a database that records individual securities issued by domestic residents. This database can reduce the burden on the respondent and confirm the data reported. This is a method successfully employed by Austria, but, as with the Canadian system, there can be considerable resource cost for the compiling agency.

13.25 Alternatively, aggregate data can be requested. As always, checks are required: for instance, with aggregate data a custodian might report the number of securities owned rather than their value. It should also be recognized when requesting aggregate information that custodians may not hold their records of nonresident ownership of domestic securities in a way that is conducive to external debt reporting. Therefore preliminary discussions are essential to ascertain which data might be readily available.

Issues of Securities by Residents in Foreign Markets

13.26 Measuring foreign investment in securities issued abroad by residents can be difficult. Foreign intermediaries will not report to the domestic compiling agency. Swapping data with foreign compilers is one option, but this approach is difficult to implement because the compiler would need to know all the compilers to approach, and the nonresident compiler would need to have the requisite data. A more promising approach is to obtain information on gross issues and redemptions of international issues either from issuers themselves or from other sources, including the domestic stock exchange or other official bodies that should be informed of any new issues by quoted companies. International sources of information, such as the BIS international securities database, discussed in Chapter 17, could also prove useful.

13.27 If a database of individual securities is maintained—or aggregate information on foreign security issuance is reported by resident issuers—so that net new issues in foreign markets—gross issues and gross redemptions—are recorded, and the outstanding amounts of the securities issued by residents in foreign markets can be calculated, a reasonable assumption could be that these securities are purchased by nonresidents, excluding those known to be purchased by residents. In other words, external debt in the form of nonresident investment in debt securities issued in foreign markets by residents, including government, could be calculated by, all other things being equal, netting out domestic ownership of resident debt securities issued in foreign markets from the total outstanding. Information on resident holdings of these debt liabilities could come from domestic respondents, either the investors themselves or financial institutions involved in this activity. Besides being a method of calculating an element of external debt, the resultant information on resident and nonresident ownership of debt securities issued in foreign markets is of interest in its own right, as explained in Chapter 7.

13.28 This approach is a perfectly acceptable compilation technique and would require the compiler to liaise with the agency that complied data on domestic investment in domestic securities for the financial accounts. Indeed, some countries employ this technique to measure inward investment into all private sector traded securities.

Information on Securities Involved in Reverse Security Transactions

13.29 If the collateralized loan approach is employed to record reverse security transactions (such as repurchase agreements, repos), a memorandum table (Table 4.5) is provided in Chapter 4 for the presentation of data on securities issued by residents that residents acquire from or provide to nonresidents under these arrangements. It is expected that the majority of such transactions will occur in the domestic market, most likely in the government securities market. Most commonly, repos are transacted by financial institutions with other financial institutions, including central banks. Requiring domestic financial institutions to report domestic and nonresident securities sold to and purchased from nonresidents under reverse transactions, perhaps in their balance-sheet returns to central banks and/or statistical agencies, is likely to cover the bulk of the business. Other entities such as nonfinancial enterprises and governments may be involved in reverse security transactions, perhaps even in domestically issued securities in foreign markets. So the compiler is advised to investigate the significance of information from these institutional sectors as well.

13.30 However, in compiling data on securities issued by residents and traded under reverse security transactions by residents with nonresidents, care needs to be taken to avoid double counting. Experience indicates that where security registers are used to identify nonresident ownership and/or where custodians report, it is not always possible to identify securities subject to repos. So, if a custodian provides information on nonresident ownership of resident securities, it may be inclusive of securities purchased and sold under reverse security transactions; that is, the information might already include resident securities acquired by nonresidents from residents under reverse transactions, contrary to the collateralized loan approach. It is very important for the compiler to understand how securities involved in reverse security transactions are recorded in the position information provided.

Possible Mismeasurement

13.31 Clearly, the more that transactions in domestic securities are concentrated in the domestic economy, the greater is the likelihood that domestic financial intermediaries can provide adequate coverage and, thus, a lower likelihood that there will be undercounting. The difficulty is then in ensuring that resident and nonresident owners are correctly identified and the concepts outlined in the *Guide* are adhered to.

13.32 On the other hand, overcounting is more possible where a number of methods are used to collect data. While more than one method may be needed to ensure comprehensive coverage—for instance, the measurement of foreign investment in government securities may differ from that for private securities—the compiler should be aware of the increased possibility for the double counting of activity when more than one method is used.

13.33 To reduce the possibility of mismeasurement, particular care needs to be taken in deciding on the respondent population; as noted in the previous chapter, a register of reporters, kept current, is essential and could be drawn from a centralized national register of reporting entities maintained for national accounts reporting purposes.

Periodic Position Surveys

13.34 As mentioned above, in the short term some economies might compile position data by accumulating transactions on a previous position. However, it is important to conduct periodic benchmark position surveys, perhaps once a year. The sources of position data could be different from those for transactions data. For instance, data on transactions might be compiled from information supplied by dealers or organized exchanges, whereas custodian information might be used for the position data. The results of the position survey can then be checked against the cumulative transactions data; in other words, reconciliation can be undertaken. This reconciliation is particularly important when financial intermediaries

are reporting transactions because it can reveal inconsistencies and errors in reporting that might not otherwise be spotted. In some ways, independent verification of the data is helpful for the robustness of the compilation system. Alternatively, the same institutions could be approached for both transactions and position data so that any discrepancies can be rectified and improvements made for future years.

Counterpart Information

13.35 Because of the need to improve the coverage of portfolio investment assets globally, and also because of the difficulty of identifying nonresident ownership of resident securities, the IMF, in cooperation with other international organizations, has promoted the development of a *Coordinated Portfolio Investment Survey* (CPIS). This survey was conducted for the first time with a reference date of end-December 1997 and was designed to collect comprehensive information, with country attribution, of resident holdings of nonresident securities, both equity and long-term debt securities. It involved 29 countries using harmonized definitions and concepts based on *BPM5*. By exchanging bilateral data, the coverage and quality of portfolio debt liabilities was also improved. The results of the first survey were published in 1999.[5]

13.36 At the time of preparation of the *Guide*, the CPIS is about to embark on its second survey, with a reference date of end-December 2001, and thereafter could become a regular undertaking. As coverage is improved, such as more major investing countries participating and the weaker areas of measurement strengthened (for example, coverage of household investment), then over time these creditor-based data could gain in importance as a source of information for external debt compilers.

---

[5]See IMF (1999), *Results of the 1997 Coordinated Portfolio Investment Survey*, and IMF (2000a), *Analysis of the 1997 Coordinated Portfolio Investment Survey Results and Plans for the 2001 Survey.*

14. Country Experience

Introduction

14.1 This chapter provides case studies of country experience in various aspects of the compilation and use of external debt data. In addition, Box 14.1 discusses the European Union statistics on the excessive deficit procedure. The country case studies are provided in alphabetical order:

- *Australia*: Experience in compiling external debt data—register compilation and form design;
- *Austria*: Measurement of IIP;
- *Canada*: Measurement of foreign portfolio investment in Canadian bonds;
- *Chile*: Reconciliation of external debt statistics with BIS International Banking Statistics;
- *India*: How debt information systems are being used for external debt management;
- *India*: Monitoring and management of nonresident deposits in India;
- *Israel*: Measurement of external debt;
- *Mexico*: Registration of private debt;
- *New Zealand*: Experience in collecting foreign currency hedging information;
- *Philippines*: System for monitoring the external debt of the private sector;
- *Turkey:* Measurement of short-term external debt; and
- *Uganda*: Data requirements for the HIPC Initiative.

Box 14.1. European Union (EU): Statistics on the Excessive Deficit Procedure

Article 104c of the 1991 Treaty on Monetary Union (the Treaty) states that EU countries should avoid excessive government deficits, and that the European Commission (the Commission) should monitor the development of the budgetary situation and of the stock of government debt. In particular, the Commission should examine compliance with budgetary discipline on the basis of whether the ratio of the planned or actual government deficit to GDP and the ratio of debt to GDP exceed a reference value. The reference values are 3 percent for government deficit, and 60 percent for debt, as specified in the Protocol on the excessive deficit procedure (the Protocol) that is annexed to the Treaty.

The Protocol defines government as general government (that is, central government, state and local government, and social security funds); the deficit as net borrowing as defined in the *European System of Accounts: ESA 1995* (Eurostat, 1996), *ESA95*; and debt as total gross debt at nominal value outstanding at the end of the year, consolidated between and within the sectors of general government. The Protocol also requires EU countries to report their planned or actual deficits and the levels of their debt promptly and regularly to the Commission, which in turn provides the statistical data used for the application of the Protocol to the Council of Finance Ministers.

This basic legislation is further developed in Council Regulation 3605/93 on the application of the Protocol (the Council Regulation). Council Regulation 475/2000 revised this Regulation, in order to introduce the references to *ESA95*. The Council Regulation defines government debt as total gross debt at nominal value (face value) outstanding at the end of the year for the general government sector, excluding those liabilities for which the corresponding financial assets are owned by the general government sector.

Government debt is constituted by the liabilities of general government in the following categories: currency and deposits; securities other than shares (excluding financial derivatives); and loans, as defined in *ESA95*.

Some debt instruments, such as trade credits, and other accounts payable, are not included in the list of debt liabilities (because of practical considerations). Liabilities denominated in foreign currency, or exchanged from one foreign currency through contractual agreements to one or more other foreign currency, shall be converted into the other foreign currency at the rate agreed upon in those contracts and shall be converted into the national currency on the basis of the representative market exchange rate prevailing on the last working day of each year. This would also apply in the case of liabilities denominated in the national currency and exchanged through contractual agreements to a foreign currency. Finally, liabilities denominated in a foreign currency and exchanged through contractual agreements to the national currency shall be converted into the national currency at the rate agreed upon in those contracts.

Box 14.1 *(concluded)*

The Council Regulation also establishes the procedure for transmitting data to the Commission. As from the beginning of 1994, EU member states were required to report their planned and actual government deficit and levels of government debt to the Commission twice a year, the first time before March 1 of the current year, and the second time before September 1 of the current year. Before March 1 of year n, EU member states report to the Commission their estimate of the level of actual government debt at the end of year $n - 1$ and their levels of actual government debt for years $n - 2, n - 3$, and $n - 4$. Concerning the deficit, they report to the Commission their planned government deficit for year n, an up-to-date estimate of their actual government deficit for year $n - 1$, and their actual government deficits for years $n - 2, n - 3$, and $n - 4$. They simultaneously provide the Commission for years $n, n - 1$, and $n - 2$ with their corresponding public accounts budget deficits according to the definition that is given most prominence nationally and the figures that explain the difference between these public accounts budget deficits data and their government deficit. Before September 1 the data required are the same, but instead of the estimate of the level of actual government debt at the end of year $n - 1$, actual data are to be provided. In member states, the exercise requires close coordination among the ministry of finance, national statistical institute, and central bank.

EU member states also provide the Commission with the figures for their government investment expenditure and interest expenditure (to calculate other ratios such as, for example, primary deficit—that is, the amount of the deficit without interest expenditure). Finally, EU member states also provide the Commission with a forecast of their GDP for year n and the actual amount of their GDP for years $n - 1, n - 2, n - 3$, and $n - 4$ (in order to calculate the ratios).

As mentioned above, the conceptual framework used for the measurement of government deficits and debt is the *ESA95*. In recent years, ensuring consistent recording treatment in all of the EU member states of economic and financial transactions that are not clearly defined in *ESA95* has been a problem. With the aim of ensuring consistency of recording practice, Eurostat has developed a well-defined procedure for dealing with these transactions, including statisticians from all member states working together through task forces, working groups, and other committees. Following this, Eurostat consults the Committee on Monetary, Financial, and Balance of Payments Statistics (CMFB), comprising senior representatives of central banks and national statistical institutes, as well as the European Central Bank, Eurostat, and other Commission services. After having heard the position of its members, the CMFB formulates, and presents to Eurostat, its (nonbinding) opinion. Eurostat makes the final decision in complete independence and neutrality, according to purely technical criteria. It does not decide on the individual cases as they relate to the EU member states, but rather decides on the principles of accounting treatment of specific transactions. Once determined, the Eurostat decision automatically applies to similar cases in all the EU countries. The decision on each issue is recorded in a methodological note addressed to the institutions concerned, notably the Commission, CMFB, central banks, and national statistical institutes. It is also disseminated through press releases and the Internet. The main methodological decisions have been collected in the *ESA95 Manual on Government Deficit and Debt* (Eurostat, 2000).

Australia

Experience in Compiling External Debt Data: Register Compilation and Form Design[1]

14.2 The Australian Bureau of Statistics (ABS) compiles and publishes balance of payments and IIP statistics quarterly according to the recommendations of both the *BPM5* and 1993 *SNA*. External debt data are a part of an extended IIP dataset, which has been augmented to provide data series that meet high-priority, domestic-user requirements.

14.3 The main data source for IIP data is the Survey of International Investment (SII). This quarterly survey collects information from business enterprises, government, investment managers, and custodians,

as appropriate, about investment activity into and out of Australia. Based on Australia's long experience, this case study provides advice on compiling a register of potential respondents to an external debt survey and on methods for survey form design that will help ensure consistent and high-quality data. Also, for information, some of the external debt data series Australia disseminates that are additional to those included in the IIP data are listed.

Developing a register of respondent entities

14.4 In an open economy with a freely floating exchange rate for nearly two decades, investment flows to or from Australia are not subject to controls or regulatory approval (although for some types of corporations, approval of foreign ownership is required). In order to measure external debt, surveys are undertaken of organizations from which the data can best be obtained. Some organizations are targeted for their

---

[1]Prepared by the Australian Bureau of Statistics.

role as end-investors/investees, and others are targeted as intermediaries (investment managers or custodians) to report on behalf of their clients. To undertake such surveys, a register of entities to approach has been developed and is maintained by the ABS.

14.5 The main ABS business register—used for surveys of the economy, and generally sourced from business taxation reports—is focused more on operating businesses with employees, rather than enterprise groups. It includes a large number of organizations that have no international investments but is deficient in its coverage of those parts of businesses involved in financing that may have no employees but through which all the international finance accessed by the group is channeled. Thus, any survey population drawn randomly from this large register for measuring international investment would be inefficient in terms of reporting load, public resources, and quality assurance. The ABS has therefore developed a separate register of enterprise groups with international involvement. Sources of information on enterprises for this specialized international investment register, and other suggested sources, are as follows:

- *Existing registers* of businesses maintained by the statistical agency or other government agencies. Enterprises on this register can be approached with brief exploratory surveys to ascertain whether they have significant external debt liabilities.
- *Existing business data collections* already run by the statistical agency or other government data-collection agencies. Information necessary for an international investment register may be elicited from another survey, either by direct inspection of the other survey's register or by adding one or two exploratory questions to that survey. A range of ABS surveys include questions that can identify potential respondents to external debt surveys, and vice versa.
- *Government administrative sources.* Depending on local legislation and administrative arrangements or the authority of the collection agency, these sources might include:
  - taxation records, files, or lists;
  - information held by foreign investment approval or monitoring boards;
  - information held by other regulatory authorities, such as lists of entities coming under their supervision and data monitored through supervision requirements (for example, registered banks, other deposit-accepting institutions,

  securities brokers, investment managers, investment advisers, and authorized pension or mutual funds);
  - listings of registered custodial businesses that can hold debt securities and other assets on behalf of nonresidents, and lists of registered investment managers that can act on behalf of nonresidents;
  - statutory company reports and company registration details;
  - records held in foreign exchange control or international transaction-reporting systems— for example, records identifying the originators or recipients of large portfolio investment flows (this source is not available in Australia);
  - submissions made to the Foreign Investment Review Board, various materials held by the Reserve Bank of Australia, and annual reports of other government bodies; and
  - other official and regulatory sources, many publicly available, that include annual statutory accounts for public companies held by the Australian Securities and Investment Commission.
- *Media reports.* Newspapers and periodicals are particularly useful sources for information on potential reporting entities. A high proportion of significant transactions are reported in the media, and these are used not only to update the register but also to confirm data reported in the SII. Apart from significant transactions, the media have a wide coverage of smaller transactions, and a high proportion of unusual transactions. The use of traditional print media can be supplemented with information obtained electronically from commercial business news services and via the Internet.
- *Publicly available databases* from which a wide variety of information is available. The information differs in completeness and accuracy, and in the extent to which it is of use for a survey of international investment. These sources include the stock exchange register, possibly packaged by the stock exchange with additional information; commercial equity registries' information services; international credit rating agencies' publications (Moody's, Standard & Poor's, etc.); and market research reports or services, such as reviews by accounting or brokerage firms. The ABS uses several Australian Stock Exchange products such as monthly updates of share issues listed on the exchange, and their prices and indices.
- *Trade associations*, and their reports and releases, can be a useful source. Apart from the public rela-

tions and liaison aspects of a close relationship between the statistical agency and trade associations, many either list publicly or can make available lists of members, often with indications of their importance or the range of services provided. Particularly in the financial sector, their members are also likely to be significant users of official statistics and thus have a vested interest in accurate data and assisting statistical or data collection agencies.

14.6 As enterprises are recognized from the various sources above as potentially engaged in cross-border finance, they are included in an "exploratory survey," which identifies if they have any foreign investment activity, and if so whether they have a parent organization in Australia from which data should be obtained. The "exploratory survey" also collects some broad investment benchmark information for use in designing the ongoing investment survey.

14.7 The international investment survey register needs to identify the legal entities in the enterprise group not only for efficiency and quality of data collection,[2] but also for the identification of direct investment relationships and the categorization of some debt as direct investment capital. Periodic requests are made to the reporting organizations regarding the legal entities covered in their survey returns. This ensures that as new acquisitions are made, the survey reports capture their external debt, and that as businesses are sold off from a group, arrangements are made to continue to capture the external debt of that business.

14.8 Other sources for maintaining the information in the international investment survey register on corporate structures include a regular review of the corporate structure of the top few hundred businesses in Australia, as well as the general press and corporate registration sources listed above.

Survey form design

14.9 In collecting and compiling external debt data, the ABS places a major emphasis on the reconcilia-

tion and consistency of data. First, external debt statistics are part of a broader system of financial accounts, which allows many checks for coherence and consistency. For instance, comparing data compiled on the total size of markets for the various debt instruments with individual institutional sectors' assets and liabilities can help identify possible gaps that might relate to external debt. Second, reporting enterprises are expected to provide balanced balance-sheet data for national accounts purposes, which helps to ensure complete coverage and accuracy in reporting and sets a framework for more detailed data on cross-border positions.

14.10 More specifically, in measuring Australia's external debt data, the SII survey form collects inward and outward investment for the full range of debt instruments entered into by direct, portfolio, and other investors. For each debt instrument, the SII survey form is structured so that data are reported in line with the IIP reconciliation format,[3] including:
- The position (level or stock) of external financial assets and liabilities of residents at the beginning and end of the survey quarter;
- Financial transactions (investment flows) resulting in increases and decreases in the levels of these assets and liabilities each quarter;
- Other changes in the levels of these assets and liabilities; and
- Income that has accrued on these assets and liabilities.

14.11 Using this IIP reconciliation format not only forces respondents to consider the consistency of the data reported, it also enables compilers to readily identify and query inconsistencies in the reported data. The ABS has found that full data on transactions, and the other reasons for the change in positions each quarter, are usually available.

14.12 The format and wording used in the collection forms, together with the wording in the detailed explanatory notes that are supplied to all respondents, are closely aligned to the wording in *BPM5*. The explanatory notes provide numerous examples of what should be included (and excluded) for each type of debt instrument.

---

[2]The enterprise groups that report are the Australian head offices on behalf of all branches, subsidiaries, and consolidated associates, rather than each legal entity that might have an element of overseas investment or debt. Approaching entities at the group level limits the number of respondent organizations to those that can best report the information.

[3]That is, the difference in opening and closing positions is "explained" by transactions, valuation changes, and "other adjustments."

14.13 One of the advantages of collecting all the data on international investment on the same form (in the case of the SII, on the same page for each instrument) is that the possibility of double counting is eliminated. Because the boundaries between debt and equity, and direct, portfolio, and other investment are subject to different interpretations, and also subject to error and mismeasurement, a valuable consistency check on the data is provided by requiring that the disaggregated data sum to a total; that is, the report form is internally consistent. Collecting debt and equity data separately, sometimes even by different agencies, inevitably creates the potential for under- and/or double counting.

14.14 To further enhance the quality of external debt statistics, a substantial proportion of Australia's domestically issued external debt securities is measured by the reporting of individual securities owned by nonresidents. These securities are held by custodians on behalf of nonresident clients, and full identification of the holdings is obtained. Information on prices is used to estimate the transactions and price changes between the reported positions.

Extensions to IIP data

14.15 As mentioned above, the ABS has extended the IIP dataset to meet domestic users' needs for external debt statistics. The more important extensions include:

- A more detailed institutional sector breakdown of the debtor so that, for example, the external debt of the financial sectors can be analyzed in more detail than set out in *BPM5*;
- A public/private ownership dissection of Australian debtors;
- A presentation of external assets held in the form of debt instruments, as well as external debt liabilities so that each institutional sector's gross debt can be seen in the context of each sector's net external debt;
- A presentation of external debt by location of issuance (debt issued in Australia and debt issued abroad); and
- The classification of external debt assets and liabilities both by type of currency and by remaining maturity (based on the final maturity date of the debt).

14.16 Remaining-maturity data on a final maturity date basis can be used to approximate debt-service

schedules for principal, given that, for Australia, the amounts of part payments of principal on external debt are small and so are not separately collected. The security-by-security reporting for debt issued by entities domiciled in Australia provides precise data for the cash-flow elements of debt amortization schedules, but the requirement for separating principal and interest in amortization schedules necessitates interest rate forecasting for other instruments.

Austria

Measurement of IIP[4]

14.17 External debt statistics of Austria are derived from the information published on the IIP. This case study sets out the process by which the Austrian IIP data are compiled, and their relationship with external debt and financial accounts data. There are three sections, covering the collection system for the IIP and balance of payments—because some IIP items are compiled by accumulation of flows; the method of compiling the IIP, including all particularities of individual items; and the links among the IIP, external debt, and the financial accounts data.

The collection system

14.18 The current collection system for balance of payments and IIP data was introduced in 1991. It is a "closed system" in that it is self-balancing, with beginning and closing stocks reported along with transactions. The stocks data are used for the compilation of the IIP (mainly other investment), and the transactions are incorporated into all areas of the balance of payments. There is continuous monitoring of foreign payments.

14.19 Reports are received from the banks and nonbanks, with the bank reports comprising information on the banks' accounts held abroad, and on accounts held with domestic banks by foreign banks and nonbanks. Nonbanks report on their accounts held abroad, intercompany working balances, and clearing accounts. Detailed transactions data reported

---

[4]Prepared by the Oesterreichische Nationalbank. For further reference, see Oesterreichische Nationalbank (2000); European Central Bank (1999); Oesterreichische Nationalbank (1995), *Reports and Summaries,* 1/1995; and Oesterreichische Nationalbank (1999), *Focus on Austria,* 1/1999.

include the nature of the counterparty, Austrian or foreign, and, if the latter, the country of residence. Reports have to be provided for all combination of currency, country, and type of accounts relevant to the balance of payments (short-/long-term, deposits/ loans, assets/liabilities, etc.). Annual and quarterly surveys of trade credits are incorporated both in the balance of payments and the IIP.

14.20 The Oesterreichische Nationalbank (ONB) maintains both a comprehensive company database and a comprehensive database of securities. The company database is used to make correct sectoral allocations of reported transactions, particularly in the area of income, transfers, and the financial account. The securities database is used in conjunction with portfolio investment collected from banks and nonbanks to produce outstanding stocks of portfolio investment (see the section "Measurement of Portfolio Investment," below).

14.21 Annual surveys of direct investment stocks are conducted, and information on the direct investment relations between Austrian and foreign companies derived from these surveys are used to identify transactions and stocks of direct investment loans, and flows of direct investment income reported elsewhere. In combination with general economic indicators (such as nominal GDP) and expectations, the survey data are used to estimate reinvested earnings. To anticipate and identify direct investment transactions, information is taken from various news sources.

Reporting agents

14.22 In order to reduce the reporting burden for respondents, direct investment below certain thresholds (below Austrian schillings (ATS) 5 million for inward investment and below ATS 10 million for outward investment) only have to be reported every two years by alternate surveys; that is, half of the enterprises concerned report in the first year and the other half in the second year. For those enterprises that do not report direct investment stocks for a certain period, estimates are made on the basis of the report of the previous year.

(i) The *banking sector*: The following entities are required to report: credit institutions, building and loan associations (*Bausparkassen*), enterprises that carry out factoring business, and all enterprises undertaking business similar to "banking." Accord-

ing to the Foreign Exchange Act (*Kundmachung* DL 1–3/91, 2/93, 1/96), banks are required to report, on a daily/monthly basis, all transactions carried out via the domestic banking system, including transactions on behalf of their customers. More specifically, they report the following:

- All settlements carried out through the accounts of domestic banks held abroad and through the accounts of foreign banks and nonbanks held by domestic banks as well as the beginning and end-of-month *stocks* of these accounts (*Devisentableaumeldung*);
- All sales/purchases and (beginning/end-of-month) stocks of foreign currency transactions (*Valutentableaumeldung*, over-the-counter or OTC money); and
- Monthly stocks of securities, as defined in the *BPM5,* that banks acting as primary custodians hold for their own account or on behalf of their resident and nonresident customers (*Wertpapierstandmeldung*).

14.23 In addition, banks (acting as a direct investor and/or as a direct investment company) are requested to respond to an annual survey concerning direct investment if the value of the nominal capital of the direct investment exceeds the threshold of ATS 1 million and 10 percent of overall nominal capital, or if the nominal capital does not exceed ATS 1 million but the balance-sheet total of the direct investment enterprise exceeds ATS 500 million and the 10 percent criterion is fulfilled.

(ii) The *nonbank sector* (enterprises and households not included in (i)): According to the Foreign Exchange Act (*Kundmachung* DL 1–3/91, 2/93, 1/96), nonbanks are required to report on a monthly basis all settlements and positions on accounts held with banks abroad as well as short-term and long-term loans granted to nonresidents or provided by nonresidents to residents, if the annual volume of transactions exceeds a certain threshold (*Auslandskontenmeldung*), or otherwise on an annual basis. Nonbank private companies and private households (acting as a direct investor and/or as a direct investment company) are requested to respond to an annual survey concerning direct investment if the value of the nominal capital of the direct investment exceeds the threshold of ATS 1 million and 10 percent of overall nominal capital. In addition, companies have to submit quarterly and annual surveys (covering a selected sample and a full range, respectively) on trade credits. In addition, nonbanks (including general government) are requested to report annually their holdings of domestic and foreign securities held outside the custody of domestic banks (held in safekeeping, held in custody with banks, etc.), unless the total market value of these holdings of securities is less than the threshold of ATS 1 million at the end of the year.

(iii) *General government*: Public authorities report all transactions of relevance to the balance of payments to the ONB. In addition, some data that are used for checking purposes are received from the Federal Ministry of Finance (particularly concerning the area of current and capital payments of the public sector vis-à-vis EU institutions).

(iv) *Monetary authority*: The ONB reports on the external monetary position and monthly flows and stocks in the same way as the banking sector. Special quarterly reports on stocks and flows are also compiled by the Accounting Department of the ONB for balance of payments and IIP purposes. These reports are mainly used to check monthly flows, to obtain data on an accrual basis, and to calculate reserve assets for the IIP.

Measurement of portfolio investment

14.24 Portfolio investment flows and stocks are measured through a comprehensive and reliable compilation system that is based on the reporting of securities on a security-by-security basis. To facilitate this work, a database of individual securities is maintained (see below). This system, developed during 1988–89, is not only reliable but provides the flexibility to meet changing user requirements and market circumstances. Previously, the experience had been that with the fast-developing international financial markets, instructions to reporting agents were becoming increasingly complicated in order to meet the needs of the balance of payments and IIP.

14.25 With the present system, the banks report transactions and stocks of individual securities, identifying each with the ISIN code. The Austrian banks appreciate using the ISIN codes since these codes are required for their own business purpose (for example, the settlement of security transactions). Once a security is reported with an ISIN code, it can be identified in the securities database that the ONB maintains. The database contains the necessary balance of payments and IIP classifications (the nature of the financial instrument, the sector and country of issuer, etc.). Because securities are reported on an individual basis, transactions and stocks can be reconciled.

14.26 The securities database was developed and is maintained by the ONB. The core of the database relies on information purchased from the Austrian and German national numbering agencies (NNAs)—the Oesterreichische Kontrollbank (OKB) and the German Wertpapiermitteilungen. The OKB provides data on securities issued by residents in the domestic market, and Austrian schilling or euro-denominated securities issued by nonresidents in Austria; the Wertpapiermitteilung provides data on securities issued in foreign markets, including securities issued by Austrian residents and denominated in currencies other than the Austrian schilling or euro. Also, reporting banks have to supply information on securities that to the best knowledge of the reporting bank do not have an ISIN code—so-called internal securities. If information on the same security is received from more than one institution, then the OKB data are usually given preference. Information on current market prices is obtained from the Telekurs. The database is updated on a weekly basis.

14.27 Using the information gathered on individual securities, the Statistics Department generates an "internal master file" of data, which is used by the ONB for the compilation of portfolio investment transaction and stock data. In early 2000, this master file contained around 150,000 debt securities and some 50,000 equity securities, thus covering around 99 percent of the securities traded by Austrian residents on a cross-border basis.

14.28 Comprehensive quality checks and amendments are made by the ONB in order to render the information received from external sources suitable for use in the IIP and balance of payments compilation. These checking procedures comprise formal controls (completeness of information), as well as plausibility checks. Detailed quality checks are required not least because the NNAs maintain their databases for their customers (banks), whose business needs for information differ from those of statistical compilers. Consequently, data fields that are particularly important for statistical purposes (for example, outstanding amount) are not always of the desired quality.

Compiling the IIP

14.29 An annual IIP statement is drawn up consistent with the recommendations of *BPM5*, with a few exceptions. A geographical attribution between euro-area and non-euro-area data is possible to a substantial extent. This section explains the compilation procedure for individual functional categories of the IIP.

Direct investment

14.30 For direct investment, Austria follows the recommendations of the international standards, including both the application of the so-called directional principle (that is, assets and liabilities reported according to the direction of the direct investment relationship) and the inclusion of reinvested earnings. The annual direct investment survey provides final position data some 18 months after the reference end-period (time *t*). Provisional position data, available six to nine months after the reference end-period (*t*), are calculated by adding accumulated flows (including reinvested earnings) to the previous end-reference period (*t*–1).

14.31 One exception is data for real estate, which are compiled exclusively using accumulated flows (approximately 7 percent on the assets side and 2 percent on the liabilities side of overall assets and liabilities of direct investment stocks, respectively).

14.32 Because the data from the annual survey are valued at book value, the reconciliation with recorded transactions (at market value) is problematic. Although price and other adjustments (in the sense of reclassifications) can be identified to a limited extent, "other adjustments" (in the sense of the residual adjustment between changes in stocks and transactions) can be very high. Exchange rate adjustments are calculated on the basis of average monthly exchange rates when IIP positions are derived from the accumulation of flows, and end-of-month exchange rates when IIP positions are directly measured.

14.33 Market valuation can be compiled additionally based on an "earning-method estimation" (that is, discounting potential future cash earnings).

Portfolio investment

14.34 Portfolio investment data are compiled in conformity with the *BPM5* recommendations, including the appropriate instrument and sector attribution. As described above, the security-by-security reporting system combined with the securities database is at the core of the compilation of these data—on both stocks and transactions, and inward and outward investment. On the asset side, the monthly bank and annual nonbank reports provide reliable position data on domestic sector asset holders.

14.35 As a consequence of the security-by-security approach, stocks, transactions, exchange rate, and price adjustments are closely reconciled, with remaining differences calculated by residual; other adjustments for sectoral and instrument adjustments can be identified; and stocks are valued at market prices, including interest costs that have accrued. Country attribution is possible for the asset information, based on the country of residence of the issuer, but the country of the owner of the domestic debt liability is not known.

Financial derivatives

14.36 IIP data for financial derivatives are a combination of stocks (approximately 20 percent of the total) and accumulated transactions (approximately 80 percent of the total). These data largely cover OTC (or off-exchange) derivatives. The stock data, reported using ISIN codes, are highly reliable and are calculated at market prices; for other reported data no clear valuation principle can be identified, although it is believed they are measured at close to market value. Stocks are available on a net basis; there are no fully reliable stock data available on a gross basis.

Other investment

14.37 Other investment data are compiled mainly in conformity with the *BPM5* recommendations, with the exception of trade credits between affiliated enterprises, which are indistinguishably included in the "other investment" item instead of being recorded under direct investment. A combination of stocks (approximately 90 percent of the total) and accumulated flows (approximately 10 percent) is used to calculate these data. The stock data are mainly derived from the settlement system with the exception of trade credits, which are measured directly from quarterly and annual surveys. For loans and other assets/liabilities where positions are below the thresholds for direct reporting by reporting agents, accumulated flows are used to calculate positions.

14.38 Reporting agents have to reconcile, in the same report, stocks and flows for "other investment" accounts. Price adjustments (mainly relating to asset trading), other adjustments (reclassifications), and residual adjustments (reporting errors or stock corrections) can be taken directly from the reports provided. Exchange rate adjustments are calculated using average monthly exchange rates for transactions and for reported adjustments, and end-of-month exchange rates for stocks. Other investment assets and liabilities are based on nominal values.

Reserve assets

14.39 The stock position for reserve assets is directly reported by the Accounting Department of the ONB in the form of special quarterly reports. These reports comprise stocks, transactions, and all kinds of adjustments. The data are taken directly from the accounting database. Stocks and transactions of currency and deposits are not included in the special quarterly reports because they are already covered by the regular monthly reports submitted by the ONB (see item (iv) under "Reporting Agents," above). Discrepancies between accounting principles and *BPM5* concepts are seen as being insignificant. Stocks are reported on a market value basis, including closing market prices for gold and closing midmarket exchange rates.

Relationship of IIP with external debt and financial accounts

Gross external debt

14.40 Austria's gross external debt position can be derived from the IIP. At present, external debt data are compiled at market price and are broken down by sector. Data on a remaining-maturity basis are available in the case of debt securities.

Financial accounts

14.41 The financial accounts implemented by the ONB in accordance with the *European System of Accounts: ESA95* (Eurostat, 1996) cover, in the form of asset and liability statements, the financial claims and liabilities of all institutional sectors. The balance sheet of the "rest of the world" sector for the financial accounts draws heavily on the IIP data. Thus, the position "nonresidents' net financial assets" (financial accounts) corresponds to the domestic sectors' "net liabilities to the rest of the world" (IIP). The latter denotes a negative net IIP position—that is, "net claims of the rest of the world sector on Austrian residents."

Canada

Measurement of Foreign Portfolio Investment in Canadian Bonds[5]

14.42 Nonresidents have been sharply increasing their investment in Canadian bonds since the 1980s. From a value of Can\$56.5 billion in 1980, the investment of foreigners reached Can\$393 billion by 1999, more than 40 percent of the value of all Canadian bonds outstanding. The interest on these debt obligations (Can\$27.5 billion in 1999) is a major factor in the deficit for investment income in Canada's current account. Given the magnitude and the wide diversity of bonds held by nonresidents, Canada has a detailed and complex statistical system to help ensure adequate and consistent statistics.

14.43 Data on nonresident investment in Canadian bonds is largely reported on a security-by-security basis by (1) major investment dealers, banks, insurance companies, and pension and mutual funds, on a monthly frequency, and (2) the largest debt issuers. These data are reported on a monthly basis, mainly on electronic tapes supplied by information service providers. Data are provided using a specific record layout describing the detailed characteristics of the instruments. Each month, more than 500,000 security transactions are collected, of which about 10,000 relate to Canadian bonds. Year-end position data are obtained from an annual census survey, with positions calculated according to four different methods of valuation.

14.44 The Canadian system is dependent on a database that maintains detailed characteristics on each specific bond issued. Indeed, each Canadian bond issue is identified by issuer, sector (federal government, private sector, etc.), and industrial classification; for each bond held by nonresidents the dates of issue and of maturity, the currency of issue, the interest rate, the timing of interest payments, etc. are identified; and nonresident holders are identified on the basis of their respective country of residence, when available, or at least by broad geographical

---

[5]Prepared by Statistics Canada.

area, and whether or not they are related to the Canadian issuers.

14.45 Using the detailed information on individual bonds, this case study reviews how these statistics are generated for the transactions and positions data and describes the various prices that are used to value bonds.[6]

Financial transactions and positions

14.46 There are four types of financial transactions that affect the position data: new issues, trade in existing securities, accrual of interest, and redemptions.

New issues

14.47 In the Canadian system, new bond issues sold to nonresidents are restricted to newly issued Canadian bonds floated directly abroad (that is, foreign issues and the portion of global issues floated in the foreign markets). Nonresident purchases of new Canadian bonds floated in the domestic market, including the domestic portion of global bonds, are classified as trade in existing issues. Transactions associated with new issues denominated in foreign currencies are entered in the system in their original currencies and are converted into Canadian dollars using the noon average exchange rate of the month in which the transactions took place. When the Canadian dollar proceeds from the new issue are known, this information is directly used as the value of the transaction.

Trading of existing bonds

14.48 Trading in Canadian bonds involving residents and nonresidents largely occurs in domestic issues, especially Government of Canada bonds. For bonds traded in the same month and year of their issue, the system deems the trading to have occurred at the date of new issue; otherwise, the trading is deemed to have occurred on the fifteenth day of the month of trading.

14.49 Bonds traded under repurchase agreements (repos) are effectively loans with the bonds used as collateral. Since respondents include them in their monthly trading, these transactions are reclassified from portfolio investment to loans. This can be eas-

ily achieved for financial intermediaries that separately identify trading of securities involving repos. Where financial intermediaries do not separately identify securities involved in repos, the system matches the sale and purchase of the same securities in a single month and evaluates a yield rate in order to identify transactions to be classified as repo transactions.

14.50 Transactions involving stripped securities—that is, the coupon payments are traded separately from the principal amount—are processed as transactions in bonds issued by the original issuer but are not linked back to the specific bond issue that was stripped. The strips are recorded as zero-coupon bonds, with income calculated as the difference between the transaction price and the redemption value.

14.51 For a number of reasons, a few security dealers do not identify transactions in existing bonds on a security-by-security basis. These bonds are regrouped by sector of issuer and are treated as a component of a synthetic single issue of the sector (for example, bonds issued by provincial governments). Once adjusted to exclude bonds under repos and strips, the system checks that each bond traded has previously been recorded in the system as having been issued. If not, an adjustment is made in the inventory to record the bond as a new issue.

Accrual of interest costs

14.52 In the Canadian system, the difference between the issue price and the redemption price accrues as interest over the life of the bond. In addition, the system computes the accrual of coupon payments on each outstanding bond issue. Until paid, these two components continuously increase the value of the bond, and Canada's stock of external debt in bonds.

Redemptions

14.53 Redemptions represent the amount of the principal payment made by the issuer at the date of maturity of the bond. Redemptions are generated automatically by the system at maturity. While there is generally one date of maturity, some bonds may have several maturity dates as the redemptions are spread over time (for example, sinking funds bond). For bonds issued in tranches, the system prorates the redemptions according to the weight of the tranches. Redemptions of bonds in foreign curren-

---

[6]A fuller description of the Canadian system is available on the Internet at the IMF website, *http://www.imf.org/external/bopage/stindex.htm.*

cies are converted into Canadian dollars at the monthly noon average rate for the month of redemption. Again, when the Canadian dollar proceeds are known, this information is used to calculate the value of redemptions.

Valuation of financial transactions and positions

14.54 From the time a bond is issued through to the time it is redeemed, its price fluctuates largely as a result of movements in interest rates in the market. In the Canadian statistical system, four prices are maintained: issue price, book value, market price at year-end, and redemption price. In turn, each of these prices is used to derive the related statistics. For example, the prices on new issues are used to derive capital flows associated with new issues, while redemption prices are used to generate redemptions data. Transactions, both sales and purchases for the month, are recorded at market prices. The stock of outstanding bonds is currently valued at book—or nominal—value and at market value.

Issue prices

14.55 At the time of issue, the bonds are generally priced at the prevailing market price. This market price is in turn equivalent to the present value of the stream of future payments, discounted at the market interest rate. If the coupon rate is set equivalent to the prevailing interest rate, the issue price will be the same as the redemption price. If the coupon rate is different from the prevailing interest rate, the issue will be priced at discount or premium to the redemption price.

14.56 In general, a bond is issued on a given date and, hence, has one issue price. There are, however, bonds, especially Government of Canada bonds, that are issued in tranches over a period of time. Each tranche has the same maturity date and coupon rate as an existing issue, but the issue price of each tranche varies according to the interest rate prevailing at the time the tranche was issued. Hence, each tranche of these bonds may have a different issue price.

Book value

14.57 The book value can be calculated from different viewpoints. From the point of view of the issuer of a bond, the book value is the issue price plus the accrual of interest costs not yet paid out. From the viewpoint of the owners of the bond, the book value

consists of the acquisition cost plus the income earned but not yet received. Given that bonds may have been purchased at various prices, there could be many book values.

14.58 In the Canadian statistical system, only the book value of the issuer is maintained. This book value is made up of the issue price plus the accrual of interest costs not paid out by the issuer. The interest is calculated as the accrual of the coupon plus the accrual of the difference between the issue price and the redemption price. Hence, at any given time, the book value—nominal value, in the terminology of the *Guide*—of the issuer is made up of three parts: the issue price, the accrual of the coupon not yet paid out, and the amortization of the discount/premium, if any, between the issue and the redemption prices.

Market prices

14.59 *Description of market prices.* At a given time, the current market price of a bond is usually calculated using a sample of recent buying and selling transactions in financial market. Throughout its lifetime, a bond will have many market prices depending on the time at which the value is observed. For instance, the issue price is, in most cases, the market price that prevailed at the time the bond was issued, and the redemption price is the market price that prevails at the time the bond matures.

14.60 *Derivation of market prices.* In the Canadian system, market prices are either observed from information obtained in the bond trading survey in the month preceding the valuation, or calculated. To the extent that bonds are traded with nonresidents in the month preceding the period of valuation, such as December trading for end-December valuation, the average price in such trading is used as the proxy for market prices when calculating transactions. For bonds whose market price are not readily available, the system estimates the present value of the future stream of payments of the bond using a market yield matrix. The matrix enables one to generate market prices for a broad range of Canadian bonds (by sector, currency, and years left to maturity) and is regularly updated in the system.

Redemption prices

14.61 The redemption price is the amount the issuer is required to pay the holder at maturity of the bond; it is the future value of the principal after the coupons have been paid out. The redemption price of a bond is the same as the market price that will prevail on that bond at the date of its maturity.

Features of the system

14.62 The degree of detail maintained and the flexibility of the Canadian system make it possible to generate numerous outputs on nonresident ownership of Canadian bonds. Canadian bonds can be valued according to four different methods: issue price, maturity price, book (nominal) value, and market value. The market value is published in Canada's IIP.

14.63 Functions are integrated in the system to derive positions, transactions, interest (paid, accrued, or payable), and commissions for a specific period of time in original currency or Canadian dollars. Exchange rate effects on the positions can also be calculated. In addition, Statistics Canada can calculate the funds that will be needed to service the debt in the years to come, taking into account the coupons to be paid as well as the retirements. The remaining term of maturity can also be calculated by type and by sector.

Chile

Reconciliation of External Debt Statistics with BIS International Banking Statistics[7]

14.64 If international capital markets are to function properly, statistics on debtor countries' external liabilities are necessary. But when the figures published by a country, from the debtor perspective, differ from those published by international agencies, from the creditor perspective, experience has shown that the credibility of the statistics published by the country is directly affected, leading to uncertainty about actual indebtedness, and so to inefficiency in the capital markets.

14.65 As with a number of other countries, Chile is one of the countries whose external debt statistics, disseminated monthly by the Central Bank of Chile (BCCH), do not coincide with the international banking statistics published by the BIS. To reconcile

the two institutions' figures, in August 1998 the Management Office of the International Division of the BCCH committed resources to undertake extensive research, and establish the necessary contacts with both the BIS and the monetary authorities of various countries, to discover reasons for the discrepancies. The work culminated in a visit by BCCH officials to the BIS in Basel, Switzerland, in late 1999. One of the conclusions of the investigation was that BIS statistics embody a broader concept than external debt as measured by the BCCH. Whereas the central bank publishes external debt statistics, the BIS data refer to claims against the country, including items such as local claims in foreign currencies to residents in Chile and other liabilities that are not within Chile's core definition of external debt.

14.66 Drawing on this work, and using data for end-June 1999, this case study explains why differences arise between the external liability figures published by the BCCH and the BIS.

14.67 As explained in Chapter 17, the BIS publishes international banking statistics on both a locational and a consolidated basis. This case study first compares BCCH data with BIS locational-based data, and then with BIS consolidated data, before drawing some conclusions.

Comparison with BIS locational data

14.68 BIS locational data provide information on the external assets and liabilities of all banks—known as BIS reporting institutions—located in what is known as the BIS reporting area.[8] Within external assets, the value of the external loans outstanding is shown separately, with an attribution by currency, institutional sector, and country of debtor. BCCH's research has discovered that the statistics published by the BCCH on debt to foreign financial institutions are more comparable with the BIS's external loans data than with the BIS's external assets data.

---

[7]Prepared by the Central Bank of Chile.

[8]At the time of writing, the reporting area comprises the G-10 plus eight countries: Austria, Belgium, Canada, Denmark, Finland, France, Germany, Ireland, Italy, Japan, Luxembourg, the Netherlands, Norway, Portugal, Spain, Sweden, Switzerland, the United Kingdom, and the United States. The quarterly reports also include the so-called offshore centers: The Bahamas, Bahrain, Cayman Islands, Hong Kong SAR, the Netherlands Antilles, and Singapore.

Table 14.1. Outstanding External Loan Claims of BIS Reporting Institutions on Chile, as at End-June 1999

	Millions of U.S. Dollars
(1) BCCH reported data	15,901
(2) BIS reported data (locational basis)	18,684
(3) Discrepancy between sources ((1) – (2))	–2,783

Table 14.2. Adjusted Data for Outstanding External Loan Claims of BIS Reporting Institutions on Chile, as at End-June 1999

	Millions of U.S. Dollars
Reported data	
(1) BCCH reported data	15,901
(2) BIS reported data (locational basis)	18,684
(3) Discrepancy between sources ((1) – (2))	–2,783
Factors explaining the discrepancy between sources[1]	
(4) *Cobranzas* (forfaiting activity)	1,900
(5) Debt with government financial institutions	721
(6) Loans used to finance operations abroad	500
(7) Total adjustment ((4) + (5) + (6))	3,121
Adjusted difference (discrepancy (3) plus total adjustment (7))	338

[1]A positive figure indicates amounts reported by the BIS as external loan claims on Chile that are not included in BCCH data for external loans from BIS reporting institutions.

14.69 Table 14.1 presents the outstanding external loan claims of BIS reporting institutions on Chile as at end-June 1999, as reported by the BCCH and BIS. As can be seen, the BIS reports a total $2,783 million higher than that reported by the BCCH.

14.70 On investigation, the difference is largely explained by three items that the BCCH does not classify as external loans from BIS reporting institutions.

14.71 First, the BIS apparently includes in its figures external loans used to finance foreign trade provided in the form of instruments issued by the debtor to the foreign supplier or third party, which are subsequently discounted by banks (thus becoming a form of forfaiting activity). In Chile these instruments are known as *cobranzas*. In contrast, at the time of writing, the external debt figures published by Chile include only those cobranzas of medium- and long-term maturity, which are classified as debt owed to suppliers.[9] According to the BCCH's estimates, total cobranzas (short-, medium-, and long-term) at end-June 1999 amounted to approximately $5,425 million, of which $1,900 million could be claims held by BIS reporting institutions, with remaining maturities up to one year,[10] and thus reported as short-term claims in BIS statistics.

14.72 Second, in its published data, the BCCH attributes lending provided to Chile by foreign government financial institutions for specific projects to government agencies. On the other hand, even though the government institutions concerned are not BIS reporters, some such lending is included in the BIS locational (and consolidated) banking statistics. For instance, lending by the Kreditanstalt für Wiederaufbau (KFW) is included in the reports sent by Germany to the BIS, while lending by the Export Development Corporation of Canada (EDC), which is also not a BIS reporter, is included in the reports prepared by the financial institutions with which it deals. For end-June 1999 data, these two agencies accounted for $721 million of the difference between BIS and BCCH data.

14.73 Third, loans contracted by Chilean enterprises and used to finance investments directly abroad are not recorded in the BCCH data but are included in both the BIS's locational and the consolidated banking statistics. At end-June 1999, these loans amounted to $500 million, of which 20 percent was of a short-term remaining maturity.

14.74 As can be seen from Table 14.2, the three factors discussed above more than account for the difference between the BIS and BCCH reported data.

---

[9]Because debtors are the source of information, these loans are classified as debt to suppliers, even though they are subsequently discounted by banks in the BIS reporting area (forfaiting).

[10]The estimate of short-term claims is derived from the BIS consolidated data, which does provide a breakdown of claims by short-term remaining maturity.

Table 14.3. Outstanding External Claims of BIS Reporting Institutions on Chile, as at End-June 1999
(Millions of U.S. dollars)

	Total	Short-term[1]	Medium- and long-term
Reported data			
(1) BCCH reported data	15,850	3,911	11,939
(2) BIS reported data (locational basis)	23,491	9,347	14,144[2]
(3) Discrepancy between sources ((1)–(2))	–7,641	–5,436	–2,205
Factors explaining the discrepancy between sources[3]			
(4) Foreign currency assets of offices of foreign banks	3,343	2,454	889
(5) Bonds	823	253	637
(6) *Cobranzas* (forfaiting activity)	1,900	1,900	0
(7) Debt with governmental financial institutions	721	84	570
(8) Loans used to finance investments abroad	500	100	400
(9) Total adjustment ((4)+(5)+(6)+(7)+(8))	7,287	4,791	2,496
Adjusted difference (discrepancy (3) plus total adjustment (9))	–354	–645	291

[1]On a remaining maturity of one year or less.
[2]Includes foreign liabilities whose maturity cannot be determined.
[3]A positive figure indicates amounts reported by the BIS as external claims on Chile that are not included in the BCCH data for external liabilities to BIS reporting institutions.

Comparison with BIS consolidated data

14.75 The BIS consolidated international banking data provide information on the external assets of banks headquartered in the reporting area, excluding banks headquartered in certain offshore centers (which are included in the locational data). Consolidation means that all the claims of each bank, including all offices throughout the world, are reported, except intrabank claims, which are excluded. Branches and subsidiaries of banks located in the reporting area but headquartered outside the reporting area provide information only on their own claims and liabilities (that is, on an unconsolidated basis). The consolidated BIS data include a breakdown by debtor sector and by short- and long-term remaining maturity and present the debtor position of each country vis-à-vis each of the creditor countries. Loans are not shown separately. Taking all this into consideration, it is clear that the asset figures of the locational and consolidated data differ substantially.

14.76 As with the locational data, it can be seen in Table 14.3 that the outstanding external claims of BIS reporting institutions on Chile as at end-June 1999 as reported by the BIS were higher than those reported by the BCCH ($23,491 million and $15,850 million, respectively).[11]

14.77 In addition to the three items discussed above, one of the reasons for the difference is that the BIS considers local foreign exchange positions of offices of foreign banks resident in Chile as external liabilities of Chile, whereas in measuring external debt, liabilities of residents to other residents are excluded. These positions amounted to $3,343 million[12] at end-June 1999, and were financed in large part by funds obtained on the local market.

14.78 The data on bond claims of BIS reporting institutions are another potential source of discrepancy. However, the value of the claims of BIS reporting institutions are unclear, since they are not separately identified in either the BIS or BCCH data. Bond liabilities to nonresidents are included by the BCCH in Chile's external debt statistics, but individ-

[11]The BCCH reported data in Table 14.3 are those for loans with BIS reporting institutions in the reporting area, converted to a consolidated basis so as to make the data comparable with those of the BIS.
[12]Source: Financial information of the Superintendency of Banks and Financial Institutions.

ual groups of creditors are not identified. At end-June 1999, Chile's total bond liabilities were valued at $4,116 million, and it is estimated that around 20 percent, or $823 million, represented claims by BIS reporting institutions, on a consolidated basis. Of this total, $253 million were thought to be of short-term maturity. It is known that many of these Chilean liabilities are held in the United States by financial institutions such as investment funds and bank holding companies. These institutions are required to report their holdings of such securities to the U.S. Federal Reserve for inclusion in the report entitled "Country Exposure Lending Survey," which is the source of the statistics reported to the BIS by the U.S. authorities.

Conclusions

14.79 From the research undertaken by the BCCH, the following conclusions can be drawn:

- To ensure proper use of data, and for comparisons to be made between figures that are conceptually measuring the same thing, the methodological framework used to compile published data should be clearly explained by each disseminating agency.
- The primary data sources (debtors for the BCCH and creditors for the BIS) are responsible for significant differences, especially in the case of debt transferred to a different creditor. In particular, for certain claims reported to the BIS, such as bonds, while they are included in Chile's external debt statistics published by the BCCH, they cannot be allocated to a specific creditor.
- There is the need to clarify the nature of the items reported to the BIS. For instance, the BIS considers local foreign exchange positions of offices of foreign banks in Chile an external liability, although they represent a claim by a resident on another resident. Whether these claims should be regarded as external liabilities is obviously debatable (they are not in this *Guide*), since the position is financed with local resources and therefore does not represent net indebtedness abroad.
- Quality control is essential and has a major impact on the comparability of statistics published by different institutions. Consequently, ensuring correct application of established methodology should always be a concern.
- To provide more complete external debt statistics, Chile is currently working on the compilation of data for instruments such as cobranzas and loans used to finance investments abroad, which,

although falling into the category of external debt, are not included in Chile's debt statistics because the necessary information is not available. To solve this problem, surveys and other data-collection methods are being introduced.

India

How Debt Information Systems Are Being Used for External Debt Management[13]

14.80 Effective monitoring is a prerequisite for successful debt management. Indeed, information on the status and composition of external debt and debt-service payments provides the basic input for debt-management decisions. With the enormous growth in the volume and complexity of loan records, debt-management decisions require the easy retrieval of information, and the ability to undertake analysis and scenario-building exercises, such as the examination of the impact of alternative debt-management strategies. In this context, manual record keeping is no longer sufficient; rather, there is a need to develop a computerized database that will facilitate both information retrieval and scenario exercises.

14.81 In India, comprehensive coverage, active monitoring, and the computerization of external debt data have all played a key role in the continuous improvement of the country's external debt position (Table 14.4). The exhaustive coverage and timely availability of data has allowed effective monitoring of the debt stock and debt-service payments. For instance, information on projected debt-service payments—that is, contractual liabilities in future years—has provided policymakers with early warning against the bunching of repayments, so that corrective steps could be taken in advance. Also, the computerized database has facilitated the evaluation of the impact of alternative borrowing strategies. Effective monitoring through computerization, therefore, has become essential to India's debt management.

Benefits of a good information system

14.82 The benefits of a good debt information system are outlined here, drawing on India's experience.

---

[13]Prepared by the Ministry of Finance of India.

Table 14.4. India's External Debt and Key Debt Indicators

	As at March 31							
	1991	1992	1995	1996	1997	1998	1999	2000P[1]
	(Billions of U.S. dollars, end-period)							
(1) Long-term debt	75.3	78.2	94.7	88.7	86.7	88.5	93.3	94.4
(2) Short-term debt	8.5	7.1	4.3	5.0	6.7	5.0	4.4	4.0
(3) Total external debt	83.8	85.3	99.0	93.7	93.5	93.5	97.7	98.4
	(Ratios, in percent)							
(4) Ratio of external debt to GDP	30.4	41.0	30.9	27.1	24.7	24.4	23.5	22.0
(5) Ratio of debt service to current receipts	35.3	30.2	25.9	26.2	23.0	19.5	19.0	16.0
(6) Ratio of short-term debt to total debt	10.2	8.3	4.3	5.4	7.2	5.4	4.5	4.1
(7) Ratio of short-term debt to foreign exchange reserves	382.1	125.6	20.5	29.5	30.1	19.4	14.9	10.6

[1]Provisional.

External debt management

14.83 One of the salient features of external debt management in India has been an annual cap or ceiling on External Commercial Borrowings (EComBs). EComBs are defined to include commercial bank loans, export credits, and bonds issued in the international capital markets. The borrowers are public sector, financial institutions, and private sector entities. As a sovereign entity the Government of India does not borrow in the international capital markets.

14.84 Every year a cap is fixed on EComB approvals, which takes into consideration the commercial borrowing requirement of different sectors of the economy, and medium-term balance of payment projections. The end-objective is to keep the debt-service ratio within the prudent limits of debt management. The exercise is undertaken with the help of computerized scenario building, the inputs for which are (1) projected debt-service payments on disbursed outstanding debt; (2) disbursements of debt "in the pipeline" and the projected debt service; (3) future EComB approvals and their impact on inflows and debt service based on an assessment of the international capital market situation.

Sovereign external debt management

14.85 India does not access international capital markets as a sovereign entity. But the need for sovereign external debt management has arisen because the World Bank now requires borrowers to make their own decisions regarding choice of currency, interest, and maturity mix on Bank borrowings. Some other multilateral institutions are also considering a similar approach. Also, with the World Bank soon to offer free-standing hedging products (derivatives products), such as interest and currency swap, interest rate caps, collars, etc., active management of sovereign external debt will become necessary.

14.86 To meet the new circumstances, India is developing a modeling exercise for sovereign external debt. The objective is to develop benchmarks that lead to an optimal currency, interest, and maturity mix of sovereign external debt so as to minimize the costs of government borrowings for any given level of risk. These benchmarks would be a guide for future borrowing and active debt-management decisions. Since the debt data for the government account are 100 percent computerized, historical data can be retrieved, and projections of future payments made readily available, for analysis and scenario-building exercises.

14.87 A separate exercise is also under way to consider the prepayment of World Bank fixed-rate loans, which have interest rates significantly above prevailing market rates.

Contingent liabilities

14.88 The Government of India has provided guarantees on a selective basis for borrowings from abroad by public sector enterprises, developmental financial institutions, and, in some instances, private sector companies. By maintaining records of such

Table 14.5. India's Central Government Guarantees on External Debt

	March 31						December 31
	1994	1995	1996	1997	1998	1999[1]	1999[1]
	(Billions of U.S. dollars, end-period)						
(1) Government debt	55.9	59.5	53.1	49.1	46.5	46.1	46.9
(2) Nongovernment debt	36.8	39.5	40.7	44.4	47.0	51.5	52.1
(3) *Of which* with government guarantee (a) + (b) + (c)[2]	12.2	12.3	10.2	8.2	7.3	7.1	7.5
(a) Financial sector	3.3	3.3	2.7	2.3	2.3	2.4	2.6
(b) Public sector	8.6	8.7	7.1	5.6	4.6	4.3	4.6
(c) Private sector	0.3	0.4	0.4	0.4	0.3	0.3	0.3
(4) Total external debt (1) + (2)	92.7	99.0	93.7	93.5	93.5	97.7	99.0
(5) Government debt and guaranteed debt (1) + (3)	68.1	71.8	63.2	57.3	53.8	53.2	54.4
	(Ratios, in percent)						
(6) Ratio of government debt and guaranteed debt to total external debt (5)/(4)	73.5	72.5	67.4	61.3	57.5	54.5	55.0
(7) Ratio of government guaranteed debt to nongovernment debt (3)/(2)	33.1	31.2	25.0	18.5	15.5	13.7	14.4

[1]Provisional.
[2]Direct guarantees on external debt provided by the central government.

explicit contingent liabilities in the computer system along with external debt data, these liabilities are regularly monitored. Because the government is now discouraging the issue of fresh guarantees, except where considered absolutely necessary (such as for certain infrastructure projects), total outstanding guarantees are on a declining trend—the share of government guaranteed debt in total nongovernment debt declined from 33.1 percent at end-March 1994 to 14.4 percent at end-December 1999. Table 14.5 provides these data and a disaggregation of guarantees by institutional sector (financial, public, and private).

Computerization and networking

14.89 Nearly 80 percent of external debt data is computerized using the Commonwealth Secretariat's Debt Recording and Management System (CS-DRMS).[14] The adoption of the CS-DRMS system, in the late 1980s, was a major step forward, marking the beginning of the use of external debt data as a management information system input for debt-management decisions. Efforts are now under way to extend the scope of computerization to the remaining data, which are currently captured on a manual reporting basis.

Interagency involvement

14.90 The main agencies involved in the compilation of external debt data are the Ministry of Finance, the Reserve Bank of India, and the Ministry of Defense. The computerized database containing data reported by all the different agencies is housed in a central server in the External Debt Management Unit (EDMU) in the Ministry of Finance. The information from the centralized database is then available for analysis and scenario-building exercises. Through Local Area Network, the database is also accessible to various users in the Ministry of Finance as an input for policy decisions.

14.91 External debt data are updated on a quarterly basis. The dissemination policy is that of full transparency of reporting, with statistics published in the *Economic Survey* of the Ministry of Finance and the *Annual Report* of the Reserve Bank of India. In addition, since 1993 the Ministry of Finance has published an annual *Status Report on External Debt*, which is circulated in the Parliament of India. This report, which provides an exhaustive analysis of external debt data, has helped raise public awareness of external debt issues.

14.92 Such transparency and awareness also leads to public feedback, which acts as an early warning system, especially in situations where key debt indi-

---

[14]The CS-DRMS is described in Chapter 18.

cators are beginning to move in the wrong direction. The transparency and comprehensive monitoring also ensures that no component of debt is unreported. This, together with low levels of short-term debt, contributed to India's success in withstanding the effects of the financial crises of 1997/98.

14.93 Senior staff in the key government agencies undertake periodic reviews of the measurement of external debt to ensure best practice and continuous improvement in the quality and coverage of data. In 1992, the Task Force/Policy Group Report on External Debt Statistics recommended adoption of internationally accepted classifications and definitions, and stressed the need for transparency of data, unusual at the time for an emerging economy. On the report's recommendation, the EDMU was set up in the Ministry of Finance to coordinate debt-monitoring activities, and provides data inputs for debt-management decisions. A World Bank Institutional Development Fund (IDF) grant of $0.475 million played a key role in providing funding support for the various debt-monitoring and management activities undertaken by the EDMU. The Report of the Technical Group on External Debt, which came out in 1998, took into consideration the changing international requirements for debt data monitoring and reporting.

14.94 There are ongoing efforts to further improve the quality of data and increase the scope of computerization. Thus, for example, given the significance of short-term debt for overall external debt management, a Study Group has been created to look into ways of ensuring its more effective monitoring and coverage. The group is expected to suggest that a computerized short-term debt database be created that is amenable to analysis and scenario exercises. Given the volatility of short-term debt flows and the possibility of their nonrenewal in times of crisis, such flows are already strictly monitored and permitted only for trade-related purposes. Another Study Group has been created to look into ways of ensuring more effective monitoring and computerization of nonresident Indian deposits data (see the next section). Further, since external debt flows are to be seen in the overall balance of payments context, other balance of payments components become important and can have a bearing on external debt flows. A separate Study Group, therefore, has been set up for streamlining monitoring and computerization of nondebt flows.

14.95 Efforts are also under way to make India a "resource center" and a "center of excellence" for external debt-management activities so that Indian experience and expertise can be shared with other countries, and learning opportunities broadened.

Monitoring and Management of Nonresident Deposits in India[15]

14.96 In the 1970s, the growth of the current account deficit prompted India to explore alternatives to the traditional source of external finance: concessional borrowing. This led to borrowing from commercial sources, and the introduction of special deposit schemes for nonresident Indians (NRIs). Different NRI deposit schemes were developed in order to meet the various asset preferences of NRIs. This section describes the features of these schemes, the method of data collection, information on their evolution during the 1990s, and some lessons from the Indian experience.

Nonresident deposit schemes

14.97 Essentially there are two types of nonresident deposit schemes: domestic-currency-denominated deposits and foreign-currency-denominated deposits. The first nonresident deposit scheme, introduced in February 1970, was a domestic currency account called the Non-Resident External Rupee Account [NR(E)RA]. Under this scheme, both principal and interest could be repatriated without any restriction, while the exchange risks were borne by the depositors. The rates of interest were initially set by the Reserve Bank of India (RBI) but were fully freed from official control by September 1997. The first foreign-currency-denominated scheme was introduced in November 1975 and was entitled the Foreign Currency Non-Resident (Account) [FCNR(A)]. This account was repatriable, with interest rates fixed by the RBI, taking into account movements in international interest rates. Although the deposit liabilities were held by the commercial banks, the exchange risk was borne by the RBI, and implemented through a mechanism of purchases and sales of foreign currency at notional exchange rates by the RBI from the banks. This scheme was withdrawn with effect from August 1994 in view of its

---

[15]Prepared in the Division of International Finance, Department of Economic Analysis and Policy, Reserve Bank of India, Mumbai.

quasi-fiscal costs and implications for the central bank's balance sheet.

14.98 Subsequently, additional schemes have been introduced, and discontinued, as circumstances have warranted. In particular, nonrepatriable deposit schemes were introduced in the early 1990s. At the time of writing, the latest in the series of non-resident rupee accounts is the Non-Resident Special Rupee Account [NR(S)RA] introduced in April 1999, and, among foreign currency accounts, the Foreign Currency Non-Resident (Bank) [FCNR(B)] scheme. The exchange risk for the latter is managed by the commercial banks and not the RBI. Furthermore, a large proportion of FCNR(B) deposits—for instance, over 90 percent at end-March 2000—are matched by foreign currency assets, which facilitates asset-liability management by accepting banks.

14.99 Also, there has occasionally been issuance of bonds by the State Bank of India, a commercial bank, aimed at nonresidents. Furthermore, nonresident Indians and Overseas Corporate Bodies can channel funds into India through direct investment, the nonresident ordinary deposit (NRO) scheme, private remittances, and a special scheme for returning citizens to import gold and silver.

Monitoring

14.100 As a part of overall financial sector management, the RBI monitors total NRI deposits, both stocks and flows, and adjusts its policies relating to these deposits as warranted by the domestic and international circumstances. Banks are required to report the necessary information on NRI deposits through various regular statements and returns provided to the RBI, including a fortnightly return. The reports are specifically designed to capture the stock and flow data on the various NRI deposits. Further, a study group financed from the IDF of the World Bank is reviewing the reporting arrangements for NRI deposits.

14.101 NRI deposits data come from a large number of branches of commercial banks at widely spread places across India, and many of these branches do not have enough communication infrastructure to submit data in electronic form. These limitations may not be serious since the flow data in respect of such branch offices do not vary significantly over short periods of time. In fact, it was estimated that about 500 large branches of commercial banks in India

accounted for over 85 percent of the overall foreign exchange business, including NRI deposits. The deficiency of coverage could, however, be addressed by remote branches reporting data to their regional or zonal offices, which, in turn, could transmit the consolidated information in electronic form to the RBI through their Head Offices. This new reporting system would provide the stock position of NRI deposits disaggregated by account type, by country of creditor, by maturity (both remaining and original) and by type of currency at the end of every quarter for principal, and, separately, interest costs that have accrued.

Evolution

14.102 Table 14.6 provides information on the evolution of various nonresident deposit accounts during the 1990s. The outstanding balances under NRI deposits have increased from $14 billion at end-March 1991 to $23 billion at end-March 2000. NRI deposits as a percentage of India's external debt remained broadly unchanged over the decade. There was a marked shift in the composition of NRI deposits from foreign currency deposits (about 74 percent of the total in 1991 to about 40 percent in 2000) to domestic-currency-denominated deposits (from about 26 percent in 1991 to 60 percent in 2000), with a significant decline in short-term deposits. Indeed, foreign-currency-denominated deposits actually fell over the decade. This shift occurred as the government decided to stop providing exchange rate guarantees on foreign currency deposits, as losses emerged; and to deregulate interest rates—previously interest rates on these deposits were held at levels significantly above interest rates prevailing in international markets. Also, while not shown in the table, nonrepatriable rupee deposits have been increasing, to over 30 percent of the total NRI deposits as at end-March 2000. Of the total repatriable NRI deposits, the proportion of short-term repatriable deposits declined from around 27 percent at end-March 1991 to about 9 percent at end-March 2000.

Lessons from the Indian experience

14.103 A number of lessons emanate from the Indian experience with nonresident deposit schemes.

14.104 First, for policy purposes, good information is required. In particular, as a part of external debt management, there needs to be careful monitoring of the currency portfolio, especially in terms of currency denomination of deposits, and of the maturity

Table 14.6. Indicators of Nonresident Deposits in India
(Millions of U.S. dollars)

Items	As at end-March					
	1991	1993	1995	1997	1999	2000
FCNR(A)[1]	10,103	10,617	7,051	2,306	0	0
FCNR(B)[2]	0	0	3,063	7,496	8,323	9,069
FC(B&O)D[3]	265	1,037	0	0	0	0
FCON[4]	0	0	10	4	0	0
NR(E)RA[5]	3,618	2,740	4,556	4,983	6,220	6,992
NR(NR)RD[6]	0	621	2,486	5,604	6,758	7,037
NR(S)RA[7]	0	0	0	0	0	0
Total NRI deposits	**13,986**	**15,015**	**17,166**	**20,393**	**21,301**	**23,098**
Domestic-currency-denominated NRI deposits	3,618	3361	7,042	10,587	12,978	14,029
(Percent of total NRI deposits)	(25.9)	(22.4)	(41.0)	(51.9)	(60.9)	(60.7)
Foreign-currency-denominated NRI deposits	10,368	11654	10,124	9,806	8,323	9,069
(Percent of total NRI deposits)	(74.1)	(77.6)	(59.0)	(48.1)	(39.1)	(39.3)
Total external debt[8]	83,801	90,023	99,008	93,470	97,666	98,435
Long-term	75,257	83,683	94,739	86,744	93,279	94,392
Short-term	8,544	6,340	4,269	6,726	4,387	4,043
Proportion of NRI deposits in India's external debt[9]	16.7%	16.0%	14.8%	15.8%	14.9%	16.3%
Proportion of long-term NRI deposits in long-term external debt[9]	13.6%	13.2%	13.1%	12.7%	12.6%	15.4%
Proportion of short-term NRI deposits in short-term external debt	43.8%	53.3%	53.4%	56.1%	50.1%	36.6%
Proportion of long-term repatriable NRI deposits in total repatriable NRI deposits	73.2%	76.7%	84.5%	74.5%	84.9%	90.8%
Proportion of short-term repatriable NRI deposits in total repatriable NRI deposits	26.8%	23.3%	15.5%	25.5%	15.1%	9.2%

Note: This table does not include amounts mobilized from nonresident Indians through issuance of bonds from time to time.
[1] Foreign Currency Non-Repatriable (Account) [FCNR(A)] was withdrawn effective August 1994.
[2] Foreign Currency Non-Resident (Banks) [FCNR(B)] was introduced in May 1993.
[3] Foreign Currency (Banks and Others) Deposits [FC(B&O)D] were withdrawn with effect from July 1993.
[4] Foreign Currency (Ordinary Non-Repatriable) Deposit Scheme [FCON] was withdrawn from August 1994.
[5] Non-Resident (External) Rupee Account [NR(E)RA] was introduced in February 1970.
[6] Non-Resident (Non-Repatriable) Rupee Deposits [NR(NR)RD] was introduced in June 1992.
[7] Non-Resident Special Rupee Account [NR(S)RA] was introduced in April 1999.
[8] Repatriable nonresident deposits (both foreign-currency- and domestic-currency-denominated—such as FCNR(A), FCNR(B), NR(E)RA and FC(B&O)D form part of India's external debt.
[9] Excludes NR(NR)RD accounts, which are not repatriable and so are not included in external debt.

profile, both in terms of original and remaining maturity. The latter data help to identify any bunching of payments, and so it is useful to program the debt-recording software systems to generate data on a remaining-maturity basis.

14.105 Second, from a policy viewpoint, the central bank or the government should refrain from providing exchange guarantee to the depositors, since such guarantees take the form of contingent external liabilities and could pose a systemic threat when reserves are low and exchange rates depreciate very sharply. The focus should be on domestic currency deposits of longer maturity. A steady repayment schedule is preferred because this enables the commercial banks to reduce the potential for serious asset-liability mismatches that may arise.

14.106 Third, when devising these schemes, interest rates on the deposits should be aligned with domestic and international rates, so as to ensure that deposits are attracted while remaining cost effective. Also, an assessment of the degree of substitution between NRI deposits and normal flows from nonresidents in the form of private transfers, workers' remittances, and other non-debt-creating flows from NRIs is required.

14.107 Finally, following the residence criterion, all nonresident deposits should be part of external debt.

However, India does not include nonresident non-repatriable deposits in its external debt statistics because the principal is not repatriable and hence no external liabilities arise, and the funds stay within the Indian economy.

Israel

Measurement of External Debt[16]

14.108 The Bank of Israel's Foreign Exchange Activity Department (FEAD) measures Israel's external debt position, using detailed loan-by-loan data provided by the Israeli Government and the nonbank private sector. Reported balance sheet data are used to compile external debt data of banks. The external debt data are published quarterly and, along with external assets owned by Israeli residents, are included in the Israeli IIP statement. This case study describes the loan-by-loan system used by the FEAD and the output it generates.

Reporting of loan-by-loan data

14.109 Most of the external debt data of the public sector are obtained, on a regular basis, from the Ministry of Finance. These data cover all loans that the government receives from creditors abroad, including government bond issues in international markets. The nonbank private sector (a private individual or a firm) must report within 15 days of receipt any loans received from abroad that have a value equivalent to $100,000 or more. These data cover all loans that firms and individuals receive from creditors abroad, including Israeli companies' issues of bonds in international markets and ownership loans received.

14.110 The following details of each loan are reported (see Figure 14.1) and entered into the FEAD's system:
- *Primary details*: Loan receipt date, amount, and currency;
- *Borrower*: Name and borrower type (such as government, central bank, firm, or individual);
- *Lender*: Name, country of residence, and lender type (such as foreign bank, branch of Israeli bank abroad, foreign government, IMF, World Bank, issue of tradable bonds, foreign firm, individual foreign resident, or ownership loan);

- *Interest rate type*: Fixed or variable rate;
- *Interest rate (percent)*: Fixed rate or spread above variable rate;
- *Principal payment schedule*: Includes final payment date; and
- *Interest payment schedule*.

14.111 Also, during the entry of these details into the database the following additional fields are automatically calculated:
- *Credit term* (months): Defined as the number of months from the date of receipt of the loan until final repayment; this field can be used to attribute the debt by loan term: short-term debt, medium-term debt, and long-term debt;
- *Grace* (months): the number of months between the date of receipt of the loan and the first repayment of the principal;
- *Calculated interest* (on loan receipt date): For fixed-rate loans, this is the interest rate figure itself; for variable-rate loans, this is equal to the value of the variable rate base plus the spread above it; and
- *Spread above LIBOR* (on loan receipt date): For fixed-rate loans, this is the calculated spread above LIBOR (London interbank offered rate).

Aggregate data compiled[17]

14.112 In addition to calculated aggregated loan and bond figures, and commercial bank balance-sheet data, the FEAD maintains aggregate external debt data on nonresidents' ownership of domestically issued bonds, and on the balance of suppliers' credit received by Israeli importers (and extended by Israeli exporters), based on an FEAD quarterly survey of companies involved in foreign trade. The same system contains figures on external assets owned by residents, including equities, bonds, loans, deposits, and direct investment (ownership loans).

14.113 Data quality checks are undertaken at the individual loan level and also by comparing the loan-by-loan data with information on transactions, which are drawn mainly from bank reports, and with the balance-sheet data of large companies. The database covers all public and banking sector loans and over 90 percent of the nonbank private sector loans.

---

[16]Prepared by the Bank of Israel.

[17]Apart from debt-related data, the same system contains data on nonresident portfolio investment in Israeli equities and direct investment of nonresidents in Israel.

Figure 14.1. Israel: Report Form on Loans Received by Local Residents from Foreign Residents[1]

1. Loan details

☐ New loan ☐ Loan particulars update ☐ Early redemption ☐ Loan renewal

Sum _____ Currency _____ Currency Code* _____ Receipt Date _____

2. Borrower details (local resident)

Borrower identifying number (identity card/corp. reg. no.)	Borrower name	Economic branch	Economic branch code*
_____	_____	_____	_____

3. Lender details (foreign resident)

Lender name	Lender type	Lender code*	Lender country	Country code*
_____	_____	_____	_____	_____

4. Principal payment schedule

1. Regular payments

First payment date	No. of payments	Frequency (months)	Final payment date
_____	_____	_____	_____

2. Irregular payments

Sum _____ Date _____

Sum _____ Date _____

Sum _____ Date _____

Sum _____ Date _____

Sum _____ Date _____

Additional payments - write below (comments)

5. Interest rate details

Interest rate type: Interest rate (%) ☐

☐ Fixed
☐ LIBOR ("interest rate" is spread above LIBOR)
☐ Interest free
☐ Other _____

6. Interest payment schedule

| 1 | Interest payment schedule coincides with principal payment schedule.

| 2 | Regular payments (equidistant payment dates)

First payment date	No. of payments	Frequency (months)
_____	_____	_____

| 3 | Interest sum discounted in advance:

Sum _____

| 4 | Irregular payments:
Dates

1 _____   4 _____

2 _____   5 _____

3 _____   6 _____

Comments: _____
_____
_____

7. Details of loan reporter

Name	Signature	Date	Telephone no.	Address
_____	_____	_____	_____	_____

*To be filled out if loan form is handled by an Israeli commercial bank.

Bank code* ☐   Branch code* ☐   Loan number (for BOI use) ☐

[1]Reporting requirement is that of the local resident—an individual or a corporation—receiving a loan of at least $100,000; with the report to be submitted within 15 days of loan receipt.

Output

14.114 From the information held on the database, the Bank of Israel publishes quarterly tables on the external debt, in U.S. dollar terms. For the public, nonbank private, and banking sectors, and by source of external debt, data are presented on the stock of outstanding external debt; the original term to maturity; the principal currency composition; and external debt receipts and principal payments. Also provided is information by sector on net debt—that is, gross debt liabilities less ownership of foreign debt liabilities by Israeli residents—and principal and interest repayment schedules.

Mexico

Registration of Private Debt[18]

14.115 The Mexican system of measuring private sector external debt has developed over the past two decades. Beginning with external debt difficulties of the early 1980s, the system has evolved as exchange controls have been repealed and economic conditions have changed. This case study explains that evolution, and sets out the present situation.

14.116 On August 5, 1982, Mexico declared a moratorium on principal payments on external debt. On September 1, 1982, across-the-board exchange controls were instituted and replaced three months later by a simple exchange control system, whereby two foreign exchange markets would operate simultaneously: one subject to control and the other not.

Data collection methods in the era of exchange controls

14.117 At the time of the introduction of exchange controls in 1982, the Mexican government had no official data on the amount of private sector external debt outstanding. So there was a need to develop a debt-registration system, whose main purpose was to facilitate exchange control operations. In the payments moratorium notice of August 5, 1982, and subsequently in the exchange control decree published on December 13, 1982, those private enterprises requesting foreign exchange to service their

debts were required to register their financing with the Secretaría de Hacienda y Crédito Público (Secretariat of Finance and Public Credit—SHCP). A special unit within the SHCP was set up to start monitoring private external debt, and this unit created a Register of Loans Payable in Foreign Exchange to Financial Institutions Abroad (the Register), and introduced a report form called the Constancia de Registro (Record of Registration) to collect the data. This report form needed to be completed for a private enterprise to receive authorization to obtain foreign exchange from national banks.

14.118 The report form identified the main contractual features of foreign exchange borrowing by private sector enterprises from foreign financial institutions. It covered the type of financing, the existing loan balance, the method of payment, and the payment schedule listing each outstanding payment with due date, and principal and interest amounts. When the registration requirement was introduced, all the enterprises quickly came forward to register their external debt because they could not otherwise obtain foreign exchange to service their debts.

14.119 In addition to the loans registered in the SHCP, a register of debt to nonbank foreign suppliers was created in October 1982 in the Secretariat of Trade and Industrial Development (SECOFI), with the same purpose as the register of foreign currency loans. In other words, the record of registration provided information on debt service to the authorities, and was a requirement for residents if they needed to obtain foreign currency from national banks. This register was closed in January 1983, and the outstanding balances were refinanced by suppliers under a long-term scheme.

14.120 Also, in 1983, the central bank set up a fund through which private sector debtors could repay foreign creditors. This helped to improve the registration of private sector debt. This fund was part of the program known as FICORCA (Trusteeship Coverage of Exchange Risk), and existed from April to October 1983. This program required private sector enterprises to restructure their foreign debts—for instance, into maturities of eight years with four years' grace, or six years with three years' grace. If the enterprise made the payments in local currency, FICORCA would pay principal and interest in foreign currency to the account of the enterprise, so that

---

[18]Prepared by the Department of Public Credit, Mexico.

the enterprise could service its restructured debts to foreign banks. A similar program was reintroduced for a short period in 1987 and 1988 and was known as the FICORCA Facility Agreement.

14.121 Once private enterprises regained access to external financing, in 1984, they were required to register new debt with the SHCP. Indeed, the authorities decided that, in order to continue to have access to foreign exchange, private enterprises would be required not only to report new debt at the time of creation, but also to report twice a year on their outstanding debt. This continued until 1991. So, twice a year the authorities made public announcements to all private sector enterprises and published in the most widely distributed major newspapers in the country the registration numbers of loans to report between January 1 and March 31 and between July 1 and September 30 of each year. Enterprises were required to provide the authorized documentation for the original borrowing and the subsequent debt servicing.

14.122 In addition to the loans registered in the SHCP, a register of debt to nonbank suppliers was created in SECOFI. Thus, in October 1982, the register of amounts owed to foreign suppliers was set up with the same purpose as the register of foreign currency loans. In other words, the record of registration provided information on debt service, and permitted the purchase of foreign currency from national banks by the debtors. This register was closed in January 1983, and the outstanding balances were refinanced by suppliers under a long-term scheme.

14.123 Outstanding amounts payable by the Mexican banking system, nationalized in September 1982, were never subject to registration. The central bank only required completion of a survey form that is still used, showing the position of the banks' accounts but not future payments.

Data collection methods following the repeal of exchange controls

14.124 An official Exchange Control Decree repealed exchange controls on November 10, 1991, since there was no longer any reason to maintain the two-tiered foreign exchange market at the controlled and market rates as established. Also, the Register of Foreign Currency Loans Payable Abroad to Financial Institutions and the Constancia de Registro were abolished. Indeed, since the termination of the exchange

control regime, private enterprises are no longer legally required to report the status of their external liabilities to the SHCP. However, the SHCP has found it necessary to continue to monitor and publish data on private sector external debt. This required the reestablishment of a means of collecting data that covered the main features of borrowing by private sector enterprises from foreign financial institutions.

14.125 Initially after the repeal of exchange controls, data were collected periodically through survey questionnaires sent to the major enterprises having a representative level of indebtedness relative to total private external debt. With the cooperation of some 100 indebted industrial groups, a database was designed for processing the data collected. This was used to draw up a statistical bulletin on private sector external debt and included a number of statistical tables that gave a clear picture of the level of external indebtedness. The level of participation by debtors was initially excellent.

14.126 However, following another crisis in the mid-1990s, it was once again necessary to implement a system whereby private enterprises provided information on an ongoing as opposed to periodic basis. An official request, similar to the public announcements mentioned above, was prepared requiring the private enterprises to report estimates of principal payments both on recent borrowing and on earlier outstanding amounts. In addition, data began to be sourced from the Mexican Stock Market (BMV) to complement the private external debt statistics; the BMV releases a quarterly financial report on borrowing by industrial corporations.

14.127 Most recently, the system has evolved such that data on private sector external debt are collected from a number of sources so as to ensure that the data published are reliable, are collected expeditiously, and are informative.

14.128 The principal source of information is now the BMV, which collects data quarterly on Mexican corporate liabilities. The BMV report form includes a breakdown of external debt by type of credit, using the following classification system: commercial banks, bonds, and foreign trade credit. The report form also provides the name of the creditor, the amount of the financing, currency of issuance, the borrowing date, the maturity date, and the estimated payments over the next four years, including the outstanding balances, the repayment schedule for the coming four years, and a classification by loan type.

14.129 Other external data sources include foreign-owned credit rating agencies, such as Duff and Phelps, Moody's, and Standard & Poor's. The publications of these agencies include information on debt they rate, which SHCP consults. Also, the debt unit frequently checks with the Undersecretariat of the SHCP for the information submitted by private enterprises when they withhold tax payments on interest payable abroad.

14.130 With this information, the SHCP reviews each credit and cross-checks the different sources, so as not to duplicate information.

14.131 Enterprises that are not listed on the BMV, have no debt ratings, and file no tax returns are requested to cooperate by completing a survey questionnaire, providing information to the SHCP on all the characteristics of their liabilities, updating the information on balances on a quarterly frequency.

14.132 All the information collected is maintained in a database, which is carefully checked to ensure that the debt of enterprises is not entered more than once, so as to avoid duplicate reports. From this database, a number of outputs can be generated, including the level of indebtedness and debt classification by enterprise, creditor, currency, and maturity.

Verification of figures

14.133 When exchange controls were established and after having registered the debt of most industrial groups, reports were produced from the database classifying the debt by creditor and with the details of each financing. This information was cross-checked with data from the major foreign creditor banks through their representative offices in Mexico. The overall balances by creditor bank were verified with the unit that received the report form from the creditor bank. This type of verification is not undertaken today, since it is mandatory for creditor banks to report to the central bank under the rules authorizing them to grant loans to Mexico. The report now covers both public sector and private sector external debt. Efforts are currently being made to have the form include information not only on the balances outstanding as traditionally reported, but also on the payment schedule for the outstanding

debt, by quarter for the first year and annually for the following three years.[19]

Dissemination

14.134 The statistical data on Mexico's total external debt, including private debt, are published in the statistical tables in *Mexico Economic and Financial Statistics—Data Book,* a biannual document published by the SHCP and distributed to foreign banks in the SHCP's quarterly review entitled *Estadísticas oportunas de finanzas públicas y deuda pública* (Timely Public Finance and Public Debt Statistics), published through the Directorate General of Financial Planning. The data also appear in the quarterly presentation on the Internet via the SHCP's webpage.

14.135 Information on private sector debt is presented for the commercial banks and the nonbank private sector, and the sources of finance are provided—commercial banks, and other liabilities for commercial bank debtors; and capital markets, commercial banks, and external trade-related debt for nonbank private sector debtors. An annual amortization schedule for the nonbank private sector external debt for the remaining portion of the current year, and the following three years, is provided.

New Zealand

Experience in Collecting Foreign Currency Hedging Information[20]

14.136 In 1998, major users of external debt statistics in New Zealand were concerned that by not taking account of hedging activity, New Zealand's published external debt statistics were overstating the extent of the economy's exposure to currency movements. As a consequence, in June 1999, Statistics New Zealand (SNZ) first published indicative information about the hedging of New Zealand's external debt denominated in foreign currency—for March 31, 1998 and 1999—alongside, and as a sup-

---

[19]While the compilation of these creditor bank data is the exclusive responsibility of the central bank, the obligation to report to the authorities and the public on the performance of external private debt is the responsibility of the Finance Secretariat. Also, the Finance Secretariat is responsible for establishing the guidelines for authorization of the operations of foreign financial institutions in Mexico, and, in conjunction with the central bank, it verifies the activity of foreign banks.

[20]Prepared by Statistics New Zealand.

plement to, New Zealand's Overseas Debt statistics.[21] These supplementary data—disaggregated by currency and into two institutional sectors—provided estimates of the extent of hedging of New Zealand's foreign currency external debt using financial derivatives contracts and natural hedges. The data also provided estimates of unhedged external debt. In addition, net market value estimates of the financial derivatives contracts were published, also with a sectoral breakdown. SNZ has continued to publish supplementary hedging information annually. This case study sets out the experience of SNZ in setting up and operating the survey in its early years, and the lessons learned.

14.137 In the presentation of external debt statistics, foreign-currency-denominated external debt is converted into New Zealand dollars at the exchange rate prevailing at the survey date (March 31). Given this methodology, and with external debt denominated in foreign currencies accounting for about half of New Zealand's gross external debt at the time, the depreciation of the New Zealand dollar between March 31, 1997 and 1998 was estimated to have accounted for 38 percent of the increase in the value of New Zealand's external debt between those two dates. Anticipating significant user interest when the March 1998 external debt statistics data were published, the SNZ gave prominence to this estimate and to the compilation methodology used. Nevertheless, some major users of the statistics questioned their relevance, believing that the total external debt statistics overstated the true external exposure of the economy, because a significant portion of the debt was probably hedged against exchange rate movements.

The project

14.138 With the collection and publication of statistics on New Zealand's net asset and liability positions in financial derivatives not due until 2001, in 1998 the SNZ felt an immediate need for hedging information that would place the published external debt statistics into a risk-management context. Consequently, the SNZ undertook a project to collect data on:

---

[21]"Overseas debt" is the term used for the SNZ survey that collects data on New Zealand's external debt, and the published statistics. The survey measures New Zealand's total overseas debt as at March 31 each year, and collects data from both private and government sector organizations.

- The extent of the foreign currency hedging of New Zealand's overseas debt; and
- Estimates of the net market value of the financial derivatives contracts.

14.139 Data were to be collected from those resident enterprises that accounted for approximately 80 percent of external debt denominated in foreign currencies. In view of the limited coverage of the hedging supplement, the results were intended to be indicative estimates.

14.140 The project began in October 1998, with the intention of collecting retrospective data as at March 31, 1998, by December 31, 1998. Thereafter, a decision would be made about whether to proceed with a further collection of data as at March 31, 1999. It was expected that the need for the hedging supplement would cease once the project to implement *BPM5* in full was completed, in 2001.

14.141 The project was undertaken by the staff of the Balance of Payments Division (BOP staff) of the SNZ. An essential feature of the early stages of the project was the close consultation between the BOP staff and Reserve Bank of New Zealand (RBNZ) staff, and, separately, a private sector bank with which the BOP staff had had previous discussions on the impact of financial derivatives on balance of payments statistics. The RBNZ offered advice and consultation on several occasions during the course of the project. The private sector bank offered advice from the perspectives of a user of the published statistics, and the perspective of being a market participant and data supplier. The cooperation and advice received from both these organizations was invaluable to the success of the project.

14.142 Initial development work within SNZ included determining an initial set of data requirements and identifying the enterprises to be surveyed from the population of the Total Overseas Debt survey. In the event, 20 enterprises (plus the official sector) were selected, of which all except one reported the data for the 1998 survey. While one further enterprise was unable to supply data for the 1999 and 2000 surveys, nevertheless the effective sample of the hedging supplement encompassed 75 to 81 percent of total foreign-currency-denominated external debt in the 1998, 1999, and 2000 surveys. While these enterprises were at first expected to be mostly banks, in fact nine of the enterprises selected were nonbank corporates. For the purposes of the survey, a two-sector classification was used: banks, and the "corporate and official" sector.

Consultations

14.143 The initial set of data requirements was discussed with the private sector bank, and separately with the RBNZ. This first round of consultations identified:

- The need for a short-term/long-term split based on original maturity, since some respondents were expected to find the reporting of hedges for short-term instruments too difficult due to daily refinancing ("rollover") and pricing;
- The need to split the data request into "hedging by financial derivatives contract" and "natural hedge";
- The need to ask respondents to report their hedging with both residents and nonresidents; by asking respondents to report all their positions, the likelihood of double counting would be reduced.

14.144 Following the amendments to the draft hedging supplement questionnaire, a second round of consultation was undertaken—an essential aspect of the project. This consultation comprised personal visits by BOP staff to ten of the enterprises selected to be surveyed, involved a discussion of the objectives of the questionnaire and its reporting requirements, and allowed BOP staff to hear the views of the respondents. Those respondents not visited personally were contacted by telephone, and a copy of the draft questionnaire sent for comment; in nearly all these cases feedback on the questionnaire was received. SNZ staff encountered a high level of cooperation among virtually all of the respondents visited or contacted, certainly once the objectives of the hedging supplement were explained.

14.145 A clear message arising from the consultations, which were reviewed with the RBNZ, was the need to customize the questionnaire, both in terms of the sector of the respondent and each individual respondent within each sector. For the nonbank corporates, it was decided to differentiate the "natural hedge" question into "hedging by balance sheet assets," and "hedging by other means—for example, expected foreign exchange receipts from exports." This made the scope of the inquiry clearer to respondents and enhanced the usefulness of the results for risk analysis purposes by separating hedges that take the form of balance-sheet assets from those that do

not. The process for the collection of retrospective data for March 31, 1998 was too far advanced for this distinction to be included in that survey, but it was incorporated into the 1999 survey.

14.146 Other features of particular interest emerging from the second round of consultations were as follows:

- Whatever the term of the underlying liability, associated derivatives contracts are often of a shorter term and rolled over (or renegotiated) through the life of the underlying liability. The effect is that at each rollover, the issuer will book to their accounts profits and losses made on their derivatives contracts. Because the survey is a snapshot of the market value of contracts in place as at March 31, the market-value results take no account of profits or losses recorded from the earlier succession of contracts.
- Banks in general, and some of the nonbanks with complex financial operations, found it difficult to extract the required market-value information. Given that frequent rollovers of debt, and the pooling of assets and liabilities for risk-management purposes characterized banks' operations, direct matching of an overseas liability to a particular hedge was often not possible, and alternative ways of providing information were established on a case-by-case basis. Therefore, the market-value results for banks were regarded as indicative estimates only. Generally, the market-value estimates for the less complex nonbanks were regarded as of better quality, since these were typically enterprises with a small number of external foreign currency liabilities matched to specific financial derivatives contracts.
- Distinguishing the residence of counterparties to the derivatives contracts was a problem for some respondents. Those nonbank corporates who dealt directly with nonresident counterparties were easily able to do this; other nonbank corporates who dealt with resident intermediaries indicated that their usual practice was to deal with a resident bank. Banks indicated that their practice was to engage with nonresident counterparties.

Hedging supplement questionnaire

14.147 Incorporating the lessons of the consultations, the data requirements were set out in two questionnaire types: one type structured for banks, the other for nonbank corporates (Figure 14.2). In

Figure.14.2. New Zealand: Foreign Currency Liabilities—Questionnaires for Banks and Nonbank Corporate Entities

Questionnaire for Banks

TABLE I

Hedging of Long-Term Foreign Currency Liabilities[1]

Currency[2] of contractual overseas liabilities **1**	Contractual overseas liabilities outstanding as at 31 March 2000 *record amounts in foreign currency (million)* **2**	Percentage of these contractual overseas liabilities as:		Not Hedged **3c**
		Hedged by:		
		financial derivatives contracts **3a**	balance sheet assets **3b**	
USD				
AUD				
JPY				
CHF				
DEM				

(1) These with original contractual maturity of 1 year or more.
(2) The following currencies are listed here as an example only.
Columns 1–4—see "Notes to Tables"

Any comments regarding information you gave in this table:

_____
_____
_____

Questionnaire for Banks

TABLE 2

Hedging of Short-Term Foreign Currency Liabilities(1)

Currency(2) of contractual overseas liabilities 1	Contractual overseas liabilities outstanding as at 31 March 2000 record amounts in foreign currency (million) 2	Percentage of these contractual overseas liabilities as:			Total NZ dollar original value of obligation on contractual overseas liabilities at 31 March 2000 $NZ(m) 4
		Hedged by:		Not Hedged 3c	
		financial derivatives contracts 3a	balance sheet assets 3b		
USD					
AUD					
JPY					
CHF					
DEM					

(1) These with original contractual maturity of less than 1 year.
(2) The following currencies are listed here as an example only. Columns 1–4–see "Notes to Tables"

Any comments regarding information you gave in this table:

THANK YOU FOR YOUR TIME.

Figure 14.2 (continued)

Questionnaire for Corporates

TABLE 3

Hedging of Long-Term Foreign Currency Liabilities[1]

Currency[2] of contractual overseas liabilities	Contractual overseas liabilities outstanding as at 31 March 2000 *record amounts in foreign currency (million)*	Percentage of these contractual overseas liabilities as:				Market value of the derivative contracts that hedge overseas liabilities as at 31 March 2000 with a			
		Hedged by:		Naturally Hedged by expected future revenues (e.g. export receipts)	Not Hedged	resident counter-party		non-resident counter-party	
		financial derivatives contracts	balance sheet assets			financial derivatives in a net asset position $NZ(m)	financial derivatives in a net liability position $NZ(m)	financial derivatives in a net asset position $NZ(m)	financial derivatives in a net liability position $NZ(m)
1	**2**	**3a**	**3b**	**3c**	**3d**	**4a**	**4b**	**4c**	**4d**
USD									
AUD									
DEM									
JPY									
CHF									

(1)These with original contractual maturity of 1 year or more.
(2)The following currencies are listed here as an example only.
Columns 1–4d—see "Notes to Tables"

Any comments regarding information you gave in this table:

_____

_____

_____

_____

Questionnaire for Corporates

TABLE 4

Hedging of Short-Term Foreign Currency Liabilities[1]

Currency[2] of contractual overseas liabilities 1	Contractual overseas liabilities outstanding as at 31 March 2000 *record amounts in foreign currency (million)* 2	Percentage of these contractual overseas liabilities as:				Market value of the derivative contracts that hedge overseas liabilities as at 31 March 2000 with a			
		Hedged by:		Naturally Hedged by expected future revenues (e.g. export receipts) 3c	Not Hedged 3d	resident counter-party		non-resident counter-party	
		financial derivatives contracts 3a	balance sheet assets 3b			financial derivatives in a net asset position $NZ(m) 4a	financial derivatives in a net liability position $NZ(m) 4b	financial derivatives in a net asset position $NZ(m) 4c	financial derivatives in a net liability position $NZ(m) 4d
USD									
AUD									
DEM									
JPY									
CHF									

(1)These with original contractual maturity of less than 1 year.
(2)The following currencies are listed here as an example only.
Columns 1–4d—see "Notes to Tables"

Any comments regarding information you gave in this table:

_____

_____

_____

THANK YOU FOR YOUR TIME.

Figure 14.2 (concluded)

GUIDE TO TABLES

General

1. Please refer to "Notes to Tables 1 & 2."

2. In column 2 of the table, please show your gross outstanding overseas liabilities by foreign currency. It's your option to report (a) grouping all your (e.g. USD) liabilities together or (b) report each (e.g. USD) liability on a separate line.

3. If possible please provide data by the term structure, long-term overseas liabilities (Table 1) and short-term overseas liabilities (Table 2). If can't distinguish, please provide all data together in one table.

Please Note: These are simplified examples for your guidance with notional exchange rates.

Example 1 Table line 1 USD

November 1999—The NZ company enters into contractual liability of $US500 million to nonresident lenders (column 1 & 2).

At the same time, the NZ borrower enters 100% of U.S. borrowings in a swap contract with a nonresident counterparty whereby the NZ borrower receives $NZ725 million in exchange for $US500 million at exchange rate 1$NZ = $US0.69.

At 31 March 2000—the exchange rate is 1$NZ = $US0.55, the market value of the derivative contract on $US500 million is $NZ909 million, and is recorded in a net assets position as positive $NZ184 million (column 4C; 909–725=184).

Example 2 Table line 2 AUD

November 1999—The NZ company enters into contractual liability of $AU100 million to non-resident lenders (column 1 & 2).

At the same time, the NZ borrower enters 85% of AU borrowings in a swap contract with a nonresident counterparty whereby the NZ borrower receives $NZ106 million in exchange for $AU85 million at exchange rate 1$NZ = $AU0.80.

At 31 March 2000—the exchange rate is 1$NZ = $AU0.83, the market value of the derivative contract on $AU85 million is $NZ102 million, and is recorded in a net liability position as negative $NZ4 million (column 4D; 85 – 106 = –4).

Example 3 Table line 3 DEM

DEM liabilities completely matched to, e.g., expected export receipts.

Example 4 Table line 4 JPY

Short-term trade credits and JPY not covered at all.

Example 5 Table line 5 CHF

CHF liabilities matched to foreign-currency-denominated assets recorded on the balance sheet—e.g., foreign currency bank deposits, export bills and foreign trade debtors, investments in overseas subsidiaries.

Hedging of Foreign Currency Liabilities

Currency[2] of contractual overseas liabilities	Contractual overseas liabilities outstanding as at 31 March 2000 *record amounts in foreign currency (million)*	Percentage of these contractual overseas liabilities as:				Market value of the derivative contracts that hedge overseas liabilities as at 31 March 2000 with a			
		Hedged by:		Naturally Hedged by expected future revenues (e.g. export receipts)	Not Hedged	resident counter-party		non-resident counter-party	
		financial derivatives contracts	balance sheet assets			financial derivatives in a net asset position $NZ(m)	financial derivatives in a net liability position $NZ(m)	financial derivatives in a net asset position $NZ(m)	financial derivatives in a net liability position $NZ(m)
1	2	3a	3b	3c	3d	4a	4b	4c	4d
USD	500	100%				0	0	184	
AUD	100	85%			15%	0	0		–4
DEM	200			100%		0	0	0	0
JPY	10				100%	0	0	0	0
CHF	300		100%						

addition, within each questionnaire type, the basic form was customized into several versions to meet the needs of various respondents. Typically, the customized form of the questionnaire was determined during the consultation meeting with a respondent, redrafted by BOP staff, and sent back to the respondent for confirmation and then completion. Additionally, a set of definitions of terms used and a guide to the questionnaire with worked examples were supplied to each respondent.

14.148 Each of the two questionnaire types had two parts; the first part requested foreign currency external debt data and established the extent and type of hedging; the second part requested market-value information. Separate tables requested data on a long-term and short-term attribution (original maturity basis).

14.149 In the section on the extent and type of hedging, respondents are asked to report:
- The currency of their original contractual overseas liabilities as at the survey date, March 31;
- The foreign currency amounts of their contractual overseas liabilities as at the survey date, March 31 (this figure was to be the same as reported in the overseas debt survey); and
- The percentage of these overseas liabilities that at the survey date were:
  – hedged, using financial derivatives;
  – hedged naturally against balance sheet assets;
  – hedged naturally against other receipts (nonbank corporates only); or
  – not hedged.

14.150 In the market-value section of the questionnaire, respondents were asked to report the market value of derivatives contracts that hedge overseas liabilities as at the survey date. Net asset and net liability positions were asked for separately, and by resident and nonresident counterparties.

Implementation

14.151 After the first survey, it was decided that the results were of sufficient quality and significance to warrant continuation of the project. So, data were collected as at March 31, 1999, and the 1998 and 1999 results were published as supplementary information alongside the 1999 Overseas Debt statistics. In line with expectations at the start of the project, the supplementary hedging information was pub-

lished with a status of "indicative estimates" (as opposed to "official statistics"), because of the limited coverage of the survey and the indicative nature of the net market-value financial derivatives data from the banks and certain nonbanks. Nonetheless, users reacted favorably to the release of these data, and there was an increase in confidence in the quality of the Overseas Debt statistics.

14.152 Therefore, the hedging supplement was repeated in 2000, with the sample of respondent enterprises updated using more recent information available from the Total Overseas Debt and Annual Capital Account surveys.

Lessons learned

14.153 Responsiveness to the needs of users of published statistics and of respondents is important. The hedging supplement project arose from user concerns, while the responsiveness to the circumstances of respondents contributed to the usefulness of the published results. For instance, customizing the questionnaire according to sector and within sectors ensured better-quality data than would have been achieved with one standard questionnaire, and discussing alternatives with respondents when they were unable to supply the market-value financial derivatives data as originally requested allowed the BOP staff to produce estimates that might not otherwise have been possible.

14.154 Consultation was essential. There were several aspects to this:
- Consultation with respondents was essential. Personal visits were of greatest value because they allowed a two-way exchange of information; increased respondent understanding of, and support for, the survey objectives; and enabled BOP staff to learn more about market practice, resulting in a better questionnaire, better-quality data, and a greater understanding of the data supplied.
- Bringing together respondents (those people who actually complete the questionnaire) and users of the published statistics from the same organization was very useful; these two groups sometimes had little knowledge of each other's positions. Bringing them together with the BOP staff provided the opportunity for all parties to better appreciate the roles of all the parties involved.
- Pooling of knowledge was key. The consultation and liaison between the SNZ and the private bank,

and the statistical office and the central bank, were an essential feature of the project. The private bank provided the perspectives of a user of the statistical output, a market participant, and a data supplier; and the central bank offered conceptual and technical advice, and an overall perspective of financial market operations. In addition, consultation between SNZ and the survey respondents gave further insight into market operations. This pooling of information was especially beneficial because the measurement of hedging was a new and highly technical subject, and new territory for a national statistical office.

Future of the supplement

14.155 The original intention had been that, provided the results warranted, the hedging supplement would continue only until 2001, when the project to implement *BPM5* in full would be completed. However, following the positive user response, it was decided to continue the supplement, but in a modified form. Net market-value data are to be collected in the new Quarterly International Investment Survey—a balance of payments form being brought into line with *BPM5* requirements—which, as originally planned, will cover both hedged and trading positions in financial derivatives. The hedging supplement will continue to be repeated annually, for data as at March 31, but will collect data only on the extent of hedging by type, sector, and currency. That is, the function of the hedging supplement will be to continue to complement the external debt statistics.

Philippines

System for Monitoring the External Debt of the Private Sector[22]

14.156 The Philippines extensively taps foreign funds to help support its large development financing requirements. Cognizant of the need for a systematic approach to managing external borrowings, the government enacted a law on foreign borrowings in the mid-1960s that instituted broad policies and safeguards on foreign borrowings. Subsequent legislation defined borrowing limits and vested

authority in the central bank to oversee compliance with the law from a foreign exchange standpoint.

14.157 Administrative mechanisms were established in the early 1970s to implement the provisions of law and rationalize the debt-management process. The monitoring system covers foreign borrowings of both the public and private sectors. The government has always recognized the important role that the private sector plays in spurring economic growth and development, and hence the need to monitor its foreign borrowing. With exchange controls then in place, it was not difficult to implement the system and ensure compliance therewith. The system has evolved over the years to address new developments, including the progressive dismantling of barriers to capital movements. The 1990s also highlighted the importance of monitoring private sector borrowings as private sector enterprises incurred substantial amounts of external debt during the period to finance their development projects and other major undertakings, including those under build-operate-transfer and similar arrangements.

14.158 Management of the country's external debt involves the concerted efforts of various government agencies, including the central socioeconomic planning body—a top-level interagency committee and the Finance Department. The Bangko Sentral ng Pilipinas (Bangko Sentral, or the Bank)[23] is at the forefront of these activities, having been mandated to ensure compliance with the provisions of law regarding foreign exchange concerns. The Bank keeps track of the debt stock, maintains outstanding liabilities within manageable levels, and ensures that borrowings are obtained on the best available terms. It currently performs these activities through the Monetary Board (its highest policymaking body) and the International Operations Department[24] (which handles the day-to-day activities of debt management).

---

[22]Prepared by the Bangko Sentral ng Pilipinas.

[23]The former Central Bank of the Philippines was reorganized into the Bangko Sentral ng Pilipinas effective July 3, 1993. As the new central monetary authority provided for in the Philippine Constitution, it enjoys fiscal and administrative autonomy.

[24]Formerly the Management of External Debt Department (MEDD), which was originally organized in 1970 as the External Debt Monitoring Office. MEDD was renamed as International Operations Department in October 1999 with the broadening of its responsibilities to include trade and investments.

Debt-management tools

14.159 The Bank presently employs a number of debt-management tools that were initiated and fine-tuned during the past three decades. These include Bangko Sentral policy issuances, which outline the rules, regulations, guidelines, and procedures for foreign borrowing activities (new issuances are promptly disseminated to the public and are complemented by press releases and structured briefing sessions, as appropriate); and administrative mechanisms, including an approval and registration process and a debt-monitoring system, both of which cover liabilities of all sectors of the economy.

Loan approval and registration

14.160 Approval for a loan proposal is applied for by a private sector borrower and must be granted by the Bangko Sentral before the covering documents may be executed and the funds disbursed. The Bank's evaluation process involves a thorough review of the proposal to determine, among other things, consistency of loan purpose with the country's overall development thrust, benefits expected from the project, reasonableness of financial terms and conditions, and the loan's impact on the country's total debt-service burden vis-à-vis the economy's capacity to meet maturing obligations.

14.161 In order to ensure compliance with the terms and conditions of the Bangko Sentral's approval, the private sector is required to register foreign loans following receipt of borrowed funds. The borrower is required to submit a copy of the signed loan documents as well as proofs of disbursement and utilization of loan proceeds. After documents are found to be satisfactory, a Bangko Sentral Registration Document (BSRD) is issued that authorizes the borrower to buy foreign exchange from local banks for debt servicing on scheduled due dates. However, purchases of foreign exchange from banks to cover any payments not consistent with the loan terms reflected in the BSRD require prior Bangko Sentral approval.

14.162 Prior to the 1990s, and consistent with existing controls on foreign exchange inflows and outflows, all foreign borrowing proposals had to be approved and registered by the old central bank. Each purchase of foreign exchange from the banking system for debt servicing was likewise subject to prior central bank approval. But with the liberalization of foreign exchange rules starting in the early 1990s, regulations were modified such that private sector borrowers[25] were, in general, given the option not to undergo the approval and registration processes, *provided* they did not purchase foreign exchange for debt servicing from the banking system.[26] This approach is consistent with the freedom residents now have in the use of their foreign exchange receipts that were previously subject to the mandatory surrender requirement.

14.163 Nonetheless, despite the relaxation of foreign exchange regulations, most borrowers (particularly those with substantial funding requirements) choose to obtain approval from the Bangko Sentral for their foreign borrowings to ensure access to banking system resources, whenever necessary, to meet maturing debt payments. A large number of international creditors also require Philippine enterprises to have their borrowings approved by and registered with the Bangko Sentral to preclude any possible difficulty in servicing the account.

Monitoring system for external debt

14.164 The current (September 2000) external-debt-monitoring system covers all external obligations under any maturity category (short-, medium-, and long-term) in any form (loans, advances, deposits, bonds, etc.) owed by the different sectors of the economy (the monetary authority, central government, bank and nonbank enterprises, both state- and privately owned) to all types of creditors (multilateral and bilateral sources, foreign banks and nonbank financial institutions, foreign suppliers and buyers, bondholders/noteholders, and others).

14.165 The system, which relies on reports from various sources, processes and stores information in a central database, and generates reports using programs developed by the Bangko Sentral. Banks transmit data electronically while others submit hard-copy reports. Steps are being undertaken for a

---

[25]There was no change in policy on public sector borrowings because the policy emanates from provisions of the Philippine Constitution and other legislation.

[26]Exceptions to this rule are borrowings that would involve or result in any liability, whether real or contingent, on the part of a public sector enterprise or a local bank to a nonresident (for example, arising from guarantees), which continue to be covered by the approval and registration process.

gradual shift to electronic reporting, at least for the major nonbank entities.

Reporting system

14.166 Report forms are designed considering the type of data required (data collected are used both for regulatory as well as statistical purposes) and the source of information. There are four major data sources that report to the Bangko Sentral on a regular basis.

- *Borrowers*: Borrowers (bank and nonbank) are important data sources because they have first-hand knowledge of transactions in, and balances of, their foreign loans. Familiarity with the reporting system, which was instituted during the era of exchange controls, facilitates compliance by borrowers because the required internal systems and procedures have long been established. With the liberalization of foreign exchange rules, the Bangko Sentral has become more aggressive in propagating information on, and compliance with, its reporting requirements. It takes a proactive approach in this regard by directly communicating with borrowers (particularly new ones with substantial funding requirements); providing advice on the Bank's reporting requirements; explaining the need for, and uses of, data requested; and exerting moral suasion to obtain the borrower's cooperation. Even with the more relaxed regulatory environment, the Bangko Sentral continues to wield substantial influence and enjoys high credibility in the country, allowing it to successfully solicit the cooperation of data providers.
- *Major foreign creditors*: Creditors' reports allow validation of data provided by the borrowers on their stock (and flows in some instances) of external debt, and also supplement data obtained from other sources.
- *Local banks (including branches/subsidiaries of foreign banks operating in the Philippines)*: Bank reports provide data on individual cross-border transactions involving purchases and sales of foreign exchange that are external-debt-related, particularly those that no longer require prior approval and/or registration. Monetary penalties and other sanctions help ensure compliance with reporting requirements.
- *Major institutional investors in the country (such as nonbank financial institutions)*: In order to produce a more accurate measure of external debt, information on investments by these institutions in Philippine debt instruments floated offshore is

used to adjust the external debt stock since these transactions are between residents.

14.167 In general, data are required in absolute values in original currencies, although the U.S. dollar equivalent is required for bank reports to facilitate comparison and cross-checking with data that are submitted in aggregate pesos and U.S. dollar equivalent to other Bangko Sentral departments/units.

14.168 Reported data on private sector accounts are strictly confidential to the Bangko Sentral; thus, figures are released only in aggregates. Disclosure of data on individual accounts or transactions requires clearance at the highest level (the Monetary Board), and the concerned party's consent to the release of data or waiver of right to confidentiality is normally sought.

The external debt database

14.169 The external debt database was designed to allow monitoring of information on individual foreign loan accounts through the entire loan cycle from approval through disbursement, registration, and repayment.

14.170 A master record for each account is created and updated for any changes in basic loan information during the life of the loan. Details of each account maintained in the database include the contracting parties (debtor, creditor, and guarantor/s) and credit terms (maturity, repayment terms, interest rate, and commitment fee).

14.171 Loan transactions (drawings, principal, and interest payments) are entered into the system after reports received have been verified for consistency and accuracy. These transaction data are reflected in the reports on external debt and on the balance of payments.

14.172 Data are maintained in original currencies but can be easily converted into U.S. dollars or other currencies. The system makes use of several libraries—foreign exchange rates of major currencies, country, and institution libraries (debtor, creditor, and guarantor).

Output reports

14.173 The system can produce consolidated or detailed reports such as basic loan information and

Table 14.7. Total Philippine External Debt[1]
(Millions of U.S. dollars, end-period)

	1990	1991	1992	1993	1994	1995	1996	1997	1998	1999	March 2000	June 2000
By borrower	**29,955**	**31,392**	**32,089**	**35,535**	**38,723**	**39,367**	**41,875**	**45,433**	**47,817**	**52,210**	**52,415**	**52,164**
Public sector	24,458	25,552	25,666	29,718	30,883	30,116	27,385	26,958	30,310	34,800	35,441	34,932
Banks	6,202	5,937	3,261	2,777	3,163	3,452	3,252	4,686	5,805	5,746	5,602	5,654
Nonbanks	18,256	19,614	22,406	26,941	27,721	26,664	24,132	22,271	24,506	29,054	29,839	29,278
Private sector[2]	5,497	5,840	6,423	5,817	7,839	9,251	14,490	18,475	17,507	17,410	16,973	17,232
Banks	1,711	1,802	1,448	521	980	2,000	5,379	5,978	5,410	4,159	3,897	3,680
Branches of foreign banks	996	1,055	603	422	376	259	348	609	494	423	383	394
Domestic banks	715	747	845	99	604	1,741	5,031	5,369	4,916	3,735	3,514	3,286
Nonbanks	3,786	4,038	4,975	5,296	6,859	7,251	9,112	12,497	12,096	13,251	13,076	13,552
By maturity	**29,955**	**31,392**	**32,089**	**35,535**	**38,723**	**39,367**	**41,875**	**45,433**	**47,817**	**52,210**	**52,415**	**52,164**
Short-term	4,376	4,827	5,256	5,035	5,197	5,279	7,207	8,439	7,185	5,745	6,009	5,932
Medium- and long-term	25,579	26,565	26,833	30,500	33,526	34,088	34,668	36,994	40,632	46,465	46,406	46,232
By creditor type	**29,955**	**31,392**	**32,089**	**35,535**	**38,723**	**39,367**	**41,875**	**45,433**	**47,817**	**52,210**	**52,415**	**52,164**
Multilateral	7,411	7,935	8,323	9,202	9,859	9,617	8,634	8,638	10,058	10,245	9,934	9,864
Bilateral	8,547	9,572	11,328	13,369	15,033	14,393	13,439	13,307	14,926	16,429	16,116	15,983
Banks and other financial institutions	10,815	10,227	5,692	5,177	5,530	6,345	8,373	10,176	9,672	10,340	10,206	10,284
Bondholders/noteholders	865	851	3,754	4,567	4,727	6,206	8,725	10,633	11,209	12,951	13,865	13,396
Suppliers/exporters	2,312	2,802	2,963	3,213	3,549	2,587	2,588	2,359	1,562	1,690	1,697	1,882
Others	5	5	29	7	25	219	116	320	390	555	598	755
By country	**29,955**	**31,392**	**32,089**	**35,535**	**38,723**	**39,367**	**41,875**	**45,433**	**47,817**	**52,210**	**52,415**	**52,164**
Japan	8,627	9,546	9,210	11,112	12,682	12,169	11,109	10,293	11,887	14,205	14,184	14,031
United States	5,808	5,552	7,156	7,064	3,812	3,771	4,190	4,569	4,566	5,314	4,704	4,993
United Kingdom	1,141	1,108	641	1,297	363	611	511	445	399	438	537	481
France	1,447	1,085	850	725	712	961	1,579	1,899	1,743	1,621	1,433	1,287
Germany	620	693	700	742	885	967	1,298	1,635	2,122	2,435	2,620	3,109
Others	4,036	4,622	1,455	826	5,682	5,065	5,829	7,321	5,832	5,001	5,138	5,003
Multilateral agencies	7,411	7,935	8,323	9,202	9,859	9,617	8,634	8,638	10,058	10,245	9,934	9,864
Bondholders/noteholders	865	851	3,754	4,567	4,727	6,206	8,725	10,633	11,209	12,951	13,865	13,396
By currency	**29,955**	**31,392**	**32,089**	**35,535**	**38,723**	**39,367**	**41,875**	**45,433**	**47,817**	**52,210**	**52,415**	**52,164**
U.S. dollar	13,016	12,931	13,471	14,247	14,953	16,573	21,660	25,946	25,600	27,381	28,206	28,069
Multicurrency loans	5,888	6,164	6,264	6,931	7,529	7,543	6,718	5,965	6,333	5,939	5,647	5,547
Japanese yen	7,193	8,273	8,530	10,605	12,263	11,635	10,600	10,260	11,878	14,480	14,392	14,340
Special drawing rights	1,258	1,554	1,683	1,910	1,824	1,576	1,192	1,680	2,425	2,700	2,654	2,644
Others	2,600	2,470	2,141	1,843	2,154	2,039	1,706	1,582	1,581	1,710	1,515	1,563

[1]Covers BSP approved/registered debt owed to nonresidents, with classification by borrower based on primary obligor per covering loan/rescheduling agreement/document.

[2]Excludes the following monitored private sector accounts:

	1994	1995	1996	1997	1998	1999	March 2000	June 2000
(1) Intercompany accounts (gross "Due to head office/branches") of Philippine branches of foreign banks	519	861	2,694	3,074	3,060	2,906	2,473	2,369
(2) Private sector loans without BSP approval/registration	100	455	562	925	1,404	1,331	1,337	1,316
(3) Private sector obligations under capital lease agreements			396	1,296	1,228	1,597	1,586	1,574

transactions; different profiles of debt stock (such as by maturity—original or remaining basis, borrower's sector, currency, and creditor's country, based either on residency or head office/citizenship); transaction summaries and projected debt-service burden. An example of a debt table generated from the system is shown in Table 14.7. The database structure allows generation of summaries of any data element—for example, outstanding balances, loan disbursements, and principal payments.

Review of debt statistics

14.174 Statistics on the debt stock produced from the system are compared with those contained in other publications such as the BIS's *Quarterly Review*, as well as the World Bank's *Global Development Finance*.

Prospects

14.175 The country's external-debt-monitoring system remains robust, enabling the Bangko Sentral to meet vital data user requirements. However, potential reporting gaps could emerge in the liberalized foreign exchange regulatory environment. Thus, the system is continuously reviewed and refined, and additional possible sources of information and mechanisms for data capture are being explored. The objective is to further strengthen the Bangko Sentral's capability to produce comprehensive, reliable, and timely debt statistics necessary for the exercise of its regulatory mandate, for policy formulation, and for meeting the requirements of other data users.

Turkey

Measurement of Short-Term External Debt[27]

14.176 In Turkey, external debt statistics are compiled in two different institutions: the Undersecretariat of Treasury, and the Central Bank (CBRT). The treasury is responsible for *medium- and long-term debt*, which mainly consists of project and program finance, international money markets credits, bond securities, as well as other private sector credits, whereas the CBRT is responsible for *short-term debt,* including that of the central bank, banks, as well as other nonbank private and public institutions (other sectors). The CBRT disseminates monthly data on short-term debt, identifying short-term debt of the central bank, banks, and other sectors; trade credit is separately identified for the other sectors.

Legal framework

14.177 Turkish legislation currently in force allows residents to borrow freely abroad. Banks can act as intermediaries to such credits by guaranteeing or not guaranteeing them. For short-term foreign borrowings, banks are responsible for reporting to the central bank on a credit information form the details of their own activity, and for collecting and reporting the details of the transactions of their clients.

---

[27]Prepared by the Central Bank of Turkey.

Definition of institutional sectors

14.178 The institutional sector classification used by the CBRT in compiling short-term external debt data is consistent with *BPM5*.

Coverage

14.179 The short-term external debt of the *central bank* consists of (1) foreign currency deposit accounts, (2) overdrafts, and (3) nonguaranteed trade arrears (NGTAs). The foreign currency accounts correspond to approximately 99 percent of the entire CBRT short-term external debt stock as of the end of 1999. These accounts are opened by Turkish citizens, over 18 years of age, who have residence or working permits abroad, and possess valid Turkish passports. Individuals in public agencies authorized to work abroad for a long term, and those employed at the representative offices and bureaus abroad of public and private sector organizations are also entitled to open such accounts.

14.180 The short-term borrowing of the *banks* includes (1) foreign exchange credits obtained abroad; (2) foreign exchange deposit accounts of nonresidents; and (3) foreign exchange deposit accounts of nonresident banks.

14.181 The short-term debt of *private and public nonbank entities* (*other secto*rs) is divided between trade credits and other credits. Trade credit includes import-related short-term debt, and prefinancing of exports. It accounted for approximately 80 percent of the other sector's short-term external debt at end-1999. Import-related debt, which has the largest share, consists of acceptance credits; letters of credit (reflecting import payments to be made, rather than actual liabilities themselves); and deferred payments for imports—essentially suppliers' credit. Other credits include foreign exchange credits extended by nonresident banks or corporations abroad.

Methods of data collection

14.182 Balance of payments data are compiled by the CBRT within the framework of the concepts and recording principles of *BPM5*. The data for short-term external debt mainly rely on banks' foreign exchange records. An exception is data on short-term debt arising from imports, which are derived from the import figures of the State Institute of Statistics (SIS) for the creation of the debt, and an estimation method for repayments.

14.183 The bank reporting system provides data on short-term foreign exchange credits obtained from nonresidents by banks and other sectors, as well as foreign exchange accounts opened with domestic banks by nonresidents and nonresident banks. Also, banks report trade financing credits in the form of acceptances and prefinancing credits for exports.

14.184 For data on credit arising from deferred payments for imports, in 1997 the central bank began using data from the SIS for the extension of credit, and data from banking records for the repayment of this credit, with the change in the stock of debt estimated as the difference between the two. This method of measuring short-term debt gave rise to sharp annual increases in the estimated stock of trade credit, which became especially noticeable in 1999, when a sharp increase occurred despite a significant decline in imports. From a survey of banks, it was discovered that these kinds of transactions have short maturity. Also, it was discovered that the data from the banks did not accurately capture all repayments, and so the stock of trade credits was overestimated. Consequently, the central bank developed a new methodology for measuring repayments, on the assumption that this form of trade credit is essentially repaid within a three-month period. Data were revised for the period 1996–99. The consequence was a significant downward revision to the stock of short-term external debt.

14.185 Data on short-term loans are provided by the banks on a transaction basis when they are received by the banks and the maturity exceeds 180 days, and, without a maturity exemption, received by other sectors for which the domestic banks act as intermediaries or as guarantors. The details reported include the creditor, the country from which the credit is received, the borrowing sector (public/private), the repayment schedule, the date of agreement, the date of last payment, the interest rate, the amount of the loan, and the currency. The outstanding value of these short-term loans is computed by accumulating the monthly flow data in U.S. dollar equivalent by applying cross-rates prevailing on the date of the transaction, and adding these cumulated transactions to the previous month's end-of-period stock data, valued at exchange rates at the end of the month.

Uganda

Data Requirements for the HIPC Initiative[28]

14.186 In 1998, Uganda became the first country to receive relief under the IMF's first Heavily Indebted Poor Countries (HIPC) Initiative, and again in 2000, it was the first country to receive assistance under the Enhanced HIPC Initiative. For Uganda, the intention of the HIPC Initiative is to reduce the external debt burden to a sustainable level, so that the savings can be used for social development. On each occasion it sought relief, Uganda was required to provide accurate external debt statistics. This case study sets out how Uganda was able to produce these data, and the external data required.

14.187 Even before the HIPC Initiative, Uganda had already taken steps to reduce its external debt burden and hence had begun the work to develop good external debt data.

- *Negotiations for debt rescheduling with Paris Club creditors.* Debt rescheduling was effected under Toronto (1989), enhanced Toronto (1992), and Naples terms (1995), where Uganda had reached an exit to any Paris Club rescheduling. But reschedulings were applied to pre-cutoff loans—which was about 4 percent of the total stock of debt, given that Uganda's cutoff date was June 1981.
- *In 1991, the government implemented the first debt strategy.* Among other things, this placed strict limits on borrowings—loans were only to be contracted for priority projects. Also, Uganda bought back a big portion of its commercial debt using a grant from the International Development Association (IDA) and other bilateral donors, totaling $153 million.
- *An enhanced debt strategy was implemented following a 1995 study undertaken by a consultant, in consultation with Ugandan officials.* The finding that the biggest burden was multilateral debt, and that it would continue to increase from 1998 onward as long-term obligations matured, resulted in the formation of the Multilateral Debt Fund. A total of $135 million was contributed to this fund—by the Netherlands, Sweden, Switzerland, Denmark, Norway, and Austria—to meet debt obligations from the four

---

[28]Prepared by the Bank of Uganda.

major multilateral creditors—IDA, the African Development Bank, the African Development Fund, and the IMF.

- *Uganda continued not to pay its non–Paris Club creditors until they accepted Paris Club comparable terms.* This is in line with the debt strategy of 1991, and the enhanced debt strategy of 1995, but excludes those creditors from whom new disbursements are received for new projects.
- *Uganda continued to adhere to borrowing on highly concessional terms (IDA terms) and requests for grants where applicable.*

14.188 Notwithstanding all of the above endeavors, Uganda found that its debt was still unsustainable and so sought relief under the HIPC Initiative, which required good external debt statistics.

Institutional arrangements

14.189 By act of parliament (the Loans and Guarantee Act), public external debt borrowing is vested in the Ministry of Finance. The minister signs all public debt loan agreements or gives powers of attorney to other senior officials to sign on his/her behalf. The ministry, therefore, performs the functions of negotiating, loan contracting, disbursement authorization and monitoring, repayment authorization, and recording of the external debt position. It also handles other aspects of the financial flows to the country, including grants and aid from nongovernmental organizations.

14.190 In the early 1980s, the ministry delegated part of the function of data recording, monitoring, and effecting payments to the Bank of Uganda (central bank) because records on loan documents in the ministry had been destroyed during the 1979 war. Once it acquired the responsibility, the central bank created the External Debt Management Office (EDMO), which was subsequently combined with the then Exchange Control Department to form the Trade and External Debt Department (TEDD) within the research function.

14.191 At that time of the handover of responsibility, debt data records were not accurate because all creditors were not known, and so what Uganda owed could not be verified easily. Therefore, the tendency was to rely on creditor billing statements, which at times were inflated. Later, in 1991, to establish Uganda's stock of debt and streamline the debt

records, a consultant—S.G. Warburg—was employed to carry out a comprehensive audit report of the external debt data. Letters were written by the minister of finance to all known creditors to avail information on their claims, and the information received was cross-checked by the consultants with records from other international institutions, and with Uganda's own data.

14.192 As part of the process the consultant, together with the central bank staff, created a new system for recording all loans, which continues to the present. UNCTAD's Debt Management and Financial Analysis System (DMFAS) was introduced,[29] with each loan given a unique DMFAS number, and loan details captured in a computerized database. The data captured are similar to those shown in Table 11.1, in Chapter 11, and cover, for each instrument, details of its type, disbursements, borrowing terms, debt-service payments, exchange and interest rates, and, if necessary, any debt-restructuring activity. Also, new filing cabinets were put in place, so that for each loan Uganda has a manual file with the loan agreement and all correspondence.

14.193 When the ministry contracts debt and signs an agreement, it sends a copy of the loan agreement to the central bank, where the loan terms are entered in the database. As the loan is disbursed, various types of disbursement information are received from the creditor, posted in the computer, and filed in the manual file. To process payments, bimonthly meetings are held between the central bank and the ministry to consider debt-service projections, which are produced from the DMFAS system. These projections are cross-checked with the billing statements received from the creditors and, according to the debt strategy, a decision is made on which creditors are to be paid.

14.194 Uganda is now using DMFAS version 5.1.1, which has the World Bank's Debt Sustainability Module Plus (DSM Plus) for calculating the (net) present value of debt, a requirement for the HIPC Initiative.

Uganda's stock of debt

14.195 Table 14.8 presents Uganda's stock of debt as at June 30, 2000. It totaled $3.57 billion. This debt

---

[29]The DMFAS system is described in detail in Chapter 18.

Table 14.8. Uganda's External Debt Obligation by Creditor as at June 30, 2000
(Millions of U.S. dollars)

Creditor	Total Debt	Percent of Total
Multilateral	**2,927.9**	**81.9**
Bilateral	**592.4**	**16.6**
Paris Club	259.0	7.2
PC pre-cutoff	110.1	3.1
PC post-cutoff	148.9	4.2
Non-OECD (Non–Paris Club)	333.5	9.3
Commercial/Other	**53.8**	**1.5**
Total	**3,574.0**	**100**

Source: Trade and External Debt Department, Bank of Uganda.

is broken down into three major categories: multilateral debt, bilateral debt, and commercial debt.

Data requirements of the HIPC Initiative

14.196 The HIPC Initiative required Uganda to undertake a debt-reconciliation exercise with all creditors as at end-June 1997 for the first HIPC, and end-June 1999 for the Enhanced HIPC.

Exposure to the HIPC Initiative

14.197 During the preparation for the first HIPC Initiative it was necessary to train TEDD and ministry staff on its requirements. Consequently, a pre-HIPC debt-sustainability analysis workshop was organized by External Finance for Africa (now Debt Relief International), the Macroeconomic and Financial Management Institute for Eastern and Southern Africa (MEFMI), the World Bank, and UNCTAD, and sponsored jointly by the Swedish International Development Agency, the Bank of Uganda, and the Ministry of Finance to help build capacity in producing the external debt data required for the HIPC Initiative.

14.198 Following attainment of the first HIPC Initiative, a workshop on post-HIPC debt-sustainability analysis, sponsored by MEFMI, Debt Relief International, UNCTAD, the Bank of Uganda, and the Ministry of Finance was held in Uganda in January 1999. From this workshop it was discovered that Uganda's debt was not sustainable, and so more relief was needed. In addition to the above work-

shops, regional workshops were organized by the same groups to enlighten Uganda's awareness on HIPC issues. Indeed, Uganda will always remain indebted to these agencies for the good work done, so allowing Ugandan officials to participate fully in the tripartite negotiations with the IMF, World Bank, and other bilateral donors.

Debt data coverage

14.199 External debt that is covered under the HIPC Initiative is limited in all cases to that owed or guaranteed by the public sector. For Uganda, this includes all medium- and long-term borrowings of the central government, the central bank, and parastatals from multilateral institutions (including the IMF), bilateral governments (Paris Club and non-OECD), and commercial credits from banks, export guarantee agencies, and suppliers' credits whether or not a government guarantees them. Therefore, all the creditors presented in Table 14.8 are covered.

Data validation

14.200 Uganda had to reconcile the debt data with all creditors, since it is normally expected under the HIPC Initiative that 95 percent of the value of external debt be fully reconciled with creditors at the decision point, with some allowance for delay in reconciling disputed debts or failure of some creditors to reply. To carry out this exercise effectively, the ministry wrote letters to all the relevant creditors requesting data on external debt outstanding and disbursed as at end-June 1997 for the first HIPC, and later for end-June 1999 for the Enhanced HIPC. The finance minister signed all the letters. They were sent to the latest-known address, but where the latest addresses could not be traced, the letters were sent to the embassies of the creditors in Uganda or Nairobi for onward transmission.

14.201 The detailed information requested was as follows:
- Creditor's name;
- Amount of the loan;
- Date of signature;
- Availability date;
- Amount disbursed;
- Undisbursed amount;
- Amount of principal paid;
- Amount of interest paid;
- Amount of principal arrears;
- Amount of interest arrears; and
- Amount canceled.

14.202 In the ministry and the central bank, a master file was opened up to store all the replies, with a copy of each reply placed in the individual files of creditors. The next step was to compare the loan position kept on the DMFAS system with that reported by the creditors. Where applicable, differences were identified for each loan, and there was correspondence with the creditors to sort out the differences. In some cases it was realized that there had been some disbursements that were not captured on DMFAS, or payments had been made that were applied differently on the maturities by the creditor (that is, payments for current maturities had been applied to arrears by the creditor), or different exchange rates had been used. Other creditors, like Egypt, said that they did not have any outstanding claims on Uganda, so their loans were removed from the database. Once the differences were resolved, where necessary, loan data were corrected.

14.203 However, complicated and controversial issues arose on the following:
- *The acknowledgement of disputed debts*, such as military debts arising from past wars. This was true for a Tanzanian loan for which a verification exercise is still required, although the amount indebted was accepted in principle by Uganda.
- *The exchange rate used for converting debts* to the currency of repayment. For instance, some debts denominated in, say, Burundi francs in which the supplies were originally quoted.
- *The "ownership" of debts that had been traded* directly or on the secondary market. For instance, the loan that was supposed to be a claim of COFACE (France) had been sold to Centenary Rural Development Bank.
- *The level of arrears on "old" loans* (for example, for Libya and commercial debts), particularly if late interest charges had been accruing.

14.204 Also, although the response was good for creditors that were being paid on schedule—such as multilateral and the bilateral Paris Club creditors— and for the Paris Club creditors that had just signed

the bilateral agreements, some bilateral non-OECD creditors were reluctant to reply. Various reminders had to be sent. On the other hand, some of them replied quickly, hoping to be repaid. The majority of commercial creditors never replied.

14.205 For those creditors who responded, the reconciled data were sent to the IMF and the World Bank as requested, for further cross-checking with data received from the creditors. For all the multilateral creditors, where the reconciliation exercise indicated that arrears had accumulated, these had to be paid off before Uganda could qualify for the HIPC Initiative. For those creditors where no information was received, IMF and World Bank figures were taken and reconciled with the information included in the database, which had been agreed upon in the S.G. Warburg audit report.

Data needs for measuring debt-burden indicators and debt relief

14.206 In Uganda's experience, a country must make realistic assumptions when projecting data for new disbursements, macroeconomic indicators, balance of payments transactions, and budget revenue and expenditures because accuracy in these projections will affect the realization of sustainability ratios. For example, the impact of El Niño rains on export projections was a factor in Uganda's external debt being unsustainable even after relief under the first HIPC Initiative was received. Also, even after making realistic assumptions and calculating the relevant balance of payments and budget projections, consideration is required about how financing gaps, either in the balance of payments or budget, will be filled.

14.207 Sensitivity analysis is important to test alternative macroeconomic scenarios and to provide government with a picture of what would happen if the central assumptions changed. Uganda uses models developed in both the World Bank's DSM Plus and in the private sector (Debt Pro) for calculating debt sustainability for the HIPC Initiative.

PART III

Use of External Debt Statistics

15. Debt Sustainability: Medium-Term Scenarios and Debt Ratios

Introduction[1]

15.1 The creation of debt is a natural consequence of economic activity. At any time, some economic entities have income in excess of their current consumption and investment requirements, while other entities are deficient in this regard. Through the creation of debt, both sets of entities are better able to realize their consumption and output preferences, thus encouraging economic growth.

15.2 The creation of debt is premised on the assumption that the debtor will meet the requirements of the debt contract. But if the income of the debtor is insufficient or there is a lack of sufficient assets to call upon in the event of income proving insufficient, debt problems ensue; the stock of debt will be such that the debtor cannot meet its obligations. In such circumstances, or in the expectation of such circumstances, the benefits arising from international financial flows—for both creditors and debtors—may not be fully realized. Hence, the need at the country level for good risk-management procedures and the maintenance of external debt at sustainable levels.

15.3 This chapter considers tools for sustainability analysis such as medium-term scenarios and the role of debt indicators in identifying solvency and liquidity problems. This is preceded by a short discussion of the solvency and liquidity aspects of sustainability.

Solvency

15.4 From a national perspective, solvency can be defined as the country's ability to discharge its external obligations on a continuing basis. It is relatively easy, but not very helpful, to define a country's theoretical ability to pay. In theory, assuming debt can be rolled over (renewed) at maturity, countries are solvent if the present value of net interest payments does not exceed the present value of other current account inflows (primarily export receipts) net of imports.[2] In practice, countries stop servicing their debt long before this constraint is reached, at the point where servicing the debt is perceived to be too costly in terms of the country's economic and social objectives. Thus, the relevant constraint is generally the willingness to pay, rather than the theoretical macroeconomic ability to pay. To establish that a country is solvent and willing to pay is not easy. Solvency is "very much like honesty: it can never be fully certified, and proofs are slow to materialize."[3]

15.5 In analyzing solvency problems, it is necessary to take into account the different implications of public and private sector debt. If there is a risk that the public sector will cease to discharge its external obligations, this in itself is likely to sharply curtail financial inflows to all economic sectors because governments can issue moratoria on debt repayment and impose exchange restrictions. Sizable public external indebtedness may undermine the government's commitment to allowing private sector debt repayment. Also, if private defaults take place on a significant scale, this too is likely to lead to a sharp reduction in financial inflows, and government intervention may follow—in the form of exchange restrictions, a general debt moratorium, or bailouts. But problems of individual private sector borrowers may be contained to the concerned lenders.

---

[1]This chapter draws on IMF (2000b), *Debt- and Reserve-Related Indicators of External Vulnerability* (Washington: March 23, 2000), available on the Internet at *http://www.imf.org/external/np/pdr/debtres/index.htm,* as well as work at the World Bank.

[2]In considering imports, it is worth noting that these are endogenous and subject to potentially severe compression (reduction).

[3]Calvo (1996), p. 208.

Liquidity

15.6 Liquidity problems—that is, when a shortage of liquid assets affects the ability of an economy to discharge its immediate external obligations—almost always emerge in circumstances that give rise to insolvency or unwillingness to pay. But it is also possible for a liquidity problem to arise independently of a solvency problem, following a self-fulfilling "run" on a country's liquidity as creditors lose confidence and undertake transactions that lead to pressures on the international reserves of the economy.[4] Liquidity problems can be triggered, for example, by a sharp drop in export earnings, or an increase in interest rates (foreign and/or domestic),[5] or prices for imports. The currency and interest rate composition of debt, the maturity structure of debt, and the availability of assets to pay debts are all important determinants of the vulnerability of an economy to external liquidity crises; these are all considered in the next chapter. Mechanisms—such as creditor "councils"—by which creditors' actions can be coordinated can be useful in preventing or limiting the impact of liquidity crises by sharing information and coordinating responses.

Medium-Term Debt Scenarios

15.7 External-debt-sustainability analysis is generally conducted in the context of medium-term scenarios. These scenarios are numerical evaluations that take account of expectations of the behavior of economic variables and other factors to determine the conditions under which debt and other indicators would stabilize at reasonable levels, the major risks to the economy, and the need and scope for policy adjustment. Macroeconomic uncertainties, such as the outlook for the current account, and policy uncertainties, such as for fiscal policy, tend to dominate the medium-term outlook and feature prominently in the scenarios prepared by the IMF in the context of Article IV consultations and the design of IMF-supported adjustment programs.

15.8 The current account balance is important because, if deficits persist, the country's external position may eventually become unsustainable (as re-flected by a rising ratio of external debt to GDP). In other words, financing of continually large current account deficits by the issuance of debt instruments will lead to an increasing debt burden, perhaps undermining solvency and leading to external vulnerability from a liquidity perspective, owing to the need to repay large amounts of debt.

15.9 One advantage of medium-term scenarios is that borrowing is viewed within the overall macroeconomic framework. However, such an approach can be very sensitive to projections for variables such as economic growth, interest and exchange rates, and, in particular, to the continuation of financial flows, which are potentially subject to sudden reversal.[6] Consequently, a range of various alternative scenarios may be prepared. Also, stress tests—"what if" scenarios that assume a major change in one or more variable—can be helpful in analyzing major risks stemming from fluctuations of these variables or from changes in other assumptions including, for example, changes in prices of imports or exports of oil. Stress tests are useful for liquidity analysis and provide the basis for developing strategies to mitigate the identified risks, such as enhancing the liquidity buffer by increasing international reserves, by establishing contingent credit lines with foreign lenders, or both.

Debt Ratios

15.10 Debt ratios have been developed mostly to help indicate potential debt-related risks, and thus to support sound debt management. Debt indicators in medium-term scenarios can usefully sum up important trends. They are used in the context of medium-term debt scenarios, as described above, preferably from a dynamic perspective, rather than as "snapshot" measures. Debt ratios should be considered in conjunction with key economic and financial variables, in particular expected growth and interest rates, which determine their trend in medium-term scenarios.[7] Another key factor to consider is the extent to which there is adequate contract

---

[4]For a discussion of self-fulfilling crises, see Krugman (1996) and Obstfeld (1994).

[5]Such as when domestic rates rise because of an economy's perceived deterioration in creditworthiness.

[6]An analysis of key indicators, such as the current account of the balance of payments, budget deficits, etc., can be particularly useful in identifying the possibility of reversals in financial flows.

[7]If barter trade is significant, and debt payments are in products that are not easily marketable, this could affect the interpretation of debt ratios, since the opportunity cost of this form of payment is different from a purely financial obligation.

enforcement—that is, creditor rights, bankruptcy procedures, etc.—that will help to ensure that private debt is contracted on a sound basis. More generally, the incentive structure within which the private sector operates could affect the soundness of borrowing and lending decisions; for example, whether there are incentives that favor short-term or foreign currency financing.

15.11 As a result, there are conceptual problems in defining on a general level what are the appropriate benchmarks for debt ratios; in other words, the scope for identifying critical ranges for debt indicators is rather limited. While an analysis over time, in relation to other macroeconomic variables, might help to develop a system of early warning signals for a possible debt crisis or debt-service difficulties, comparing the absolute value of overall debt ratios across heterogeneous countries is not very useful. For instance, a high or low debt-to-exports ratio in a particular year may have limited use as an indicator of external vulnerability; rather, it is the movement of the debt-to-exports ratio over time that reflects the debt-related risks.

15.12 For more homogeneous country groupings and for debt of the public sector, there is more potential to identify ranges for debt-related indicators that suggest that debt or debt-service ratios are approaching levels that in other countries have resulted in suspension or renegotiations of debt-service payments, or have caused official creditors to consider whether the debt burden may have reached levels that are too costly to support. For example, assistance under the HIPC Initiative is determined on the basis of a target for the ratio of public debt to exports (150 percent), or the ratio of debt to fiscal revenue (250 percent). In these ratios, the present value of debt is used, and only a subset of external debt is taken into consideration, namely medium- and long-term public and publicly guaranteed debt.[8]

15.13 Several widely used debt ratios are discussed in somewhat greater detail later. Table 15.1 provides a more comprehensive list. Broadly speaking, there are two sets of debt indicators: those based on flow variables (for example, related to exports or GDP)—

these are called flow indicators because the numerator or denominator or both are flow variables; and those based on stock variables—that is, both numerator and denominator are stock variables.

Ratio of Debt to Exports and Ratio of Present Value of Debt to Exports

15.14 The debt-to-exports ratio is defined as the ratio of total outstanding debt at the end of the year to the economy's exports of goods and services for any one year. This ratio can be used as a measure of sustainability because an increasing debt-to-exports ratio over time, for a given interest rate, implies that total debt is growing faster than the economy's basic source of external income, indicating that the country may have problems meeting its debt obligations in the future.

15.15 Indicators that use the stock of debt have several shortcomings in common. First, countries that use external borrowing for productive investment with long gestation periods are more likely to exhibit high debt-to-exports ratios. But as the investments begin to produce goods that can be exported, the country's debt-to-exports ratio may start to decline. So for these countries, the debt-to-exports ratio may not be too high from an intertemporal perspective even if in any given year it may be perceived as large. Therefore, arguably this indicator can be based on exports after the average gestation lag— that is, using projected exports one or several time periods ahead as a denominator.[9] More generally, this also highlights the need to monitor debt indicators in medium-term scenarios to overcome the limitations of a "snapshot."

15.16 Second, some countries may benefit from highly concessional debt terms, while others pay high interest rates. For such countries, to better capture the implied debt burden—in terms of the opportunity cost of capital—it is useful to report and analyze the average interest rate on debt or to calculate the present value of debt by discounting the projected stream of future amortization payments including interest, with a risk-neutral commercial reference rate. As noted above, in analyzing debt

---

[8]See Andrews and others (1999); available on the Internet at http://www.imf.org/external/pubs/cat/longres.cfm?sk=3448.0. Appendix V discusses the HIPC approach and includes information on the debt ratios monitored.

[9]To average out idiosyncratic or irregular swings in export performance, multiyear period averages are frequently used, such as the three-year averages used in the debt-sustainability analysis for HIPCs.

Table 15.1. Overview of Debt Indicators

Indicator	Evaluation/Use
Solvency	
Interest service ratio	Ratio of average interest payments to export earnings indicates terms of external indebtedness and thus the debt burden
External debt to exports	Useful as trend indicator closely related to the repayment capacity of a country
External debt over GDP	Useful because relates debt to resource base (for the potential of shifting production to exports so as to enhance repayment capacity)
Present value of debt over exports	Key sustainability indicator used, for example, in HIPC Initiative assessments comparing debt burden with repayment capacity
Present value of debt over fiscal revenue	Key sustainability indicator used, for example, in HIPC Initiative assessments comparing debt burden with public resources for repayment
Debt service over exports	Hybrid indicator of solvency and liquidity concerns
Liquidity	
International reserves to short-term debt	Single most important indicator of reserve adequacy in countries with significant but uncertain access to capital markets; ratio can be predicted forward to assess future vulnerability to liquidity crises
Ratio of short-term debt to total outstanding debt	Indicates relative reliance on short-term financing; together with indicators of maturity structure allows monitoring of future repayment risk
Public sector indicators	
Public sector debt service over exports	Useful indicator of willingness to pay and transfer risk
Public debt over GDP or tax revenues	Solvency indicator of public sector; can be defined for total debt or for external debt
Average maturity of nonconcessional debt	Measure of maturity that is not biased by long repayment terms for concessional debt
Foreign currency debt over total debt	Foreign currency debt including foreign currency indexed debt; indicator of the impact of a change in the exchange rate on debt
Financial sector indicators	
Open foreign exchange position	Foreign currency assets minus liabilities plus net long positions in foreign currency stemming from off-balance-sheet items; indicator for foreign exchange risk, but normally small because of banking regulations
Foreign currency maturity mismatch	Foreign currency liabilities minus foreign currency assets as percent of these foreign currency assets at given maturities; indicator for pressure on central bank reserves in case of a cutoff of financial sector from foreign currency funding
Gross foreign currency liabilities	Useful to the extent that assets are not usable to offset withdrawals in liquidity
Corporate sector indicators	
Leverage	Nominal (book) value of debt over equity (assets minus debt and derivatives liabilities); key indicator of sound financial structure; high leverage aggravates vulnerability to other risks (for example, low profitability, high ratio of short-term debt/total debt)
Interest over cash flow	Total prospective interest payments over operational cash flow (before interest and taxes); key cash flow indicator for general financial soundness
Short-term debt over total term debt (both total and for foreign currency only)	In combination with leverage, indicator of vulnerability to temporary cutoff from financing
Return on assets (before tax and interest)	Profit before tax and interest payments over total assets; indicator of general profitability
Net foreign currency cash flow over total cash flow	Net foreign currency cash flow is defined as prospective cash inflows in foreign currency minus prospective cash outflows in foreign currency; key indicator for unhedged foreign currency exposure
Net foreign currency debt over equity	Net foreign currency debt is defined as the difference between foreign currency debt liabilities and assets; equity is assets minus debt and net derivatives liabilities; indicator for balance sheet effect of exchange rate changes

sustainability for HIPCs, the IMF and World Bank use such a present value of debt measure—notably present value of debt to exports, and to fiscal revenue (see below). A high and rising present value of the debt-to-exports ratio is considered to be a sign that the country is on an unsustainable debt path.

Ratio of Debt to GDP and Ratio of Present Value of Debt to GDP

15.17 The debt-to-GDP ratio is defined as the ratio of the total outstanding external debt at the end of the year to annual GDP. By using GDP as a denominator, the ratio may provide some indication of the potential to service external debt by switching resources from production of domestic goods to the production of exports. Indeed, a country might have a large debt-to-exports ratio but a low debt-to-GDP ratio if exportables comprise a very small proportion of GDP.

15.18 While the debt-to-GDP ratio is immune from export-related criticisms that mainly focus on the differing degree of value added in exports and price volatility of exports, it may be less reliable in the presence of over- or undervaluations of the real exchange rate, which could significantly distort the GDP denominator. Also, as with the debt-to-exports ratio, it is important to take account of the country's stage of development and the mix of concessional and nonconcessional debt.

15.19 In the context of debt ratios, the numerator in the present value of debt-to-GDP ratio is again estimated using future projections of debt-service payments discounted by market-based interest rates (that is, a risk-neutral commercial reference rate).

Ratio of Present Value of Debt to Fiscal Revenue

15.20 The ratio of the present value of debt to fiscal revenue is defined as the ratio of future projected debt-service payments discounted by market-based interest rates (a risk-neutral commercial reference rate) to annual fiscal revenue. This ratio can be used as a measure of sustainability in those countries with a relatively open economy facing a heavy fiscal burden of external debt. In such circumstances, the government's ability to mobilize domestic revenue is relevant and will not be measured by the debt-to-exports or debt-to-GDP ratios. An increase in this indicator over time indicates that the country may have budgetary problems in servicing its debt.

Ratio of Debt Service to Exports[10]

15.21 This ratio is defined as the ratio of external debt-service payments of principal and interest on long-term and short-term debt to exports of goods and services for any one year. The debt-service-to-exports ratio is a possible indicator of debt sustainability because it indicates how much of a country's export revenue will be used up in servicing its debt and thus, also, how vulnerable the payment of debt-service obligations is to an unexpected fall in export proceeds. This ratio tends to highlight countries with significant short-term external debt. A sustainable level is determined by the debt-to-exports ratio and interest rates, as well as by the term structure of debt obligations. The latter may affect creditworthiness because the higher the share of short-term credit is in overall debt, the larger and more vulnerable is the annual flow of debt-service obligations.

15.22 By focusing on payments, the debt-service-to-exports ratio takes into account the mix of concessional and nonconcessional debt, while its evolution over time, especially in medium-term scenarios, can provide useful information on lumpy repayment structures. Moreover, a narrow version of the debt-service ratio, focused on government and government-guaranteed debt service, can be a useful indicator of government debt sustainability and transfer risk (the risk that exchange rate restrictions are imposed that prevent the repayment of obligations) because it may provide some insight into the political cost of servicing debt.[11]

15.23 The debt-service-to-exports ratio has some limitations as a measure of external vulnerability, in addition to the possible variability of debt-service payments and export revenues from year to year. First, amortization payments on short-term debt are typically excluded from debt service,[12] and the coverage of private sector data can often be limited, either because the indicator is intentionally focused on the public sector or because data on private debt service are not available.

15.24 Second, many economies have liberalized their trade regimes and are now exporting a larger proportion of their output to the rest of the world. But at the same time they are importing more, and

---

[10]This ratio, in addition to the total debt-to-exports and the total debt-to-GNP (national output) ratios, is provided for individual countries in the World Bank's annual *Global Development Finance* publication.

[11]A version of this indicator that focuses on official debt is used, for instance, in the HIPC Initiative.

[12]This is the approach taken in the World Bank's *World Development Report* and *Global Development Finance,* and the IMF's *World Economic Outlook.* Lack of data, as well as the assumption that short-term debt mainly constituted trade credit that was easy to roll over, contributed to this practice. As experience shows, this assumption is in some cases questionable.

the import content of exports is rising. Thus, a debt-service-to-exports ratio not corrected for the import intensity of exports is biased downward for economies with a higher propensity to export;[13] this argument applies similarly to the debt-to-exports ratio.

15.25 Finally, the concept summarizes both liquidity and solvency issues, which may make it analytically less tractable than measures that track only solvency (such as the ratio of interest payments to exports) or liquidity (the ratio of reserves to short-term debt).

Ratio of International Reserves to Short-Term Debt

15.26 This ratio is a pure liquidity indicator that is defined as the ratio of the stock of international reserves available to the monetary authorities to the short-term debt stock on a remaining-maturity basis. This could be a particularly useful indicator of reserve adequacy, especially for countries with significant, but not fully certain, access to international capital markets.[14]

15.27 The ratio indicates whether international reserves exceed scheduled amortization of short-, medium-, and long-term external debt during the following year; that is, the extent to which the economy has the ability to meet all its scheduled amortizations to nonresidents for the coming year using its own international reserves. It provides a measure of how quickly a country would be forced to adjust if it were cut off from external borrowing—for example, because of adverse developments in international capital markets. All scheduled debt amortization payments on both private and public debt to nonresidents over the coming year are covered in such a ratio under short-term debt, regardless of the instrument or currency denomination. A similar ratio can be calculated focusing on the foreign currency debt of the government (and banking sector) only. This may be especially relevant for economies with very open capital markets, and significant public sector foreign currency debt.

15.28 Interestingly, in most theoretical models the maturity structure of public debt is irrelevant because it is assumed that markets are complete.[15] But markets are rarely complete, even in developed countries. And, as several currency crises in developing and emerging market countries in the mid-to-late 1990s have shown, the risk associated with an excessive buildup of the stock of short-term debt relative to international reserves can be quite severe, even in countries that were generally regarded as solvent. One conclusion drawn has been that countries with excessively large short-term debt in relation to international reserves are more susceptible to liquidity crisis.[16]

15.29 However, various factors need to be taken into account when interpreting the ratio of international reserves to short-term debt. First, a large stock of short-term debt relative to international reserves does not necessarily lead to a crisis. Many advanced economies have higher ratios of short-term debt to reserves than many emerging economies, which have shown vulnerability to financial crisis. Factors such as an incentive structure that is conducive to sound risk management, and a proven track record of contract enforcement, can help develop credibility, and help to explain this difference. Moreover, macroeconomic fundamentals, in particular the current account deficit and the real exchange rate, play an important role. Consideration should also be given to the exchange rate regime. For example, a flexible regime can reduce the likelihood and costs of a crisis. Finally, the ratio assumes that measured international reserves are indeed available and can be used to meet external obligations; this has not always been true historically.

---

[13]See Kiguel (1999) for more reasons why the ratio of debt service to exports may not be a highly reliable indicator of the external vulnerability of a country under special circumstances.

[14]The potential importance of other residents' external assets in relation to debt is highlighted in the table for the net external debt position presented in Chapter 7 (Table 7.11).

---

[15]See Lucas and Stokey (1983) and Calvo and Guidotti (1992).

[16]See Berg and others (1999); Bussière and Mulder (1999); and Furman and Stiglitz (1998).

16. External Debt Analysis: Further Considerations

Introduction

16.1 The type of debt ratios discussed in the previous chapter focus primarily on overall external debt and external debt service and the potential to meet debt obligations falling due on an economy-wide basis. However, in assessing the vulnerability of the economy to solvency and liquidity risk arising from the external debt position, a more detailed examination of the composition of the external debt position and related activity may be required. In this chapter, the relevance of additional data on the composition of external debt, external income, external assets, financial derivatives, and on the economy's creditors is explored, drawing particularly on data series described in Part I of the *Guide*. The discussion in this chapter, however, is not intended to be exhaustive.

Composition of External Debt

16.2 The relevance for debt analysis of the different data series presented in the *Guide* is set out below. In particular this section focuses on the following issues:

- Who is borrowing?
- What is the composition of debt by functional category?
- What type of instrument is being used to borrow?
- What is the maturity of debt?
- What is the currency composition of the debt?
- Is there industrial concentration of debt?
- What is the profile of debt servicing?

16.3 Traditionally in debt analysis, the focus has been on official sector borrowing, not least in the form of loans from banks or official sources. But the 1990s saw a tremendous expansion in capital market borrowing by the private sector. This has had significant implications for debt analysis, including the need to gather and analyze external debt data by the **borrowing sector**.

16.4 If there is a risk that the **public sector** will cease to discharge its external obligations, this is likely in itself to lead to a sharp curtailment of financial inflows to the economy as a whole, in part because it also casts severe doubt on the government's commitment to an economic environment that allows private sector debt repayment. Thus, information on public sector total, and short-term, external debt is important. Especially in the absence of capital controls or captive markets, information on short-term domestic debt of the government is important, since capital flight and pressure on international reserves can result from a perceived weak financial position of the public sector.

16.5 Also, beyond its own borrowing policies, the government has a special role to play in ensuring that it creates or maintains conditions for sound risk management in other sectors; for instance, avoiding policies that create a bias toward short-term foreign currency borrowing.

16.6 Most of the financial sector, notably **banks**, is by nature highly leveraged—that is, most assets are financed by debt liabilities. Banks may take on liabilities to nonresidents by taking deposits and short-term interbank loans. These positions can build up quickly and, depending also on the nature of the deposits and depositors, be run down quickly. How well banks intermediate these funds has implications for the ability to withstand large-scale withdrawals. More generally, information on the composition of assets and liabilities is important for banks (and **nonbank financial corporations**)—notably information on the maturity structure and maturity mismatch (including in foreign currency)—because it provides insight about their vulnerability to such withdrawals and their sensitivity to changing exchange and interest rates.[1]

16.7 As mentioned in Chapter 15, large-scale defaults by **nonfinancial corporations** that borrow from abroad, depending on their importance to the economy, could result in financially expensive government intervention, an impact on the credit risk of the financial sector, and an undermining of asset prices in the economy. In any case, the debt-service needs of corporations will affect the economy's liquidity situation. As with banks, the regulatory regime and incentive structure within which the corporate sector operates is important. For instance, overborrowing in foreign currency, particularly short-term, in relation to foreign currency assets or hedges (be they natural hedges in the form of foreign currency cash flow or through derivatives products such as forwards), exposes the corporate sector to cash-flow (liquidity) problems in case of large exchange rate movements. Overborrowing in foreign currency in relation to foreign currency assets could potentially expose corporations to solvency problems in the event of a depreciation of the domestic exchange rate. Ensuing corporate failures, in the event of sharp exchange rate depreciation, can reduce external financing flows and depress domestic activity, especially if contract enforcement is poor or the procedures are overwhelmed.

16.8 The provision of **guarantees** can influence economic behavior. Invariably, the government provides implicit and explicit guarantees, such as deposit insurance, and sometimes also guarantees on private sector external borrowing (classified as **publicly guaranteed private sector debt** in the *Guide*). Also, domestic corporations may use offshore enterprises to borrow, and provide guarantees to them, or have debt payments guaranteed by domestic banks. Similarly foreign corporations may guarantee part of domestic debt. Where possible, direct and explicit guarantees should be monitored because they affect risk assessment.

16.9 The **functional classification of debt instruments** is a balance of payments concept, grouping

instruments into four categories: direct investment, portfolio investment, financial derivatives, and other investment. Direct investment takes place between an investor in one country and its affiliate in another country and is generally based on a long-term relationship. Recent crises have tended to support the view that this category of investment is less likely to be affected in a crisis than other functional types.[2] Portfolio investment, by definition, includes tradable debt instruments; other investment, by definition, includes all other debt instruments. The relevance of financial derivatives instruments for external debt analysis is discussed below.

16.10 The type of **instrument** that a debtor will issue depends on what creditors are willing to purchase as well as the debtor's preferences. Borrowing in the form of loans concentrates debt issuance in the hands of banks, whereas securities are more likely to be owned by a wider range of investors. Trade credit is typically of a short-term maturity. Although equity issues are not regarded as debt instruments, declared dividends on equity are included in debt servicing, and so it remains necessary to monitor activity in these instruments. At the least, sudden sales of equity by nonresidents or residents can have important ramifications for an economy and its ability to raise and service debt.[3]

16.11 The **maturity composition** of debt is important because it can have a profound impact on liquidity. Concentration of high levels of short-term external debt is seen to make an economy particularly vulnerable to unexpected downturns in financial fortune.[4] For instance, an economy with high levels of short-term external debt may be vulnerable to a sudden change in investor sentiment. Interbank lines are particularly sensitive to changes in risk perception, and early warning signals of changes in investor sentiment towards the economy might be

---

[1]Banks are subject to moral hazard risk through explicit or implicit deposit insurance and limited liability. The potential moral hazard risk arising from deposit insurance schemes is that by "protecting" from loss an element of their deposit base, banks might be provided with an incentive to hold portfolios incorporating more risk, but potentially higher returns, than they otherwise would. Monitoring the risks taken by banks is a central element of banking supervision, a subject beyond the scope of the *Guide*.

[2]However, direct investment enterprises may place additional pressure on the exchange rate in a crisis situation through the hedging of domestic currency assets. Moreover, foreign investors can repatriate rather than reinvest profits, thereby effectively increasing the domestically (debt) funded part of their investments.

[3]In analyzing the securities transactions, both debt and equity, changes in prices (rather than in quantities) may equilibrate the market.

[4]The compilation of average maturity data might disguise important differences in the sectoral composition of debt and in the dispersion of maturities. However, data on average maturity by sector and by debt instrument might alert policymakers and market participants to maturity structures that are potentially problematic.

detected through the monitoring of the refinancing ("rollover") rate.[5]

16.12 Debt analysis needs to make a distinction between short-term debt on an original maturity basis—that is, debt issued with a maturity of one year or less—and on a remaining-maturity basis—that is, debt obligations that fall due in one year or less. Data on an **original maturity** basis provides information on the typical terms of debt and the debt structure, and monitoring changes in these terms provides useful information on the preferences of creditors and the sectoral distribution of debtors. Data on a **remaining** (residual) **maturity** basis provides the analyst and policymaker with information on the repayment obligations (that is, the liquidity structure). For the policymaker, to ensure sufficient liquidity, such as indicated by an appropriate ratio of international reserves to short-term debt, requires avoiding a bunching of debt payments.

16.13 The debtor will be interested in the **nominal value** of its debt because at any moment in time it is the amount that the debtor owes to the creditor at that moment. Also, the debtor is well advised to monitor the **market value** of its debt. The market value and the spreads over interest rates on "risk-free" instruments provide an indication to the borrower of the market view on its ability to meet debt obligations as well as current market sentiment toward it.[6] This is important information because it might influence future borrowing plans: whether it is advantageous to borrow again while terms seem good, or whether there are early warning signs of possible increased costs of borrowing, or even refinancing difficulties. However, for those countries with debt that has a very low valuation or is traded in markets with low liquidity (or both), a sudden swing in sentiment might cause a very sharp change in the market value of external debt, which might also be reversed suddenly. Because it would be unaffected by such swings, information on the nominal value of external debt would be of particular analytical value in such circumstances.

16.14 The **currency composition** of external debt is also important. There is a significant difference between having external debt payable in domestic cur-

rency and having external debt payable in foreign currency. In the event of a sudden depreciation of the domestic currency, foreign currency external debt (including foreign-currency-linked debt) has potentially important wealth and cash-flow effects for the economy. For instance, when public debt is payable in foreign currency, a devaluation of the domestic currency could aggravate the financial position of the public sector, so creating an incentive for the government to avoid a necessary exchange rate adjustment. Information on the currency composition of debt at the sectoral level, including resident and nonresident claims in foreign currency, is particularly important because the wealth effects also depend on foreign currency relations between residents.

16.15 But any analysis of the foreign currency composition of external debt needs to take account of the size and composition of foreign currency assets, and income, together with foreign-currency-linked financial derivatives positions. The latter instruments can be used to change the exposure from foreign to domestic currency or to a different foreign currency.

16.16 The **interest rate composition** of external debt, both short- and long-term, may also have significant implications. Sharp increases in short-term interest rates, such as those experienced in the early 1980s, can have profound implications for the real cost of debt, especially if a significant share of debt pays interest that is linked to a floating rate such as LIBOR. As with the foreign currency position, it is necessary to take account of financial derivatives positions, since these may significantly change the effective interest composition of debt. For instance, interest-rate-based financial derivatives can be used to swap variable-rate obligations into fixed-rate liabilities, and vice versa. The relevance of financial derivatives in analyzing external debt is considered in more detail below.

16.17 The **industrial concentration** of debt should also be monitored. If debt is concentrated in a particular industry or industries, economic shocks such as a downturn in worldwide demand for certain products could increase the risk of a disruption in debt-service payments by that economy.[7]

---

[5]This type of monitoring is discussed in more detail in Chapter 7, Box 7.1.

[6]Increasingly, information from credit derivatives, such as default swaps and spread options, also provides market information on an entity's credit standing.

[7]While the *Guide* does not explicitly include guidance for the measurement of the industrial composition of external debt, these data can be compiled using the concepts set out in the *Guide* together with the International Standard Industrial Classification (*1993 SNA*, pp. 594–96) as the "sector" classification.

16.18 To monitor **debt service**, the amounts to be paid are important, rather than the market value of the debt. Debt servicing involves both the ongoing meeting of obligations—that is, payments of interest and principal—and the final payment of principal at maturity. However, it is most unlikely that the debt-service schedule will be known with certainty at any given time. Estimates of the amounts to be paid can vary over time because of variable interest and foreign currency rates, and the repayment dates for debt containing embedded put (right to sell) or call (right to buy) options that can be triggered under certain conditions add further uncertainty. So, in presenting data on the debt-service payment schedule, it is important that the assumptions used to estimate future payments on external debt liabilities be presented in a transparent manner along with the data.

16.19 One indication of an economy that is beginning to have difficulty servicing its external debt is when the level of **arrears** is on a rising trend both in relation to the external debt position and to the amount of debt service falling due. In such circumstances, detailed data by institutional sector and by type of instrument might help to identify the sources of the difficulty.

The Role of Income

16.20 In analyzing debt, the future trend of income is clearly relevant because it affects the ability of the debtor to service debt. Traditionally, the focus has been on **earnings from exports of goods and services**. To what extent is debt, or are debt-service payments, "covered" by earnings from the export of goods and services? Diversification of products and markets is positive because it limits exposure to shocks, in turn limiting the possibility that the private sector as a whole will get into difficulties, and that the public sector will lose revenues, thus affecting the willingness to pay. The currency composition of export earnings may also be of relevance.

16.21 While the willingness to pay is an important factor in determining whether debt-service payments are made, the **use of external borrowing** will affect the future income from which those payments are made.[8] If debt is used to fund unproductive activity,

future income is more likely to fall short of that required to service the debt. The question to address is not so much the specific use of the borrowed capital but rather the efficiency of total investment in the economy, considered in the context of indicators for the economy as a whole, such as the growth rates of output and exports, and total factor productivity—all data series potentially derivable from national accounts data. From another perspective, if an economy is unwilling to service its debts, and defaults, production losses might ensue as the economy ceases to be integrated with international capital markets.

The Role of Assets

16.22 As indicated above, the external debt position needs to be considered in the context of external assets because these help to meet debt-servicing requirements—assets generate income and can be sold to meet liquidity demands. In the IIP, the difference between external assets and external liabilities is the net asset (or liability) position of an economy.

16.23 For all economies, **international reserve assets** are, by definition, composed of external assets that are readily available to and controlled by the monetary authorities for direct financing of payments imbalances, for indirectly regulating the magnitude of such imbalances through intervention in exchange markets to affect the currency exchange rate, and for other purposes. Because of this role, in March 1999, the IMF's Executive Board, drawing on the work of the IMF and the Committee on Global Financial Systems of the G-10 central banks, strengthened the Special Data Dissemination Standard requirements for the dissemination of data on international reserves, and foreign currency liquidity. A data template on international reserves and foreign currency liquidity was introduced that provides a considerably greater degree of transparency in international reserves data than was hitherto available.[9]

---

[8]Dragoslav Avramovic and others (1964, p. 67) noted that while the debt-service ratio "does serve as a convenient yardstick for

passing short-term creditworthiness judgments, that is to say, judgments of the risk that default may be provoked by liquidity crises," in fact "the only important factor, from the long-run point of view, is the rate of growth of production." Indeed, "it is only in the interest of the borrowers as well as of the lenders that output and savings be maximized, since they are the only real source from which debt service is paid."

[9]See Kester (2001).

16.24 But as private entities in an economy become increasingly active in international markets, they are likely to acquire external assets as well as liabilities. The diverse nature of private sector external assets suggests that they are of a different nature than reserve assets. For instance, private sector external assets may not be distributed among sectors and individual enterprises in such a way that they can be used to absorb private sector liquidity needs. But the presence of such assets needs to be taken into account in individual country analysis of the external debt position. One approach is to present the net external debt position for each institutional sector, thus comparing the institutional attribution and concentration of external assets in the form of debt instruments with external debt (see Chapter 7).

16.25 But in comparing assets with debt, it is necessary to also consider the liquidity and quality of assets, their riskiness, and the functional and instrument composition of assets.

16.26 Most important, assets should be capable of generating income or be liquid so that they could be sold if need be, or both. The **functional composition of assets** provides important information in this regard. For instance, direct investment assets may generate income but are often less liquid, especially if they take the form of fully owned nontraded investments in companies or subsidiaries. Typically, direct investment assets are either illiquid in the short term (such as plant and equipment) or, if they are potentially marketable, the direct investor needs to take into account the implications on direct investment enterprises of withdrawing assets. The latter will be a countervailing factor to any selling pressures. Nonetheless, some direct investment assets may be closer to portfolio investments and relatively tradable—such as nonmajority shares in companies in countries with deep equity markets.

16.27 Portfolio investment is by definition tradable. Investments—such as loans and trade credit—while generating income can be less liquid than portfolio investment, but the maturity of these investments may be important because the value of short-term assets can be realized early. Increasingly, loans can be packaged into a single debt instrument and traded. Trade credit may be difficult to withdraw without harming export earnings, a very impor-

tant source of income during situations of external stress.

16.28 In assessing assets in the context of debt analysis, the **quality of assets** is a key factor. In principle the quality of the assets is reflected in the price of the assets. Some knowledge of the issuer and the country of residence may provide a further idea of the quality of the asset and its availability in times of a crisis; availability is often correlated with location or type of country. Knowledge of the geographic spread of assets can help one to understand the vulnerability of the domestic economy to financial difficulties in other economies.

16.29 The **currency composition** of assets, together with that of debt instruments, provides an idea of the impact on the economy of changes in the various exchange rates; notably, it provides information on the wealth effect of cross exchange rate movements (such as changes in the dollar-yen exchange rate for euro-area countries). The BIS International Banking Statistics (see next chapter), and the IMF's Coordinated Portfolio Investment Survey (see Chapter 13), at the least, encourage the collection of data on the country of residence of the nonresident debtor, and the currency composition of assets.

Relevance of Financial Derivatives and Repurchase Agreements (Repos)

16.30 The growth in financial derivatives markets has implications for debt management and analysis. They are used for a number of purposes including risk management, hedging, arbitrage between markets, and speculation.

16.31 From the viewpoint of managing the risks arising from debt instruments, **derivatives** can be both cheaper and more efficient than other tools. This is because they can be used to directly trade away the specific risk to be managed. For instance, a foreign currency borrowing can be hedged through a foreign-currency-linked derivative and so eliminate part or all of the foreign currency risk. Thus, aggregate information on the notional position in foreign currency derivatives is important in determining the wealth and cash-flow effects of changing exchange rates. Similarly, the cash-flow uncertainties involved in borrowing in variable interest rates can be reduced by swapping into "fixed-rate" payments with an interest rate swap.[10] In both instances the derivatives contract will involve the borrower in additional counterparty credit risk, but it facilitates good risk-management practices.

16.32 Derivatives are also used as speculative and arbitrage instruments.[11] They are a tool for undertaking leveraged transactions, in that for relatively little capital advanced up front, significant exposures to risk can be achieved, and differences in the implicit price of risk across instruments issued by the same issuer, or very similar issuers, can be arbitraged.[12] However, if used inappropriately, financial derivatives can cause significant losses and so enhance the vulnerability of an economy. Derivatives can also be used to circumvent regulations, and so place unexpected pressure on markets. For instance, a ban on holding securities can be circumvented by foreign institutions through a total-return swap.[13]

16.33 Derivatives positions can become very valuable or costly depending on the underlying price movements. The value of the positions is measured by the market value of the positions. For all the above reasons, there is interest in market values, gross assets and liabilities, and notional (or nominal) values of financial derivatives positions.[14]

16.34 Risk-enhancing or -mitigating features that are similar to financial derivatives may also be embedded in other instruments such as bonds and notes. Structured bonds are an example of such enhanced instruments. These instruments could, for example,

be issued in dollars, with the repayment value dependent on a multiple of the Mexican peso–U.S. dollar exchange rate. Borrowers may also include a put—right to sell—option in the bond contract that might lower the coupon rate but increase the likelihood of an early redemption of the bond, not least when the borrower runs into problems. Also, for example, credit-linked bonds may be issued that include a credit derivative, which links payments of interest and principal to the credit standing of another borrower. The inclusion of these derivatives can improve the terms that the borrower would otherwise have received, but at the cost of taking on additional risk. Uncertainty over the repayment terms or the repayment schedule is a consequence, so there is analytical interest in information on these structured bond issues.

16.35 Repurchase agreements (repos) also facilitate improved risk management and arbitrage. A repo allows an investor to purchase a financial instrument, and then largely finance this purchase by on-selling the security under a repo agreement. By selling the security under a repo, the investor retains exposure to the price movements of the security, while requiring only modest cash outlays. In this example, the investor is taking a "long" or positive position. On the other hand, through a **security loan**, a speculator or arbitrageur can take a "short" or negative position in an instrument by selling a security they do not own and then meeting their settlement needs by borrowing the security (security loan) from another investor.

16.36 While in normal times all these activities add liquidity to markets and allow the efficient taking of positions, when sentiment changes volatility may increase as leveraged positions may need to be unwound, such as the need to meet margin requirements. Position data on securities issued by residents and involved in repurchase and security lending transactions between residents and nonresidents help in understanding and anticipating market pressures. These data can also help in understanding the debt-service schedule data. For example, if a nonresident sold a security under a repo transaction to a resident who then sold it outright to another nonresident, the debt-service schedule would record two sets of payments to nonresidents by the issuer for the same security, although there would be one set of payments for the one security. In volatile times, when large positions develop in one direction, this might result in

---

[10]The risk might not be completely eliminated if at the reset of the floating rate the credit risk premium of the borrower changes. The interest rate swap will eliminate the risk of changes in the market rate of interest.

[11]Speculation and arbitrage activity can help add liquidity to markets and facilitate hedging. Also, when used for arbitrage purposes, derivatives may reduce any inefficient pricing differentials between markets and/or instruments.

[12]Leverage, as a financial term, describes having the full benefits arising from holding a position in a financial asset without having had to fund the purchase with own funds. Financial derivatives are instruments that can be used by international investors to leverage investments, as are repos.

[13]A total-return swap is a credit derivative that swaps the total return on a financial instrument for a guaranteed interest rate, such as an interbank rate, plus a margin.

[14]While the *Guide* explicitly presents data only on the notional (or nominal) value for foreign-currency- and interest-rate-linked financial derivatives, information on the notional value of financial derivatives, for all types of risk category, by type and in aggregate, can be of analytical value.

apparent very significant debt-service payments on securities; the position data on resident securities involved in cross-border reverse transactions could indicate that reverse transactions are a factor.

Information on the Creditor

16.37 In any debt analysis an understanding of the creditor is relevant because different creditors have different motivations and influences upon them.

16.38 The **sector and country of lender** are important factors in debt analysis. Debt analysis has traditionally focused on sectors—in particular, on the split between the official sector, banking, and other, mostly private, sectors. The importance of this sectoral breakdown lies in the different degrees of difficulty for reaching an orderly workout in the event of payment difficulties. For instance, negotiations of debt relief will differ, depending on the status of the creditor. The official sector and the banks constitute a relatively small and self-contained group of creditors that can meet and negotiate with the debtor through such forums as the Paris Club (official sector), and London Club (banks). By contrast, other private creditors are typically more numerous and diverse.

16.39 Also, the public sector may be a **guarantor** of debts owed to the foreign private sector. Often this is the case with export credit, under which the credit agency pays the foreign private sector participant in the event of nonpayment by the debtor, and so takes on the role of creditor. These arrangements are intended to stimulate trade activity, and premiums are paid by the private sector. In case of default, the ultimate creditor is the public sector, if the credit agency is indeed in the public sector. The **country of creditor** is important for debt analysis because overconcentration of the geographic spread of creditors has the potential for contagion of adverse financial activity. For instance, if one or two countries are main creditors, then a problem in their own economies or with their own external debt position could cause them to withdraw finance from the debtor country. Indeed, concentration by country and sector, such as banks, could make an economy highly dependent on conditions in that sector and economy.

PART IV

Work of International Agencies

17. External Debt Statistics from International Agencies

Introduction

17.1 External debt and related statistics are disseminated by four international agencies:

- The BIS, from its locational and consolidated International Banking Statistics (creditor reporting) and International Securities Statistics (based on market information), in the BIS *Quarterly Review*;
- The IMF, according to balance of payments and IIP (*BPM5*) framework, in *International Financial Statistics* and the *Balance of Payments Statistics Yearbook*;
- The OECD, through its Creditor Reporting System for the external debt of developing and transition countries, in *External Debt Statistics*; and
- The World Bank, through its Debtor Reporting System for the external debt of low- and middle-income countries, in *Global Development Finance*.

17.2 These collections have developed for different reasons and for different purposes. This chapter outlines the BIS, IMF, OECD, and World Bank reporting systems, as at the end of 2000, and compares the data disseminated by the BIS, OECD, and World Bank with that from the IIP of the IMF. Also, this chapter provides some explanations for the differences between the OECD and World Bank data, and describes the quarterly release, *Joint BIS-IMF-OECD-World Bank Statistics on External Debt*.

Bank for International Settlements

17.3 The BIS produces two main sets of data: the International Banking Statistics (IBS) and the International Securities Statistics. These data are available at *http://www.bis.org/statistics/index.htm*, and published quarterly in the BIS publication, *Quarterly Review*, and in the *Joint BIS-IMF-OECD-World Bank Statistics on External Debt* (see below).

International Banking Statistics

17.4 Table 17.1 shows the coverage of the BIS International Banking Statistics. The IBS system has two main sets of data.[1] The first, which was developed in the late 1970s as a by-product of the need for monitoring overall market developments, is based on the country of location, or residence, of creditor banks (termed locational statistics). The second, which was introduced in the wake of the Latin American debt crisis in the early 1980s and was therefore explicitly designed to measure credit risk, is based on the country of origin, or nationality, of creditor banks. Its underlying principle is the worldwide consolidation of the outstanding exposures of reporting banking institutions. While the locational statistics have been available on a quarterly basis since the inception of the system, the reporting frequency of the consolidated data increased from semiannual to quarterly in 2000.

17.5 Although in both sets of statistics debtor counterparties are identified according to their country of residence, regardless of the location of the ultimate guarantor of the borrowed funds, only the locational banking statistics are consistent with the IIP framework. First, creditors are also identified according to their country of location and, therefore, reported by the host lending country (as opposed to the home country of the head office in the case of the nationality/consolidated statistics). This approach permits a statistical reconciliation on a country-by-country bilateral basis. Second, the

---

[1] See BIS (2000a). Although the BIS also collects data on syndicated loan facilities, this information cannot be used for measuring external debt. First, facilities may be used as a backup for other types of fund-raising and may therefore remain undrawn or only partially used. Second, in some instances the funds are used to replace past banking debt, without therefore entailing any increase in borrowers' debt. Third, syndicated loans are but one of the various forms of international bank lending. Thus, whereas syndicated loan data may help to assess current market conditions, they cannot be used to measure external debt.

Table 17.1. Coverage of BIS International Banking Statistics

Basis for Defining Creditor	Basis for Defining Debtor	Available Breakdown
Residence/location	Residence	Sector, currency, instrument
Nationality/consolidated	Residence	Sector, maturity
Nationality/consolidated	Nationality	None

breakdown by instrument—namely, between loans and debt securities holdings—comes close to the IIP distinction between portfolio and other investment positions. Third, the currency breakdown makes it possible to derive flows from stock data, which can be used as a proxy for measuring balance of payments transactions.[2] Also, there is a sectoral breakdown between banks and nonbanks. Keeping in mind that domestic debt compilers face difficulties reporting comprehensively on domestic nonbank financial transactions, this breakdown is particularly useful to national debt compilers for comparative or estimation purposes.[3]

17.6 In contrast, the nationality/consolidated statistics are not consistent with the IIP framework. Their main objective is to measure the credit risk faced by reporting institutions, with the reporting on a worldwide-consolidated basis being the main underlying principle. Consolidation implies that the country exposure of individual reporting institutions covers that of their affiliates in all countries, including in the debtor country itself. Also as part of the process of consolidation, positions between the related offices of the same banking groups (intrabank positions) are netted out, which eliminates a number of cross-border positions. Finally, country exposure under this reporting system includes local claims denominated in foreign currencies, which clearly fall outside the scope of balance of payments statistics.

17.7 At the same time, the BIS nationality/consolidated statistics provide an insight into some important categories of countries' external debt not available elsewhere. Prime among these is short-term debt (with a remaining maturity of up to one year), which had not been the original focus of debtor reporting systems. Another important piece of information is the sectoral breakdown (banks, the public sector, and private nonbanks). Moreover, as from end-June 1999, the reporting system includes a reallocation of claims according to the country of domicile of the guarantor, either the head office of the borrowing entity itself (for branches) or of borrowed funds with explicit (legally binding) guarantees—so-called "ultimate risk" data. Also included, in principle, under guarantees is collateral that is liquid and available in a country other than that of the borrower; that is, if the collateral provided is issued by a resident of the United States, then the ultimate risk data reallocates the claim to the United States from the country of residence of the provider of the collateral. This reclassification from immediate to ultimate counterparties will therefore exclude claims with implicit guarantees, or those perceived as such, as is the case of independent banking or corporate subsidiaries (unless explicitly covered by the head office).

17.8 As part of the BIS consolidated statistics, information is available on certain potential claims that do not appear on the balance sheet ("undisbursed credit commitments"). Such off-balance-sheet exposures include legally binding commitments to provide funds, such as the drawdown of loans according to a predefined calendar and the undrawn part of credit lines. Unfortunately, the heterogeneous nature of items covered by the definition (which may, for instance, include certain guarantees) might limit the use of this category for debt-measurement purposes.

17.9 The introduction of data on exposures to ultimate counterparties does not aim to replace those on exposures to immediate counterparties, but to provide a useful complement for the purpose of evaluat-

---

[2]Changes adjusted to exclude the impact of currency movements on stock data using average exchange rates for the period under consideration can only serve to approximate actual transactions.
[3]See also IMF (1992), pp. 54–62.

Table 17.2. Coverage of BIS International Security Statistics

Basis for Defining Creditor	Basis for Defining Debtor	Available Breakdown
Residence	n.a.	Maturity, currency, instrument, sector
Nationality	n.a.	Maturity, currency, instrument, sector

ing country risk. Indeed, in view of the difficulty of measuring where the final risk lies and of the significance of borderline cases, the Basel Committee on Banking Supervision has explicitly recommended that banks calculate their country exposure on both bases (dual exposure measurement).[4] The ultimate risk exposure tends to provide a better measure of the ability of creditors to recoup their claims.

International Securities Statistics

17.10 Table 17.2 shows the coverage of the BIS International Securities Statistics, which are derived from a database containing detailed information about all issues of international securities,[5] which are obtained from various commercial market sources. Each individual issuer of securities is assigned two country fields. One is location, determined by the residence of the issuer. The second field is nationality, corresponding to the country of residence of the head office or owner of the issuing entity. Thus, debt data are available on both a residence and a nationality basis. However, since holders of debt securities are difficult to identify (not least because international bonds are generally bearer securities), there is no equivalent classification for creditors. As a result, no allowance is made for international securities purchased by residents of the debtor country. At the same time, the fact that only international securities are reported means that domestic securities purchased by nonresidents are not covered by the reporting system.

17.11 The statistics comprise four types of basic information, pertaining to individual quarters: announcements of new issues, completions of new issues, net new issues (corresponding to the difference between completed issues and redemptions), and end-quarter stocks. The nationality and residence of issuers are readily available for these four types of basic information, as are the maturity breakdown (remaining maturity) and the sectoral breakdown. In addition, computer programs have been developed to read and aggregate individual issues to produce data such as original maturity and type of issues.

17.12 When aggregating the international banking and securities statistics for the purpose of measuring external debt, the breakdown of the locational (but not the consolidated) banking statistics into bank loans and securities holdings should in principle enable double counting in debt securities to be eliminated. However, the banking data include holdings of an unknown volume of securities issued on local markets (as opposed to international issues), which can be significant and/or volatile in some instances. As a result, the actual size of the overlap between the international banking and securities data cannot be fully ascertained.

International Monetary Fund

17.13 In the field of external debt statistics, the IMF collects and publishes annual and quarterly data on the IIP. These data are published in the monthly *International Financial Statistics (IFS)* publication, and in the annual *Balance of Payments Statistics Yearbook (BOPSY)*. Data on the IIP were first published in *BOPSY* in 1984. The recommended concepts for the measurement of the IIP are outlined in *BPM5*. The concepts are consistent with the *1993 SNA*, and hence with the concepts introduced in this *Guide*. At the time of writing, data were available for 63 countries.

---

[4]See Basel Committee on Banking Supervision (1982). Also, in this context and as mentioned in Chapter 12, the collection of semiannual statistics on open positions in the global over-the-counter (OTC) derivatives market was introduced by the BIS in June 1998. However, these data are not available with a country-by-country breakdown of counterparties.

[5]International securities issues are defined as those raised outside the debtor country itself, whether in the international bond (formerly Eurobond) market or in foreign markets, such as the Yankee bond market.

17.14 The IIP is a measure of the stock of a country's external financial assets and liabilities at one moment in time, such as year-end.[6] In other words, the IIP is a statistical statement of the value and composition of the stock of an economy's external financial assets (that is, the economy's financial claims on the rest of the world) and the value and composition of the stock of an economy's liabilities to the rest of the world. The financial items that comprise the position consist of claims on nonresidents, liabilities to nonresidents, monetary gold, and SDRs. In relation to the balance sheet (as delineated in the *1993 SNA*) of an economy, the net IIP (the stock of external financial assets minus the stock of external liabilities) combined with an economy's stock of nonfinancial assets comprises the net worth of that economy.

17.15 The position at the end of a specific period reflects financial transactions, valuation changes, and other adjustments that occurred during the period and affect the level of assets and/or liabilities.[7] Because of the consistency of conceptual approach, the financial transactions are those recorded in the balance of payments. The valuation changes in the IIP are holding gains and losses arising from market price changes of such instruments as equities and debt securities, as well as from exchange rate changes. In nominal value terms, changes in the market price of a debt instrument do not affect the nominal amount outstanding. The other adjustments item, which is equivalent to "other changes in volume" in the *1993 SNA*, are changes that are not transactions or valuation changes, but items that affect the levels of assets and liabilities, such as reclassifications.

17.16 Thus, the IIP provides a framework that allows transactions in external debt, such as disbursements and repayments of loans, the accrual of interest costs, etc., that are recorded in the balance of payments to be related to changes in outstanding positions in external debt liabilities, as recorded in the change in the IIP between reporting periods. Because stock levels are sometimes utilized in the determination of investment income receipts and payments in balance of payments accounts, consistent classification and valuation throughout the income category of the current account, the financial account, and the position components allows for meaningful analysis of yields and rates of return on external investments. In addition, the reconciliation between the IIP and the rest-of-the-world balance sheet in the national accounts provides a framework for analyzing developments in the IIP in the context of the financial behavior of all institutional sectors of the economy.[8] These various reconciliations support debt analysis work.

Organisation for Economic Co-operation and Development

17.17 The OECD collects two sets of data that include information on external indebtedness:

- Aggregate information on official and officially supported (that is, guaranteed or insured by the official sector) export credits, and individual transactions data on all other official loans from the Creditor Reporting System (CRS)—these data are published in the OECD publication, *External Debt Statistics*, and the *Joint BIS-IMF-OECD-World Bank Statistics on External Debt* (see below); and
- Aggregate data on flows of aid loans and grants, other official flows, private market transactions, and assistance from nongovernmental organizations to each recipient country and recipient countries combined, from the Development Assistance Committee (DAC) annual questionnaire—these data are published in *Geographical Distribution of Financial Flows to Developing Countries* and in the *Development Co-operation Report*.

17.18 The main external debt publication of the OECD is the annual publication *External Debt Statistics*, which provides data on debt for developing and transition economies. These data are based largely on creditor sources, with the CRS data on loans (including export credits), the BIS international banking and security statistics, and the World Bank's data on multilateral lending providing the core data series. Some additional debtor data are obtained from the World

---

[6]For a full description of the IIP, see Chapter XXIII of *BPM5*.

[7]While the financial transactions are shown in *IFS* and *BOPSY* as part of the balance of payments statement, the valuation changes and other adjustments are not collected or published by the IMF.

[8]There are differences in classification between the rest-of-the-world account and the IIP that reflect, inter alia, differences in analytical requirements. For instance, the national accounts focus on instruments, while the IIP focuses on functional categories. The detailed reconciliation is provided in Appendix IV.

Bank for debt owed to non-OECD official creditors and from various sources for nonresident nonbank deposits in banks. The data are presented by maturity, creditor sector, and/or instrument. The classifications are not the same as in the IIP and, while in theory they should be similar, the external debt data totals in the two presentations will differ because of differences in concepts and methodology used, and in completeness of reporting.

OECD Reporting Systems

17.19 The CRS was established in 1967 with the aim of supplying "participants with a regular flow of data on indebtedness and capital flows." Consequently, over the years it has become a major source of information not only on official lending but also on the terms and conditions of external lending, as well as the sectoral and geographic distribution of flows to developing economies.

17.20 The CRS comprises separate report forms for commitments and loans. Three report forms cover commitments: grants (Form 1A); aid and other official loans excluding export credits (Form 1B); and guaranteed and direct export credits extended for a period of five years or more (Form 1C). Four forms cover loans: the status of individual aid and other official loans, excluding export credits (Form 2); the status of aggregated medium- and long-term guaranteed export credits (Form 3); the status of aggregated medium- and long-term direct export credits (Form 3A); and the outstanding amounts of short-term export credits on an original maturity basis (Form 3B). Form 2 provides individual transaction data, and Forms 3, 3A, and 3B provide aggregate data on outstanding amounts at the end of the period and transactions during the period. Forms 3, 3A, and 3B also provide expected payments.

17.21 Reporting frequency for the CRS differs among forms. Whereas respondents report official loan commitments continuously, and export credit debt semiannually, data on the status of individual aid and other official loans are reported annually. Because these loans are not closely affected by financial market developments, this frequency is considered adequate.

17.22 The annual DAC questionnaires provide aggregated flow data that are based largely on balance of payments principles, with the exceptions noted below.[9] Thus, there is a broad correspondence between balance of payments and DAC flows data. Where CRS reporting is incomplete, debt flow data may be obtained from the DAC reporting system, and debt stock data may be estimated on the basis of previous stocks and DAC flows.

Comparison of OECD Data with Balance of Payments/IIP Data

Presentation of data

17.23 Unlike the presentation in the IIP, OECD categories show different types of debt, based partly on the creditor and partly on the instrument. They include official bilateral lending (excluding export credits), official development assistance (ODA)/official aid, officially supported export credits, official multilateral lending, bank lending, debt securities, other claims, and short-term debt.

17.24 Historically, the collection of data on ODA and other official loans has reflected analytical interest in recording development finances, especially aid. ODA is defined as those flows to countries on Part I of the DAC List of Aid Recipients that are (1) provided by official agencies, including state and local governments, or by their executive agencies; and (2) each transaction is administered with the promotion of the economic development and welfare of developing countries as its main objective, and is concessional in character and conveys a grant element of at least 25 percent (calculated at a rate of discount of 10 percent). Flows to countries on Part II of the DAC List (transition countries) that meet the above criteria are classified as official aid.[10] Although it is rare, such loans may also be made to the private sector in the borrowing country.

17.25 The collection of export credit data arose from the needs of the OECD Trade Committee to follow the activities of export credit agencies. Also of interest to creditors and debtors is the scale of multilateral lending from the World Bank and related organizations, as are loans made by other non-OECD creditors, although these data are compiled from the Debtor Reporting System (DRS).

---

[9]Further information on the DAC reporting system is available on the Internet at the following website: *http://www1.oecd.org/dac/htm/crs.htm.*

[10]The DAC list essentially includes all non-OECD members and some OECD members.

17.26 The presentation of the data allows creditors to consider country risk. Debtors and creditors can identify amounts that may be renegotiated in such fora as the Paris Club, the London Club, or may be the object of bilateral debt relief, and examine such questions as burden sharing by creditors, or the relative importance of different categories of creditors in a debtor country's borrowing.

Concepts

17.27 In both the OECD's reporting systems, the balance of payments criteria of residence is generally required. Creditors identify their debtor counterparts according to their country of residence, although in cases such as offshore centers, flag of convenience countries, or aircraft leases, the ultimate borrower may be in a third country. In the OECD reporting systems, all debt stocks and flows are valued at face value, unlike market value in the balance of payments and IIP. Although this may seem like a major divergence, there is in practice little difference because nontraded instruments are invariably valued at nominal value in the IIP.

17.28 A significant difference between the OECD and IIP data is that, unlike the IIP, OECD data are not reported on a full accrual basis. Both the OECD and IIP data record disbursements at the time they occur, whereas repayments are reported in OECD data when they take place, not when they are due (as in the IIP). OECD debt stock is calculated as the amount of disbursed principal outstanding plus interest in arrears, whereas the IIP debt stocks are the amounts outstanding including all interest costs that have accrued and have not yet been paid.

17.29 The IIP and OECD data define long-term and short-term debt identically. Thus in the OECD data, short-term debt includes all debt contracted for a period of one year or less plus, wherever possible, arrears of both principal and interest on all debt. In the OECD data, the maturity breakdown is available for only two categories: banks and export credits. For other categories, all debt is classified as long-term. Using data in *External Debt Statistics*, debt with a remaining maturity of one year or less can be estimated by combining short-term debt with the amount of principal payments due in the next year on long-term debt.

17.30 The nonresident creditor sector is published in the OECD data, whereas the IIP publishes the res-

ident debtor sector. Also, the sector classification in the OECD data does not correspond with the IIP, or the *1993 SNA*. In the OECD data, there is the official sector and the private sector, of which banks are separately identified. Although not published, the OECD does have some data on the resident debtor sector. The classification of borrowers is not reported for official lending other than export credits, but it can be assumed that the vast majority of borrowers of these funds belong to the general government sector. In the case of export credits, reporters distinguish between public and private borrowers, although a further distinction between bank and other private sector is not available. Rescheduled export credits are assumed to be claims on public borrowers; the rescheduled debt notified to the OECD is generally debt rescheduled by the public sector of the debtor and the official sector of the creditor.

Specific items

Trade credits

17.31 The concept of "trade credits" is wider in the OECD data than in the IIP, which "only" includes claims and liabilities arising from the direct extension of credit by suppliers and buyers for transactions in goods and services, and for work in progress (or to be undertaken). The OECD data cover three types of export credits—officially supported suppliers credits, officially supported bank credits, and official direct credits. They do not cover private sector credits that do not have official support in the form of insurance or guarantee.

Arrears

17.32 The recording treatment of arrears of principal and interest is the same in the IIP and OECD debt data; arrears arise when payments are past due, and are classified as short-term debt. However, in the OECD data, late interest (interest on arrears) is reported and included in the debt stock only when the interest is capitalized under a rescheduling, whereas in the IIP interest costs accrue on arrears (although *BPM5* is not very clear on this issue).

Write-offs

17.33 A write-off is a unilateral creditor action that is an accounting procedure that removes a debt from a creditor's books. As such, it should be reflected in the notification of creditors' debt stocks to the OECD, thus affecting the level of claims. The IIP is silent on the treatment by the debtor, so a discrepancy could arise between the debtor and creditor data. While write-offs are rare for official and officially supported debt, they are a more common procedure for banks.

Debt forgiveness

17.34 In the DAC statistics debt forgiveness is a similar but different concept from that used in *BPM5*. Unlike *BPM5*, only relief implemented for the purpose of promoting the development or welfare of the recipient qualifies as debt forgiveness in the DAC data. However, if this condition is fulfilled, like *BPM5*, a voluntary cancellation of debt within the framework of a bilateral agreement is classified in the DAC statistics as debt forgiveness, and is reported as an ODA grant (capital transfer in *BPM5*). Unlike *BPM5*, the DAC system's concept of debt forgiveness also includes a reduction in the present value of debt achieved by concessional rescheduling or refinancing, and the discount in a debt conversion occurring within the framework of a bilateral agreement between governments (although in certain circumstances *BPM5* also records such discounts as debt forgiveness; see Chapter 8 of the *Guide*, paragraph 8.33).

17.35 Most OECD reporters follow balance of payments principles in reporting forgiveness when debt is canceled—the amount forgiven is valued as the amount of debt stock canceled and is reported in a lump sum at the time the creditor enters the forgiveness on its books. However, a few reporters only report the forgiveness of the debt annually when debt-service payments would have fallen due. This approach results in differences in timing (forgiveness spread out over many years) and amounts (interest not yet due at the time of forgiveness included in addition to principal and interest arrears) between the DAC forgiveness grants and the balance of payments capital transfers. Because some already forgiven amounts may remain included in the outstanding debt stock until the period in which their payments would have fallen due, this approach may also have the consequence of overstating the OECD measured debt stock in the intervening period after the forgiveness agreement.

Debt rescheduling

17.36 Debt rescheduling is reflected in both the debt stock and flow data collected by the OECD. The rescheduling flows are recorded at the time of actual implementation of the rescheduling, which should correspond to the time they are entered into the books (of both the creditor and the debtor), the same approach as the IIP. The rescheduling of any future maturities is therefore recorded at the time of the actual implementation of their rescheduling, rather than when the rescheduling as a whole is agreed. When short-term debt, including arrears, is rescheduled into long-term maturities, this is reflected in the OECD data, as in the IIP. Also as in the IIP, if the rescheduling involves a shift in creditor or debtor sectors—for example, a Paris Club rescheduling of debt lent by the private sector (under a creditor government guarantee) to the private sector (under a borrower government guarantee) could become government to government—the OECD data record the legal change of ownership.[11] However, when the rescheduling is within the official sector, only the capitalization of interest is reported as a flow (in order to avoid two offsetting entries for the principal rescheduled). While rescheduled export credit debt owed to public creditors can be identified as such in the OECD database, in *External Debt Statistics* it is classified under *nonbank export credits*.

17.37 Although there is much similarity in the principles, in practice the complexity of restructuring makes full and correct reporting difficult to implement for both creditors and debtors and can give rise to discrepancies between OECD data and the IIP. Genuine differences in the timing of book entries between creditors and debtors, and practical difficulties in tracing restructuring that can lead to problems such as misclassification of arrears and rescheduled debts, and omission of capitalized interest, sometimes produce different figures in creditors' reports and the debtor's IIP.

Debt conversions

17.38 In OECD data, when official debt is exchanged for equity or counterpart funds to be used for development purposes, this should be reported as an ODA grant for debt conversion, with debt forgiveness recorded only if there is a discount on the exchange. Also when, in the framework of a bilateral

---

[11]The counterentry to the governments' assumption of external debt might well be a claim on their private sector or capital transfer. Because of guarantees or insurance provided by the government's export credit agency, the creditor government may acquire the claim from their private sector.

agreement for development purposes, the official sector sells debt at a discount to a private sector entity that is then exchanged for equity or counterpart funds to be used for the benefit of the private sector entity for development purposes, the official sector's loss should be reported as debt forgiveness. In both cases, and as in the IIP, the debt stock is reduced by the value of the debt converted.

World Bank

17.39 The World Bank collects data on external indebtedness from debtor countries through the Debtor Reporting System (DRS). These reported data form the core of the detailed country-level debt stock and flow data that are published annually in the *Global Development Finance* (*GDF*) publication (formerly *World Debt Tables*). Selected debt data are also available in the annual *World Development Indicators* publication, and in the *Joint BIS-IMF-OECD-World Bank Statistics on External Debt* (see further, below).

17.40 The World Bank's interest in debt statistics is both analytical and operational. At the analytical level, the Bank is a leading international source of information and analysis on the economic situation of developing countries. Bank staff make extensive use of debt statistics in analyzing the economic prospects, financing needs, creditworthiness, and debt sustainability of developing economies. At the operational level, the lending and borrowing activities of the Bank demand a close monitoring of the overall financial situation of each borrower, such as debt-servicing capacity. To this end, the Bank's General Conditions (of borrowing) require a borrowing or guaranteeing member country to report external debt information to the Bank. As a condition of presentation of loans and credits to the World Bank's Executive Board, each borrowing or guaranteeing country must submit a complete report (or an acceptable plan of action for such reporting) on its external debt.

Debtor Reporting System

17.41 The DRS was established in 1951 and is the World Bank's principal means of monitoring external debt. Through the DRS, countries—typically low- and middle-income—that borrow from the Bank report data on long-term external indebtedness.

17.42 The number of countries covered and the data to be reported have expanded over time. At the time of writing, 136 countries submitted two kinds of reports: loan-by-loan data on long-term debt of the public sector and debts guaranteed by the public sector; and summary reports on long-term debt of the private sector that is not publicly guaranteed. The data are supplied on special reporting forms. For public and publicly guaranteed debt, individual new loan commitments are reported (quarterly) on Forms 1 and 1A, and the status of each loan at the end of the recording period and the transactions recorded during the recording period are reported on Form 2. For private nonguaranteed debt, aggregate figures on the stock of debt, transactions during the recording period, and future debt services are reported on Form 4. Short-term debt data are either obtained from the country or estimated separately using creditor and other sources, the most important source being remaining-maturity data from the BIS consolidated International Banking Statistics, which are adjusted to come into line with the original-maturity concept.[12]

17.43 *Form 1* is used for reporting the terms and conditions of each external public and publicly guaranteed debt obligation incurred during a calendar quarter with an original maturity of more than one year. This report allows a wide range of information to be captured and disseminated for statistical and analytical purposes within and outside the World Bank.

17.44 Information is collected on creditor name, type, and residence and is used in classifying external debt owed to official and private creditors, assessing creditor exposure, analyzing net resource flows from official and private creditor sources, and identifying Paris Club debt eligibility.

17.45 On the debtor side, borrower name and type, guarantor name, economic sector of borrower, and whether funds for debt servicing are to come from the budget of the central government are also reported on Form 1. This information is used in several ways, including measuring public and private sector borrowings, identifying uses of funds, and assessing the central government's debt burden.

---

[12]Described in detail in the notes and definitions to the *Global Development Finance* report; on the Internet, see *http://www.worldbank.org/prospects/gdf2002/vol1.htm*. The *GDF* database is also available on-line, by subscription, at *http://publications.worldbank.org/ecommerce/catalog/product?item_id=1023868.*

17.46 Form 1 allows compilation of detailed information on loan terms, including interest rates and spreads, grace period, maturity, debt-service pattern, and currencies in which the loan amounts are denominated and repaid. This information is used in calculating the grant element component, projected debt service, present value of debt, and other debt and economic indicators.

17.47 *Form 1A* captures future payments due when the terms of repayments cannot be adequately described in Form 1, and amounts rescheduled in multiyear rescheduling agreements that will become effective on future specified dates.

17.48 *Form 2* is used for reporting the annual status of each external debt liability with an original maturity of more than one year. This annual summary report presents stock and flow information for each public or publicly guaranteed debt extant at the end of the reporting period or repaid or canceled during the period. For each debt, the amount of debt committed, undisbursed, and outstanding and disbursed is presented along with the transactions that have taken place during the year. Also presented is information on any accumulation of arrears and debt reschedulings. All amounts are reported in the currency in which the debt is payable. Based on the Form 2 report, a wide range of stock and flow accounts as well as economic indicators are derived and disseminated in the *GDF*. The report is due within three months after the end of the reporting period.

17.49 *Form 4* is used for submitting annual information on the status of private sector external debt that has an original maturity of more than one year and that does not have a public sector guarantee. The information is aggregated by type of debtor institution—commercial banks, direct investment enterprises, and other—and a separate form is submitted for each type of institution. The creditor information for each type of debtor institution is provided for the following types of creditors: private banks and other financial institutions, foreign parents and affiliates, exporters and other private, and official (governments and international organizations).

17.50 Form 4 contains both stock and flow accounts and, for each type of debtor institution, estimated future payments of principal and interest for the first ten years following the end of the reporting period.

Comparison of World Bank and Balance of Payments/IIP data

Presentation of data

17.51 The presentation of debtor data, as shown in the *GDF*, responds to a different set of analytical requirements from that of the IIP. The aim is to provide a detailed view of a country's borrowing activities, accessibility to external funds, and borrowing costs, as well as to facilitate a comprehensive analysis of the debt burden, debt-servicing capacity, financing needs, and creditworthiness of the country. To this purpose, both stock and flow data are provided at different levels of breakdown. The first breakdown is that between long- and short-term debt, and the second between public (and publicly guaranteed) and private borrowing. Special attention is paid to identifying private borrowing with direct government guarantees. Also, projected repayment profiles are viewed as critical to analysis and management of obligations, and these are included in the presentation of data.

17.52 The creditor breakdown goes beyond a breakdown by instrument. For instance, for official creditors, multilateral and bilateral, the more detailed breakdown identifies concessional lending by this sector. These data are particularly useful in debt work. Official credits with an original grant element of 25 percent or more using a 10 percent rate of discount are characterized as concessional (as defined by the DAC). The exception are credits from major regional development banks—African Development Bank, Asian Development Bank, European Bank for Reconstruction and Development, and the Inter-American Development Bank—and from the IMF and World Bank, where concessionality is determined on the basis of each institution's own classification of concesssional lending.

17.53 The disaggregation of private lending is a mixture—by institution, such as banks, and by instrument, such as bonds. Trade-related borrowing, such as export credits and supplier credits, is included within "other private," and so not separately identified. The presentation of the data distinguishes between private-sourced debt that is owed by public entities or owed by private entities but with explicit government guarantees, and that which is owed by the private sector.

17.54 Projected debt-service payments and debt-disbursement profile are based on current debt transactions and loan terms. Projected debt-service payments are projections of payments due on existing debt outstanding, including undisbursed amounts of existing external debt, taking account of implemented multiple-year restructuring agreements. Future disbursements and debt-service payments refer only to existing debt and do not reflect any assumptions about future borrowing.

Concepts

17.55 The principal concepts used by the DRS in compiling debt stocks are consistent with the conceptual framework of the *Grey Book* (BIS and others, 1988) and there is consistency with several elements of the IIP as well. The level of detail of the information required from reporting countries and the presentation of debt data are influenced by the analytical and operational application of the data (see paragraph 17.40). The DRS includes all debt with an original maturity of more than one year owed to nonresidents and short-term debt. Total external debt is derived as the aggregate of long-term and short-term debt (and use of IMF credit).

17.56 Like the IIP, external debt statistics in the DRS are compiled on a residence basis (as opposed to a nationality basis)—external debt is that owed by entities physically located in the reporting country to entities located outside the reporting area, irrespective of nationality. So, branches of foreign banks are resident to the reporting country, whereas foreign offices of domestic banks are not. Also, bank deposits held in domestic banks by nationals living abroad are included in external debt data.

17.57 In a few cases the DRS deviates from the residence criteria, and hence the IIP framework, for analytical and operational reasons. For instance, the DRS excludes from a country's external debt the indebtedness of banks located in a resident offshore banking center; this indebtedness can often be very large in relation to the host economy.[13]

17.58 Debts payable in both foreign and domestic currency to nonresidents are required information to be reported under the DRS. In practice, the DRS's focus is on foreign currency debt; domestic currency

debt owed to nonresidents has not been included. This is a departure from the IIP framework. Also, currency—notes and coins—held by nonresidents are not captured by the DRS.

17.59 A point of departure from the IIP is the valuation of stocks. The DRS measures all stocks at nominal value rather than at traded or current market value. For nontraded or nontransferable debt instruments such as loans and deposits, there is in practice little difference because nontraded instruments are invariably valued at nominal value in the IIP. However, this is not true for traded debt instruments.

17.60 Short-term and long-term debt are similarly defined in the DRS and the IIP: short-term debt includes all debt with an original maturity of one year or less, and long-term debt includes all debt with an original maturity greater than one year; interest arrears are included under short-term debt. There is a difference in the treatment of principal arrears; the DRS classifies these arrears by the original type of the debt, whereas the IIP classifies them as short-term debt.

17.61 The DRS sectoral classification of external long-term debt has two categories: debt of the public sector and private debt with a public sector guarantee; and all other private, nonguaranteed debt. This classification is not equivalent to the IIP breakdown, although with the available information it is possible to relate the DRS's debtor classifications—the nine types are central government, local government, central bank, private bank, direct investment, public corporation, mixed enterprise, official development bank, and private—to those of the IIP. Within the debtor category the DRS provides a further breakdown by creditor sector. The IIP does not provide a creditor sector breakdown.

17.62 The DRS measures debt stocks and flows on a cash transaction basis as opposed to the accrual method recommended in the IIP. Thus, reported flows are the result of a cash (or in-kind) transaction, such as an actual loan disbursement or repayment, and debt outstanding is the amount disbursed less amount repaid (and any interest arrears). Projections are on a debt-due basis. In the IIP framework, disbursements are recorded when they occur, but repayments are reported when due. Debt stocks in the IIP include interest costs that have accrued and have not yet been paid.

---

[13]The same can be true for countries that sponsor "flag of convenience" companies.

Comparison of World Bank Data with OECD Data

17.63 There are notable differences for data users, both in presentation and in the recording of categories of debt between the debt statistics of the debtor and creditor data. This is because the breakdowns chosen by the different reporting systems reflect the analytical requirements of users. This section discusses and explains the reasons for some of the differences.

17.64 One classification that is consistent in both systems is the concept of short- and long-term based on original maturity. Both systems also provide data on long-term debt due within the year, as well as short-term debt data on an original-maturity basis, thus allowing for a measure of remaining maturity to be estimated.

17.65 The compilers of the DRS and CRS do compare the two sets of data series to see why there are differences in reported debt figures. From their work, certain reporting differences have emerged.

17.66 First, certain borrowing countries apply the definition of short- and long-term debt differently from creditors. For instance, certain creditors may classify short-term loans that are rolled over as long-term loans. Second, the DRS does not classify arrears of principal as short-term debt but, as noted above, by the original type of debt. However, this does not pose a problem for reconciling debtor and creditor data because principal arrears are separately identified in the debtor data so to allow comparability with creditor information.

17.67 Second, bilateral ODA in the CRS and bilateral concessional debt in the DRS are not entirely comparable. The difference emerges because of the coverage of loans. In the debtor data, bilateral direct export credits may be included under bilateral concessional loans if the grant element on the loans is 25 percent or more, whereas they are classified as export credits and not ODA in the creditor data. When export credits are subsidized by ODA loans—mixed credits—the subsidies for such credits would appear as ODA loans in the creditor data.

17.68 Third, loan-by-loan comparisons between the DRS and CRS have sometimes shown a different perception of the timing of disbursements and repayments

between debtor and creditor, resulting in a difference in the reported outstanding debt at any given time.

17.69 Fourth, differences arise due to restructuring. In the case of forgiveness, the DRS may, for analytical purposes, anticipate the timing of cancellation, whereas the creditor usually waits for the signing of the bilateral agreement, which may entail delayed parliamentary approval. In the case of rescheduling of guaranteed export credits, the rescheduled loan may remain classified as an export credit rather than a new official loan on the creditor side, whereas the debtor records it as a bilateral official loan.

Joint BIS-IMF-OECD-World Bank Statistics on External Debt

17.70 The *Joint BIS-IMF-OECD-World Bank Statistics on External Debt* were first released on March 15, 1999 on the website of the OECD[14] with hyperlinks available from the websites of the BIS, the IMF, and the World Bank.[15] This release is an initiative of the Inter-Agency Task Force on Finance Statistics (TFFS); it is updated quarterly. The purpose of the site is to facilitate timely and frequent access by a broad range of users to one dataset that brings together external debt data that are currently compiled and published by the contributing international agencies (BIS, IMF, OECD, and World Bank).

17.71 The types of debt primarily covered in the Joint Statistics comprise loans from banks, debt securities issued abroad, Brady bonds, officially supported nonbank trade credits (that is, export credits extended by nonbank institutions of the exporting country), multilateral claims,[16] and official bilateral loans (loans provided mainly for development purposes excluding export credits). Data on total liabilities to banks and on officially supported bank and nonbank trade credits are available as the memorandum items. The BIS, IMF, OECD, and World Bank provide the data. The statistics are mostly from creditor and market sources but also include data pro-

---

[14]See *http://www1.oecd.org/dac/Debt/index.htm*.

[15]Respectively, at *http://www.bis.org/statistics/index.htm*, *http://www.imf.org/external/np/sta/ed/joint.htm*, and *http://www.worldbank.org/data/databytopic/debt.html*.

[16]At the time of writing, the multilateral claims covered by the data in the Joint Table were loans from the African Development Bank, Asian Development Bank, and Inter-American Development Bank, use of IMF credit, and IBRD loans and IDA credits from the World Bank.

Box 17.1. Joint BIS-IMF-OECD-World Bank Statistics on External Debt

The sources, definitions and coverage of individual series are explained in detail in this box. See also Table 17.3 and *http://www1.oecd.org/dac/Debt/index.htm.*

The columns of the table cover stocks—the amounts outstanding at the end of each period—and flows—disbursements net of repayments during the period. Flows are available for debt securities, Brady bonds, multilateral claims, and bilateral loans (lines B, C, E, and F of the table). For the banking and trade credit figures (lines A, D, J, L, and M of the table), the change in stocks, adjusted for changes in exchange rates to the U.S. dollar during the period, is given. For other series, flow data are not available.

Line A: Bank loans

Line J: Total liabilities to banks (locational)

Line M: Total claims on banks (locational)

Data above are derived from the BIS locational banking statistics.

Line B: Debt securities issued abroad

Line H: Debt securities issued abroad (due within a year)

Data are derived from quarterly BIS statistics on international securities.

Line C: Brady bonds

Brady bonds comprise commercial bank debt restructured under the Brady Plan, introduced in early 1989. Data on Brady bonds are provided from the World Bank's Debtor Reporting System (DRS). Annual data on stocks and flows (issues less repayments) are as reported by the debtor country and include buybacks. Quarterly data on stocks and flows are estimates based on repayment terms of the bonds and reflect adjustments for buybacks during the quarter. In the World Bank's *Global Development Finance* (*GDF*), data are included (but not shown separately) under public and publicly guaranteed debt.

Line D: Nonbank trade credits

Data are derived from the semiannual reports to the OECD made by OECD member countries' export credit guarantee agencies. Nonbank trade-related credits comprise official export credits, which are long-term, and officially guaranteed or insured suppliers' credits, which are credits extended by exporters to importers abroad. They also include arrears and officially rescheduled amounts on officially guaranteed or insured financial credits, since these are taken over by export credit agencies from the original bank creditors. Guaranteed financial credits made by banking institutions that do not report to the BIS are also included here. These data only cover trade credits that have been guaranteed or insured by the official sector in the creditor country. They include credits extended to both the public and private sector in the borrowing country.

Line E: Multilateral claims

Multilateral claims cover data for African Development Bank (AfDB), Asian Development Bank (ADB), Inter-American Development Bank (IADB), IMF, and World Bank claims. Stocks are the total of loans from AfDB, ADB, and IADB, use of IMF credit, and IBRD loans and IDA credits from the World Bank. Flows are the sum of disbursements less principal repayments on loans and IDA credits, and IMF purchases less IMF repurchases.

Line F: Official bilateral loans (DAC creditors)

This line shows the outstanding debt from the OECD's Credit Reporting System (CRS) on loans, other than direct export credits, extended by governments that are members of the OECD's Development Assistance Committee (DAC). Direct export credits extended by the official sector are included in nonbank trade credits (lines D and I). In addition to straightforward loans, official bilateral loans include loans payable in kind, and eligible loans in Associated Financing packages.

Line G: Liabilities to banks (due within a year)

Line K: Total liabilities to banks (consolidated)

Data are derived from the BIS consolidated banking statistics.

Line I: Nonbank trade credits (due within a year)

These data are derived from the OECD's CRS. They comprise official and officially guaranteed or insured suppliers' credits extended by exporters to importers abroad that have a remaining maturity of one year or less. They include (1) export credits with an original maturity of one year or less and (2) the amounts of principal due in the next year on credits with an original maturity of over one year. These data only cover trade credits that have been guaranteed or insured by the official sector in the creditor country. They include credits extended to both the public and private sector in the borrowing country.

Line L: Total trade credits

These data are derived from the OECD's CRS. This line covers all official and officially supported trade credits; that is, trade credits that have been guaranteed or insured by the official sector in an OECD reporting country. The credits include those extended to both the public and private sector in the borrowing country. In addition to the nonbank trade credits shown in line D, this line includes financial or buyer credits extended by banks that are guaranteed or insured by an official export credit guarantee agency. These guaranteed bank credits are also included in the amounts shown in line A (Bank loans), line G (Liabilities to banks), line J (Total liabilities to banks—locational), and line K (Total liabilities to banks—consolidated).

Line N: International reserve assets (excluding gold)

Data are those published in the IMF's *International Financial Statistics* (*IFS*).

vided by debtor countries. At the time of writing, data were available for more than 175 countries. Data are also shown on external financial assets in the form of claims on banks and holdings of interna-

tional reserve assets, which are prepared by the BIS and the IMF, respectively. A detailed description of the data in the Joint Statistics as at mid-2001 is provided in Box 17.1.

Table 17.3. Example of Joint BIS-IMF-OECD-World Bank Statistics on External Debt (1)

(In millions of U.S. dollars)	2000 December	March	June	September	December	2002 March	2000 Year	2001 Year	Third Quarter	Fourth Quarter

Stocks (end of period) with 2001 spanning March–December. *Flows (2)* 2001.

COUNTRY A
External debt—all maturities
A Bank loans (3)
B Debt securities issued abroad
C Brady bonds
D Nonbank trade credits (4)
E Multilateral claims
F Official bilateral loans (DAC creditors)
Debt due within a year
G Liabilities to banks (5)
H Debt securities issued abroad (6)
I Nonbank trade credits (4)
Memorandum items
J Total liabilities to banks (7) (locational)
K Total liabilities to banks (6) (consolidated)
L Total trade credits
M Total claims on banks (8)
N International reserve assets (excluding gold)

COUNTRY B
External debt—all maturities
A Bank loans (3)
B Debt securities issued abroad
C Brady bonds
D Nonbank trade credits (4)
E Multilateral claims
F Official bilateral loans (DAC creditors)
Debt due within a year
G Liabilities to banks (5)
H Debt securities issued abroad (6)
I Nonbank trade credits (4)
Memorandum items
J Total liabilities to banks (7) (locational)
K Total liabilities to banks (6) (consolidated)
L Total trade credits
M Total claims on banks (8)
N International reserve assets (excluding gold)

COUNTRY C
External debt—all maturities
A Bank loans (3)
B Debt securities issued abroad
C Brady bonds
D Nonbank trade credits (4)
E Multilateral claims
F Official bilateral loans (DAC creditors)
Debt due within a year
G Liabilities to banks (5)
H Debt securities issued abroad (6)
I Nonbank trade credits (4)
Memorandum items
J Total liabilities to banks (7) (locational)
K Total liabilities to banks (6) (consolidated)
L Total trade credits
M Total claims on banks (8)
N International reserve assets (excluding gold)

Source: OECD, on the Internet at http://www1.oecd.org/dac/debt.
(1) From creditor and market sources, except for data on Brady bonds which are from debtor sources, all currencies included.
(2) Flow data for items B, C, E, F and L; exchange rate adjusted changes for items A, J, and M; no data available for items D, G, H, I, K and N.
(3) From BIS locational banking statistics, which are based on the country of residence of reporting banks.
(4) Official and officially guaranteed. Break in series at end-1998 due to reallocation of rescheduled export credits from line F to line D.
(5) From BIS consolidated banking statistics, which are based on the country of head office of reporting banks and which include banks' holdings of securities.
(6) Including debt securities held by foreign banks, which are also included in line G.
(7) From BIS locational banking statistics, which are based on the country of residence of reporting banks and which include banks' holdings of securities.

17.72 Table 17.3 (on preceding page) shows a sample table from the Joint Statistics: the stock of debt, with a minimum two-month lag, for the past five quarters and the previous December; and flow figures for the latest complete two years and two recent quarters. Whenever available, data on short-term debt, based on the remaining-maturity concept, are also provided. Free access to an on-line database, which provides longer time series and permits manipulation of the figures, is also available. Some of the data are only available semiannually, and no attempt is made to provide quarterly inter- or extrapolations of these data. The data are published 22 weeks after the end of the quarter.[17]

17.73 With a view to making users aware of the data limitations and promoting best practice in using the data, a set of metadata has been prepared, along with the data, indicating how the data relate to internationally agreed concepts. These data are mostly from creditor and market sources but also include information provided by the debtor countries themselves. These data do not provide a completely comprehensive and consistent measure of total external debt.

---

[17]The lag refers to the BIS International Banking Statistics, which are the core series in the Joint Statistics.

For example, these data do not cover (1) nonofficially guaranteed suppliers credit not channeled through banks; (2) direct investment: intercompany lending; (3) private placements of debt securities; (4) domestically issued debt securities held by nonresidents; (5) deposits of nonresidents in domestic institutions; and (6) amounts owed to non-DAC governments. Nevertheless, the Joint Statistics do bring together the best international comparative data currently available on external debt that are compiled and published separately by the contributing institutions.

17.74 The user needs to be careful in comparing data series. For instance, there are overlaps between data sources such as the international securities data and the nationality/consolidated banking statistics, which indistinguishably include securities. Thus, for debt due within a year, the data relating to debt securities issued abroad include securities held by foreign banks that are also included under the data relating to liabilities to banks. Also, there can be inconsistencies. For example, the data on loans from banks and on total liabilities to banks due within a year are drawn from different data sources—the BIS locational and consolidated international banking statistics, respectively. Thus, creditor and market-based statistics are not a substitute for setting up appropriate reporting systems by the debtor countries themselves.

18. External Debt Monitoring Systems

Introduction

18.1 This chapter describes the debt recording systems of the Commonwealth Secretariat and the UN Conference on Trade and Development (UNCTAD) as at end-2000. Both systems are widely used and are designed to assist countries in capturing and storing instrument-by-instrument information in a computerized system. Both include features that can analyze the stored information.

Commonwealth Secretariat's Debt Recording and Management System (CS-DRMS)

18.2 The CS-DRMS, first released in 1985, assists countries to record and manage debt by providing a comprehensive repository for external and domestic debt data, both public and private, on an instrument-by-instrument basis, as well as tools to analyze and manage the loan portfolios. It is regularly enhanced to reflect changes in instruments, creditor practices, debt reporting standards, and technology in order to represent best practice in debt-management. The main functions of the CS-DRMS are set out in Table 18.1.

18.3 The CS-DRMS system is used in some 50 Commonwealth and non-Commonwealth countries, across 70 sites in ministries of finance and planning and central banks. It is provided as part of the Commonwealth Secretariat's advisory services in debt and development resources management, which cover the following areas:
- Strengthening the legal and institutional arrangements for contracting and managing debt;
- Advice to governments in areas such as debt policy and strategy, debt restructuring, loan evaluation, and assistance in negotiations with creditors;
- Assistance in debt data compilation and in the review of the quality of databases;
- Capacity building through training courses and workshops in various areas of debt management as well as in the use of CS-DRMS; and
- Development and maintenance of CS-DRMS, including user support.

Functionality

18.4 The CS-DRMS is an integrated system that records various types of flows—external and domestic debt, grants and government lending—for day-to-day administration and management. It has a comprehensive **External debt** module that allows for the recording of a wide range of official and commercial instruments, including short-term and private sector debt; and a comprehensive **Domestic debt** module that allows for the recording of the full issuance cycle of domestic debt instruments such as treasury bills, bonds, and notes, and for the planning of issues, auctions, and analysis of bids. Both actual and forecasted transactions data as well as that on arrears are captured in a manner that meets the international external debt data guidelines. Also, there are comprehensive facilities within CS-DRMS to handle debt restructuring, including refinancing and Paris Club rescheduling.

18.5 The special **Management tools** module assists debt managers in debt strategy formulation and analysis, such as portfolio analysis, sensitivity testing for risk management, monitoring debt sustainability indicators, and other early warning signals. Also, there are extensive querying and reporting facilities, including over 60 standard reports, as well as a custom-built report generator that allows users to write their own reports quickly.

18.6 There are multilayer security features to meet individual country requirements, including the ability to configure access screens and reports to differentiate among front, middle, and back office functions.

Table 18.1. Major Functions of the Commonwealth Secretariat Debt Recording and Management System (CS-DRMS)

Debt Recording	Debt Reporting	Debt Analysis	Other Functions
• Maintain an inventory of all external and domestic debt instruments including: — public debt and grants; — short-term and private sector debt; — restructuring agreements including rescheduling • Record basic details and terms on an instrument • Record other relevant debt-related information such as exchange rates, interest rates, and macroeconomic data • Forecast debt-service payments, both by instrument and in aggregate terms, with and without future disbursements • Record actual transactions of debt service and disbursements on a transaction-by-transaction basis • Identify loans in arrears and calculate penalty payments • Monitor loan and grant utilization and disbursements • Monitor government lending including on-lending	• Provide information and reports on any group or class of instruments • Produce standard reports for various data requirements including government finance, balance of payments, and IIP • Provide easy generation of custom reports using a purpose-built report generator • Respond to specific user enquiries into the database	• Perform sensitivity analysis on interest and exchange rate variations under various scenarios • Test the implications of new borrowings, based on different assumptions of currencies, interest, and repayment terms • Undertake debt sustainability analysis in conjunction with other packages such as the World Bank's DSM Plus • Evaluate different loan offers • Evaluate different proposals for refinancing and rescheduling of loans and compute debt relief • Combine CS-DRMS debt data with exogenous economic data to project critical debt indicators, both on nominal and a present value basis • Evaluate exposure to exchange and interest rate risk	• Transfer debt data electronically to the World Bank's DRS, as well as to spreadsheets and other packages such as asset and liability management and government accounting systems • Browse CS-DRMS data using Debt Manager—a Windows-based add-on product developed for debt managers • Use validation utilities to ensure database integrity and accuracy • Integrate front, middle, and back office functions via the database and security management options • Perform housekeeping functions such as backup and restore and setting up modem access **Future Developments:** • Web-enabled for on-line recording and reporting • Full accrual and market valuation computation • Contingent Liability Module

Technological Characteristics

18.7 The CS-DRMS has a number of technical features to assist debt managers and compilers. For instance, the **Loans Explorer** facility (similar to Windows Explorer) allows quick display, interrogation, and report of data stored in the database. More generally, the CS-DRMS is designed to cater to both small and larger databases and can be run on various types of relational databases including INFORMIX, ORACLE, and SQL-Server. CS-DRMS is based on open, industry-standard technology and can export information to the DSM Plus, World Bank DRS, as well as other packages, such as MS Excel, accounting, and other management information systems. The CS-DRMS functions in both English and French and has language-independent design to facilitate translation into other languages.

18.8 CS-DRMS has a **Help** facility, both on-line and on hard copy, that is to be augmented by Internet support from the CS-DRMS website. For further information, see the CS-DRMS website at: *www.csdrms.org* or contact:

Director
Economic and Legal Advisory Services Division
Commonwealth Secretariat
Marlborough House
Pall Mall, London SW1Y 5HX, United Kingdom
Tel: 44-(0) 20–7747 6430
Fax: 44-(0) 20–7799 1507
E-mail: *csdrms@commonwealth.int.*

UNCTAD's Debt Management and Financial Analysis System (DMFAS)

18.9 The DMFAS is a computer system designed for use by ministries of finance and/or central banks for the management of public debt. It is regularly enhanced so that it remains current with, and helps establish, best practice in debt management.

18.10 The DMFAS allows the user to monitor public short-, medium-, and long-term debt, external and domestic, as well as on-lending operations. Private debt and grants may also be registered within the system. DMFAS is designed to satisfy three distinct debt-management needs: the day-to-day operational needs of the debt manager (see UNCTAD, 1993), the aggregate statistical requirements of the debt office, and the analytical needs of the policymaker. In connection with public expenditure, the DMFAS is easily linked to the budget execution system, when there is one in use at the ministry of finance.

18.11 DMFAS version 5.2 is a Windows-based application[1] that uses all the advantages of this standard graphical user-interface. It also uses ORACLE's Relational Database Management System (RDBMS)[2] and ORACLE Development Tools.[3] The Standard DMFAS version 5.2 exists in four different languages—English, French, Spanish, and Russian—and can be used both in a single-user and in a networked environment.

Operational Management

18.12 Operational debt management is the day-to-day management of debt in accordance with executive direction and organization, and involves the recording, analytical, controlling, and operating functions. The operational features of DMFAS 5.2 put the main emphasis on the recording and analytical functions, including compilation of aggregated debt figures and analysis of key indicators. This information, in turn, serves as a basis for control of public borrowing.

---

[1]Windows is licensed software from Microsoft Corporation.

[2]A relational database is a collection of "relations," whereby a relation is a two-dimensional table in which the entries in the table are single-valued; each column has a distinct name; all the values in the same column are values of the same attribute; the order of the columns is immaterial; each row is distinct; and the order of the rows is immaterial.

[3]ORACLE is a registered trademark of Oracle Corporation.

DMFAS 5.2 Recording Function

18.13 The DMFAS main menu follows the typical operational life cycle of a loan agreement. Loan details are registered in the **Administration** section and, based on the contract information, amortization tables are calculated and initial drawing estimates made. The Administration section also contains a **Reference files** menu where the user enters information on daily exchange rates, variable interest rates, commercial interest reference rates, budget line identification numbers, as well as creditors/debtors and other participants to the agreements. As disbursements take place, these will be registered into the loan **Mobilization** section of the system. This section may also, upon the user's request, be programmed to print drawing requests automatically. Thereafter, all transactions related to the servicing of loans, including operations on arrears, penalty (late) interest, rescheduling, swaps, etc., are recorded in the **Servicing** section of the system. The servicing section contains links to budget allocations. The automatic registry of arrears function enables the user to create blocks of arrears for a given subset of loans.

Types of agreements that can be registered in the DMFAS

18.14 The DMFAS version 5.2 has facilities to register and establish the required links between the following types of agreements:

* *Loans.* The system can record all loan-type contracts, including bonds, in their original currency. The system can store quantitative information (such as financial terms) and qualitative information (such as notes for specific comments or memorandum items, like the type of legal clauses in the contract). Furthermore, the loans "module" has facilities for:
  — recording of *secondary market shares* and share movements for syndicated loans in order to report the exposure of each member of the syndicate at a given point in time;
  — maintaining records of *amendments* to loan agreements;
  — maintaining records of the *loan status* throughout the lifetime of the loan (when the loan was agreed but disbursement had not occurred), the period when the loan was in existence, and when it was fully repaid;
  — recording *currency pool* loans (World Bank and regional development bank loans);

— linking loans and grants information to specific *projects*, *agreed minutes*, *on-lending* agreements, and *budget allocations*.

- *Grants*. The "module" for registration of grants contains the same facilities as the loans module, except for repayment conditions.
- *On-lending agreements*. The system can record **On-lending** of loans and the relation between the on-lent loans and the original loan.
- *Composite agreements*. The facility for recording **Composite agreements** permits the user to register the global information on agreements incorporating several individual credits (and/or grants) and to link this global agreement to the individual loans or grants stemming from it.
- *Projects*. The **Project information** facilities of the system permit easy identification of individual projects and their relationship to loans and grants financing them, as well as the individual disbursements related to them.
- *Debt reorganization agreements*. The **Debt reorganization** facility links the reorganized bilateral loans to the relevant "Agreed Minutes" and is designed to provide supporting data for reorganization negotiations, to facilitate recording of the reorganized terms received, and to facilitate identification and reporting of reorganized transactions.

How is this information registered into DMFAS 5.2?

18.15 The DMFAS captures financial terms of individual credits as specified in each loan contract; the characteristics to be entered include, among others, the principal terms, interest terms, as well as interest and exchange rates. On the basis of this information, the system automatically calculates estimated disbursements and amortization tables. Loan information is entered on two levels, **General information** and **Tranches**; these are subsets of administration. Each loan has one general information section and at least one tranche section.

Administration

18.16 The section **Administration** registers all the basic data related to specific loan or grant agreements, projects financed through loans and/or grants, general agreements (for example, composite agreements, Paris Club Agreed Minutes, etc.), and rescheduling agreements. The following **Reference** information is stored within this section:

- The **Participants** (debtors, creditors, etc.) in the different agreements. The system requires the availability of a set of information on each one of the participants (for example, institution type, country of residence, telecommunications data, etc.).
- The **Common variable interest rates** for projection purposes.
- The **Commercial interest reference rates** (CIRR) for a present-value calculation, which is especially useful within the framework of the HIPC Initiative. The OECD publishes these interest rates.
- The system can record **Daily exchange rates**. These rates are entered into the common exchange rate file for the entire loan portfolio in the system.
- The **Budgetary lines** are loaded here for use in the disbursement and debt-servicing processes, as required. In other words, the budget lines refer to the budget account numbers that are used to service the different loans.
- The **Interest rate groups** and **Maturity groups** allow the user to customize the range of these loan attributes for selection and sorting needs.

General information

18.17 All the information that is general to the loan agreement and a grant is entered under this heading. The links to the loan participants or clients (borrowers, lenders, guarantors, beneficiaries, etc.) are also entered in this section, although there are facilities for entering loan participant links at the tranche level if the agreement has participants who only relate to a specific tranche. Some of the important features include:

- The system uses flexible **Loan identification** so that the user can use his or her own codification standards and is not limited to predefined numeric loan numbers.
- The role of the **Participants** to the different agreements (loan, grant, etc.) is defined here with reference to the participants file.
- The **Amendments** to the different agreements (loan, grant, etc.) are registered and monitored here.
- The **Creditor's participation shares** in a syndicated loan are registered and monitored here with reference to the participants' file.
- The record of the **Loan status** throughout the lifetime of the loan is registered and monitored here.
- The recording of the **Currency pool** loans (World Bank and regional development bank loans) is made here.

- **User-defined fields** allow the debt officers to cater to country-specific loan details that can then be used as selection and sorting criteria when generating reports.

Tranche information

18.18 Information on interest payment and principal repayment terms is registered on a detailed level in so-called **Tranches**, and allows more accurate recording of loans in several currencies and with several interest rates. Multilateral borrowing, for instance, often has several currency tranches under the same credit. These different tranches may or may not have the same rate of interest. Each currency will therefore be registered as a separate tranche with its own amortization schedule. The system captures specific floating interest rates for the tranches. These rates are either entered into the common exchange rate file for the entire loan portfolio in the system or they are entered as characteristics of a loan tranche. This will depend on the level of accuracy of calculations that are required by the user. It was conceived in this way because different creditors will be using different interest rates for the same currency on the same date.

18.19 The DMFAS system provides three different options for manual and/or automatic management of tranches: one tranche only, known multiple numbers of tranches, and unknown number of tranches:
- *One tranche* only. There will be only one tranche; all disbursements will belong to this tranche. The transactions of this tranche will always be in the base currency of this tranche, which must be the same as the loan currency.
- *Multiple known tranches.* The user creates each tranche, defining the disbursement profile and amount of each tranche (the system will automatically manage the distribution of the undisbursed amount of each tranche as theoretical disbursements).
- *Unknown number of tranches until the loan is fully disbursed.* The DMFAS system assists in this case in the creation of a tranche by automatically generating the so-called 0 (zero) tranche containing the estimated disbursements based on the remaining undisbursed amount of the loan. Each time a disbursement is registered, it will generate an actual amortization table starting in the number 1 tranche. Disbursements may also be entered into existing tranches, in which case the estimated disbursements in the existing

0 tranche will be recalculated, but no new tranche is created.

DMFAS 5.2 Operating and Controlling Functions

Operating function

18.20 The DMFAS records all types of individual transactions: disbursements (registered in **Mobilization**) and repayments of principal, payment of interest and commissions, etc. (registered in **Servicing**).

Mobilization

18.21 The section **Mobilization** is for registering **Disbursements**. The system can handle disbursements in the same (or different) currency as that of the tranche and registers the equivalent value in the loan currency, in the tranche currency, and in the local currency. For validation all the figures are checked for consistency against the exchange rates registered in the corresponding files. The disbursement can also be related to a project or a program allocation.

18.22 The system has a facility for identifying estimated disbursements in the past and automatically redistributing these into the future—the **Roll forward estimated disbursements**—which is also activated from this option. When a large number of estimated disbursements have not taken place, the user can update the future undisbursed amounts in batch mode from this option starting at a given date. The system will thus automatically update the amortization tables as a result of projecting future disbursements.

Servicing

18.23 The **Debt-service operations** are handled in this section. There is an option dealing with principal and interest and two other options for commissions and penalty (late) interest. All debt-service operations can be entered and/or followed in six currencies: local, tranche, effective, euro, U.S. dollar, and SDR. The user will have access to the following functionalities:
- The debt-service operations will be ordered by scheduled date, and the field status will inform the user of the current stage in the servicing process for the maturity concerned (scheduled, waiting, paid, written-off, rescheduled, payment ordered but no feedback received from the payer, etc.).

- The generation of the list of **Debt-service** maturities is based on the amortization tables. The user must verify these lists and that the maturities in the waiting list (those whose scheduled date are before today's date) are registered as paid, rescheduled, written-off, swapped, or confirmed as arrears. The system might confirm the overdue maturities as arrears automatically if the user has chosen this option.

- The accumulation of arrears will eventually also lead to accumulation of a stock of **Penalty (late) interest** due to different creditors. The DMFAS system estimates this penalty interest based on each individual confirmed arrears transaction in the database. The penalty interest "module" allows the user to record payments, rescheduled, and written-off operations on penalty interest.

- This section is also where the **Budgetary allocation amounts** are registered. The system allows entry of budget allocations for comparison with actual payments. The user defines the budget periods (within the fiscal year) and loads the budget line identifications and the allocation to each budget line. The allocation is then linked to tranches and individual transactions, and in this way the system automatically monitors the allocation against the accumulated amount of actual transactions during the specified budget period. So, the budgeting of payments may be monitored on loans, interest, principal, and commissions—one line for each item as defined in the budget—and can easily be adjusted to the needs of individual countries. The system will issue a warning if the sum of actual transactions exceeds the allocation.

- The **Adjustment factors** used in some of the currency pool loans from multilateral institutions are registered here. These factors will be used for reporting, since the system will always keep the currency pool loan in book values, using the factors to reevaluate the outstanding amount and debt servicing at a given date stated by the user.

- The **Payment order**, a country-specific facility, can also be either printed or electronically transmitted from this option. If there is a linkage with a budget system, the payment order can be processed through the corresponding budget allocations.

Historical data

18.24 A public debt system should be able to show and calculate the historical data. Loading the information about the individual transactions in order to fulfill this requirement can be very tedious and, in some cases, an overwhelming task. The DMFAS, in order to overcome this problem, permits the user to load balances on a loan-by-loan and tranche-by-tranche basis at a given date (the user-defined DMFAS cutoff date). The **Historical amount** balances will include total principal repaid, total interest paid, etc., at the cutoff date. This will allow the system to calculate, at any date after the cutoff date, stocks and flows at any level of aggregation.

Controlling and monitoring functions

18.25 The first controlling function is on the data accuracy and data validation. Once the data are entered, they will be updated regularly or deleted, as the case may be. To ensure consistency among data for a particular loan, a certain number of controls have been incorporated in the system. By means of a number of error messages appearing on the user's computer screen, the user will correct and validate data. The user may also produce different reports to check the data for correctness.

18.26 The system can also produce a large number of reports for the purpose of control and monitoring the debt-management operations.[4] Examples include reports of payments falling due in the next month, in order to pay them on time, and the selection facility that permits the user to select loans by economic sector, type of creditor, type of financing, etc., that can be used for controlling ceilings on outstanding debt or debt servicing.

DMFAS 5.2 Analytical Function

Reporting facilities

18.27 This function provides a flexible and comprehensive set of reports that, when generated in aggregate, can be produced in local currency, in U.S. dollars, in euros, or in SDRs. The DMFAS 5.2 can produce a large number of reports of four types, as described below.

Predefined reports without parameters

18.28 The user cannot modify this type of format. The report concerns a very specific topic and will present all available information on the selected

---

[4]The system cannot perform these functions properly without the proper institutional environment; that is, the administrative and institutional arrangements of the debt office, as well as its relationships and information flows with other institutions.

"block" of loans. No parameters are therefore required. The **Amortization table** is one example of this type of report.

Predefined reports with parameters

18.29 The user also cannot modify this type of format. The report, however, potentially covers large amounts of data, and the user therefore can define the reporting period covered. DMFAS version 5.2 produces Form 1 and Form 2 of the World Bank's DRS, which are examples of this type of report,[5] as is the loan account statement that is extensively used by debt officers.

User-defined reports

18.30 Customized reports permit users to create their own self-designed reports. In addition to a different set of parameters that the user can choose—such as the currency, the level of aggregation, the period, etc.—it is possible for the user to select the contents of the columns from among a list of available debt totals from the stored information and/or projections. For certain formats, the report can contain up to 12 columns as well as include percentages as debt totals. The report format, once the user has created it, is stored by DMFAS 5.2, so that the user can retrieve it in order to print it out with the original or new data, as well as to modify its format if needed.

18.31 To create reports in DMFAS the user starts by defining a subset of loans to work with, then sorts this subset and finally defines the report parameters, such as the currency, the periodicity, the level of detail, etc., as well as the hierarchical order in which the selected criteria appear in the report and how their subtotals are calculated. DMFAS version 5.2 uses a customized Oracle Browser to create subsets of loans and to sort the subsets. These subsets may, if the user wishes, be given a name and saved for later use.

18.32 When creating a user-defined report, the user has to select the report's format:
- Format 1: Aggregates in columns, and each aggregate for a specific period;
- Format 2: Aggregates in columns, and time periods in rows;
- Format 3: Aggregates in rows, and time periods in columns.

18.33 The user names each new report in order to be able to retrieve the report for later use. When retrieving previously saved reports, however, the user still has the option of changing the corresponding subset or the report parameters. The report parameters include, among others:
- *Period base.* The user may produce reports based on the fiscal year, the calendar year, or according to an exact period defined by him. The budgetary year is defined separately as one of the system parameters of DMFAS version 5.2.
- *Adjusted amount.* For loans that have been registered as currency pool loans, the system allows the user to adjust the amounts of the report by the registered currency pool adjustment factors.
- *Selection of the individual columns.* The user can select from a list of columns, defined by the DMFAS staff, and put them together according to the user's own needs. This enables, for instance, the combination of stock and flows columns in the same report, either for previous transactions or for projections.
- *Specification of the columns.* The user not only has access to the existing variables or aggregates for the columns but also can create his or her own aggregates and include them on the list of predefined columns. The users can, in this way, free themselves from waiting for the DMFAS staff to include new aggregates in the system's reports.

Specific reports

18.34 *Through direct access to the database.* With the help of Oracle Browser and Oracle Reports and other tools like Microsoft Access and Microsoft Query, the user can create reports by accessing directly the different DMFAS 5.2 database tables. In addition, any program supporting ODBC (**O**pen **D**ata**B**ase **C**onnectivity) may connect to the DMFAS version 5.2 database, giving the user with the appropriate access authorization the possibility to use the calculating, sorting, formatting, and graphics capabilities of the user's software on the DMFAS version 5.2 database. Most popular spreadsheets and database programs such as Excel, Lotus 1–2–3, and Access support ODBC. The links can be based on queries so that the result will change when new entries into the database are made. The contents of an Excel spreadsheet with a query selecting the outstanding amounts of all loans with U.S. dollars as loan currency will therefore automatically change without the Excel user's intervention as the outstanding nominal amounts of these loans in the database changes, and the same applies to graphs based on the same data.

---

[5]The World Bank Forms 1 and 2 can also be "printed" and reported electronically. See Chapter 17, paragraph 17.39 ff.

18.35 The DMFAS 5.2 therefore has no limit to the number of report formats the user may create.

18.36 *By exporting the generated results into Excel.* The DMFAS system allows the easy export of the generated results into Excel for further manipulation of the data. However, contrary to the above ODBC option, the data in Excel or other similar spreadsheets is not automatically updated when modifications are made in the DMFAS database.

Analytical facilities

18.37 The analysis module has been specifically designed to calculate projections based on the outstanding nominal amount, and the present-value amount using CIRR interest rates as the rate of discount, of a debt portfolio. The use of present value instead of nominal value allows the user to take into account the terms and concessionality of a debt portfolio and to eliminate the effects of the concessionality. The module on projections based on the outstanding nominal amount is used, among other things, to calculate debt-service payments effectively owed, excluding future and hypothetical disbursements.

18.38 This module enables the user to choose between different parameters and calculation methods (the pro-rata and the truncation methods) of particular interest to produce and compare different scenarios for the debt-sustainability analysis of HIPC.

18.39 An interface has been created between the DMFAS system and DSM Plus of the World Bank, which is a tool designed to help officials analyze the external financing requirements of a country and to quantify the effects of debt-relief operations or new borrowing. This interface provides the DMFAS user with the means to export data from the DMFAS system for subsequent import into the DSM Plus system. The interface enables the DMFAS user to benefit directly from the data in the DMFAS database, avoiding the need to reenter that data in DSM Plus.

18.40 The DMFAS system also provides analytical support for debt managers by, for example:
- Facilitating easy **Registration of potential new debt** and analyzing the effect of these new debts on the future debt-service pattern;

- Permitting easy **Simulations** to determine the effect of interest rate fluctuations and exchange rate variations over a period of time;
- Calculating and giving information on **Detailed penalty (late) interest** from the scheduled date of a maturity registered as an arrear to a given date; and
- Calculating **Accrued interest costs**, which allows debt officers to generate automatically such information for, and at the end of, the previous month for use by other departments, including the accounting unit.

Executive Management

18.41 Executive debt-management features of the DMFAS, in combination with the World Bank's DSM Plus, include specialized reports to:
- Provide debt managers and planners with easy-to-use tools to assist in policy decision making, evaluation of alternative strategies, and development of negotiation strategies. These analytical and decision-support tools integrate debt data with other economic variables (for example, balance of payments components), allowing simulations of debt reorganizations and taking into account hypothetical new loans and financing.
- Provide debt managers with decision-support systems and analytical tools to assist in portfolio management and optimization of composition, maturities, and interest and exchange rate exposure. Such tools allow for sensitivity analysis through simulations that take into account, for example, exchange rate variations or fluctuations in floating interest rates.

Technical Characteristics

Overview

18.42 The DMFAS system has to be portable and easy to use because it has to work in an environment where its users may not be computer specialists. Therefore, significant effort has been devoted to making the system as user-friendly and as flexible as possible so that the user, to the largest extent feasible, can operate it independently of the technical staff of UNCTAD. In this light, the following features have been made standard:[6]

---

[6]For further information on hardware and software requirements, please refer to UNCTAD (2000). This document is regularly updated to include the most recent developments in software and hardware technology.

- Windows-based **Graphical user interface** that includes field-to-field navigation, color screens, Windows standards with "Shortcut Keys" and mouse support, easy selection of menu options from selection lists, etc.
- The **Code** file of the system is divided into standard and user-defined codes. This allows country-specific customization of codes, such as Location, Economic Sector codes, etc.
- **Language independence** permits the language-dependent parts of the system—for example, menus—to be separated from the system itself. In addition, the DMFAS is delivered with four standard languages included, and the user may easily switch from one language to another. This feature is particularly important for countries operating the system in languages (such as Russian) that they cannot use for reporting to the World Bank and other international organizations or creditors. In this way, they will have the option of producing the reports in English.
- **Access to system codes** allows the user to add, delete, or modify user-updatable system codes, provided he or she has sufficient "privileges" (see below).
- The user also fixes **Tolerance limits** for data validation in the system.

Security

18.43 The **Security** features in DMFAS 5.2 include preventing unauthorized personnel from viewing or editing data by assigning different access rights to different users—for instance, to ensure that only the database administrator has access to administrative functions of the system. If required, this **Access control** can be refined to permit the definition and enforcement per individual end-user of groups of data with which that user may work—particular creditors, for example—and, for each group of data, the operations that the user may perform. A facility of **Double control** allows managers to enforce validation of initial registry or modification of data by nominated people other than the user who first registered or modified the data. Among other advantages, the system, if calibrated that way, would not allow the entered or modified data to be used before the data were validated (for reporting purposes, for example).

18.44 ORACLE provides the possibility to keep and consult logs detailing the types of operations performed by each user and keeping track of what the data looked like before an operation in case of a modification.

18.45 ORACLE also provides backup and restore procedures as well as automatic recovery functions in case of power failure. This considerably diminishes the risk of corrupted data files.

Conversion software

18.46 For users of DMFAS versions 4.1 Plus or 5.0 who want to upgrade their installation to DMFAS version 5.2, UNCTAD has developed an interface for automatic conversion of data to version 5.2 format with minimum manual intervention by the user.

Support to other information systems

18.47 DMFAS 5.2 can be linked with other computer systems. The system may therefore provide debt data for other information systems, such as those dealing with balance of payments, budget, public and/or central bank accounting, government revenue and expenditure, currency management, etc.

Compatibility with network operating systems

18.48 As mentioned, DMFAS 5.2 is built on ORACLE's RDBMS relational client/server architecture. Consequently, DMFAS 5.2 can be run on any network operating system that supports the ORACLE 7.1 RDBMS server and can have Windows workstations as clients. This includes Novell, Windows NT, and UNIX.

Documentation and Training

18.49 A comprehensive set of *documentation* is available for DMFAS version 5.2. This includes:
- A comprehensive User's Guide;
- A DMFAS Glossary (see UNCTAD, 1998);
- A Database Administrator's Manual; and
- Technical documentation of interfaces when appropriate.

Training available from UNCTAD is described in the next chapter.

19. Provision of Technical Assistance in External Debt Statistics

Introduction

19.1 This chapter provides an introduction to the technical assistance in external debt statistics, and related macroeconomic statistics, provided by the international agencies involved in the production of the *Guide*. This chapter is not comprehensive of all the technical assistance provided in external debt statistics and is accurate as of the time of writing.

Commonwealth Secretariat

19.2 In addition to supporting the CS-DRMS[1] debt system in user countries, the Commonwealth Secretariat provides technical assistance to ministries of finance and central banks in various aspects of debt management related to data compilation, loan operations and analysis, capacity building, and policy advice. In the field of debt statistics, targeted assistance is available for:
- *Compiling debt data* extracted from various sources: Local staff are exposed to the techniques of making an inventory of loans through the interpretation of loan documents (loan agreements, creditor statements, general conditions and other creditor practices, etc.) so that all relevant debt information can be compiled/retrieved.
- *Recording loan instruments* using appropriate methodologies: Training is provided on the CS-DRMS system, which has taken into account different creditor practices and the agreed norms on compilation of debt statistics. The system allows user countries to record debt information (details, terms, and transactions) on a loan-by-loan basis. Subsequent developments, such as debt restructuring resulting from Paris Club agreements, can also be captured in the system.

---

[1]The main features of the Commonwealth Secretariat's Debt Recording and Monitoring System (CS-DRMS) are described in Chapter 18.

- *Validating and reconciling* stocks, flows, and other details on a loan-by-loan basis, including with creditor records: Once a database is created, local staff are trained to validate the data and reconcile debt stock and debt-service levels with other sources (creditors or other agencies, including the World Bank). Any inconsistencies in classifying the data are addressed during this exercise.
- *Disseminating debt data* in the various formats required by different users: In recent years, dissemination of external debt data to various users, and in the format the information is required, has been a focal point of assistance. Users of CS-DRMS are trained in the various facilities that can provide data to users, both within and outside the country. These facilities include the 100 reports that are available in CS-DRMS; the facility to export information into spreadsheet for further manipulation; and the add-on facilities and built-in electronic links with other systems.

19.3 Also, as part of its capacity-building efforts, the Commonwealth Secretariat has developed a comprehensive training program in debt management aimed at enhancing the skills and knowledge of local staff with different levels of responsibilities, so that they are able to carry our their debt-management functions in an effective manner. These training modules, which can be customized to meet specific country needs, can be grouped under the following broad categories:
- Basic training programs such as the interpretation of loan/credit agreements (external and domestic debt); debt-restructuring operations, including for Paris Club and London Club; and debt data validation techniques;
- Basic and advanced courses in the use of CS-DRMS (and add-on software) for loan recording and administration; for timely reporting of debt statistics, including data extraction to other systems; and for supporting debt analysis such as portfolio analysis or debt-sustainability analysis;

- Specialized courses and workshops on debt-management techniques and strategies, new debt initiatives, and new practices and standards; these are aimed at different audiences ranging from senior officials in governments to those involved in actual debt operations; and
- Seminars and consensus-building meetings on issues with wider implication for debt management—for example, the HIPC Initiative and debt sustainability in a liberalizing economic environment.

19.4 In delivering its advisory services to countries, the Commonwealth Secretariat has actively collaborated with various institutions—regional and international—especially in undertaking joint activities in specific countries (for instance, data validation) and in regional training programs.

European Central Bank

19.5 The Eurosystem,[2] under the coordination of the ECB, provides technical assistance to the central banks of the countries that are candidates to join the European Union (EU), the so-called accession countries,[3] with a view to preparing for their future integration into the European System of Central Banks (ESCB), and later into the Eurosystem. The ECB's technical assistance is primarily intended to help these countries implement data collection and compilation systems that will allow them in due course to meet the ECB's statistical requirements, and to contribute to properly articulated (aggregated and consolidated) statistics for the euro area. The assistance takes the form of seminars organized at the ECB or in different countries, and country visits conducted by ECB staff. The seminars may call on experts in national central banks of the EU and are targeted essentially at economists-statisticians and/or managerial staff of central banks and of national statistical institutes, where relevant. In cooperation with other institutions—notably, the European Commission (Eurostat) and the IMF—the ECB seeks to promote the adoption of current international statistical standards, in particular *1993 SNA*, *ESA95*, and *BPM5*.

19.6 The assistance provided by the ECB covers the various statistical areas of its competence within the EU: money and banking statistics, securities issues, interest rates, balance of payments and the IIP, and related issues—Special Data Dissemination Standard (SDDS), international reserves, external debt, etc. Within the EU, the ECB is solely responsible for money and banking and related statistics. Where competence is shared—which is the case for balance of payments statistics, with the European Commission (Eurostat) having responsibility within the EU for the current and capital accounts (and for compiling EU aggregates), and the ECB being responsible for the financial account (and for compiling euro-area aggregates)—the assistance is organized in close cooperation between the two institutions; close cooperation is also sought with other international organizations.

19.7 The ECB will also cooperate with the accession countries in the field of financial accounts, including time series for the rest-of-the-world account as specified in the *1993 SNA* and *ESA95*; compilation of financial accounts helps to promote consistency across statistical areas. External debt data are embedded in this framework on an instrument, rather than a functional, approach.

19.8 In addition to the assistance to accession countries, the ECB participates in seminars and workshops organized by regional institutions and forums (for example, Mercosur, West African Economic and Monetary Union, South African Customs Union) to share the experience gained in compiling aggregates for a group of countries.

International Monetary Fund

19.9 The IMF offers technical assistance for statistics including balance of payments, IIP and external debt, government finance, money and banking, and national accounts and price statistics. This work is reinforced by training courses and seminars for member country officials on statistical methodologies and their applications, including external debt and international reserves and related information. In addi-

---

[2]The Eurosystem comprises the ECB plus the National Central Banks (NCBs) of the 12 EU countries that had adopted the euro as of January 1, 2001. The ESCB comprises the Eurosystem and the central banks of the three other EU countries (Denmark, Sweden, and the United Kingdom).

[3]The term refers exclusively to countries that have started such negotiations with the EU, which at the time of writing the *Guide* were: Bulgaria, Cyprus, the Czech Republic, Estonia, Hungary, Latvia, Lithuania, Malta, Poland, Romania, Slovenia, and the Slovak Republic. Turkey is also a candidate country, but negotiations have not yet started.

tion, the IMF provides information on statistical topics via its public website, at *http://www.imf.org/external/np/sta/index.htm.*

19.10 In all areas, technical assistance is designed to improve the collection, compilation, and dissemination of official statistics. In addition to providing assessments with respect to accuracy, coverage, and timeliness, technical assistance missions in each area often deliver on-the-job training, help design reporting forms and spreadsheets to facilitate correct classification, and lay out short- and medium-term action plans for the improvement of statistical procedures. Missions may pay particular attention to assisting countries in their efforts to comply with the requirements of the SDDS or participate in the General Data Dissemination System (GDDS). Technical assistance missions generally discuss a draft report with country authorities while in the field, which is later finalized with the benefit of the authorities' comments.

19.11 The main vehicle for the delivery of technical assistance is short-term single-topic missions, which are conducted by IMF staff and externally recruited experts. A Panel of Experts is established to recognize those experts who have, by virtue of their experience and qualifications, demonstrated their capacity to contribute to the technical assistance program of the Statistics Department in one or more areas of macroeconomic statistics. The IMF also undertakes multisectoral statistical missions, which provide overall assessments and recommendations for strengthening institutional arrangements, methodology, collection, and compilation practices in the major areas of macroeconomic statistics. These missions not only address the issues related to each sector, but also consider the consistent treatment of data and coordination arrangements across sectors, and provide short- and medium-term action plans for improving statistics, including follow-up missions in the topical areas.

19.12 Technical assistance is provided only when requested by a country's authorities. Since the demand for such assistance normally exceeds the resources available from the IMF, a number of considerations are taken into account in prioritizing country requests for technical assistance, including the extent to which (1) the country's authorities are strongly supportive of obtaining the assistance and committed to ensuring its implementation; (2) the technical assistance addresses those weaknesses in a

country's institutional capacity for macroeconomic policy implementation that have been identified in the course of the IMF's surveillance and other work; (3) the assistance contributes to strengthening a country's capacity to design and implement an IMF-supported program; and (4) the assistance supports a country's efforts to comply with internationally agreed standards and codes of transparency. The IMF recognizes that at times the systemic or regional importance of the requesting country and/or the emergence of a need as a result of a post-crisis situation may influence a decision to provide technical assistance.

19.13 The IMF also offers training courses in statistical methodology at the IMF Institute in Washington, D.C., the Joint Vienna Institute, the IMF-Singapore Regional Training Institute, the Joint Africa Institute in Abidjan, the Regional Training Program in the United Arab Emirates, and at several other regional sites. These seminars are up to six weeks in length and generally include a series of lectures, discussions, practical exercises, and case studies. During the lectures, participants are afforded an opportunity to discuss problems that they have actually encountered in the course of their work in their respective countries.

19.14 For further information on the IMF's technical assistance and training courses, please contact:

> Director
> Statistics Department
> International Monetary Fund
> Washington, D.C. 20431, U.S.A.

Organisation for Economic Co-operation and Development

19.15 There is no formal program of technical assistance by the division responsible for the Creditor Reporting System (CRS) of the OECD. However, Secretariat staff provide technical support to member country creditor reporters, both in Paris and through missions to capitals of reporting countries. In addition, non-OECD members occasionally visit Paris to discuss reporting problems, and differences between debtor and creditor reporting. For example, staff from the Indian Ministry of Finance and from the Federal Reserve Bank in Mumbai are regular visitors to the OECD.

19.16 The OECD hosts PARIS21—the Partnerships in Statistics for development in the 21st Century. Created in 1999, PARIS21 is a global consortium of statisticians, policymakers, and other users of statistics that supports the development of statistics in developing and transition countries. Not a new agency, it works through existing global, regional, and national structures. Its members share an interest in strengthening national statistical capacity as the foundation for effective policymaking. PARIS21 promotes dialogue between users and producers of statistics, initially in subregional workshops. This dialogue leads to country action plans—known as Strategic Statistical Development Plans—for the development of sustainable statistical capacity for a wide range of data—economic (including external debt statistics), social, and environmental. The production of such plans, and their implementation, usually requires technical assistance. By working with the DAC, which brings together the bilateral donors and the European Commission, the IMF, the United Nations Development Programme (UNDP), and the World Bank, PARIS21 emphasizes the importance of statistics in attaining and monitoring development goals, and promotes closer coordination among donor programs of statistical capacity building assistance. For more details see the PARIS21 website, *http://www.paris21.org.*

United Nations Conference on Trade and Development

19.17 UNCTAD's training program in debt management consists of a number of individual predefined training modules that are organized according to orientations, "blocks," and level of management. This module approach allows a great deal of flexibility in the design of training programs and is used by UNCTAD to communicate with DMFAS[4] users in order to design programs customized for individual countries, debt offices, and/or groups of users.

19.18 The UNCTAD training framework has three orientations:
- Internal capacity building within the national debt-management framework;

---

[4]The DMFAS (Debt Management and Financial Analysis System) is a computer system designed for use in the management of public debt. It was described in detail in Chapter 18.

- Software and computer (including DMFAS training); and
- General debt management.

19.19 These orientations are organized within two different categories of training blocks:
- **Block 1** is what may be described as the *general knowledge base*, which is the minimum knowledge any participant should have on each one of the orientations. General knowledge base training comprises all basic knowledge and is of general applicability for all those working in the field of public debt.
- **Block 2** is what may be described as the *specialized knowledge base*, which is the targeted training given to different officers so that they can exercise their specific mandated functions or tasks. Specialized knowledge base training has specific applicability for those working in the field of public debt.

19.20 Within each component and block, the training activities are designed for three levels of management: senior management, middle management, and operational staff. The delivery of the different training modules will, in general, follow a progressive approach within each level and will evolve from general knowledge to specialized knowledge base training over time. In all cases, the training is always based on the latest version of DMFAS and the different information it can produce.

World Bank

19.21 The World Bank offers technical assistance in statistical capacity building to its client countries so as to facilitate the production and wide dissemination of key economic, social, and environmental statistics. Such data support economic management and poverty-reduction strategies.

19.22 Technical assistance is provided through institutional capacity-building projects, advisory functions, training, and related activities. Whatever the modality through which technical assistance is delivered, these programs are essentially country-oriented, although regional programs are sponsored when similar issues are encountered within regional groups and where a common approach can be effective. In all areas, technical assistance draws on international statistical standards and methodologies, good practices in statistical capacity building, and recent technological developments.

19.23 Technical assistance activities are usually demand driven and are in response to needs and priorities identified by member countries, in collaboration with Bank staff in the course of their country economic and sectoral work, or other international organizations. The goal of coordination among stakeholders—between donors and between entities in the national statistical system—is, most importantly, to avoid duplication of effort and improve harmonization of procedures, thereby reducing transaction costs. As a mechanism for donor and recipient coordination, the World Bank has supported the creation of a consortium, PARIS21, which provides a forum for policymakers and statisticians from around the world to discuss issues of statistical capacity building and to agree on modalities for delivering assistance to strengthen statistical capacity.

19.24 The thrust of the Bank's technical assistance work has increasingly been on promoting coordinated, demand-led, and knowledge-based technical assistance for building sustainable statistical capacity and covering both comprehensive (or integrated) statistical capacity building as well as programs relating to specific aspects of the national statistical system.

19.25 A comprehensive approach to statistical capacity building covers all dimensions of the national statistical system (see Figure 19.1). The objective here is to:

- Strengthen statistical infrastructure by establishing sound legal and institutional frameworks for the collection, processing, and compilation of statistics;
- Enhance organizational arrangements through improved organizational structure and better coordination among statistical agencies and through managerial reforms involving emphasis on strategic management and corporate planning;
- Improve staffing methods through better human resource management and development;
- Upgrade technical and physical resources through newer data collection techniques, application of newer statistical methodologies, and modern information management systems (with appropriate customization on a country-specific basis); and
- Provide training in new data concepts and in international standards for reliable and consistent data compilation, quality control, and widespread dissemination.

19.26 By contrast, specific programs address gaps in segments of a country's statistical system such as national income accounts, environmental statistics, or debt data systems. But like comprehensive programs, specific programs also address organizational and functional issues.

19.27 Bank-sponsored technical assistance activities are financed by grants or loans. Grant financing is through World Bank grants[5] and grants from Bank-administered trust funds.[6]

19.28 Small and medium-sized technical assistance programs may be part of a large World Bank project loan. For larger programs, stand-alone loans in the form of a Learning and Innovation Loan (LIL) or a Specific Investment Loan (SIL), often with cofinancing through partnership arrangements with bilateral donors and other international agencies, are also possible. The country technical assistance program preparation is normally financed through grants and the implementation and monitoring through a combination of grants, and loans with appropriate burden sharing by the client country (often in-kind). For some middle- and high-income countries, technical assistance participation is encouraged on a reimbursable basis.[7]

---

[5]The World Bank's Institutional Development Fund (IDF) was established in FY1993 to provide technical assistance grants for "upstream" institutional development not directly linked to the lending operations of the Bank. The IDF is used for funding small, action-oriented schemes identified in the course of country economic and sectoral work and policy dialogue.

[6]Includes trust funds that finance advisory services and technical assistance. These trust funds cover a wide range of activities, including project preparation and preinvestment studies, economic and sectoral work, institution building, pilot projects, training, and conferences. The advisory services may support recipient activities directly or support Bank activities and may be provided through trust fund programs or through free-standing trust funds. In FY2000, bilateral donors established a new global technical assistance facility to promote statistical capacity building. The Bank on behalf of donors manages the Trust Fund for Statistical Capacity Building.

[7]Under "reimbursable arrangements," Bank services are specifically requested, and their costs are fully reimbursed. Such arrangements are undertaken with member countries that are no longer active Bank borrowers but still require technical assistance, and with partner development institutions that contract with the Bank to provide assistance for loan preparation, appraisal, or supervision services.

Figure 19.1. World Bank Technical Assistance (TA) in Institutional Capacity Building in Statistics

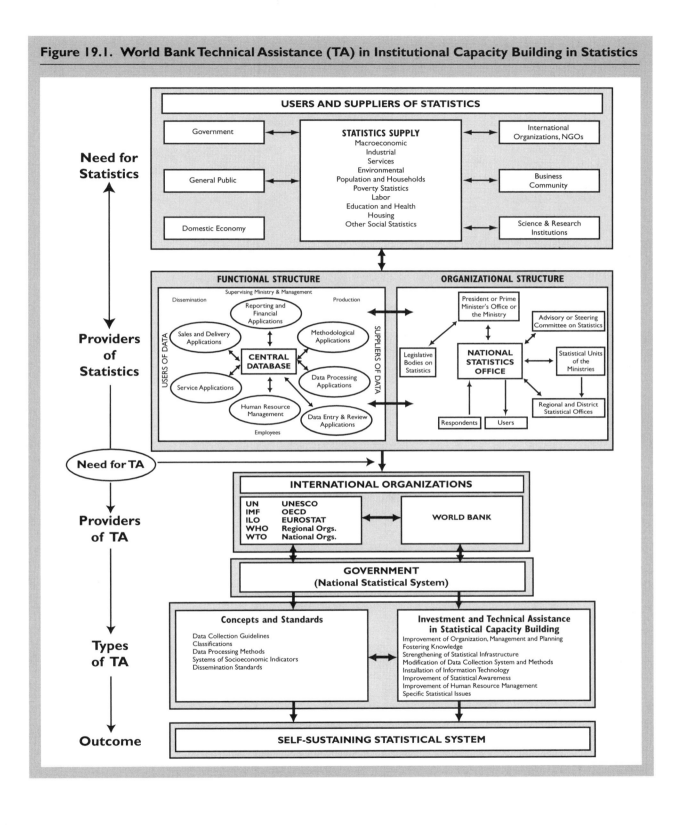

19.29 Technical assistance in improving the coverage and quality of debt statistics has been an essential component of Bank technical assistance programs in public debt management in several countries—for example, as a component of a public debt-management LIL, a Technical Assistance Loan (TAL), or a Public Sector Reform Loan (PSRL).

Technical assistance activity in debt statistics is likely to cover a wide range of items, including organizational structure of the national debt office, data collection methods, database management systems, data needs for strategic debt management, dissemination practices, and training of debt office staff.

Appendices

Appendix I. Specific Financial Instruments and Transactions: Classifications

The purpose of this appendix is to provide detailed information on specific instruments and transactions and to set out their classification treatment in the gross external debt position. There are two sections. The first provides a description of specific financial instruments and how they should be classified in the gross external debt position; the second sets out the classification treatment of some specific transactions that, experience suggests, require particular clarification.

Part 1. Financial Instruments: Description and Classification in the Gross External Debt Position[1]

A

American Depository Receipt (ADR)

An ADR is a negotiable certificate that represents ownership of the securities of a non-U.S. resident company. Although the securities underlying ADRs can be debt or money market instruments, the large majority are equities. An ADR allows a non-U.S. resident company to introduce its equity into the U.S. market in a form more readily acceptable to U.S. investors, such as in U.S. dollars, without needing to disclose all the information normally required by the U.S. Securities and Exchange Commission. A U.S. depository bank will purchase the underlying foreign security and then issue receipts in dollars for those securities to the U.S. investor. The receipts are registered. The investor can exchange the ADRs for the underlying security at any time. See also *Bearer Depository Receipts* and *Depository Receipts*.

Classification

These instruments are classified by the nature of the underlying instrument backing the ADR. This is because the "issuing" intermediary does not take the underlying security onto its balance sheet but simply acts as a facilitator. So, the debtor is the issuer of the underlying security—that is, an ADR is regarded as a non-U.S. resident issue. If owned by nonresidents, these instruments are to be included in the gross external debt position if the underlying security is a debt security. The security is classified as *long-term, bonds and notes (debt securities, portfolio investment* in the IIP) or, depending on the relationship between debtor and creditor, as *direct investment, intercompany lending* (see the description of *direct investment* in Chapter 3). If the underlying item is an equity investment it should be classified in the memorandum item, *equity liabilities*.

Arrears

Amounts that are past due-for-payment and unpaid. These include amounts of scheduled debt-service payments that have fallen due but have not been paid to the creditor(s).

In the context of the Paris Club, arrears are the unpaid amounts that fall due before the consolidation period. See *Paris Club, Creditor,* and *Consolidation Period* in Appendix III.

Classification

Arrears of principal and/or interest are reported as new short-term liabilities. If owned by nonresidents, these new instruments are to be included in the gross external debt position as *arrears*. Regarding the original borrowing, the debt outstanding is to be reported as though the principal and interest were paid on schedule.

---

[1]This appendix has drawn significantly upon the Bank of England (1998), *Financial Terminology Database*.

Asset-Backed Securities

Asset-backed securities are bonds whose income payments and principal repayments are dependent on a pool of assets. Securities may be backed by various assets—for example, mortgages, credit card loans, automobile loans—in effect, converting illiquid assets into tradable securities. An asset-backed security enables the original lending institution to devolve credit risks to investors. There are several key features of asset-backed securities: the original lender will usually sell the assets to a trust or other form of intermediary (special purchase vehicle) and so, in the case of a bank, this frees "capital" that regulatory guidelines require a bank to hold against the assets. The intermediary will finance the purchase of the assets by issuing securities. Because income and the repayment of principal are dependent on the underlying assets, if the underlying assets are prepaid so is the security. Issuers often provide different tranches of the security so that if there are prepayments, the first tier will be repaid first, the second tier next, etc. The pricing of the various tranches will reflect the probability of early repayment. Asset-backed securities have also been developed that securitize future income streams—such as the earnings of musicians.

Classification

Asset-backed securities owned by nonresidents are to be included in the gross external debt position. They should be classified as *long-term, bonds and notes (portfolio investment, debt securities* in the IIP) unless they have an original maturity of one year or less, in which instance they are to be classified as *money market instruments*. Alternatively, depending on the relationship between debtor and creditor, these securities could be classified as *direct investment, intercompany lending* (see the description of *direct investment* in Chapter 3). These securities present a special problem regardless of the amount outstanding because there can be partial repayments of principal at any time. So, simply revaluing the original face value to end-period market prices will cause overvaluation of the position data if there has been a partial repayment.

B

Balances on Nostro and Vostro Accounts

A vostro (your) account is another bank's account with a reporting bank, while a nostro (our) account is a reporting bank's account with another bank.

Classification

Liability positions in nostro and vostro accounts are to be included in the gross external debt position. They are classified as *banks, short-term, currency and deposits,* or *loans (other investment* in the IIP) depending on the nature of the account.

Bank Deposits

Bank deposits are claims on banks that are either transferable or are "other deposits." Transferable deposits consist of deposits that are exchangeable on demand at par without restriction, or penalty, and directly usable for making payments by check, giro order, direct debit/credit, or other payment facility. "Other deposits" comprise all claims represented by evidence of deposit—for example, savings and fixed-term deposits; sight deposits that permit immediate cash withdrawals but not direct third-party transfers; and shares that are legally (or practically) redeemable on demand or on short notice in savings and loan associations, credit unions, building societies, etc.

Classification

Bank deposits are liabilities of banks and other depository institutions, and if owned by a nonresident are to be included in the gross external debt position. They should be classified as *banks, short-term, currency and deposits (other investment* in the IIP) unless detailed information is available to make the short-term/long-term attribution.

Banker's Acceptances

A negotiable order to pay a specified amount of money on a future date, drawn on and guaranteed by a bank. These drafts are usually drawn for international trade finance purposes as an order to pay an exporter a stated sum on a specific future date for goods received. The act of a bank stamping the word "accepted" on the draft creates a banker's acceptance. The acceptance represents an unconditional claim on the part of the owner and an unconditional liability on behalf of the accepting bank; the bank has a claim on the drawer, who is obliged to pay the bank the face value on or before the maturity date. By writing the word "accepted" on the face of the draft the bank carries primary obligation, guaranteeing payment to the owner of the acceptance. Banker's acceptances can be discounted in the secondary market, the discount reflecting the time to maturity and credit quality of the guaranteeing bank. Since the banker's acceptance carries a banker's obligation to pay (in effect "two-name paper") and is negotiable, it becomes an attractive asset. Banker's acceptances are always sold at a discount and have maturities of up to 270 days.

Classification

Banker's acceptances are money market instruments that are claims on the accepting bank, with the bank owning a claim on the issuer of the bill. As recommended in the *1993 SNA*, flexibility in the application of this recommendation is required to take national practices and variations in the nature of these instruments into account.

If owned by nonresidents, banker's acceptances should be included in the gross external debt position. They should be classified as *short-term, money market instruments* (*portfolio investment, debt securities* in the IIP) unless they have an original maturity of over one year, in which instance they are to be classified as *bonds and notes*. Alternatively, depending on the relationship between debtor and creditor, these securities could be classified as *direct investment, intercompany lending* (see the description of *direct investment* in Chapter 3).

Bearer Depository Receipt (BDR)

A form of depository receipt issued in bearer rather than registered form. See *Depository Receipts*.

Classification

A BDR is classified according to the nature of the underlying instrument backing it. This is because the "issuing" intermediary does not take the underlying security onto its balance sheet but simply acts as a facilitator. So, the debtor is the issuer of the underlying security. If owned by nonresidents, these instruments are to be included in the gross external debt position. They should be classified as *long-term, bonds and notes* (*portfolio investment, debt securities* in the IIP) unless they have an original maturity of one year or less, in which instance they are to be classified as *money market instruments*. Alternatively, depending on the relationship between debtor and creditor, these securities could be classified as *direct investment, intercompany*

lending (see the description of *direct investment* in Chapter 3).

Bonds and Notes

Bonds and notes are debt securities with an original maturity of over one year. They are usually traded (or tradable) in organized and other financial markets. Bonds and notes usually give the holder the unconditional right to fixed money income or contractually determined variable money income. With the exception of perpetual bonds, bonds and notes also provide the holder with an unconditional right to a fixed sum as repayment of principal on a specified date or dates.

Classification

Bonds and notes owned by nonresidents are to be included in the gross external debt position. They should be classified as *long-term, bonds and notes* (*portfolio investment, debt securities* in the IIP). Alternatively, depending on the relationship between debtor and creditor, these securities could be classified as *direct investment, intercompany lending* (see the description of *direct investment* in Chapter 3).

Bonds with an Embedded Call Option

A bond that gives the issuer a right to buy back the bonds on or by a particular date. The value of this right is usually reflected in the interest rate on the bond.

Classification

Bonds with embedded call options owned by nonresidents are to be included in the gross external debt position. They should be classified as *long-term, bonds and notes* (*portfolio investment, debt securities* in the IIP) unless they have an original maturity of one year or less, in which instance they are to be classified as *money market instruments*. Alternatively, depending on the relationship between debtor and creditor, these securities could be classified as *direct investment, intercompany lending* (see the description of *direct investment* in Chapter 3).

Bonds with an Embedded Put Option

A bond whereby the creditor has the right to sell back the bonds to the issuer on or by a particular date, or under certain circumstance, such as a credit downrating of the issuer. This right is usually reflected in the interest rate on the bond.

Classification

Bonds with embedded put options owned by nonresidents are to be included in the gross external debt position. They should be classified as *long-term, bonds and notes (portfolio investment, debt securities in the IIP)* unless they have an original maturity of one year or less, in which instance they are to be classified as *money market instruments.* Alternatively, depending on the relationship between debtor and creditor, these securities could be classified as *direct investment, intercompany lending* (see the description of *direct investment* in Chapter 3). The option is regarded as an integral part of the bond and is not separately valued and classified.

Brady Bonds

Brady bonds, named after U.S. Treasury Secretary Nicholas Brady, arose from the Brady Plan. This plan was a voluntary market-based approach, developed in the late 1980s, to reduce debt and debt service owed to commercial banks by a number of emerging market countries. Brady bonds were issued by the debtor country in exchange for commercial bank loans (and in some cases unpaid interest). In essence they provided a mechanism by which debtor countries could repackage existing debt. They are dollar denominated, "issued" in the international markets. The principal amount is usually (but not always) collateralized by specially issued U.S. Treasury 30-year zero-coupon bonds purchased by the debtor country using a combination of IMF, World Bank, and the country's own foreign currency reserves. Interest payments on Brady bonds, in some cases, are guaranteed by securities of at least double-A-rated credit quality held with the New York Federal Reserve Bank. Brady bonds are more tradable than the original bank loans but come in different forms. The main types are as follows.

* *Par bonds*: Bonds issued to the same value as the original loan, but the coupon on the bonds is below market rate. Principal and interest payments are usually guaranteed.
* *Discount bonds*: Bonds issued at a discount to the original value of the loan, but the coupon is at market rate. Principal and interest payments are usually guaranteed.

* *Debt-conversion bonds*: Bonds issued to the same value as the original loan but on condition that "new" money is provided in the form of new-money bonds.
* *Front-loaded interest reduction bonds*: Bonds issued with low-rate fixed coupons that step up after the first few years.

There are also other, less common types.

Classification

Brady bonds owned by nonresidents are to be included in the gross external debt position. They should be classified as *long-term, bonds and notes (portfolio investment, debt securities in the IIP).* When a Brady bond is issued, the original loan is assumed to have been redeemed unless the terms of the issue of the Brady bond state otherwise. Any debt reduction in nominal value terms should be recorded—see Chapter 8. The initial purchase of the principal collateral (U.S. Treasury bonds) is a separate transaction and is classified as debt of the United States.

C

Certificate of Deposit (CD)

A certificate issued by a bank acknowledging a deposit in that bank for a specified period of time at a specified rate of interest; CDs are essentially a form of negotiable time deposit (evidenced by the certificate). CDs are widely issued in the domestic and international markets, and are typically bearer instruments, issued at face value with original maturities of one to six months, although there have been maturities of up to seven years. Typically, interest costs are payable at maturity for issues of one year or less, and semiannually on longer issues. The rate of interest on a given CD depends on several factors: current market conditions, the denomination of the certificate, and the market standing of the bank offering it. Typically, CDs are highly liquid instruments, which allows banks access to a cheaper source of funds than borrowing on the interbank market.

Classification

CDs owned by nonresidents are to be included in the gross external debt position. Those with an original maturity of one year or less should be classified as *short-term, money market instruments (portfolio investment, debt securities* in the IIP), while those with an original maturity of over one year should be classified as *bonds and notes*. A small minority of CDs are known to be nonnegotiable—not tradable—and if owned by nonresidents are to be classified as *banks, short-term, currency and deposits (other investment* in the IIP). Alternatively, depending on the relationship between debtor and creditor, these securities could be classified as *direct investment, intercompany lending* (see the description of *direct investment* in Chapter 3).

Collateralized Debt Obligations (CDOs)

CDOs are bonds whose income payments and principal repayments are dependent on a pool of instruments. Typically, a CDO is backed by a diversified pool of loan and bond instruments either purchased in the secondary market or from the balance sheet of a commercial bank. The diversified nature of the instruments differentiates a CDO from an asset-backed security, which is backed by a homogeneous pool of instruments, such as mortgages and credit card loans. Because income and the repayment of principal are dependent on the performance of the underlying instruments, there is a probability of early repayment. Issuers are often provided with different tranches of the security, so that if there are prepayments the first tier will be repaid first, the second tier next, etc. The pricing of each tranche reflects the probability of repayment.

Classification

CDOs owned by nonresidents are to be included in the gross external debt position. They should be classified as *long-term, bonds and notes (portfolio investment, debt securities* in the IIP) unless they have an original maturity of one year or less, in which instance they are to be classified as *money market instruments*. Alternatively, depending on the relationship between debtor and creditor, these securities could be classified as *direct investment, intercompany lending* (see the description of *direct investment* in Chapter 3). These securities present a special problem regardless of the amount outstanding because there can be partial repayments of principal at any time. So, simply revaluing the original face value to end-period market prices will cause overvaluation of the position data if there has been a partial repayment.

Commercial Paper (CP)

Commercial paper is an unsecured promise to pay a certain amount on a stated maturity date, issued in bearer form. CP enables corporations to raise short-term funds directly from end investors through their own in-house CP sales team or via arranged placing through bank dealers. Short-term in nature, with maturities ranging from overnight to one year, CP is usually sold at a discount. A coupon is paid in a few markets. Typically, issue size ranges from $100,000 up to about $1 billion. In bypassing financial intermediaries in the short-term money markets, CP can offer a cheaper form of financing to corporations. But because of its unsecured nature, the credit quality of the issuer is important for the investor. Companies with a poor credit rating can obtain a higher rating for the issue by approaching their bank or insurance company for a third-party guarantee, or perhaps issue CP under a MOF (Multiple Option Facility), which provides a backup line of credit should the issue be unsuccessful.

Classification

Commercial paper owned by nonresidents is to be included in the gross external debt position. Such paper should be classified as *short-term, money market instruments (portfolio investment, debt securities* in the IIP). Alternatively, depending on the relationship between debtor and creditor, these securities could be classified as *direct investment, intercompany lending* (see the description of *direct investment* in Chapter 3). When CP is issued at a discount, this discount represents interest income.

Commodity-Linked Bonds

A bond whose redemption value is linked to the price of a commodity. Typically, issuers whose income stream is closely tied to commodity earnings issue these bonds.

Classification

Bonds with payoffs linked to movements in commodity prices and owned by nonresidents are to be included in the gross external debt position. They should be classified as *long-term, bonds and notes (portfolio investment, debt securities* in the IIP) unless they have an original maturity of one year or less, in which instance they are to be classified as *money market instruments*. Alternatively, depending on the relationship between debtor and creditor, these securities could be classified as *direct investment, intercompany lending* (see the description of *direct investment* in Chapter 3).

Commodity-Linked Derivatives

Derivatives whose value derives from the price of a commodity. These include:

- *Commodity future*—traded on an organized exchange, in which counterparties commit to buy or sell a specified amount of a commodity at an agreed contract price on a specified date;
- *Commodity option*—gives the purchaser the right but not the obligation to purchase (call) or sell (put) a specified amount of a commodity at an agreed contract price on or before a specified date; and
- *Commodity swap*—a swap of two payment streams, where one represents a currently prevailing spot price and the other an agreed contract price for a specified quantity and quality of a specified commodity.

Net cash settlements are usually made.

Classification

Commodity-linked derivatives in which the counterparty is a nonresident are included indistinguishably in the memorandum item, *financial derivatives.*

Convertible Bonds

A convertible bond is a fixed-rate bond that may, at the option of the investor, be converted into the equity of the borrower or its parent. The price at which the bond is convertible into equity is set at the time of issue and typically will be at a premium to the market value of the equity at the time of issue. The conversion option on the bond may be exercised at one specified future date or within a range of dates—"the window period." The conversion right cannot be separated from the debt. The instrument allows the investor to participate in the appreciation of the underlying asset of the company while limiting risk. A convertible bond will generally pay a coupon rate higher than the dividend rate of the underlying equity at the time of issue but lower than the rate of a comparable bond without a conversion option. For the investor, the value of the convertible bond lies in the excess return of the bond yield over the dividend yield of the underlying shares.

Classification

Convertible bonds owned by nonresidents are to be included in the gross external debt position. They should be classified as *long-term, bonds and notes (portfolio investment, debt securities* in the IIP) unless they have an original maturity of one year or less, in which instance they are to be classified as *money market instruments.* Alternatively, depending on the relationship between debtor and creditor, these securities could be classified as *direct investment, intercompany lending* (see the description of *direct investment* in Chapter 3). As bonds are converted into equity, so the debt is extinguished. The equity issued is recorded in the memorandum item, *equity liabilities.* If the nonresident is in a direct investment relationship with the issuer, then the equity is classified as *Direct investment in reporting economy: equity capital and reinvested earnings* in the memorandum item.

Credit Derivatives

Derivatives that provide a market in credit risk. Investors will use credit derivatives to gain or reduce exposure to credit risk. With a credit derivative the investor is taking a view on the creditworthiness of the issuer(s) of the underlying instrument(s) without necessarily risking principal (although credit derivatives may be embedded in a security). For instance, a creditor may lend to a debtor but wants to protect against the risk of default by that debtor. The creditor "buys" protection in the form of a credit default swap—the risk premium inherent in the interest rate is swapped by the creditor for a cash payment in event of default. Also, these instruments are used to circumvent local investment rules; for example, if a foreign investor cannot invest in equity securities and so enters into a total return swap where the foreign investor pays a reference rate, say LIBOR, against the total return—dividends and capital gain/loss—on an equity security. The other most common structure is a spread option whose payoff structure depends on the interest rate spread between emerging country debt and, say, U.S. Treasury bonds.

Classification

Credit derivatives in which the counterparty is a nonresident are included indistinguishably in the memorandum item, *financial derivatives.*

Credit-Linked Note

A so-called structured security that combines a credit derivative and a regular bond.

Classification

Credit-linked notes owned by nonresidents are to be included in the gross external debt position. They should be classified as *long-term, bonds and notes (portfolio investment, debt securities* in the IIP). Alternatively, depending on the relationship between debtor and creditor, these securities could be classified as *direct investment, intercompany lending* (see the description of *direct investment* in Chapter 3). The credit derivative is regarded as an integral part of the bond and is not separately valued and classified.

Currency

Currency consists of notes and coin that are in circulation and commonly used to make payments.

Classification

Domestic currency owned by nonresidents is included within the gross external debt position as *monetary authorities* (or perhaps *banks), short-term, currency and deposits (other investment* in the IIP).

Currency-Linked Bonds

A bond in which the coupon and/or redemption value are linked to the movement in an exchange rate. Examples of these types of bonds were the *tesobonos* issued by Mexican banks in 1994. These bonds, issued and payable in pesos, had a redemption value linked to the movement in the U.S. dollar/Mexican peso exchange rate. When the Mexican peso depreciated, the redemption value increased.

Classification

Bonds with payoffs linked to movements in exchange rates and owned by nonresidents are to be included in the gross external debt position. They should be classified as *long-term, bonds and notes (portfolio investment, debt securities* in the IIP) unless they have an original maturity of one year or less, in which instance they are to be classified as *money market instruments.* Alternatively, depending on the relationship between debtor and creditor, these securities could be classified as *direct invest-*

ment, intercompany lending (see the description of *direct investment* in Chapter 3).

Currency Pool Loans

Currency pool loans, provided by the World Bank and regional development banks, are multicurrency obligations committed in U.S. dollar-equivalent terms whose currency composition is the same (pooled) for all borrowers. The World Bank guarantees that at least 90 percent of the U.S. dollar-equivalent value of the currency pool is maintained in fixed currency ratios of 1 U.S. dollar: 125 Japanese yen: 1 euro. These ratios have been maintained since 1991, and prior to the introduction of the euro, the currency ratios were maintained in a fixed ratio of 1 U.S. dollar: 125 Japanese yen: 2 deutsche mark equivalent (consisting of deutsche mark, Netherlands guilders, and Swiss francs). The currency amount disbursed is converted into a U.S. dollar equivalent amount, using the applicable exchange rate on the day of disbursements. The U.S. dollar equivalent amount is then divided by the pool unit value on the day of disbursement to determine the pool units disbursed. The pool units are what the borrower will have to repay. When pool units are to be repaid, they are converted back into the dollar equivalent amount using the prevailing pool unit value. Thus, the pool unit value may be thought of as an exchange rate used to convert the units into their equivalent value in U.S. dollars, and it changes daily in accordance with movements of the exchange rates of the currencies in the pool. The pool unit value is calculated by dividing the U.S. dollar equivalent of the currencies in the pool by the total number of pool units outstanding. As the U.S. dollar appreciates relative to other currencies in the pool, the pool unit value decreases.

Classification

Currency pool loans of the borrowing economy are to be included in the gross external debt position. They should be classified as *loans (other investment* in the IIP).

D

Deep-Discount Bond

A bond that has small interest payments and is issued at a considerable discount to its par value. See also *Zero-Coupon Bonds.*

Classification

Deep-discount bonds owned by nonresidents are to be included within the gross external debt position. They should be classified as *long-term, bonds and notes* (*portfolio investment, debt securities* in the IIP) unless they have an original maturity of one year or less, in which instance they are to be classified as *money market instruments*. Alternatively, depending on the relationship between debtor and creditor, these securities could be classified as *direct investment, intercompany lending* (see the description of *direct investment* in Chapter 3).

Depository Receipts

A depository receipt allows a nonresident entity to introduce its equity or debt into another market in a form more readily acceptable to the investors in that market. A depository bank will purchase the underlying foreign security and then issue receipts in a currency more acceptable to the investor. The investor can exchange the depository receipts for the underlying security at any time. See also *American Depository Receipts* and *Bearer Depository Receipts*.

Classification

A depository receipt is classified according to the nature of the underlying instrument backing it. This is because the "issuing" intermediary does not take the underlying security onto its balance sheet but simply acts as a facilitator. So, the debtor is the issuer of the underlying security. If owned by non-residents, these instruments, if a debt security is the underlying instrument, are to be included in the gross external debt position. They should be classified as *long-term, bonds and notes* (*portfolio investment, debt securities* in the IIP) unless they have an original maturity of one year or less, in which instance they are to be classified as *money market instruments*. Alternatively, depending on the relationship between debtor and creditor, these securities could be classified as *direct investment, intercompany lending* (see the description of *direct investment* in Chapter 3). If the underlying item is an equity investment, it should be classified in the memorandum item, *equity liabilities*. If the nonresident is in a direct investment relationship with the issuer, then the equity is classified as *Direct investment in reporting economy: equity capital and reinvested earnings* in the memorandum item.

Deposits in Mutual Associations

Deposits in the form of shares or similar evidence of deposit issued by mutual associations such as savings and loans, building societies, credit unions, and the like are classified as bank deposits. See *Bank Deposits*.

Classification

Deposits in mutual associations owned by nonresidents are to be included in the gross external debt position. They should be classified as *banks, short-term, currency and deposits* (*other investment* in the IIP).

Dual-Currency Bonds

Dual-currency bonds are a group of debt securities where the interest and/or principal payments differ from the currency in which the bond is issued. The issue of currency-linked bonds followed the development of the currency swap market that broadened the range of currencies in which international bonds were issued.

Classification

Dual-currency bonds owned by nonresidents are to be included in the gross external debt position. They should be classified as *long-term, bonds and notes* (*portfolio investment, debt securities* in the IIP) unless they have an original maturity of one year or less, in which instance they are to be classified as *money market instruments*. Alternatively, depending on the relationship between debtor and creditor, these securities could be classified as *direct investment, intercompany lending* (see the description of *direct investment* in Chapter 3).

E

Equity

Equity securities cover all instruments and records acknowledging, after the claims of all creditors have been met, claims to the residual values of incorporated enterprises.

Classification

Equity securities are included in the memorandum item, *equity liabilities*. If the nonresident is in a direct investment relationship with the issuer, then the equity is classified as *Direct investment in reporting economy: equity capital and reinvested earnings* in the memorandum item.

Equity-Linked Bond

An equity-linked bond comprises features of both debt and equity. Equity-linked bonds are debt instruments that contain an option to purchase (either by conversion of existing debt or by exercising the right to purchase) an equity stake in the issuer, its parent, or another company at a fixed price. These instruments are usually issued when stock market prices are rising because companies can raise funds at lower than market interest rates while investors receive interest payments, and potentially lock into capital gains.

Classification

Equity-linked bonds, if owned by nonresidents, are to be included in the gross external debt position. They should be classified as *long-term, bonds and notes* (*portfolio investment, debt securities* in the IIP) unless they have an original maturity of one year or less, in which instance they are to be classified as *money market instruments*. Alternatively, depending on the relationship between debtor and creditor, these securities could be classified as *direct investment, intercompany lending* (see the description of *direct investment* in Chapter 3). If the bonds are converted into equity, the debt is extinguished. The equity issued is recorded in the memorandum item, *equity liabilities*. If the nonresident is in a direct investment relationship with the issuer, then the equity is classified as *Direct investment in reporting economy: equity capital and reinvested earnings* in the memorandum item. See also *Equity Warrant Bond* and *Warrants*.

Equity-Linked Derivatives

Derivatives whose value derives from equity prices. These include:
- Equity future—traded on an organized exchange, in which counterparties commit to buy or sell a specified amount of an individual equity or a basket of equities or an equity index at an agreed contract price on a specified date;

- Equity option—gives the purchaser the right but not the obligation to purchase (call) or sell (put) a specified amount of an individual equity or a basket of equities or an equity index at an agreed contract price on or before a specified date; and
- Equity swap—in which one party exchanges a rate of return linked to an equity investment for the rate of return on another equity investment.

Net cash settlements are usually made.

Classification

Equity-linked derivatives in which the counterparty is a nonresident are included indistinguishably in the memorandum item, *financial derivatives*.

Equity Warrant Bond (Debt-with-Equity Warrants)

Equity warrant bonds are debt securities that incorporate warrants, which give the holder the option to purchase equity in the issuer, its parent company, or another company during a predetermined period or on one particular date at a fixed contract price. The warrants are detachable and may be traded separately from the debt security. The exercise of the equity warrant will normally increase the total capital funds of the issuer because the debt is not replaced by equity but remains outstanding until the date of its redemption. The issue of equity warrant bonds reduces the funding costs for borrowers because the investor will generally accept a lower yield in anticipation of the future profit to be gained from exercising the warrant.

Classification

Because the warrant is detachable and may be traded separately from the debt security, the two instruments should be separately recorded. Bonds owned by nonresidents are to be included in the gross external debt position. They should be classified as *long-term, bonds and notes* (*portfolio investment, debt securities* in the IIP) unless they have an original maturity of one year or less, in which instance they are to be classified as *money market instruments*. Alternatively, depending on the relationship between debtor and creditor, these securities could be classified as *direct investment, intercompany lending* (see the description of *direct investment* in Chapter 3). Warrants owned by nonresidents are to be included indistinguishably in the memorandum item, *financial derivatives*.

F

Fixed-Rate Bond

A bond whose coupon payments remain unchanged for the life of the bond or for a certain number of years. See also *Variable-Rate Bond*.

Classification

Fixed-rate bonds owned by nonresidents are to be included in the gross external debt position. They should be classified as *long-term, bonds and notes (portfolio investment, debt securities* in the IIP) unless they have an original maturity of one year or less, in which instance they are to be classified as *money market instruments*. Alternatively, depending on the relationship between debtor and creditor, these securities could be classified as *direct investment, intercompany lending* (see the description of *direct investment* in Chapter 3).

Foreign Bonds

A foreign bond is a security issued by a nonresident borrower in a domestic capital market, other than its own, usually denominated in the currency of that market. Issues are placed publicly or privately. These bonds generally adopt the characteristics of the domestic market of the country in which they are issued, such as in terms of registration—bearer or registered form—settlement, and coupon payment arrangements. Common foreign bonds are Yankee bonds (U.S. market), Samurai bonds (Japan), and Bulldog bonds (U.K.).

Classification

If the owner of the foreign bond is a nonresident, and this is most likely given that the bonds are issued in foreign markets, the bonds are to be included in the gross external debt position. They should be classified as *long-term, bonds and notes (portfolio investment, debt securities* in the IIP) unless they have an original maturity of one year or less, in which instance they are to be classified as *money market instruments*. Alternatively, depending on the rela-

tionship between debtor and creditor, these securities could be classified as *direct investment, intercompany lending* (see the description of *direct investment* in Chapter 3).

Foreign-Currency-Linked Derivatives

Derivatives whose value is linked to foreign currency exchange rates. The most common foreign-currency-linked derivatives are:

- Forward-type foreign exchange rate contracts, under which currencies are sold or purchased for an agreed exchange rate on a specified day;
- Foreign exchange swaps, whereby there is an initial exchange of foreign currencies and a simultaneous forward purchase/sale of the same currencies;
- Cross-currency interest rate swaps, whereby—following an initial exchange of a specified amount of foreign currencies—cash flows related to interest and principal payments are exchanged according to a predetermined schedule; and
- Options that give the purchaser the right but not the obligation to purchase or sell a specified amount of a foreign currency at an agreed contract price on or before a specified date.

Classification

Foreign-currency-linked derivatives in which the counterparty is a nonresident are included indistinguishably in the memorandum item, *financial derivatives*.

Forward-Type Derivatives

A contract in which two counterparties commit to exchange an underlying item—real or financial—in a specified quantity, on a specified date, at an agreed contract price or, in the specific example of a swaps contract, agree to exchange cash flows, determined by reference to the price(s) of, say, currencies or interest rates according to predetermined rules. In essence, two counterparties are trading risk exposures of equal market value.

Classification

Forward-type derivatives in which the counterparty is a nonresident are included in the memorandum item, *financial derivatives*.

G

Gold Swaps

A gold swap involves an exchange of gold for foreign exchange deposits with an agreement that the transaction be reversed at an agreed future date at an agreed gold price. The gold taker (cash provider) will not usually record the gold on its balance sheet, while the gold provider (cash taker) will not usually remove the gold from its balance sheet. In this manner, the transaction is analogous to a repurchase agreement and should be recorded as a collateralized loan. See Appendix II; see also *Repurchase Agreements* in Part 2 of this appendix.

Classification

For the cash taker, a gold swap is classified as a loan; so borrowing under a gold swap from a nonresident is included within the gross external debt position. The debt should be classified as a *loan (other investment* in the IIP).

I

Index-Linked Securities

Index-linked securities are debt instruments with coupon and/or principal payments linked to commodity prices, interest rates, stock exchange, or other price indices. The benefits to the issuer of indexing include a reduction in interest costs if the deal is targeted at a particular group of investors' requirements, and/or an ability to hedge an exposed position in a particular market. The benefit to investors is in the ability to gain exposure to a wide range of markets (for example, foreign exchange or property markets) without the same degree of risk that may be involved in investing in the markets directly. Issues linked to a consumer price index also provide investors with protection against inflation.

Classification

Index-linked securities owned by nonresidents are to be included within the gross external debt position. They should be classified as *long-term, bonds and notes (portfolio investment, debt securities* in the IIP) unless they have an original maturity of one year or less, in which instance they are to be classi-

fied as *short-term, money market instruments*. Alternatively, depending on the relationship between debtor and creditor, these securities could be classified as *direct investment, intercompany lending* (see the description of *direct investment* in Chapter 3). When interest payments are index linked, the payments are treated as interest. If the value of the principal is index linked, the issue price should be recorded as principal, and any subsequent change in value due to indexation should be treated as an interest cost, and added to the value of the underlying instrument.

Interest-Rate-Linked Derivatives

Derivatives whose value is linked to interest rates. The most common are:

- Interest rate swaps, which involve an exchange of cash flows related to interest payments, or receipts, on a notional amount of principal in one currency over a period of time;
- Forward rate agreements, in which a cash settlement is made by one party to another calculated by the difference between a market interest rate of a specified maturity in one currency on a specific date and an agreed interest rate, times a notional amount of principal that is never exchanged (if the market rate is above the agreed rate, one party will agree to make a cash settlement to the other, and vice versa); and
- Interest rate options that give the purchaser the right to buy or sell a specified notional value at a specified interest rate—the price traded is 100 less the agreed interest rate, with settlement based on the difference between the market rate and the specified rate times the notional value.

Classification

Interest-rate-linked derivatives in which the counterparty is a nonresident are included indistinguishably in the memorandum item, *financial derivatives*.

L

Land Ownership

By convention, land can only be owned by residents. So if a nonresident purchases land, then a notional resident entity is created on which the nonresident has a financial claim.

Classification

The financial claim the nonresident has on the notional resident entity is assumed to be a direct investment equity investment, so the equity investment is classified in the memorandum item, *Direct investment in reporting economy: equity capital and reinvested earnings.*

Letters of Credit

Letters of credit provide a guarantee that funds will be made available, but no financial liability exists until funds are actually advanced.

Classification

Because letters of credit are not debt instruments, they are not included within the gross external debt position.

Loans

Loans comprise those financial assets created through the direct lending of funds by a creditor to a debtor through an arrangement in which the lender either receives no security evidencing the transaction or receives a nonnegotiable document or instrument. Included are loans to finance trade, other loans and advances (including mortgages), use of IMF credit, and loans from the IMF. In addition, finance leases and repurchase agreements are covered under loans. Loans may be payable in the domestic or foreign currency(s).

Classification

Loans extended by nonresidents to residents are to be included in the gross external debt position as *loans (other investment* in the IIP). Alternatively, depending on the relationship between debtor and creditor, the debt could be classified as *direct investment, intercompany lending* (see the description of *direct investment* in Chapter 3).

M

Medium-Term Notes (MTNs)

These are debt instruments of usually one- to five-year maturity issued in bearer form under a program agreement through one or more dealers. Once a program is set up, issues can be made quickly to take advantage of market conditions, with issues structured more closely to investors' needs than in the public bond markets. Typically, the MTN market is not as liquid as the international bond market, so issuers may have to pay a higher interest rate.

Classification

Medium-term notes owned by nonresidents are to be included within the gross external debt position. They should be classified as *long-term, bonds and notes (portfolio investment, debt securities* in the IIP) unless they have an original maturity of one year or less, in which instance they are to be classified as *money market instruments.* Alternatively, depending on the relationship between debtor and creditor, these securities could be classified as *direct investment, intercompany lending* (see the description of *direct investment* in Chapter 3).

Military Debt

Loans and other credits extended for military purposes.

Classification

Military debt owed to nonresidents is to be included in the gross external debt position, allocated by the nature of the debt instrument.

Miscellaneous Accounts Payable and Receivable

See *Other Accounts Payable and Receivable.*

Money Market Instruments

Money market instruments are debt securities that generally give the owner the unconditional right to receive a stated, fixed sum of money on a specified date. These instruments usually are traded, at a discount, in organized markets; the discount is dependent upon the interest rate and the time remaining to maturity. Included are such instruments as treasury bills, commercial and financial paper, banker's acceptances, negotiable certificates of deposit (with original maturities of one year or less), and short-term notes issued under note issuance facilities.

Classification

Money market instruments owned by nonresidents are to be included in the gross external debt position. They should be classified as *short-term, money market instruments (portfolio investment, debt securities* in the IIP). Alternatively, depending on the relationship between debtor and creditor, these securities could be classified as *direct investment, intercompany lending* (see the description of *direct investment* in Chapter 3).

Mortgage-Backed Securities

A mortgage-backed security is a form of asset-backed security. See *Asset-Backed Securities*.

Classification

Mortgage-backed securities owned by nonresidents are to be included in the gross external debt position. They should be classified as *long-term, bonds and notes (portfolio investment, debt securities* in the IIP).

Mutual Fund Shares

Mutual funds are financial institutions through which investors pool their funds to invest in a diversified portfolio of securities. The shares in the fund purchased by individual investors represent an ownership interest in the pool of underlying assets—that is, the investors have an equity stake. Because professional fund managers make the selection of assets, mutual funds provide individual investors with an opportunity to invest in a diversified and professionally managed portfolio of securities without the need of detailed knowledge of the individual companies issuing the stocks and bonds. Usually, fund managers must adequately inform investors about the risks and expenses associated with investment in specific funds.

Classification

Because nonresidents own mutual fund shares, the shares are equity investments to be included in the memorandum item, *equity liabilities*.

N

Nondeliverable Forward Contracts (NDFs)

A nondeliverable forward contract is a foreign currency financial derivative instrument. An NDF differs from a normal foreign currency forward contract in that there is no physical settlement of two currencies at maturity. Rather, based on the movement of two currencies, a net cash settlement will be made by one party to the other. NDFs are commonly used to hedge local currency risks in emerging markets where local currencies are not freely convertible, where capital markets are small and undeveloped, and where there are restrictions on capital movements. Under these conditions, an NDF market might develop in an offshore financial center, with contracts settled in major foreign currencies, such as the U.S. dollar.

Classification

NDF contracts in which the counterparty is a nonresident are included indistinguishably in the memorandum item, *financial derivatives*.

Nonparticipating Preferred Shares

These are a type of preferred shares in which the payment of a "dividend" (usually at a fixed rate) is calculated according to a predetermined formula and not determined by the earnings of the issuer. In other words, the investor does not participate in the distribution of profits to equity investors (if any), nor share in any surplus on dissolution of the issuer. See also *Preferred Shares* and *Participating Preferred Shares*.

Classification

Nonparticipating preferred shares are debt instruments, and so if owned by a nonresident are to be included in the gross external debt position. They should be classified as *long-term, bonds and notes (portfolio investment, debt securities* in the IIP) unless they have an original maturity of one year or less, in which instance they are to be classified as *money market instruments*. Alternatively, depending on the relationship between debtor and creditor, these securities could be classified as *direct investment, intercompany lending* (see the description of *direct investment* in Chapter 3).

Nontraded Debt

Debt instruments that are not usually traded or tradable in organized and other financial markets.

Classification

Depends on the nature of the instrument.

Note Issuance Facilities (NIFs) / Revolving Underwriting Facilities (RUFs)

A note issued under an NIF/RUF is a short-term instrument issued under a legally binding medium-term facility—a form of revolving credit. A bank, or banks, underwrite, for a fee, the issuance of this three- or six-month paper and may be called upon to purchase any unsold paper at each rollover date, or to provide standby credit facilities. The basic difference between an NIF and an RUF is in the underwriting guarantee: under an RUF the underwriting banks agree to provide loans should the issue fail, but under an NIF they could either lend or purchase the outstanding notes. First developed in the early 1980s, the market for NIFs grew substantially for a short period in the mid-1980s. It was a potentially profitable market for international banks at a time when the syndicated credits market was depressed, following the debt crisis of the early 1980s. By the early 1990s, euro commercial paper (ECP), and euro medium-term notes (EMTNs) had become more popular forms of finance.

Classification

Notes issued under an NIF/RUF that are owned by a nonresident are to be included in the gross external debt position. They should be classified as *short-term, money market instruments* (*portfolio investment, debt securities* in the IIP). This is because the contractual maturity is less than one year's maturity. Alternatively, depending on the relationship between debtor and creditor, these securities could be classified as *direct investment, intercompany lending* (see the description of *direct investment* in Chapter 3).

O

Operational Leases

Operational leases are arrangements in which machinery or equipment is rented out for specified periods of time that are shorter than the total expected service lives of the machinery or equipment. Typically under an operational lease, the lessor normally maintains the stock of equipment in good working order, and the equipment can be hired on demand or at short notice; the equipment may be rented out for varying periods of time; and the lessor is frequently responsible for the maintenance and repair of the equipment as part of the service which he provides to the lessee. Under an operational lease, ownership of the equipment does not change hands; rather, the lessor is regarded as providing a service to the lessee, on a continuous basis.

Classification

Operational leases are not financial instruments, but rather the provision of a service, the cost of which accrues continuously. Any payments under an operational lease are either classified as prepayments for services—creating a trade credit claim on the lessor—or postpayments for services rendered—extinguishing a trade credit liability to the lessor.

Options

An option is a contract that gives the purchaser the right but not the obligation to buy (call) or sell (put) a specified underlying item—real or financial—at an agreed contract (strike) price on or before a specified date from the writer of the option.

Classification

Options owned by nonresidents are to be included in the memorandum item, *financial derivatives*.

Other Accounts Payable and Receivable

Other accounts payable and receivable—see also *Trade Credit*—include amounts due in respect of taxes, dividends, purchases and sales of securities, rent, wages and salaries, and social contributions.

Classification

Other accounts payable owed to nonresidents are to be included in the gross external debt position. They should be classified as *other debt liabilities (other investment* in the IIP). Alternatively, depending on the relationship between debtor and creditor, these securities could be classified as *direct investment, intercompany lending* (see the description of *direct investment* in Chapter 3).

P

Participating Preferred Shares

Also known as a participating preference share. These are a type of preferred share where the investor has some entitlement to a share in the profits or a share of any surplus on dissolution of the issuer (in addition to the fixed dividend payment received). See also *Preferred Shares* and *Nonparticipating Preferred Shares.*

Classification

Because of the claim on the residual value of the issuer, participating preference shares are classified as equity instruments, and so are included in the memorandum item, *equity liabilities.* If the nonresident is in a direct investment relationship with the issuer, then the equity is classified as *Direct investment in reporting economy: equity capital and reinvested earnings* in the memorandum item.

Permanent Interest-Bearing Shares (PIBS)

These are deferred shares issued by mutual societies, which rank beneath ordinary shares (which are more akin to deposits than equity in mutual societies) and all other liabilities (including subordinated debt) in the event of a dissolution of the society. They provide "permanent" capital. In the United Kingdom these instruments are non-profit-participating by regulatory requirement; rather, predetermined (but not necessarily fixed) interest costs are payable, with the amounts to be paid not linked to the issuer's profits; interest costs are not to be paid if this would result in the society breaching capital adequacy guidelines and are noncumulative; but more PIBS can be issued in lieu of a cash dividend.

Classification

PIBS are debt instruments because they are a form of nonparticipating preferred share (defined as such because the holders of the instruments do not participate in the profits of the society). PIBS owned by nonresidents are to be included within the gross external debt position. They should be classified as *long-term, bonds and notes (portfolio investment, debt securities* in the IIP) unless they have an original maturity of one year or less, in which instance they are to be classified as *money market instruments.* Alternatively, depending on the relationship between debtor and creditor, these securities could be classified as *direct investment, intercompany lending* (see the description of *direct investment* in Chapter 3).

Perpetual Floating-Rate Notes

A debt security whose coupon is refixed periodically on a refix date by reference to an independent interest rate index such as three-month LIBOR. Generally, these instruments are issued by financial institutions, particularly banks, and are perpetual so as to replicate equity and qualify as tier-two capital under the Basel capital adequacy requirements. Investor demand for perpetual floating-rate notes has been weak in recent years.

Classification

Despite the perpetual nature of these instruments, they are debt securities because the instruments give the holder a contractually determined money income. Perpetual floating-rate notes owned by nonresidents are to be included within the gross external debt position. They should be classified as *long-term, bonds and notes (portfolio investment, debt securities* in the IIP) unless they have an original maturity of one year or less, in which instance they are to be classified as *money market instruments.* Alternatively, depending on the relationship between debtor and creditor, these securities could be classified as *direct investment, intercompany lending* (see the description of *direct investment* in Chapter 3).

Preferred Shares

Also known as a preference share. Preferred shares are a class of equity capital that rank ahead of common equity in respect of dividends and distribution of assets upon dissolution of the incorporated enterprise. Investors have little control over the decisions of the company: voting rights are normally restricted to situations where the rights attached to preferred shares are being considered for amendment. Preferred shares are registered securities. Preferred share issues typically pay a fixed-rate dividend payment that is calculated according to a predetermined formula, but some preferred shares participate in the profits of the issuer.

Classification

Preferred shares are classified as equity securities if the shares are participating and debt securities if the shares are nonparticipating. See *Nonparticipating* and *Participating Preferred Shares* for specific classification requirements.

Promissory Note

An unconditional promise to pay a certain sum on demand on a specified due date. Promissory notes are widely used in international trade as a secure means of payment. They are drawn up (issued) by an importer in favor of the exporter. When the latter endorses the note, provided the importer is creditworthy, a promissory note is traded.

Classification

Promissory notes are money market instruments that are claims on the issuer. If owned by nonresidents, promissory notes should be included in the gross external debt position. They should be classified as *short-term, money market instruments (portfolio investment, debt securities* in the IIP) unless they have an original maturity over one year, in which instance they are to be classified as *bonds and notes*. Alternatively, depending on the relationship between debtor and creditor, these securities could be classified as *direct investment, intercompany lending* (see the description of *direct investment* in Chapter 3).

R

Reverse Security Transactions

See Appendix II.

S

Stripped Securities

Stripped securities are securities that have been transformed from a principal amount with periodic interest coupons into a series of zero-coupon bonds, with the range of maturities matching the coupon payment dates and the redemption date of the principal amount. Strips can be created in two ways. Either the owner of the original security can ask the settlement or clearing house in which the security is registered to "create" strips from the original security, in which case the strips replace the original security and remain the direct obligation of the issuer of the security; or the owner of the original security can issue strips in its own name, "backed" by the original security, in which case the strips represent new liabilities and are not the direct obligation of the issuer of the original security. Usually, short-term strips are bought by money managers as gov-

ernment bill or note substitutes; intermediate maturity strips will be purchased by investors who believe that the yield curve might become more positive. Whereas demand is strongest for the longer maturities because these instruments have longer duration than the original bonds and are leveraged investments, a relatively small up-front payment gives the investor exposure to a larger nominal amount.

Classification

Stripped securities owned by a nonresident are to be included in the gross external debt position. Depending on their maturity, a stripped security is to be classified as either *short-term, money market instruments* (original maturity of one year or less) or *long-term, bonds and notes* (original maturity of over one year) (*portfolio investment, debt securities* in the IIP). Alternatively, depending on the relationship between debtor and creditor, these securities could be classified as *direct investment, intercompany lending* (see the description of *direct investment* in Chapter 3). The residence of the issuer depends on who has issued the strips. If the owner of the original security issues the stripped bonds, then the residence of the issuer is that of the entity issuing the strips; the underlying securities remain extant. If the strips remain the direct obligation of the original issuer, then the issuer is the original issuer, and the strips "replace" the original securities that have been stripped.

Structured Bonds

Structured bonds have characteristics that are designed to attract a certain type of investor and/or take advantage of particular market circumstances. However, structuring securities to appeal to a particular type of investor risks the possibility of a loss of liquidity if the market moves in such a way as to make the structured features of the issue no longer attractive. Typically the structured features are achieved through the use of derivatives—for instance, a credit-linked note is a bond with an embedded credit derivative.

Classification

Structured bonds are debt instruments, and if owned by a nonresident are to be included in the gross external debt position. They should be classified as *long-term, bonds and notes (portfolio investment, debt securities* in the IIP) unless they have an original maturity of one year or less, in which instance they are to be classified as *money market instruments*. Alternatively, depending on the relationship between debtor and creditor, these securities could be classified as *direct investment, intercompany lending* (see the description of *direct investment* in Chapter 3). Any embedded derivative is regarded as an integral part of the bond and not separately valued and identified.

Structured Floating-Rate Notes

The structured floating-rate note is a variation of a standard variable-rate bond (that is, a long-dated debt security whose coupon payment is reset periodically by reference to an independent interest rate index such as six-month LIBOR). The structured issue includes a derivative that allows the coupon calculation to be tailored to meet investors' interest rate expectations. For instance, there may be an interest rate collar or band—the interest rate cannot increase above an upper specified rate or fall below a lower specified rate. The issue of structured floating-rate notes has grown as borrowers have used financial derivatives to tailor financing products to investor demands while meeting their own funding needs.

Classification

Structured floating-rate notes are debt instruments, and if owned by a nonresident are to be included in the gross external debt position. They should be classified as *long-term, bonds and notes* (*portfolio investment, debt securities* in the IIP) unless they have an original maturity of one year or less, in which instance they are to be classified as *money market instruments*. Alternatively, depending on the relationship between debtor and creditor, these securities could be classified as *direct investment, intercompany lending* (see the description of *direct investment* in Chapter 3). Any embedded derivative is regarded as an integral part of the note and not separately valued and identified.

Swaps

A forward-type financial derivative contract in which two counterparties agree to exchange cash flows determined with reference to prices of, say, currencies or interest rates, according to predeter-

mined rules. At inception, this instrument typically has zero market value, but as market prices change the swap acquires value.

Classification

Swaps in which the counterparty is a nonresident are included in the memorandum item, *financial derivatives*.

T

Total Return Swap

A credit derivative that swaps the total return on a financial instrument, cash flows and capital gains and losses, for a guaranteed interest rate, such as an interbank rate, plus a margin.

Classification

Total return swaps in which the counterparty is a nonresident are included in the memorandum item, *financial derivatives*.

Trade Credit

Trade credits consist of claims and liabilities arising from the direct extension of credit by suppliers for transactions in goods and services, and advance payments by buyers for goods and services and for work in progress (or to be undertaken). The direct extension of trade credit by buyers arises when they prepay for goods and services; the debt is extinguished when the supplier provides the goods and/or services.

Classification

Trade credit owed to nonresidents is to be included in the gross external debt position. Such credit should be classified as *trade credit* (*other investment* in the IIP). Alternatively, depending on the relationship between debtor and creditor, the credit could be classified as *direct investment, intercompany lending* (see the description of *direct investment* in Chapter 3). *1993 SNA* regards trade credit as a form of accounts payable/receivable (*1993 SNA*, paragraph 11.100).

Treasury Bills

A common form of sovereign short-term debt; many governments of the world issue treasury bills. Typically issued through the central bank with maturities ranging from four weeks to two years, they are typically issued at a discount to face value and are redeemed at par.

Classification

Treasury bills are debt instruments, and so if owned by a nonresident are to be included in the gross external debt position. These bills should be classified as *short-term, money market instruments (portfolio investment, debt securities* in the IIP) unless they have an original maturity of more than one year, in which instance they are to be classified as *long term, bonds and notes.*

U

Use of IMF Credit and Loans

These comprise members' drawings on the IMF other than those drawn against the country's reserve tranche position. Use of IMF credit and loans includes purchases and drawings under Stand-By, Extended, Structural Adjustment, Enhanced Structural Adjustment, and Systemic Transformation Facility Arrangements, together with Trust Fund loans.

Classification

Use of IMF credit and loans is to be included in the gross external debt position as *monetary authorities, loans (other investment* in the IIP). Because of the particular accounting procedures of the IMF, the use of IMF credit might be considered to have some of the characteristics of a swap of currencies. However, since the IMF has lent in SDR terms, with payments in SDR terms, at an interest rate that is SDR-related, the recommended classification reflects the economic nature of the transaction—a loan.

V

Variable-Rate Bond

A bond whose interest payments are linked to a reference index (for example, LIBOR), or the price of a specific commodity, or the price of a specific financial instrument that normally changes over time in a continuous manner in response to market pressures.

Classification

Variable-rate bonds owned by nonresidents are to be included in the gross external debt position. They should be classified as *long-term, bonds and notes (portfolio investment, debt securities* in the IIP) unless they have an original maturity of one year or less, in which instance they are to be classified as *money market instruments.* Alternatively, depending on the relationship between debtor and creditor, these securities could be classified as *direct investment, intercompany lending* (see the description of *direct investment* in Chapter 3).

Variable-Rate Notes (VRNs)

These securities adopted the standard characteristics of a variable-rate bond. However, whereas a standard characteristic of a variable-rate bond is that it carries a fixed spread over a referral index, the spread over LIBOR on a VRN varies over time depending on the change in the perceived credit risk of the issuer. The spread is reset at each rollover date—normally every three months—by means of negotiation between the issuer and arranging house. VRNs are usually issued with no maturity date (perpetual VRNs) but fixed five-year and longer-dated issues are in existence. VRNs generally have a put option for the existing holders of notes to sell the issue back to the lead manager of the issuing syndicate, at par, at any interest payment date.

Classification

VRNs owned by nonresidents are to be included in the gross external debt position. They should be classified as *long-term, bonds and notes (portfolio investment, debt securities* in the IIP) unless they have an original maturity of one year or less, in which instance they are to be classified as *money market instruments.* Alternatively, depending on the relationship between debtor and creditor, these securities could be classified as *direct investment, intercompany lending* (see the description of *direct investment* in Chapter 3). The put option, embedded in the instrument, is not valued and classified separately.

W

Warrants

Warrants are a form of financial derivative giving the owner the right but not the obligation to purchase or sell from the issuer of the warrant a fixed amount of an underlying asset, such as equities and bonds, at an agreed contract price for a specified period of time or on a specified date. Although similar to traded options, a distinguishing factor is that the exercise of the warrants can create new securities, thus diluting the capital of existing bond or shareholders, whereas traded options typically grant rights over assets that are already available. Warrants can be issued in their own right or with equity or bonds to make the underlying issue more attractive. They can be quoted and traded separately in the secondary market.

Classification

Warrants owned by nonresidents are to be included in the memorandum item, *financial derivatives*.

Z

Zero-Coupon Bonds

A single-payment security that does not involve interest payments during the life of the bond. The bond is sold at a discount from par value, and the full return is paid at maturity. The difference between the discounted issue price and the face or redemption value reflects the market rate of interest at the time of issue and time to maturity. The longer the maturity of the bond and the higher the interest rate, the greater the discount against the face or redemption value. Zero-coupon, and deep-discount bonds, have four particular advantages for investors:

- There may be some tax advantage in receiving a capital gain rather than an income payment;
- There is no or little (deep-discount bond) reinvestment risk (the possibility that when coupon payments fall due, and need to be reinvested, interest rates will be lower);
- The bond has a longer "duration" than a bond of comparable maturity that pays fixed- or variable-rate interest, so making the zero-coupon bond's price more sensitive to interest rate changes; and
- A zero-coupon bond is a leveraged investment in that a relatively small initial outlay gives exposure to a larger nominal amount.

See also *Deep-Discount Bond.*

Classification

Zero-coupon bonds owned by nonresidents are to be included in the gross external debt position. They should be classified as *long-term, bonds and notes (portfolio investment, debt securities* in the IIP) unless they have an original maturity of one year or less, in which instance they are to be classified as *money market instruments.* Alternatively, depending on the relationship between debtor and creditor, these securities could be classified as *direct investment, intercompany lending* (see the description of *direct investment* in Chapter 3).

Part 2. Classification of Specific Transactions

This section discusses the classification treatment within the gross external debt position of specific transactions.

Arrears: When Should They Be Recorded?

Arrears should be recorded from the day after a required payment has not been made. It is recognized that, in some instances, arrears arise for operational reasons rather than a reluctance or inability to pay. Nonetheless, in principle such arrears when outstanding at the reference date should be recorded as arrears.

Collateralization of External Debt

To provide additional assurance to the creditor, the debtor may set aside either financial assets or future streams of income as collateral for the debt incurred. In other words, payments on the debt might be "backed" by future export earnings, such as receipts from petroleum sales, or the creditor may have a claim on certain financial assets held with third parties if the debtor defaults. Alternatively, the debtor might invest funds in a zero-coupon instrument that at maturity will equal the value of the principal debt incurred, which is then due for repayment. In all cases, external debt should be recorded gross—that is, separately from the collateral. For instance, where the debtor has invested funds in a zero-coupon bond, both the external debt and the zero-coupon bond are recorded on a gross basis, the zero-coupon bond being an asset of the debtor. Also, when debt is contractually to be serviced by an income source of the debtor (for example, future export earnings), the debtor continues to record the receipt of income and the payment of principal and/or interest even if the income is passed directly from "source" (for example, the purchaser of the exports) to the account of the creditor, without directly involving the debtor. There may well be analytical interest in information on the value of external debt that has been collateralized, and in the type of financial asset or income stream used to back the external debt.

Consignment Trade

No debt is created for goods on consignment—that is, goods intended for sale but not actually sold at the time of crossing a frontier—because ownership of the goods has not changed hands.

Defeasement

Defeasance is a technique by which a debtor unit removes liabilities from its balance sheet by pairing them with financial assets, the income and value of which are sufficient to ensure that all debt service payments are met. Defeasance may be carried out by placing the paired assets and liabilities in a separate account within the institutional unit concerned or by transferring them to another unit. The *Guide* does not recognize defeasance as affecting the outstanding debt of the debtor as long as there has been no change in the legal obligations of the debtor. In other words, provided the payment obligations remain de jure with the original debtor, ownership of the liabilities remains unchanged, and should be reported as external debt of the original debtor.

Financial Leases: Treatment of Residual Values

As explained in Chapter 3, under a financial lease, ownership of the underlying item is considered to have changed hands because the risks and rewards of ownership have, de facto, been transferred from the legal owner to the user; this de facto change of ownership is financed by a financial claim, which is the asset of the lessor and a liability of the lessee. However, even though the rentals may enable the lessor over the period of the contract to recover most of the costs of goods and the carrying charges, there may be a residual amount. The lessee may have an option to pay the residual value to gain legal ownership of the underlying item. How should the residual amount be recorded?

The residual amount is part of the debt obligation that arises when the goods are assumed to have changed ownership. In other words, under statistical convention, the debt at the inception of the lease is defined as the full value of the good, inclusive of the residual amount. This debt obligation is recorded as a *loan*. The loan liability arising from the residual value is extinguished either when the goods are returned or when a payment is made and legal ownership changes hands. The IMF's *Balance of Payments Textbook* (IMF, 1996, page 126) provides an example of the circumstance in which there is a final residual payment.

This issue also raises the question of whether there is a point at which the residual value is such a large percentage of the total value of the goods that the lease should be regarded as operational and not financial. There is no firm percentage; rather, these arrangements are determined more by their nature. When a lease is a financial arrangement, it is usually evident from the roles and obligations of the transactors—for example, the lessee is responsible for repairs and maintenance, and the lessor is a financial institution, etc.

Fundamental to the assumption of a change of ownership is the idea that, de facto, the lessee assumes the risks and rewards of ownership from the legal owner. But if there is option rather than agreement to purchase the residual value, or if it is agreed that the lessee will pay a market price for the residual amount, the greater the percentage size of the residual amount at inception, the more diminished the extent to which the de facto risks and rewards of ownership can be said to have changed hands.

Guaranteed External Debt

The provision by one institutional unit of a guarantee to make future debt-service payments to a nonresident creditor if certain conditions are met, such as a default by the debtor, does not negate the claim the creditor has on the debtor. Thus, the debtor on whom the nonresident creditor has a claim, and not the guarantor, should record an external debt liability, unless and until the guarantor assumes the external debt. Chapter 8 provides guidance on the classification of debt assumption.

Islamic Banking[2]

Activities of Islamic financial institutions differ from those of standard commercial depository cor-

---

[2]Islamic banking is described in detail in Appendix 2 of the IMF's *Monetary and Financial Statistics Manual* (IMF, 2000d).

porations in that predetermined interest on financial transactions is prohibited. As is evident from the definition of external debt in Chapter 2, the nonpayment of interest on liabilities does not in itself preclude instruments from being classified as external debt. The classification of Islamic banking instruments as external debt, or not, can be determined by the following general guidance.

Islamic instruments—deposits include conventional and transferable deposits, such as Amanah and Qard-hasan deposits—as well as various investment participation certificates that are not investments in the permanent capital of a financial institution and do not have the characteristics of tradable securities.

Islamic instruments—debt securities consist of various investment participation certificates that have the characteristics of tradable securities and are not permanent capital of an institutional unit. Included in this category are the most tradable investment certificates recorded as liabilities of a financial corporation.

Islamic instruments—loans cover arrangements in which a financial institution makes prepayments for clients, finances ventures or trade, or supplies working capital to clients. The arrangements may include short-term or other partnerships in which a financial institution is not making permanent, equity-type investments.

Nonlife Insurance

For nonlife insurance the following transactions result in external debt:
- Any prepayments of premiums by nonresidents are classified as external debt of the insurance company, under *other debt liabilities.*
- Reserves that are held against outstanding claims of nonresidents—that is, claims that have arisen because an event has occurred that results in a valid claim—are also external debt of the insurance company. Again, these reserves are included in *other debt liabilities.*

Nonresident Deposits

Because of exchange control or other restrictions, nonresident deposits in domestic banks may not be transferable out of the economy. Such restrictions may be introduced after the deposits have been made or may have been established when the accounts were opened. All such nonresident deposit claims on resident banks should be classified as external debt. Nonetheless, if the amounts are significant and are of analytical interest in their own right, it is recommended that additional information be provided.

On-Lending of Borrowed Funds

An institutional unit within an economy might borrow funds from a nonresident(s) and then on-lend the funds to a second institutional unit within the economy. In such instances, the first institutional unit—that is, the institutional unit that borrowed from the nonresident(s)—should record an external debt liability, with any subsequent on-lending classified as a domestic claim/liability. As set out in Chapter 2, the decisive consideration is whether the creditor has a claim on the debtor, and in this example the nonresident creditor has a claim on the first institutional unit.

If an institutional unit within an economy borrowed from a nonresident(s) and on-lent the funds to a nonresident, the unit should record both external debt and an external claim. The nonresident borrower would also record an external debt liability in that economy's measure of external debt.

Part-Payments for Capital Goods

For capital goods with long delivery periods, such as ships, the purchaser may make part-payments to the builder or exporter while the good is being produced. These part-payments should be recorded as trade credit debt of the exporter. The debt is extinguished when the purchaser takes delivery of the good.

Penalties Arising from Commercial Contracts

Under the terms of a commercial contract, one party (resident) may be required to compensate another party (nonresident) (that is, pay a penalty) in the event of the first party failing to meet its obligations, or some of its obligations, under the contract. Once the penalty is owed and until it is paid to the nonresident, it is external debt, and recorded under other debt liabilities. The debt should be recorded from the time when the resident becomes liable under the contract for the penalty.

Prepayments of Goods and Services

When an importer makes a prepayment to an exporter for goods and services, the exporter has a liability to the importer that remains outstanding until ownership of the goods changes hands or the service is provided. Similarly, when an importer makes a postpayment some time after he acquires goods or services, the importer has a liability to the exporter that remains outstanding until the postpayment is made. These liabilities should be recorded as debt liabilities because future payments are required; in the case of the prepayment, the principal amount outstanding is repaid in goods or in a service provided, whereas in the case of the postpayment, it is likely that a financial payment will be made, although in the instance of barter, goods or services may be provided to extinguish the debt. Unless the prepayment is for more than one year hence, these debt liabilities should be recorded as *short term, trade credit*. Also, unless the agreed date for payment is past, neither the prepayment nor postpayment of goods and services should be recorded as arrears.

Processing of Goods

In *BPM5*, when goods are exported across a border for processing with the intention that the processed goods are returned to the exporting economy, a goods transaction should be recorded in the balance of payments—an import of the processing economy from the original economy. In such circumstances, a corresponding financial liability is established and recorded as external debt under *trade credit*. When the processed good is returned, the financial liability is extinguished. If the amounts are significant, it is recommended that such trade credit be separately identified (as is recommended in the trade account of the balance of payments).

Project Loans: Disbursements

Disbursements of project loans can take the form of
- Advances to the borrowing entity—disbursements are to be recorded when the lender advances funds to the borrower;
- Direct payment by the lender to suppliers of goods and services—disbursements are to be recorded when the lender pays the supplier; and
- On a reimbursement basis after the borrower has already paid the suppliers—disbursements are to be recorded when the lender makes reimbursements to the borrower.

Public Investment Projects

Public investment projects involve the construction and operation by private corporations of assets of a kind that are usually the responsibility of the general government sector, or public corporations. These commonly include, for example, roads, bridges, water supply and sewerage treatment works, hospitals, prison facilities, electricity generation and distribution facilities, and pipelines. In many such instances, such transactions are likely to be classified as resident to resident, particularly if the private corporation creates a separate unit to construct and/or operate the asset (although in such instances that unit may incur external debt liabilities to its nonresident parent, which need to be recorded). But if the private sector corporation is a nonresident, the classification of the transactions as external debt depends on the nature of the arrangement:
- Where an asset is constructed by a corporation and transferred to government on completion, any prepayments by the government are claims on a nonresident enterprise—that is, external debt of the private nonresident corporation. If the government only pays on completion and needs to borrow abroad to finance this purchase, then the government will incur external debt when it borrows.
- Where there are lease arrangements between the government and corporation, these are classified in the normal way as operating or finance leases, and hence external debt or not, depending on whether the government or corporation gains most of the risks and benefits of ownership as a result of the contracts entered into. For instance, if the private corporation continues to own the asset but will transfer ownership to the government at a later date, and in the meantime the government makes payments both to cover the costs of operating the asset and to meet the financing costs, then a finance lease, and hence external debt, arises for the government and should be recorded as such.

As with all finance leases, at the time of effective change of ownership, the market value of the good is recorded and represents the external debt of the government. The payments to be made need to be separated into operating and financing costs. If a market value is available, the total amount paid in financing costs over the life of the lease in relation to that price will determine the implicit rate of interest on the loan. Otherwise, the financing costs discounted by a representative interest rate of the government—the present value of the finance payments—could represent the market value of the asset in the absence of other information, and generate data on the future interest and principal payments—Appendix to Chapter 2, examples 1 and 2, provides calculations that illustrate the principles involved.

Reinsurance

Positions arising from reinsurance are treated in the same way as those arising from insurance.

For reinsurance relating to life insurance, any technical reserves held by insurance companies that are assets of nonresident policyholders are external debt of the insurance company. As with claims of households in life insurance companies, any such external debt should be included under *other debt liabilities* in the gross external debt position.

For nonlife insurance, prepayment of premiums by nonresidents, and reserves held against claims of nonresidents that have arisen, are also external debt. In both instances, any such external debt is included under *other debt liabilities* (see also *Nonlife Insurance*, above).

Repurchase Agreements: Delay in Returning the Security

If the security taker fails to return the security to the security provider, then the recording treatment depends on whether the failure is simply a delay or whether there is a default. If the failure is due to a delay (for example, the result of another party in the chain of repo securities being unable to access the specific security at that particular date), it has no impact on the gross external debt position, although in line with common market practice the security provider may retain the funds without paying any interest. If there is a default, usually under the terms of the reverse agreement the security provider's loan liability to the security taker is extinguished—the security taker no longer has a claim on the security provider. If the security provider defaults on returning the cash, then the security provider's security holdings fall, and those of the security taker increase, and the loan is extinguished. In either event, because the security provided is likely to be of greater value than the cash provided, residual claims may still continue to exist.

The Value of Debt After Consolidation Is Greater Than the Value of the Consolidated Debts Combined

If the terms of a loan are changed, a new contract is created. Thus, if two or more old debts are consolidated into one debt, the new debt replaces the two or more old debts and is classified by type of instrument (loan, security, etc.). If the total value of the new debt is greater than the old debts combined—for example, because of extra charges arising from rescheduling—the gross external debt position increases.

Appendix II. Reverse Security Transactions

1. A reverse securities transaction is defined in the *Guide* to include all arrangements whereby one party legally acquires securities and agrees, under a legal agreement at inception, to return the same or equivalent securities on or by an agreed date to the same party from whom the securities were acquired initially. These arrangements are known as repurchase agreements (repos), securities lending, and sell-/buybacks.[1] Where cash is involved, the economic nature of the agreement is similar to that of a collateralized loan in that the purchaser of the security is providing funds collateralized by the securities to the seller for the period of the agreement and is receiving a return from these funds through the agreed fixed price at which the securities are resold when the agreement is reversed.

2. As outlined in Chapter 3, securities that are provided under a reverse securities transaction are reported as remaining on the balance sheet of the security provider. If the security taker sells outright these securities so acquired, the security taker reports a negative (or "short") position in the security.

3. This appendix provides some background information on reverse security transactions and some examples of how these positions should be recorded in the gross external debt position.

What Are These Instruments?

Repurchase Agreements (Repos)

4. Under a repo, securities are provided for cash with a commitment by the seller (security provider) to repurchase the same or similar securities for cash at a fixed price on a specified future date. The security taker views the transaction as a *reverse repo*. The security taker earns interest on the cash advanced through the difference between the selling and buying rates for the securities; interest is related to the current interbank rate and not that of the security being "repoed."[2] Full, unfettered ownership passes to the security taker, who can on-sell the security, but the market risk—the benefits (and risks) of ownership (such as the right to holding gains—and losses)—remains with the security provider, who also receives the property/investment income attached to the security, albeit from the security taker rather than the security issuer. Originally, it was intended that the security taker's right to on-sell would be invoked only in the event of a default by the security provider, but as the market has developed, the right to on-sell at the security taker's option has become commonplace.

5. Repos are actively used in international financial markets. They often have a very short overnight maturity, but are also for longer maturities (sometimes up to several weeks), or have an "open" maturity (that is, the parties agree daily to renew or terminate the agreement). Several different types of institutions are involved. Most commonly, financial institutions transact with other financial institutions, both domestic and nonresident, and central banks with domestic financial institutions and other central banks. However, nonfinancial enterprises and governments may also use repos.

6. Repos are undertaken for a variety of reasons:
* To finance security purchases—that is, the security provider acquires a security outright and then sells it under a repo to help finance the position;

---

[1]Sell-/buybacks are the same as repos in economic effect, but are less sophisticated operationally. If the seller acquires an option rather than an obligation to buy back the security, the arrangement is sometimes called a *spurious repurchase agreement*. Such a transaction is not considered to be a reverse security transaction in the *Guide*.

[2]In the event that a coupon payment is made during the life of the repo, this is taken into account when determining the funds to be repaid. However, market participants endeavor to avoid such a situation if possible.

- To increase liquidity by raising funds while retaining exposure to market price movements in the security—that is, the security provider may want a longer-term position in the security but may also require cash in the short term;
- To acquire securities in order to cover a negative (or "short") position—that is, the security taker takes a negative position in the security, thus benefiting from market price declines;
- To take leverage positions in securities through a program of buying securities, repoing them out, purchasing more securities with the cash acquired and so on, with only the requirement for margins limiting this activity—that is, the security provider creates a large positive exposure to movements in the price of the securities without having to fully fund this exposure with own funds;
- Central banks use repos as an operational tool to ease or drain liquidity in the domestic financial markets—in many countries, the repo rate (the rate paid by the borrower in a repo transaction) is the benchmark rate for central bank market lending.

7. Chains of repos and reverse repos are common practice in financial markets as highly creditworthy market players raise funds at lower rates than they are able to on-lend. In this manner, the repo market is part of broader financial intermediation activity.[3] The development of repo markets can increase the liquidity of a money market while, at the same time, deepening the market for the underlying securities used (frequently government securities, but not necessarily), leading to finer borrowing rates both for money market participants and governments.

8. Usually, the security provider in a repo is the initiator of the transaction, which tends to place the security taker in a slightly stronger negotiating position. These are called "cash-driven" repos. In these circumstances, the security provider is not required to provide a specific security—a list of acceptable securities is generally available. Frequently, substitution of the security is permitted during the life of the repo—that is, the security provider may wish to access the security repoed and so usually is permitted to do so by substituting it for another of equal quality (generally, one on the list of acceptable securities). The right to substitute securities will usually affect the rate of interest charged on the repo.

9. In certain circumstances, one party may have need for a specific type of security. These transactions are known as "securities-driven" repos. They result when a particular security goes "special"—that is, is in very high demand and there is insufficient supply to meet commitments. In these circumstances, cash is provided as collateral (noncash collateral is discussed under *Securities Lending,* below) and the security provider is in a stronger bargaining position. In essence, when a security-driven transaction takes place, the security provider is prepared to accept cash in return for the security "lent," provided that the provider can be compensated for the risk of lending by obtaining a sufficient spread between the interest to be paid on the cash received and what can be earned in the money market. In extreme cases, when the security may be unavailable from any other source, the interest rate on the cash received may fall to zero.

10. Whether a transaction is cash-driven or securities-driven will affect which party pays *margin.* Margin payments provide one party with collateral of greater market value than the instrument being provided—the term "haircut" is sometimes used to describe this difference. Margin payments may be made at the outset—known as *initial margins*—and during the life of a repo—known as *variation margin.*[4] As the market value of the collateral falls, so variation margin is paid, restoring the margin to its original market value. If the transaction is cash-driven, the security provider will provide the margin; if the transaction is securities-driven, the security taker will provide the margin. Margin may be cash or securities.

11. Market and credit risk affect the amount of margin provided. The market risk is that of the underlying security—the more variable the market price of the security, the greater the margin; the credit risk is that of the two counterparties to the repo to each other—the greater the perceived credit risk of the

---

[3]Repo market players may have matched or unmatched books: in a matched book, maturities of all repos out are the same as those for repos in; in an unmatched book, the maturities differ, in which case the market player is speculating on movements in the yield curve.

[4]Sale-/buybacks do not have margin payments.

margin provider, the higher the margin. In both instances, the higher margin protects the margin taker against the higher probability of adverse developments. Because each party at the inception of a repo is equally exposed to risk, in many developed financial markets, initial margin may not be required if the credit standing is approximately equal (monetary authorities usually ask for initial margin and rarely, if ever, pay initial margin), but variation margin is usually provided when the market price of the security falls. On the other hand, when the value of the security rises, the security taker may or may not return part of the security's value as a "reverse variation margin," depending on the market's practices in any given country. In less developed capital markets, and depending on the depth and price volatility of the market of the security underlying the repo, initial margins of substantially more (possibly up to 25 percent) than the value of the cash provided may be required.

12. The legal and market arrangements for repos, including the payments of margin (whether initial or variation), the ability to substitute securities, and the retention of market risk by the security provider, support the view that repos are classified as loans, with the security remaining on the balance sheet of the security provider. This is certainly the way repos are viewed by market participants. On the other hand, given the change of ownership of the security, some argue that a security transaction should be recorded—the security provider no longer has a legal claim on the security issuer. In Chapter 4 a memorandum table to the gross external debt position is provided that can be used to present data on resident-issued debt securities that residents (1) provided to and (2) acquired from nonresidents under outstanding reverse transactions, including repo agreements. This table helps in tracking the change of ownership of these debt securities between residents and nonresidents and, more generally, the positions acquired under reverse transactions.

Securities Lending

13. Under a *securities lending agreement*, securities are provided under a legal agreement that requires the security taker to return the same or similar securities on or by an agreed date to the same party from whom the securities were acquired initially. No cash is provided by the security taker to the security provider in return for the acquisition of the securities, although a fee may be paid by the security taker and collateral provided (as in the form of other securities). If cash collateral is provided, the transaction has the same economic impact as a repo.

14. As with repos, full, unfettered ownership passes to the security taker, who can on-sell the security, but the market risk—the benefits (and risks) of ownership (such as the right to holding gains—and losses)—remains with the original owner of the security, who also receives the property/investment income attached to the security, albeit from the security taker rather than the security issuer. Because securities lending is a securities-driven activity, so the security taker initiates the transaction, which means that the bargaining advantage lies with the "lender" of the security. The level of the fee charged depends on the availability of the security. The payment may be made at inception or at the closeout of the contract. In most cases, the original security owner considers the arrangements to be temporary and does not remove the securities or include the collateral on its balance sheet, since the owner retains the rights to any dividends or interest while the securities are on loan, albeit from the security taker rather than the security issuer.[5]

15. Security loans are actively used in financial markets. In many cases, the transfer of securities between holders is conducted by security depositories. The security owner will provide the depository with the general right to on-lend the securities subject to certain legal safeguards. As a consequence, frequently the owner of the security will be unaware that the security it owns has been sold under a securities loan agreement.

16. The primary purposes of securities lending are:
- For the security taker, the security is acquired in order to meet a commitment to sell the security— that is, to cover a negative (or "short") position.

---

[5]In instances where equities are loaned, the period of the loan usually avoids coinciding with a shareholders' meeting, or any other instance where voting rights are required to be exercised (such as for a takeover bid). However, it is not always possible to know when these situations will arise, and the arrangements usually permit the return of the equities to the original owner in such circumstances.

The security taker can take leverage positions by selling securities it does not own and then covering the position with securities acquired under securities loans.

• For the security provider, the fee paid by the security taker generates income—the owner has a long-term position in the security, but through a securities loan earns additional income.

• The depository can earn extra fee income, which might be partially passed on to the security owner through lower custodial fees. The depository is more likely to be able to manage the collateral provided by the security taker than the security owner, who, in return for allowing securities to be lent, may pay lower custodial fees and not have the responsibility of managing the collateral provided.

17. Like repos, chains of securities lending can be established whereby brokers successively on-lend securities to brokers, dealers, or other parties. The lending chains are reversed when the securities are returned. Securities lending involves securities that may be issued by residents or nonresidents, by governments or by corporations, and can be either equities or debt instruments. Securities lending increases liquidity in the securities market as well as the timeliness of some trade settlements—especially for securities that trade infrequently or in small volume.

18. The securities taker will usually provide collateral in the form of other securities of equal or greater value to the securities "lent," providing initial margin, although in some instances no collateral is provided. If cash collateral is provided, the transaction has the same economic impact as a repo (discussed above). If the market value of securities placed as collateral falls relative to the value of the securities "loaned," the securities taker is usually required to place variation margin, to restore the relative position. If the value of the securities placed as collateral increases, the securities provider may or may not be required to return part of the collateral, depending on country practice.

19. Because of the requirement for the securities to be returned, the payments of margin, the retention by the original security owner of the market risks of the securities, and the right to receive income payments on the security, securities lent under security loans remain on the balance sheet of the original owner. If a security taker sells the security acquired under a security loan, a negative (or "short") position is recorded in the security, reflecting the obligation to return the security to the security provider. As noted above, Chapter 4 provides a memorandum table to the gross external debt position that can be used to present data on resident-issued debt securities that residents (1) provided to and (2) acquired from nonresidents under outstanding reverse transactions, including security lending agreements.

Recording Examples

20. To help compilers, some examples are set out in Table A2.1 of how different types of reverse security transactions should be recorded in the gross external debt position and in the memorandum table, when debt securities are involved.[6] These examples show the change in the position when resident-issued debt securities are acquired by a nonresident from a resident, or vice versa, under a reverse security transaction. In all these examples, it is assumed that debt securities involved in the transactions are valued at 100, and any cash provided is valued at 95. Each example involves a transaction in a debt security issued by a resident of A. Each example specifies an initial transaction, followed by different subsequent transactions. For each subsequent transaction, the recorded entries include both the initial transaction and the subsequent transaction. So, the entries for example 1(b) include both the sale of the debt security under a repo by a resident of A to a nonresident (1(a)), and the subsequent sale under a repo by the nonresident to another resident of A (1(b)); the entries for example 1(c) include both the sale of the debt security under a repo by a resident of A to a nonresident (1(a)), and the subsequent sale under a repo by the nonresident to another nonresident (1(c)).

---

[6]When equity securities are involved in reverse security transactions, external debt is affected only if the equity securities are used as collateral to raise cash from a nonresident. In this instance, a loan is recorded.

Table A2.1. External Debt: Recording of Reverse Security Transactions

Transaction	Change in the Gross External Debt Position		Memorandum Items: Debt Securities Acquired Under Reverse Security Transactions: Change in the Position	
	Debt securities (+ = increase)	Loans (+ = increase)	Acquired by nonresidents from residents (+ = increase)	Acquired by residents from nonresidents (− = increase)
Example 1: Repurchase agreement (repo)				
(a) Resident of A sells the security under a repo to a nonresident	—	+95	+100	—
(b) Following 1(a), the nonresident sells the security under a repo to another resident of A	—	+95	+100	−100
(c) Following 1(a), the nonresident sells the security under a repo to another nonresident	—	+95	+100	—
(d) Following 1(a), the nonresident sells the security outright to a resident of A	−100	+95	+100	—
(e) Following 1(a), the nonresident sells the security outright to another nonresident	—	+95	+100	—
Example 2: Repurchase agreement (repo)				
(a) Resident of A buys the security under a repo from a nonresident	—	—	—	−100
(b) Following 2(a), the resident sells the security under a repo to another resident of A	—	—	—	−100
(c) Following 2(a), the resident sells the security under a repo to a nonresident	—	+95	+100	−100
(d) Following 2(a), the resident sells the security outright to another resident	—	—	—	−100
(e) Following 2(a), the resident sells the security outright to a nonresident	+100	—	—	−100
Example 3: Security loan				
(a) Resident of A "sells" the security under a security loan to a nonresident	—	—	+100	—
(b) Following 3(a), the nonresident "sells" the security under a security loan to another resident of A	—	—	+100	−100
(c) Following 3(a), the nonresident "sells" the security under a security loan to another nonresident	—	—	+100	—
(d) Following 3(a), the nonresident sells the security outright to a resident of A	−100	—	+100	—
(e) Following 3(a), the nonresident sells the security outright to another nonresident	—	—	+100	—
Example 4: Security loan				
(a) Resident of A "buys" the security under a securities loan from a nonresident	—	—	—	−100
(b) Following 4(a), the resident "sells" the security under a security loan to another resident of A	—	—	—	−100
(c) Following 4(a), the resident "sells" the security under a security loan to a nonresident	—	—	+100	−100
(d) Following 4(a), the resident sells the security outright to another resident of A	—	—	—	−100
(e) Following 4(a), the resident sells the security outright to another nonresident	+100	—	—	−100

Appendix III. Glossary of External Debt Terms

A

Accrual of Interest Costs

Continuous recording of interest costs, so matching the cost of capital with the provision of capital.

Affiliated Enterprises

Enterprises related through direct investment ownership structures, such as branches, subsidiaries, associates, and *joint ventures*. Affiliated enterprises include those in a direct ownership relationship but also those that are related through a third enterprise and/or a chain of direct investment relationships. For a fuller exposition of direct investment relationships, see the *OECD Benchmark Definition of Foreign Direct Investment* (OECD, 1996, pp. 9–12).

Agreed Minute

Paris Club document detailing the terms for a *debt rescheduling* between *creditors* and the debtor. It specifies the coverage of *debt-service* payments (types of debt treated), the cutoff date, the *consolidation period*, the proportion of payments to be rescheduled, the provisions regarding the down payment (if any), and the repayment schedules for rescheduled and deferred debt. Creditor governments commit to incorporate these terms in the bilateral agreements negotiated with the debtor government that implements the Agreed Minute. Paris Club *creditors* will agree to reschedule only with countries that have an IMF upper credit tranche arrangement (*Stand-By Arrangement* or *Extended Fund Facility* (EFF)), a *Poverty Reduction and Growth Facility* (PRGF) arrangement, or a *Rights Accumulation Program*.

Amortization Schedule

The schedule for the repayment of *principal* and payment of *interest* on an ongoing basis. For loans,

the amortization schedule is normally included in an annex to the contract or can be estimated from the contract.

Arbitrage

Buying (or borrowing) in one market and selling (or lending) in the same or another market to profit from market inefficiencies or price differences.

Arrangement on Guidelines for Officially Supported Export Credits (OECD Consensus)

The Arrangement (sometimes known as the Consensus) is a gentleman's agreement governing the provision of officially supported *export credits* with a credit period of two years or more. It is negotiated by an international body called the Participants to the Arrangement on Guidelines for Officially Supported Export Credits, which meets in Paris under the auspices, and with the administrative support, of the Secretariat of the OECD. The Participants are Australia, Canada, the European Union (including all the Member States), Japan, Korea, New Zealand, Norway, Switzerland, and the United States. Additionally, there are three Observers: the Czech Republic, Hungary, and Poland.

B

Balance of Payments

The balance of payments is a statistical statement that systematically summarizes, for a specific period of time, the economic transactions of an economy with the rest of the world. Transactions, for the most part between residents and nonresidents, consist of those involving goods, services, and income; those involving financial claims and liabilities to the rest of the world; and those (such as gifts) classified as transfers.

Bank for International Settlements (BIS)

Established in 1930 by intergovernmental convention, the Bank for International Settlements promotes cooperation among central banks. In this capacity it carries out four main functions: it holds and manages deposits from a large number of central banks throughout the world; it serves as a forum for international monetary cooperation; it assists as agent or trustee in the execution of various international financial agreements; and it carries out research and issues publications on monetary and economic subjects.

Berne Union

The International Union of Credit and Investment Insurers. This Union is an informal association of export credit insurance agencies, founded in 1934. The two main objectives of the Berne Union are the promotion of the international acceptance of sound principles in export credit insurance and investment insurance, and the exchange of information relating thereto. The almost 50 members meet twice a year to exchange information and seek to establish common standards, for instance on the appropriate down payment and repayment periods for various kinds of exports. Informal credit ratings of the borrowing countries are maintained. They also consult with each other on a continuing basis, and cooperate closely. All members participate as insurers and not as representatives of their governments.

Bilateral Deadline

In the context of Paris Club reschedulings, the date by which all bilateral agreements must be concluded. It is set in the *Agreed Minute* and is typically about six months later, but can be extended upon request.

Bilateral Debt

Loans extended by a bilateral creditor.

Bilateral Rescheduling Agreements

Rescheduling agreements reached bilaterally between the debtor and *creditor* countries. These are legally the equivalent of new loan agreements. After a Paris Club rescheduling, such agreements are required to put into effect the *debt restructuring* set forth in the multinational *Agreed Minute*.

Bullet Repayment

The repayment of *principal* in a single payment at the maturity of the debt.

Buyer's Credit

A financial arrangement in which a bank or financial institution, or an *export credit agency* in the exporting country, extends a loan directly to a foreign buyer or to a bank in the importing country to pay for the purchase of goods and services from the exporting country. Also known as financial credit. This term does not refer to credit extended directly from the buyer to the seller (for example, through advance payment for goods and services).

C

Capital Account

In the *balance of payments*, the capital account covers *capital transfers* and the acquisition or disposal of nonproduced nonfinancial items (for example, patents).

Capital Transfers

Capital transfers consists of the transfer—without a quid pro quo—of ownership of a fixed asset or the forgiveness, by mutual agreement between *creditor* and debtor, of the debtor's financial liability when no counterpart is received in return by the creditor.

Capitalized Interest

Capitalized interest is the conversion of accrued *interest* costs or future interest payments, by a contractual arrangement with the creditor, into a new *debt instrument* or the *principal* amount. The most common form of capitalization is the reinvestment of interest costs into the principal amount, either because of an explicit agreement regarding the specific debt instrument or as part of a *rescheduling agreement*. Frequently as part of a rescheduling agreement, some percentage of interest due during the *consolidation period* (see below) is converted, through an agreement made with the *creditor*, into principal.

Claim Payments

Payments made to exporters or banks, after the *claims-waiting period*, by an *export credit agency* on insured or guaranteed loans when the original borrower or borrowing-country guarantor fails to pay. These are recorded by the agencies as unrecovered claims until they are recovered from the debtor or the debtor's guarantor.

Claims-Waiting Period

The period that exporters or banks must wait after the due-date of payment before the *export credit agency* will pay on the corresponding claim.

Cofinancing

The joint or parallel financing of programs or projects through loans or grants to developing countries provided by commercial banks, *export credit agencies*, other official institutions in association with other agencies or banks, or the World Bank and other multilateral financial institutions.

Commercial Credit

In the context of the Paris Club, loans originally extended on terms that do not qualify as *official development assistance* (ODA) credits. These are typically export credits on market terms but also include other non-ODA loans by governments.

Commercial Interest Reference Rates (CIRRs)

A set of currency-specific interest rates for major OECD countries. CIRRs have been established for 13 currencies, the majority of which are based on either the five-year government bond yields or on three-, five- and seven-year bond yields, according to the length of the repayment period. CIRRs are adjusted monthly and are intended to reflect commercial rates.

Commercial Risk

In the context of *export credits*, the risk of nonpayment by a nonsovereign or private sector buyer or borrower in his or her domestic currency arising from default, insolvency, and/or a failure to take up goods that have been shipped according to the supply contract (contrasted with *transfer risk* arising from an inability to convert domestic currency into the currency in which the *debt service* is payable, or with broader political risk).

Commitment

Generally, a firm obligation to lend, guarantee, or insure resources of a specific amount under specific financial terms and conditions. However, in the OECD's *Arrangement on Guidelines for Officially Supported Export Credits* (see above), commitment simply refers to any statement, in whatever form, whereby the willingness or intention to provide official support is communicated to the recipient country, the buyer, the borrower, the exporter, or the financial institution.

Commitment Charge (or Fee)

This is the charge made for holding available the *undisbursed* balance of a loan commitment. Typically, it is a fixed-rate charge (for example, 1.5 percent a year) calculated on the basis of the undisbursed balance.

Commitment, Date of

The date on which the commitment is made.

Comparable Treatment

An understanding in a *debt-restructuring* agreement with the Paris Club creditors that the debtor will secure at least equivalent *debt relief* from other creditors.

Complete Market

A financial market place is said to be complete when a market exists with an equilibrium price for every asset in every possible state of the world.

Completion Point

In the context of the *HIPC Initiative* (see below), when the IMF and World Bank Executive Boards decide that a country has met the conditions for assistance under the Initiative. The timing of the completion point depends on the satisfactory implementation of key structural policy reforms agreed at the *decision point*, the maintenance of macroeconomic stability, and the adoption and implementation of a poverty reduction strategy developed through a broad-based participatory process. (See also *Decision Point*.)

Concessional Loans

These are loans that are extended on terms substantially more generous than market loans. The concessionality is achieved either through interest rates below those available on the market or by *grace periods*, or a combination of these. Concessional loans typically have long grace periods.

Concessional Restructuring

Debt restructuring with a reduction in *present value* of the *debt service*. In the context of the Paris Club, concessional restructuring terms have been granted to *low-income countries* since October 1988 with a reduction in the *present value* of *eligible debt* of up to one-third (Toronto terms); since December 1991, with a present value reduction of up to one-half (London terms or "enhanced concessions" or "enhanced Toronto" terms); and, since January 1995, with a present value reduction of up to two-thirds (Naples terms). In the context of the *HIPC Initiative, creditors* agreed in November 1996 to increase the present value reduction to up to 80 percent (Lyon terms) and then in June 1999 to 90 percent (Cologne terms). Such restructuring can be in the form of *flow restructuring* or *stock-of-debt operations*. While the terms (*grace period and maturity*) are standard, creditors can choose from a menu of options to implement the *debt relief.*

Concessionality Level

A *net present value* calculation, measured at the time the loan is extended, that compares the outstanding nominal value of a debt and the future *debt-service* payments discounted at an *interest* rate applicable to the currency of the transaction, expressed as a percentage of the nominal value of the debt. The concessionality level of *bilateral debt* (or tied aid) is calculated in a similar manner, but instead of using the nominal value of the debt, the face value of the loan is used—that is, including both the *disbursed* and *undisbursed* amounts, and the difference is called the *grant element.* (See also *Grant Element* and *Net Present Value.*)

Consolidated Amount or Consolidated Debt

The *debt-service payments* and arrears, or debt stock, restructured under a Paris Club *rescheduling agreement.*

Consolidated Reporting

Reporting covering the claims and liabilities of all offices worldwide of the same entity, but excluding positions between offices of the same entity. Offices include head offices, branch offices, and subsidiaries. A consolidated balance sheet refers to a balance sheet grouping of assets and liabilities of a parent company and all its offices, after elimination of all unrealized profits on intragroup trading and of all intragroup balances.

Consolidation Period

In Paris Club restructuring agreements, the period in which *debt-service* payments to be restructured (the "current maturities consolidated") have fallen or will fall due. The beginning of the consolidation period may precede, coincide with, or come after the date of the *Agreed Minute*. The standard consolidation period is one year, but sometimes debt payments over a two- or three-year period have been consolidated, corresponding with a multiyear arrangement with the IMF.

Contingent Asset/Liability (Contingencies)

The principal characteristic of a contingency is that one or more conditions must be fulfilled before a financial transaction takes place.

Cover

Provision of *export credit* guarantee or insurance against risks of payment delays or nonpayments relating to export transactions. Cover is usually, though not always, provided for both *commercial risk* and *political risk*. In most cases, cover is not provided for the full value of future *debt-service* payments; the percentage of cover is typically between 90 percent and 95 percent. (See also *Quantitative Limits.*)

Coverage of Rescheduling Agreements

The *debt service* or arrears rescheduled. Comprehensive coverage implies the inclusion of most or all *eligible debt service* and arrears.

Credit

An amount for which there is a specific obligation of repayment. Credits include loans, trade credits, bonds, bills, etc., and other agreements that give rise to specific obligations to repay over a period of time usually, but not always, with *interest*. Credit is extended to finance consumption and investment expenditures, and financial transactions.

Credit Guarantee

Commitment by an *export credit agency* to reimburse a lender if the borrower fails to repay a loan. The lender pays a guarantee fee.

Credit Insurance

The main business of most *export credit agencies* is insurance of finance provided by exporters or banks (although some major agencies lend on their own account). Insurance policies provide for the export credit agency to reimburse the lender for losses up to a certain percentage of the *credit* covered and under certain conditions. Lenders or exporters pay a premium to the export credit agency. Insurance policies typically protect the lender against political or *transfer risks* in the borrowing country that prevent the remittance of *debt-service* payments.

Creditor

An entity with a *financial claim* on another entity.

Creditor Country

The country in which the creditor resides. In Paris Club terminology, it is an official bilateral creditor.

Creditor Reporting System

A statistical reporting system, maintained by the OECD, to monitor the debt of developing countries. Major creditor countries, primarily the 22 member countries of the Development Assistance Committee (DAC), together with the European Commission, supply information. The data are published in the OECD's annual *External Debt Statistics* publication.

Cross-Border Positions

Asset and liability positions of residents of an economy vis-à-vis residents of all other economies.

Currency of Reporting

The unit of account in which amounts are reported either to the compiling agency and/or to an interna-

tional agency compiling debt statistics. See Chapter 2 for details on unit of account.

Currency of Transaction

The medium of exchange in which an individual transaction occurs. It may be currency, goods, or services. The medium of exchange of one transaction (for example, disbursement) does not necessarily determine the medium of exchange of another (for example, repayment).

Current Account

The current account of the *balance of payments* covers all transactions (other than those in financial items) that involve economic values and occur between residents and nonresident entities. Also covered are offsets to current economic values provided or acquired without a quid pro quo. Included are goods, services, income, and *current transfers*. The balance on goods, services, income, and current transfers is commonly referred to as the "current balance" or "current account" balance.

Current Maturities

In the context of restructuring agreements, *principal* and *interest* payments falling due in the *consolidation period*.

Current Transfers

Current transfers are all transfers—that is, the transfer of a real resource or a financial item without a quid pro quo—that are not transfers of capital. Current transfers directly affect the level of disposable income and should influence the consumption of goods and services.

Cutoff Date

The date (established at the time of a country's first Paris Club *debt reorganization/restructuring*) before which loans must have been contracted in order for their *debt service* to be eligible for restructuring. New loans extended after the cutoff date are protected from future restructuring (*subordination strategy*). In exceptional cases, arrears on post-cutoff-date debt can be deferred over short periods of time in restructuring agreements.

D

De Minimis Creditors (or Clause)

Minor creditors that are exempted from *debt restructuring* to simplify implementation of the Paris Club restructuring agreements. Their claims are payable in full as they fall due. An exposure limit defining a minor creditor is specified in each *Agreed Minute*.

Debt- and Debt-Service-Reduction (DDSR) Operations

Debt-restructuring agreements are typically undertaken for bank loan debt obligations and involve the buyback and exchange of *eligible debt* either for financial instruments that are valued at a substantial discount (simple cash buyback) or for new bonds featuring a *present value* reduction. In some instances, the principal portion of new financial instruments is fully collateralized with zero-coupon bonds issued by the treasury of an industrial country, while interest obligations are also partially secured. DDSR operations are characterized by a "menu approach," allowing individual creditors to select from among several DDSR options. Under the Brady plan of March 1989, some of these arrangements have been supported by loans from official creditors.

Debt Assumption

The assumption of a debt liability of one entity by another entity, usually by mutual agreement.

Debt Buyback

The repurchase by a debtor of its own debt, usually at a substantial discount. The debtor's obligations are reduced while the *creditor* receives a once-and-for-all payment. Although in apparent contravention of standard commercial bank loan agreements, some debtors have bought back their own debt on the secondary market.

Debt Conversion

The exchange of debt for a nondebt liability, such as equity, or for counterpart funds, such as can be used to finance a particular project or policy.

Debt Default

Failure to meet a debt obligation payment, either *principal* or *interest*. A payment that is overdue or in arrears is technically "in default," since by virtue of nonpayment the borrower has failed to abide by the terms and conditions of the debt obligation. In practice, the point at which a debt obligation is considered "in default" will vary.

Debt-for-Charity Swap

The purchase by a nonprofit organization such as a nongovernmental organization (NGO) of the *external debt* of a country at a discount in the secondary market, which the NGO then exchanges for local currency to be used for philanthropic purposes.

Debt-for-Commodity Swap

The repayment in kind by a debtor country of all or part of its *external debt*. Typically, the lender takes a specific, earmarked percentage of the receipts from the exports of a particular commodity or group of commodities to service the debt.

Debt-for-Development Swap

Financing part of a development project through the exchange of a foreign-currency-denominated debt for local currency, typically at a substantial discount. The process normally involves a foreign nongovernmental organization (NGO) that purchases the debt from the original creditor at a substantial discount using its own foreign currency resources, and then resells it to the debtor country government for the local currency equivalent (resulting in a further discount). The NGO in turn spends the money on a development project, previously agreed upon with the debtor country government.

Debt-for-Equity Swap

A transaction in which debt of an economy is exchanged, usually at a discount, for equity in an enterprise in the same economy. Although variable in form, such arrangements usually result in the extinction of a fixed-rate liability (for example, a debt security or loan) denominated in foreign currency and the creation of an equity liability (denominated in domestic currency) to a nonresident. There may be clauses in the agreement to prevent the repatriation of capital before some specified future date.

Debt-for-Nature Swap

Similar to a debt-for-development swap, except that the funds are used for projects that improve the environment.

Debt Forgiveness

The voluntary cancellation of all or part of a debt within a contractual arrangement between a *creditor* in one economy and a debtor in another economy.

Debt Instrument(s)

Existing debt instruments typically arise out of contractual relationships under which an institutional unit (the debtor) has an unconditional liability to another institutional unit (the creditor) to repay principal with or without interest, or to pay interest without principal. These instruments include debt securities, loans, trade credit, and currency and deposits. Debt instruments may also be created by the force of law—in particular, obligations to pay taxes or to make other compulsory payments—or through rights and obligations that results in a debtor accepting an obligation to make future payment(s) to a *creditor*.

Debt-Reduction Option

Option under concessional Paris Club *debt restructurings* where *creditors* effect the required debt reduction in *present value* terms through a reduction of the *principal* of the *consolidated amount*. A commercial *interest* rate and standard repayment terms apply to the remaining amounts. (See *Concessional Restructuring*.)

Debt Refinancing

Debt refinancing refers to the conversion of the original debt including arrears, into a new *debt instrument*. In other words, overdue payments or future *debt-service* obligations are "paid off" using a new debt obligation. In the *Guide*, as in *BPM5*, a change in the terms of a debt instrument is to be reported as the creation of a new debt instrument, with the original debt extinguished.

Debt Relief

Any form of *debt reorganization* that relieves the overall burden of debt. Debt relief results where there is a reduction in the *present value* of these *debt-service* obligations and/or a deferral of the payments due, thus providing smaller near-term debt-service obligations. This can be measured, in most cases, by an increase in the duration of these obligations; that is, payments become weighted more

toward the latter part of the *debt instrument*'s life. However, if debt reorganization results in changes in present value and duration that are countervailing in their impact on the debt burden, then there is no debt relief, unless the net impact is significant—such as could occur if there was a deep reduction in present value (together with small decrease in duration) or a sharp increase in duration (together with a small increase in present value).

Debt Reorganization/Restructuring

Debt reorganization arises from bilateral arrangements involving both the *creditor* and the debtor that alter the terms established for the servicing of a debt. This includes debt rescheduling, refinancing, forgiveness, conversion, and prepayments.

Debt Rescheduling

Debt rescheduling refers to the formal deferment of *debt-service* payments and the application of new and extended maturities to the deferred amount. Rescheduling debt is one means of providing a debtor with *debt relief* through a delay and, in the case of concessional rescheduling, a reduction in debt-service obligations.

Debt Service

Refers to payments in respect of both *principal* and *interest*. Actual debt service is the set of payments actually made to satisfy a debt obligation, including principal, interest, and any late payment fees. Scheduled debt service is the set of payments, including principal and interest, that is required to be made through the life of the debt.

Debt-Service (-to-Exports) Ratio

The ratio of debt service (*interest* and *principal* payments due) during a year, expressed as a percentage of exports (typically of goods and services) for that year. Forward-looking debt-service ratios require some forecast of export earnings. This ratio is considered to be a key indicator of a country's debt burden.

Debt-Service-Reduction Option

Option under concessional Paris Club *debt reschedulings* where creditors effect the required debt reduction in *present value* terms through a reduction in the applicable interest rate. (See *Concessional Restructuring*.)

Debt-Sustainability Analysis

A study of a country's medium- to long-term debt situation. A country's eligibility for support under the *HIPC Initiative* is determined on the basis of such an analysis, jointly undertaken by the staffs of the IMF, the World Bank, and the country concerned.

Debt Swaps

Debt swaps are exchanges of debt, such as loans or securities, for a new debt contract (that is, debt-to-debt swaps), or exchanges of *debt-for-equity*, debt-for-exports, or debt-for-domestic currency, such as to be used for projects in the debtor country (also known as *debt conversion*).

Debt Workout

The process of working out a satisfactory method whereby the debtor country can repay external debt, including restructuring, adjustment, and the provision of new money.

Debtor Country

The country in which the debtor resides.

Debtor Reporting System (DRS)

A statistical reporting system maintained by the World Bank to monitor the debt of developing countries. Information is supplied through reports from debtor countries. The data supplied are the basis for the annual World Bank report, *Global Development Finance* (formerly *World Debt Tables*).

Decision Point

In the context of the *HIPC Initiative*, the point at which a country's eligibility for assistance is determined by the IMF and World Bank Executive Boards on the basis of a *debt-sustainability analysis* and three years of sound performance under IMF- and World Bank-supported adjustment programs. The international community enters into a commitment at the decision point to deliver assistance at the completion point, provided that the debtor adheres to its policy commitments. The debt-sustainability analysis is

essentially a medium-term *balance of payments* projection that assesses the debt burden of the country and its capacity to service those obligations. If external debt ratios for that country fall within or above applicable targets, it will be considered for special assistance: the target is 150 percent for the ratio of the *present value* of debt to exports, with exceptions to this target in the special case of very open economies with a high debt burden in relation to fiscal revenues. (See also *Completion Point*.)

At the decision point, the Executive Boards of the IMF and World Bank will formally decide on a country's eligibility, and the international community will commit to provide sufficient assistance by the completion point for the country to achieve debt sustainability calculated at the decision point. The delivery of assistance committed by the IMF and Bank will depend on satisfactory assurances of action by other creditors.

Deferred Payments

In the context of Paris Club *debt reschedulings*, obligations that are not consolidated but postponed nonconcessionally, usually for a short time, as specified in the *Agreed Minute*.

Development Assistance Committee (DAC) of the OECD

Established in 1960 as the Development Assistance Group, with the objective of expanding the volume of resources made available to developing countries and to improve their effectiveness. The DAC periodically reviews both the amount and the nature of its members' contributions to aid programs, both bilateral and multilateral. The DAC does not disburse assistance funds directly, but is concerned instead with promoting increased assistance efforts by its members. The members of the DAC are Australia, Austria, Belgium, Canada, Denmark, Finland, France, Germany, Greece, Ireland, Italy, Japan, Luxembourg, the Netherlands, New Zealand, Norway, Portugal, Spain, Sweden, Switzerland, the United Kingdom, the United States, and the Commission of the European Communities.

Disbursed Loans

The amount that has been disbursed from a loan but has not yet been repaid or forgiven.

Disbursements

The transactions of providing financial resources. The two counterparties must record the transaction simultaneously. In practice, disbursements are recorded at one of several stages: provision of goods and services (where trade credit is involved); placing of funds at the disposal of the recipient in an earmarked fund or account; withdrawal of funds by the recipient from an earmarked fund or account; or payment by the lender of invoices on behalf of the borrower. The term "utilized" may apply when the credit extended is in a form other than currency. Disbursements should be recorded gross—the actual amount disbursed.

Domestic Currency

The domestic currency is that which is legal tender in the economy and issued by the monetary authority for that economy, or for the common currency area to which the economy belongs.

Duration

Duration is the weighted average term to maturity of a *debt instrument*. The time period until the receipt/payment of each cash flow, such as six months, is weighted by the *present value* of that cash flow, as a proportion of the present value of total cash flows over the life of the instrument. Present value can be calculated using the yield to maturity or another interest rate. The more the cash flows are concentrated toward the early part of a debt instrument's life, the shorter the duration relative to the time to maturity.

E

Eligible Debt or Debt Service

In the context of the Paris Club, debt that can be rescheduled—namely, debt that is contracted before the *cutoff date*, with maturities of one year or longer.

Enhanced Concessions (or Enhanced Toronto Terms)

See *Concessional Restructuring*.

Enhanced Structural Adjustment Facility (ESAF)

See *Structural Adjustment Facility* (SAF). Renamed the *Poverty Reduction and Growth Facility* (PRGF) in November 1999.

ESAF-HIPC Trust

A trust established by the IMF in February 1997 to provide assistance to the countries deemed eligible for assistance under the *HIPC Initiative* by the Boards of the IMF and the World Bank. Through this trust, the IMF will provide grants (or, in exceptional circumstances, highly concessional loans) that will be used to retire a country's obligations falling due to the IMF after the *completion point*.

Escrow Accounts

In the context of *external debt* payments, accounts typically held in banks outside of the *debtor country* through which a portion of the export proceeds of a debtor is channeled. Typically involve balances of one-year maturity to cover future *debt-service* payments. *Creditors* who are the beneficiaries of such accounts thus obtain extra security for their loans and effective priority in *debt service*.

Exceptional Financing

As an alternative to—or in conjunction with—the use of reserve assets, IMF credit and loans, and liabilities constituting foreign authorities' reserves, to deal with payments imbalance, exceptional financing denotes any other arrangements made by the authorities of an economy to finance *balance of payments* needs. The identification of exceptional financing transactions is linked to an analytical concept rather than being based on precise criteria. Among the transactions regarded as exceptional financing transactions are *debt forgiveness*, *debt-for-equity swaps*, and other types of transactions relating to *debt reorganizations*. Under certain circumstances, some borrowings by the government or other sectors might meet the criterion.

Export Credit

A loan extended to finance a specific purchase of goods or services from within the *creditor country*. Export credits extended by the supplier of goods—such as when the importer of goods and services is allowed to defer payment—are known as supplier's credits; export credits extended by a financial institution, or an export credit agency in the exporting country are known as *buyer's credits*. (See also *Officially Supported Export Credits*.)

Export Credit Agency

An agency in a *creditor country* that provides insurance, guarantees, or loans for the export of goods and services.

Extended Fund Facility (EFF)

An IMF lending facility established in 1974 to assist member countries in overcoming *balance of payments* problems that stem largely from structural problems and require a longer period of adjustment than is possible under a *Stand-By Arrangement.* A member requesting an Extended Arrangement outlines its objectives and policies for the whole period of the arrangement (typically three years) and presents a detailed statement each year of the policies and measures it plans to pursue over the next 12 months. The phasing and performance criteria are comparable to those of Stand-By Arrangements, although phasing on a semiannual basis is possible. Countries must repay EFF resources over a period of 4½ to 10 years. (See *Stand-By Arrangement.*)

External Debt

Gross external debt, at any given time, is the outstanding amount of those actual current, and not contingent, liabilities that require payment(s) of *interest* and/or *principal* by the debtor at some point(s) in the future and that are owed to nonresidents by residents of an economy.

F

Face Value

The amount of *principal* to be repaid (for example, the redemption amount of a bond). Sometimes called initial contractual value, for loans, the face value is the original amount of the loan as stated in the loan contract. If the loan is not fully disbursed, then the face value will include future disbursements, just as the face value of a zero-coupon bond includes interest that has not yet accrued.

Financial Account

The financial account of the *balance of payments* consists of the transactions in foreign financial assets and liabilities of an economy. The foreign financial assets of an economy consist of holdings of monetary gold, IMF Special Drawing Rights, and claims on nonresidents. The foreign liabilities of an economy consist of claims of nonresidents on residents. The primary basis for classification of the financial account is functional: direct, portfolio, and other investment, financial derivatives, and reserve assets.

Financial Asset

Financial assets are stores of value, over which ownership rights are enforced and from which their owners may derive economic benefits—such as property income and/or holding gains and losses—by holding them over a period of time. Most financial assets differ from other assets in the system of national accounts in that they have counterpart liabilities on the part of another institutional unit.

Financial Claim

A financial claim (1) entitles a creditor to receive a payment, or payments, from a debtor in circumstances specified in a contract between them; or (2) specifies between the two parties certain rights or obligations, the nature of which requires them to be treated as financial.

Financial Derivatives

Financial derivatives are financial instruments that are linked to a specific financial instrument or indicator or commodity, and through which specific financial risks can be traded in financial markets in their own right. The value of a financial derivative derives from the price of an underlying item, such as an asset or index. Unlike *debt instruments*, no principal amount is advanced to be repaid, and no investment income accrues. Financial derivatives are used for a number of purposes including risk management, hedging, *arbitrage* between markets, and speculation. Transactions in financial derivatives should be treated as separate transactions rather than integral parts of the value of underlying transactions to which they may be linked.

Financial Liability

A financial liability (1) requires a debtor to make a payment, or payments, to a *creditor* in circumstances specified in a contract between them; or (2) specifies between the two parties certain rights or obligations, the nature of which requires them to be treated as financial.

Flag-of-Convenience Countries

Countries with favorable tax rules and other regulations attracting companies whose main business (originally, primarily shipping—but increasingly, production or services) is outside the country.

Flow Rescheduling

In the context of the Paris Club, the rescheduling of specified *debt service* falling due during the *consolidation period* and, in some cases, of specified arrears outstanding at the beginning of the consolidation period. (See *Stock-of-Debt Operation.*)

Foreign Currency

In this *Guide*, a foreign currency is a currency other than the domestic currency.

Forfaiting

A mechanism, most commonly used in medium- and long-term credit, involving the purchase of promissory notes or bills of exchange by the forfaiter, at a discount. Banks or other financial services entities often own forfait companies.

Fund Credit

See *Use of IMF Credit and Loans* in Appendix I.

G

Geographical Distribution of the Flows of Financial Resources to Aid Recipients (Annual)

An annual publication of the OECD that shows the sources of official development financing to individual developing countries and territories. Included in this publication are detailed data on the geographical distribution of net and gross disbursements, commitments, terms, and the sectoral allocation of commitments.

Goodwill Clause

Clause used in Paris Club agreements under which *creditors* agree in principle, but without commit-

ment, to consider favorably subsequent *debt-relief* agreements for a *debtor country* that remains in compliance with the restructuring agreement as well as with its IMF arrangement, and has sought comparable debt relief from other creditors. The clause can be intended for a future *flow restructuring* or a *stock-of-debt operation.*

Grace Period and Maturity

The grace period for *principal* is the period from the date of signature of the loan or the issue of the financial instrument to the first repayment of principal. The repayment period is the period from the first to last repayment of principal. Maturity is the sum of both periods: grace plus repayment periods.

Graduated Payments (or "Blended Payments")

In the context of Paris Club reschedulings, the term refers to a repayment schedule where principal repayments gradually increase over the repayment period, reflecting an expected improvement in the repayment capacity of a debtor country. Creditors have made increasing use of the graduated payments, replacing flat payment schedules where equal amounts of principal repayments were made over the repayment period: from the creditor perspective, graduated payments provide for principal repayments starting earlier, and, from the debtor perspective, they avoid a large jump in *debt service.*

Grant Element

Measure of the concessionality of a loan, calculated as the difference between the *face value* of the loan and the sum of the discounted future *debt-service* payments to be made by the borrower expressed as a percentage of the face value of the loan. A 10 percent rate of discount is used by the Development Assistance Committee (DAC) and the World Bank to measure the grant element of official loans. (See also *Development Assistance Committee, Concessionality Level,* and *Official Development Assistance.*)

Grant-Like Flows

Loans for which the original agreement stipulates that payments to service the debt are to be placed into an account in the borrowing country and used in the borrowing country to the benefit of that country. These transactions are treated as grants in the OECD-DAC statistics because their repayment does not require a flow of foreign currency across the exchanges. They are nevertheless counted as external debt because the creditor is nonresident.

(The classification of these transactions as grants is not consistent with *BPM5* recommendations. In *BPM5*, grants are regarded as transfers: transactions where a real resource or financial item is provided but no quid pro quo is received. In the above transaction, in return for a reduction in outstanding debt, domestic currency is provided.)

Gross Domestic Product (GDP)

Essentially, the sum of the gross value added of all resident producer units. For further details, see *1993 SNA*, paragraphs 2.171–2.174.

Gross National Product (GNP)

GDP plus net income from abroad. For further details, see *1993 SNA*, paragraphs 7.16 and 7.17. In the *1993 SNA*, GNP was renamed gross national income.

H

Heavily Indebted Poor Countries (HIPCs)

Group of 41 developing countries classified as being heavily indebted poor countries. These are those countries that are eligible for highly concessional assistance from the *International Development Association* (IDA), and from the IMF's *Poverty Reduction and Growth Facility* (PRGF, previously the Enhanced Structural Adjustment Facility, ESAF), and that face an unsustainable debt situation even after the full application of traditional *debt-relief* mechanisms.

Helsinki Package

Agreement that came into force in 1992. This agreement prohibits (with some exceptions) the provision of *tied aid loans* to *high-income countries* (based on World Bank per capita income), and for commercially viable projects. (See also *Arrangement on Guidelines for Officially Supported Export Credits*.)

High-Income Countries

The World Bank classifies as high-income those countries with GNP per capita income of $9,266 or more in 2000.

HIPC Initiative

Framework for action to resolve the external debt problems of *heavily indebted poor countries* (HIPCs) that was developed jointly by the IMF and the World Bank and was adopted in September 1996. The Initiative envisaged comprehensive action by the international financial community, including multilateral institutions, to reduce to sustainable levels the *external debt* burden on HIPCs, provided they build a track record of strong policy performance.

Following a comprehensive review of the HIPC Initiative, a number of modifications to the Initiative were approved in September 1999 to provide faster, deeper, and broader *debt relief* and strengthen the links between debt relief, poverty reduction, and social policies.

HIPC Trust Fund

The Trust Fund administered by the International Development Association (IDA) to provide grants to eligible *heavily indebted poor countries* (HIPCs) for relief on debt owed to participating multilaterals. The Trust Fund will either prepay, or purchase, a portion of the debt owed to a multilateral creditor and cancel such debt, or pay *debt service*, as it comes due. The HIPC Trust Fund receives contributions from participating multilateral creditors and from bilateral donors. Contributions can be earmarked for debt owed by a particular debtor or to a particular multilateral creditor. Donors can also provide contributions to an unallocated pool and participate in decisions regarding the use of these unallocated funds. The Trust Fund allows multilateral creditors to participate in the Trust Fund in ways consistent with their financial policies and aims to address the resource constraints for certain multilateral creditors. (See also *ESAF-HIPC Trust*.)

Home Country

The country of residence of the head office of the institutional entity.

Host Country

The country in which the institutional entity is located.

Houston Terms

See *Lower-Middle-Income-Country Terms.*

I

IMF Adjustment Program

An adjustment program in a member country of the IMF. An IMF-supported program is a detailed economic program that is based on an analysis of the economic problems of the member country. It specifies the policies being implemented or that will be implemented by the country in the monetary, fiscal, external, and structural areas, as necessary, in order to achieve economic stabilization and set the basis for self-sustained economic growth. It usually, though not necessarily, refers to a program that is supported by the use of IMF resources.

IMF Arrangement

Agreement between the IMF and a member country on the basis of which the IMF provides financial assistance to a member country seeking to redress its *balance of payments* problems and to help cushion the impact of adjustment. Nonconcessional resources are provided mainly under *Stand-By Arrangements* and the *Extended Fund Facility* (EFF), and concessional resources are provided under the *Poverty Reduction and Growth Facility* (PRGF).

Institutional Sector

The grouping of institutional units with common economic objectives and functions. (See also S*ector Classification.*)

Institutional Unit

In the *1993 SNA* institutional units are the entities that undertake the activities of production, consumption, and the accumulation of assets and liabilities. In other words, economic activity involves transactions between institutional units be they households or corporations. An institutional unit is defined in the *1993 SNA* as "an economic entity that is capable, in its own right, of owning assets, incurring liabilities and engaging in economic activities and in transactions with other entities" (*1993 SNA*, paragraph 4.2).

Insured (Guaranteed) Export Credit

An *export credit* that carries a guarantee, issued by an *export credit agency*, protecting the *creditor* against political, commercial, or *transfer risks* in the *debtor country* that may prevent the remittance of *debt-servic*e payments. (See also *Export Credit Agency.*)

Interbank Positions

Asset and liability positions that banks have with other banks.

Interest

For the use of *principal*, interest can, and usually does, accrue on the principal amount, resulting in an interest cost for the debtor. When this cost is paid periodically, as commonly occurs, it is known in this *Guide* as an interest payment. Interest can be calculated either on a fixed-interest-rate or on a variable-interest-rate basis. In this *Guide*, in contrast to a fixed interest rate, which remains unchanged over a period of years, a variable interest rate is linked to a reference index (for example, the *London interbank offered rate*, LIBOR), or the price of a specific commodity, or the price of a specific financial instrument that normally changes over time in a continuous manner in response to market pressures. (See also *Principal.*)

International Bank for Reconstruction and Development (IBRD)

The International Bank for Reconstruction and Development (IBRD) was set up as an intergovernmental financial institution in 1946 as a result of the Bretton Woods Accord. It is the original agency of the *World Bank Group* and is commonly referred to as the World Bank. (See also *World Bank Group.*)

International Banking Business (BIS Data)

For these data, the term "international" refers to banks' transactions in any currency with nonresidents plus their transactions in foreign (nonlocal) currency with residents.

International Development Association (IDA)

IDA, established in 1960, is the concessional lending arm of the *World Bank Group*. IDA provides low-income developing countries with long-term loans on highly concessional terms: typically a 10-year grace period, a 40-year repayment period, and only a small servicing charge.

International Interbank Market

An international money market in which banks lend to each other—either cross-border or locally in foreign currency—large amounts of funds, usually at short term (between overnight and six months).

International Investment Position (IIP)

The IIP is the stock of external financial assets and liabilities on a specified reference date, usually the end of the quarter or year. The change in position between two end-periods reflects financial transactions, valuation changes, and other adjustments occurring during the period.

International Monetary Fund (IMF)

Following the Bretton Woods Accords and established in 1945, the IMF is a cooperative intergovernmental monetary and financial institution with 184 member countries. Its main purpose is to promote international monetary cooperation so to facilitate the growth of international trade and economic activity more generally. The IMF provides financial resources to enable its members to correct payments imbalances without resorting to trade and payments restrictions.

International Security Identification Number (ISIN)

The ISIN is a unique international security code issued by National Numbering Agencies (NNAs) to securities issued in their jurisdiction. The Association of National Numbering Agencies (ANNA) is the authority responsible for coordinating all aspects of the implementation of the ISIN numbering system. More information on the ISIN code system is avail-

able in Appendix VII of the IMF's *Coordinated Portfolio Investment Survey Guide*, 2nd ed. (IMF, 2002).

J

Joint Venture

An enterprise in which two or more parties hold major interests.

L

Late Interest Charges

The additional interest that may be levied on obligations overdue beyond a specified time; in some Paris Club agreements, late interest charges have been specifically excluded from the debt consolidation.

Leverage

Having exposure to the full benefits arising from holding a position in a financial asset, without having to fully fund the position with own funds.

Line of Credit

An agreement that creates a facility under which one unit can borrow credit from another up to a specified ceiling usually over a specified period of time. Lines of credit provide a guarantee that funds will be available, but no financial asset/liability exists until funds are actually advanced.

Loan Agreement

The legal evidence and terms of a loan.

Loan Guarantee

A legally binding agreement under which the guarantor agrees to pay any or all of the amount due on a loan instrument in the event of nonpayment by the borrower.

London Club

A group of commercial banks whose representatives meet periodically to negotiate the restructuring of debts of sovereign borrowers. There is no organizational framework for the London Club comparable to that of the Paris Club.

London Interbank Offered Rate (LIBOR)

The London interbank offered rate for deposits, such as the six-month dollar LIBOR. LIBOR is a reference rate for the international banking markets and is commonly the basis on which lending margins are fixed. Thus, an original loan agreement or a *rescheduling agreement* may set the interest rate to the borrower at six-month dollar LIBOR plus 1.5 percent, with semiannual adjustments for changes in the LIBOR rate. Also, interest rate swap rates are quoted in reference to LIBOR; that is, the quoted rate is the fixed-rate side of the swap because the floating-rate side is LIBOR.

London Terms

See *Concessional Restructuring.*

Long-Maturities Option

In the context of the Paris Club, an option under which the consolidated amount is rescheduled over a long period of time, but without a reduction in the *present value* of the debt.

Long-Term External Debt

External debt that has a maturity of more than one year. Maturity can be defined either on an original or remaining basis. (See also *Original Maturity* and *Remaining Maturity.*)

Low-Income Countries

In the context of the Paris Club, countries eligible to receive concessional terms. The Paris Club decides eligibility on a case-by-case basis, but only countries eligible to receive highly concessional IDA credits from the *World Bank Group* are included. The World Bank classifies as low-income those countries with GNP per capita income of $755 or less in 2000.

Lower-Middle-Income-Country Terms

In the context of the Paris Club, refers to the rescheduling terms granted, since September 1990, to lower-middle-income countries. These terms are nonconcessional and originally provided for flat repayment schedules, but in recent years graduated payment schedules have often been agreed upon for *commercial credits*, namely, with a maturity of up to 18 years, including a grace period of up to 8 years.

Official development assistance credits are rescheduled over 20 years, including a grace period of up to 10 years. This set of rescheduling terms also includes the limited use of debt swaps on a voluntary basis. The World Bank classifies as lower-middle income those countries with GNP per capita income of between $756 and $2,995 in 2000.

Lyon Terms

See *Concessional Restructuring.*

M

Market Valuation

Amounts of money that willing buyers pay to acquire something from willing sellers; the exchanges are made between independent parties on the basis of commercial considerations only. The market value of a *debt instrument* should be based on the market price for that instrument prevailing at the time to which the position statement refers; that is, current market prices as of the dates involved (beginning or end of the reference period). Chapter 2 provides more details. (See also *Nominal Value.*)

Maturity Date (Final)

The date on which a debt obligation is contracted to be extinguished. (See also *Original Maturity* and *Remaining Maturity.*)

Maturity Structure

A time profile of the maturities of claims or liabilities. Also known as "maturity profile" or "maturity distribution."

Mixed Credits

A credit that contains an aid element, so as to provide concessional credit terms—such as a lower rate of interest or a longer credit period.

Moratorium Interest

Interest charged on rescheduled debt. In the Paris Club, moratorium interest rates are negotiated bilaterally between the *debtor* and *creditor countries* and thus can differ among creditors. In the London Club, where all creditors are deemed to have access to funds at comparable rates, the moratorium interest rate applies equally to all rescheduled obligations under an agreement.

Multilateral Creditors

These creditors are multilateral institutions such as the IMF and the World Bank, as well as other multilateral development banks.

Multiyear Rescheduling Agreement (MYRA)

An agreement granted by official creditors that covers *consolidation periods* of two or more years in accordance with multiyear *IMF arrangements*, such as the *Extended Fund Facility* (EFF) and the *Poverty Reduction and Growth Facility* (PRGF). The modalities of the agreement are that a succession of shorter consolidations (*tranches*) are implemented after certain conditions specified in the *Agreed Minute* are satisfied, such as full implementation to date of the *rescheduling agreement* and continued implementation of the IMF arrangements.

N

Naples Terms

See *Concessional Restructuring.*

Nationality

Country of residence of the head office of an institutional entity.

National Numbering Agencies (NNAs)

NNAs have the sole right to allocate *International Security Identification Number* (ISIN) codes to securities within their own jurisdiction.

Net Flow

From the viewpoint of a loan, the net flow is gross *disbursements* less *principal* repayments.

Net Present Value (NPV) of Debt

The nominal amount outstanding minus the sum of all future *debt-service* obligations (*interest* and *principal*) on existing debt discounted at an interest rate different from the contracted rate.

The concept is closely related to that of opportunity cost: if the debtor has a loan that bears a 3 percent rate of interest, it is clear that the debtor is better off than by borrowing at 10 percent. But by discounting the future debt-service obligations at 10 percent and comparing the outcome with the amount borrowed, the NPV will tell how much the opportunity to borrow at 3 percent, rather than at 10 percent, is worth to the debtor. The NPV can be used to assess the profitability of buying back bonds, although account needs to be taken of how the buyback is to be financed.

The *Development Assistance Committee* (DAC) OECD *grant element* is an NPV concept, since the grant element is the percentage that the NPV, using a 10 percent rate of discount, represents of the *face value* of the loan. In the context of the Paris Club and the *HIPC Initiative*, sometimes *present value* is misdescribed as NPV. (See *Present Value, Concessionality Level,* and *Grant Element.*)

Net Resource Transfer

A net resource transfer is a current account deficit excluding any net interest payments.

Nominal Value

The nominal value of a *debt instrument* is the amount that at any moment in time the debtor owes to the creditor at that moment; this value is typically established by reference to the terms of a contract between the debtor and creditor. The nominal value of a debt instrument reflects the value of the debt at creation, and any subsequent economic flows, such as transactions (for example, repayment of *principal*), valuation changes (independent of changes in its market price), and other changes. Conceptually, the nominal value of a debt instrument can be calculated by discounting future *interest* and principal payments at the existing contractual interest rate(s) on the instrument; the latter may be fixed-rate or variable-rate. Chapter 2 provides more details. (See also *Market Valuation.*)

Nonconsolidated Debt

The debt that is wholly or partly excluded from rescheduling. It has to be repaid on the terms on which it was originally borrowed, unless creditors agree otherwise.

Notional (Nominal) Amount of a Financial Derivatives Contract

The notional amount is that underlying a *financial derivatives* contract and is necessary for calculating payments or receipts, but which may or may not be exchanged.

O

OECD Working Party on Export Credits and Credit Guarantees

This is a forum for discussing *export credit* issues and for exchanging information among 28 of the 29 member countries of the OECD (only Iceland does not participate).

Official Development Assistance (ODA)

Flows of official financing administered with the promotion of the economic development and welfare of developing countries as the main objective, and which are concessional in character with a *grant element* of at least 25 percent (using a fixed 10 percent rate of discount). By convention, ODA flows comprise contributions of donor government agencies, at all levels, to developing countries ("bilateral ODA") and to multilateral institutions. ODA receipts comprise *disbursements* by bilateral donors and multilateral institutions. Lending by *export credit agencies*—with the pure purpose of export promotion—is excluded.

Official Development Assistance (ODA) Loans

Loans with a maturity of over one year meeting the criteria set out in the definition of ODA, provided by governments or official agencies and for which repayment is required in convertible currencies or in kind.

Official Development Bank

A nonmonetary financial intermediary controlled by the public sector. It primarily engages in making long-term loans that are beyond the capacity or willingness of other financial institutions.

Official Development Finance (ODF)

Total official flows to developing countries excluding (1) *officially supported export credits*, (2) official

support for private export credits (both are regarded as primarily trade promoting rather than development oriented), and (3) grants and loans for nondevelopmental purposes. ODF comprises official development assistance (ODA) and other official development finance flows.

Officially Supported Export Credits

Loans or credits to finance the export of goods and services for which an official *export credit agency* in the creditor country provides guarantees, insurance, or direct financing. The financing element—as opposed to the guarantee/insurance element—can be extended by an exporter (supplier's credit), or through a commercial bank in the form of trade-related credit provided either to the supplier, or to the importer (buyer's credit). It can also be extended directly by an export credit agency of the exporting countries, usually in the form of medium-term finance as a supplement to resources of the private sector, and generally for export promotion for capital equipment and large-scale, medium-term projects. Under the rules of the *Arrangement on Guidelines for Officially Supported Export Credits* covering export credits with duration of two years or more, up to 85 percent of the export contract value can be officially supported.

Offshore Financial Center

Countries or jurisdictions with financial centers that contain financial institutions that deal primarily with nonresidents and/or in foreign currency on a scale out of proportion to the size of the host economy. Nonresident-owned or -controlled institutions play a significant role within the center. The institutions in the center may well gain from tax benefits not available to those outside the center.

Organisation for Economic Co-operation and Development (OECD)

The OECD provides governments of its member countries with a setting in which to discuss, develop, and perfect economic and social policy. The exchanges may lead to agreements to act in a formal way, but more often, the discussion makes for better-informed work within government on the spectrum of public policy and clarifies the impact of national policies on the international community. The chance to reflect and exchange perspectives with other countries similar to their own is provided. The OECD's objectives are to promote growth, employment, free trade, and a rising standard of living in both member countries and nonmember countries.

Original Maturity

The period of time from when the financial asset/liability was created to its final maturity date.

Other Official Flows (OOFs)

Official flows of a *creditor country* that are not undertaken for economic development purposes or, if they are mainly for development, whose grant element is below the 25 percent threshold that would make them eligible to be recorded as ODA. They include *export credits* extended or rescheduled by the official sector.

Own Offices

Different offices of the same entity, including head offices, branch offices, and subsidiaries. Also sometimes called "related offices."

P

Paris Club

An informal group of creditor governments that has met regularly in Paris since 1956 to reschedule bilateral debts; the French treasury provides the secretariat. Creditors meet with a debtor country to reschedule its debts as part of the international support provided to a country that is experiencing debt-servicing difficulties and is pursuing an adjustment program supported by the IMF. The Paris Club does not have a fixed membership, and its meetings are open to all official creditors that accept its practices and procedures. The core creditors are mainly OECD member countries, but other creditors attend as relevant for a debtor country. Russia became a member in September 1997.

Political Risk

The risk of nonpayment on an export contract or project due to action taken by the importer's host government. Such action may include intervention to prevent transfer of payments, cancellation of a license, or events such as war, civil strife, revolution,

and other disturbances that prevent the exporter from performing under the supply contract or the buyer from making payment. Sometimes physical disasters such as cyclones, floods, and earthquakes come under this heading.

Post-Cutoff-Date Debt

See *Cutoff Date.*

Poverty Reduction and Growth Facility (PRGF)

An IMF facility known until November 1999 as the *Enhanced Structural Adjustment Facility* (ESAF). The PRGF is available to those countries that are facing protracted balance of payments problems and are eligible to borrow on concessional terms under the *International Development Association* (IDA). The PRGF supports programs that are consistent with strategies elaborated by the borrowing country in a Poverty Reduction Strategy Paper (PRSP). The PRSP is a comprehensive, nationally owned strategy that is prepared by the borrowing country and endorsed in their respective areas of responsibility by the Boards of the IMF and World Bank. Funds are provided at an annual interest rate of 0.5 percent. They are repayable over 10 years, including a grace period of 5½ years. (See *Structural Adjustment Facility.*)

Premium

In the context of *export credits*, the amount paid, usually in advance, by the party to an export agency for its facilities. Cover will often not be fully effective until the premium has been paid. Premiums are normally calculated on the basis of the exposure, length of credit, and the riskiness of transacting with the importing country. Premium income, an important source of revenue for *export credit agencies*, is intended to cover the risk of nonpayment of the credit.

Prepayment

The partial or full repayment by the borrower, perhaps at a discount, of an outstanding debt obligation in advance of the maturity date. The prepayment may be at a discount from the current outstanding *principal* amount.

Present Value

The present value is the discounted sum of all future *debt service* at a given rate of *interest*. If the rate of interest is the contractual rate of the debt, by construction, the present value equals the *nominal value*, whereas if the rate of interest is the market interest rate, then the present value equals the market value of the debt.

In *debt-reorganization* discussions, the present value concept is used to measure, in a consistent manner, the burden sharing of debt reduction among *creditors*. This can be illustrated by the following example.

Debtor A owes 100 to both creditor B and creditor C. The maturity of both loans is the same. Creditor B's loan has an interest rate of 3 percent and that of C an interest rate of 6 percent. The "market rate" is assumed to be 8 percent—that is, B and C could have lent the money at this higher rate. So, for both B and C, the opportunity cost of lending at their respective interest rates, rather than at the market rate, can be calculated by discounting future payments at the market rate of 8 percent (present value), and comparing the outcome with the outstanding nominal value of 100. If PV(B) represents the present value for B and PV(C) represents the present value for C, then:

$$PV(B) < PV(C) < 100$$

PV(B) is less than PV(C) because the size of the future payments to be made by A to B is less than those to be made to C. In turn, the payments by A to C are less than would have been the case if a market rate of interest had been charged. This is illustrated by the annual interest payments. Debtor A would annually pay 3 to B; 6 to C; and 8 at the market rate of interest.

In deciding upon burden sharing of debt reduction, since B's claims on A are already lower than those of C, despite the same nominal value, debt reduction required from B might well be less than that required from C. So, it can be seen that by using a common interest rate to discount future payments, the burden on the debtor of each loan can be quantified in a comparable manner.

Present Value of Debt-to-Exports Ratio (PV/X)

Present value (PV) of debt as a percentage of exports (usually of goods and services) (X). In the context of the Paris Club and *HIPC Initiative*, sometimes present value is misdescribed as *net present value* (NPV). In this context NPV/X has the same meaning as PV/X.

Previously Rescheduled Debt

Debt that has been rescheduled on a prior occasion. This type of debt was generally excluded from further rescheduling in both the Paris and London Clubs until 1983. Since then, however, previously rescheduled debt has frequently been rescheduled again for countries facing acute payment difficulties.

Principal

The provision of economic value by the *creditor*, or the creation of debt liabilities through other means, establishes a principal liability for the debtor, which, until extinguished, may change in value over time. For *debt instruments* alone, for the use of the principal, *interest* can, and usually does, accrue on the principal amount, increasing its value.

Principal Repayment Schedule

The repayment schedule of *principal* by due date and installment amount.

Private Creditors

Creditors that are neither governments nor public sector agencies. These include private bondholders, private banks, other private financial institutions, and manufacturers, exporters, and other suppliers of goods that have a financial claim.

Provisioning

Funds set aside in an entity's account for potential losses arising from financial claims that are not serviced by the debtor, and/or from claims on the entity arising out of insurance cover and/or guarantees given. In many *export credit agencies*' accounts, provisions are divided into general and specific provisions. General provisions apply to the overall business, while specific provisions are on a case-by-case basis. Banks make provisions.

Public Debt

The debt obligations of the public sector.

Public External Debt

The *external debt* obligations of the public sector.

Q

Quantitative (or Cover) Limits

A ceiling on the amount of insurance or credit that an *export credit agency* will provide under certain circumstances. Limits can apply to individual buyers or to total exposure on buying countries or to maximum contract sizes.

R

Recoveries

Repayments made to an *export credit agency* by a borrowing country after the agency has paid out on claims by exporters or banks.

Refinancing

See *Debt Refinancing*.

Reinsurance by Export Credit Agencies

Export credit agencies may reinsure amounts originally insured by a private sector insurer or commercial bank (some large official agencies are also providing reinsurance for smaller official agencies). For example, a private insurer might keep the *commercial risk* of a loan on its own books, but seek reinsurance against specific political risks. Also, some *export credit agencies* may receive reinsurance from their governments or purchase it in the private reinsurance market.

Remaining (Residual) Maturity

The period of time until debt payments fall due. In the *Guide*, it is recommended that short-term remaining maturity of outstanding *external debt* be measured by adding the value of outstanding short-term external debt (original maturity) to the value of outstanding long-term external debt (original maturity) due to be paid in one year or less.

Repayment Period

The period during which the debt obligation is to be repaid.

Rephasing

A revision of the terms of repayment of a debt obligation.

Reporting Banks

In *BIS* terminology, all those deposit-taking institutions (plus some non-deposit-taking financial institutions) that submit data to be included in the *BIS* International Banking Statistics.

Repudiation of Debt

A unilateral disclaiming of a *debt instrument* obligation by a debtor.

Rescheduling

See *Debt Rescheduling*.

Rescheduling Agreement

An agreement between a creditor, or a group of creditors, and a debtor to reschedule debt. This term is sometimes used loosely to apply to a debt-reorganization/restructuring agreement, one element of which is rescheduling.

Rights Accumulation Program

An IMF program of assistance established in 1990 whereby a member country with long overdue obligations to the IMF, while still in arrears, may accumulate "rights" toward a future disbursement from the IMF on the basis of a sustained performance under an IMF-monitored adjustment program. Countries incurring arrears to the IMF after end-1989 are not eligible for assistance under this program. Rights Accumulation Programs adhere to the macroeconomic and structural policy standards associated with programs supported by the *Extended Fund Facility* (EFF) and the *Poverty Reduction and Growth Facility* (PRGF), and performance is monitored, and rights accrue, quarterly.

S

Sector Classification

In the *1993 SNA* and *BPM5*, institutional sectors are formed by the grouping of similar kinds of institutional units according to their economic objectives and functions.

Short-Term Commitments or Credits

In the context of *export credits*, short-term commitments are those that provide for repayment within a short period, usually six months (although some *export credit agencies* define short-term credits as those with repayment terms of up to one or two years). Short-term business represents the bulk of that of most export credit agencies and normally includes transactions in raw materials, commodities, and consumer goods.

Short-Term Debt

Debt that has maturity of one year or less. Maturity can be defined either on an original or remaining basis. (See also *Original Maturity* and *Remaining Maturity*.)

Special Accounts

In the context of the Paris Club, deposits into special accounts were first introduced in 1983 for debtor countries that had a history of running into arrears. After signing the *Agreed Minute*, the debtor makes monthly deposits into an earmarked account at the central bank of one of the *creditor countries*. The deposit amounts are roughly equal to the *moratorium interest* that is expected to fall due on the rescheduled debt owed to all Paris Club creditors combined, and any other payments falling due during the *consolidation period*. The debtor then draws on the deposited funds to make payments as soon as the bilateral agreements with the individual Paris Club creditors are signed and as other payments fall due.

Stand-By Arrangement

An IMF lending facility established in 1952 through which a member country can use IMF financing up to a specified amount to overcome short-term or cyclical *balance of payments* difficulties. Installments are normally phased on a quarterly basis, with their release conditional upon the member's meeting performance criteria, such as monetary and budgetary targets. These criteria allow both the member and the IMF to assess the member's progress in policy implementation and may signal the need for further corrective policies. Stand-By Arrangements typically cover a period of one to two years (although they can extend up to three years). Repayments are to be made over a period of 3¼ to 5 years. The expected repayment period is shortened to 2¼–4 years if the country's external position allows it to repay earlier.

Stand-By Credit

A commitment to lend up to a specified amount for a specific period, to be used only in a certain contingency.

Standstill

This is an interim agreement between a *debtor country* and its commercial banking creditors that defers principal repayments of medium- and long-term debt and rolls over short-term obligations, pending agreement on *debt reorganization*. The objective is to give the debtor continuing access to a minimum amount of trade-related financing while negotiations take place and to prevent some banks from abruptly withdrawing their facilities at the expense of others.

Stock Figures

The value of financial assets and liabilities outstanding at a particular point in time.

Stock-of-Debt Operation

In the context of the Paris Club, restructuring of the eligible stock of debt outstanding. These restructuring operations were granted to Egypt and Poland in 1991 and, partially, for Russia and Peru in 1996 and are being implemented for low-income countries under Naples, Lyon, and Cologne terms (see *Concessional Restructuring*), provided that certain conditions are met: the debtor country has implemented earlier flow rescheduling agreements for at least three years and has an appropriate arrangement with the IMF.

Stress Test

A stress test is a "what if" scenario that takes the world as given but assumes a major change in one or more variables in order to see what effect this would have on various indicators. For instance, for an economy, the impact on growth, inflation, and external debt of a huge change in oil prices could be considered. Stress tests are particularly useful for financial institutions: for instance, an individual entity might consider the impact on net worth of a sharp movement in financial market prices, in order to help determine the appropriate level of capital to hold.

Structural Adjustment Facility (SAF)/ Enhanced Structural Adjustment Facility (ESAF)

The SAF was established by the IMF in 1986 and is no longer operational. The ESAF was established by the IMF in 1987 and was made a permanent, rather than a temporary, facility in September 1996. It was renamed the *Poverty Reduction and Growth Facility* in November 1999. (See *Poverty Reduction and Growth Facility*.)

Subordination Strategy

The policy of Paris Club creditors is that loans extended after the cutoff date are not subject to rescheduling; therefore, pre-cutoff date loans are effectively subordinated to post-cutoff loans. (See *Cutoff Date*.)

Supplier's Credit

A financing arrangement under which an exporter extends credit to the buyer.

T

Technical Cooperation Grants

There are two basic types of technical cooperation: (1) free-standing technical cooperation (FTC), which is the provision of resources aimed at the transfer of technical and managerial skills or of technology for the purpose of building up general national capacity without reference to the implementation of any specific investment projects; and (2) investment-related technical cooperation (IRTC), which denotes the provision of technical services required for the implementation of specific investment projects.

Terms-of-Reference Rescheduling

Paris Club rescheduling involving only a small number of creditors. Typically this does not require a rescheduling meeting between the debtor country and its creditors, with the agreement being reached through an exchange of letters.

Tied-Aid Loans

Bilateral loans that are linked to purchases of goods and services by the *debtor country* from the *creditor country*.

Toronto Terms

See *Concessional Restructuring*.

Total Official Flows (Gross or Net)

The sum of *official development assistance* (ODA) and *other official flows* (OOF). Represents the total (gross or net) *disbursements* by the official sector of the creditor country to the recipient country.

Tranche

A particular portion of a financial claim or liability with its own specific terms as opposed to the general terms governing the whole claim or liability.

Transfer Clause

A provision that commits the debtor government to guarantee the immediate and unrestricted transfer of foreign exchange in all cases, provided that the private sector pays the local currency counterpart for servicing its debt.

Transfer Risk

The risk that a borrower will not be able to convert local currency into foreign exchange, and so be unable to make *debt-service* payments in foreign currency. The risk normally arises from exchange restrictions imposed by the government in the borrower's country. This is a particular kind of *political risk*.

Transfers

Transfers are transactions where there is a transfer of a real resource or a financial item without a quid pro quo.

U

Undisbursed

Funds committed by the creditor but not yet utilized by the borrower. In BIS terminology, this refers to open lines of credit that are legally binding on lending banks. A transaction in the *balance of payments* or a position in the *international investment position* (IIP) is only recorded when an actual *disbursement* takes place.

Unrecovered Claims

See *Claim Payments*.

Upper-Middle-Income Countries

In the context of the Paris Club, countries not considered *lower-middle-income* or *low-income countries*. These countries receive nonconcessional rescheduling terms, originally with flat repayment schedules, but in the 1990s increasingly with graduated payment schedules that have a maturity of up to 15 years and a grace period of 2–3 years for *commercial credits*. Official development assistance credits are rescheduled over 10 years, including a grace period of 5–6 years. The World Bank classifies as upper-middle income those countries with GNP per capita income of between $2,996 and $9,265 in 2000.

W

World Bank Group

Founded in 1944, the World Bank Group (or World Bank) consists of five closely associated institutions: the *International Bank for Reconstruction and Development* (IBRD), the *International Development Association* (IDA), the International Finance Corporation (IFC), the Multilateral Investment Guarantee Agency (MIGA), and the International Centre for Settlement of Investment Disputes (ICSID). The World Bank is the world's largest source of development assistance; its main focus is on helping the poorest people and the poorest countries through IDA credits (concessional lending) and on providing IBRD loans to low- and middle-income countries for developmental purposes. To achieve its poverty-reduction mission, the World Bank focuses on investing in people, particularly through basic health and education; protecting the environment; supporting and encouraging private business development; and promoting reforms to create a stable macroeconomic environment and long-term economic growth.

Write-Off

A financial claim that a creditor regards as unrecoverable and so no longer carries on its books.

Appendix IV. Relationship Between the National Accounts and the International Investment Position (IIP)

1. In the *Guide*, linkages between external debt statistics, the IIP, and the national accounts have been developed and explained. This appendix goes further and explains the relationship between the national accounts and the IIP, such that data on the IIP can be incorporated into the external account components of the rest of the world account of the national accounts system, bringing compilation and collection efficiency gains as well as analytical benefits.

2. There is virtually complete concordance between the *1993 SNA* and *BPM5* with respect to such issues as the delineation of resident units, valuation of transactions and of the stock of external assets and liabilities, time of recording of transactions in goods and services, income flows, current transfers, capital transfers, external assets and liabilities, and coverage of the IIP. There are, however, differences in classification between the rest of the world account and *BPM5*. These reflect, inter alia, differences in analytical requirements and the need in the *1993 SNA* to adopt a uniform classification scheme for all sectors of the economy. In this appendix, the financial account element of the national accounts is examined, followed by a detailed comparison between the financial accounts and the IIP.

Financial Accounts

Features of Financial Accounts

3. The key features of financial accounts are that (1) they identify the liabilities that net borrowing institutional sectors use to finance their deficits, and the financial assets that net lending sectors use to allocate their surpluses; (2) they facilitate analysis of the flow of funds between different institutional sectors of the economy; (3) they place emphasis on stock variables such as financial assets and debt; and (4) they are developed from detailed information on the various institutional sectors and their activities in financial assets/liabilities.

4. The complete system of financial accounts, including flow of funds accounts,[1] has considerable analytical power. For instance, corporate sector gross debt-equity ratios can be calculated; related shifts by households or companies into financial deficit (defined relative to GDP) can be observed; and increases in income gearing (interest payments as a proportion of income), shifts in the pattern of intermediation toward or away from the banking sector (as shown by the total assets of banks relative to nonbank financial institutions), and rapid growth of lending in any individual market to a given sector can be monitored. Furthermore, information on investment patterns of institutional investors, the balance between sources of corporate debt finance in banking and bond markets (to assess vulnerability to crises in different institutions or markets), and the maturity of debt (on an original maturity basis) is also available.

Financial Assets

5. Financial accounts deal with stocks of financial assets owned by institutional sectors and transactions in these assets through financial markets. In the *1993 SNA* and the *European System of Accounts 1995 (ESA95)*,[2] financial assets are defined as entities over which ownership rights are enforced and from which economic benefits may be derived by their owners by holding them or using them, over a period of time (paragraph 11.16 of the *1993 SNA*). In short, financial assets are stores of economic value. Most financial assets differ from other assets in that there are counterpart liabilities on behalf of another institutional unit.

6. The *1993 SNA* distinguishes eight types of financial assets:

---

[1]Flow of funds accounts provide information on financial transactions among institutional sectors (for more details, see paragraphs 11.103–11.111 and Table 11.3a of the *1993 SNA*).

[2]The *ESA95* (Eurostat, 1996) is the system of national accounts used by member states of the European Union. Unless otherwise stated, the *ESA95* treatment is consistent in all aspects with the *1993 SNA*.

Table A4.1. Classification by Sector in *1993 SNA*

Nonfinancial corporations (S.11)

Financial corporations (S.12)
• Central bank (S.121)
• Other depository corporations (S.122)
• Other financial intermediaries (except insurance corporations and pension funds) (S.123)
• Financial auxiliaries (S.124)
• Insurance corporations and pension funds (S.125)

General government (S.13)[1]
• Central government (S.1311)
• State government (S.1312)
• Local government (S.1313)
• Social security funds (S.1314)

Households (S.14)

Nonprofit institutions serving households (S.15)

Rest of the world (S.2)

Note: The abbreviations given in brackets are the sectors as they are numbered in the *1993 SNA*.
[1]The *1993 SNA* also includes an alternative presentation of the general government sector. This alternative presentation attributes social security funds to the level of government at which they operate, leaving three subsectors: Central government plus social security funds operating at the central government level (S.1321); State government plus social security funds operating at the state government level (S.1322); and Local government plus social security funds operating at the local government level (S.1323).

Table A4.2. Link Between the Accounts

Flows (change to financial assets and liabilities)
    Financial account transactions
    Other changes in volume of assets account
    Revaluation account
Stocks (stocks of financial assets and liabilities)

distinction is made between the central bank, other depository corporations (other monetary financial institutions in the *ESA95*), other financial institutions (except insurance corporations and pension funds), financial auxiliaries, and insurance corporations and pension funds. The general government is also divided in four subsectors: central government, state government, local government, and social security funds. In the *ESA95* (paragraph 2.49) the central bank and other financial corporations are grouped together in the monetary financial institutions (MFIs) sector. Also, the *ESA95* divides the rest of the world sector into European Union (EU), and nonmember countries and international organizations.

The Link Between the Accounts

8. Changes in stocks of financial assets and liabilities from one accounting point to another are the consequence of a combination of economic flows. These include financial transactions, valuation changes, and other changes, such as write-offs and transfers of assets/liabilities resulting from, say, an institutional unit changing sectors. In the *1993 SNA* flows and stocks are completely integrated—that is, changes in the stock or balance sheet positions[3] of the institutional units can be fully explained by recorded flows (Table A4.2).

A Simplified Version of Financial Account Balance Sheets

9. As mentioned above, the economy consists of five resident sectors—nonfinancial and financial corporations, general government, households, and NPISH—all of which have relationships with the rest of the world sector. Figure A4.1 is a matrix of

• Monetary gold and special drawing rights (SDRs) (AF.1);
• Currency and deposits (AF.2);
• Securities other than shares (AF.3);
• Loans (AF.4);
• Shares and other equity (AF.5);
• Insurance technical reserves (AF.6);
• Financial derivatives (AF.7); and
• Other accounts receivable/payable (AF.8).

Most financial assets are further disaggregated, in particular according to maturity and market type. Thus, transferable deposits and other deposits (for example, nontransferable savings deposits) are included within currency and deposits, while within securities other than shares, a distinction is made between short-term and long-term securities.

Institutional Sectors

7. The *1993 SNA* groups the institutional units of a national economy into five mutually exclusive institutional sectors: nonfinancial corporations, financial corporations, general government, households, and nonprofit institutions serving households (NPISH) (Table A4.1). With regard to financial corporations, a

[3]Balance sheets are statements, at a particular point in time, of the value of the stock of nonfinancial assets and financial assets and liabilities of an economy, sector, or institutional unit. For an economy, gross assets less gross liabilities, the balancing item for a balance sheet, equals the "net worth" of the economy.

Figure A4.1. Simplified Version of Balance Sheet Accounts¹

Assets								Stocks and balancing items	Liabilities and Net Worth							
Total	Rest of the world	Total economy	NPISH	House-holds	General govern-ment	Financial corpo-rations	Non-financial corpo-rations		Non-financial corpo-rations	Financial corpo-rations	General govern-ment	House-holds	NPISH	Total economy	Rest of the world	Total
9,922		9,922	324	2,822	1,591	144	5,041	**AN Nonfinancial assets**								
6,047		6,047	243	1,698	1,001	104	3,001	AN.1 Produced assets								
5,544		5,544	231	1,423	913	99	2,878	AN.11 Fixed assets								
231		231	2	97	47		85	AN.12 Inventories								
272		272	10	178	41	5	38	AN.13 Valuables								
3,875		3,875	81	1,124	590	40	2,040	AN.2 Nonproduced assets								
3,809		3,809	81	1,124	578	37	1,989	AN.21 Tangible nonproduced assets								
66		66			12	3	51	AN.22 Intangible nonproduced assets								
7,573	618	6,955	173	1,821	416	3,598	947	**AF Financial assets/liabilities²**	1,852	3,469	712	291	122	6,446	357	6,803
770		770			80	690		AF.1 Monetary gold and SDRs²								
1,587	105	1,482	110	840	150		382	AF.2 Currency and deposits	40	1,281	102	10	38	1,471	116	1,587
1,388	125	1,263	25	198	115	950	90	AF.3 Securities other than shares	44	1,053	212	2		1,311	77	1,388
1,454	70	1,384	8	24	12	1,187	50	AF.4 Loans	897		328	169	43	1,437	17	1,454
1,409	113	1,296	22	411	20	651	200	AF.5 Shares and other equity	687	715	4		5	1,406	3	1,409
396	26	370	4	291	20	30	25	AF.6 Insurance technical reserves	12	335	19	2	5	371	25	396
208	45	163	1	2	20	90	50	AF.7 Financial derivatives	35	85	25	2	1	148	60	208
361	134	227	3	55	19		150	AF.8 Other accounts receivable/payable	137		22	108	35	302	59	361
								B.90 Net worth	4,136	273	1,295	4,352	375	10,431	261	10,692

Note: Shaded areas indicate cells that are not applicable; codes from the *1993 SNA* balance sheets are shown in the center column. Data are derived from the *1993 SNA* Table 13.1: Balance sheets—a line for financial derivatives has been added to reflect the 1999 revision to the *1993 SNA*. In addition, data differ slightly due to small errors in the *1993 SNA* table.

¹In the *1993 SNA*, other accounts receivable/payable are accorded the code AF.7, but following the revision to the *1993 SNA* in 1999, financial derivatives are accorded the code AF.7, while other accounts receivable/payable are accorded AF.8.

²Monetary gold and SDRs are external assets of the total economy, but there are no counterpart liabilities for the rest of the world sector.

Figure A4.2. Balance Sheets of the Total Economy and the Rest of the World

Assets		Stocks and balancing items	Liabilities and Net Worth	
Rest of the world	Total economy		Total economy	Rest of the world
	16,714	**Assets**		
	9,922	**AN Nonfinancial assets**		
	6,047	AN.1 Produced assets		
	5,544	AN.11 Fixed assets		
	231	AN.12 Inventories		
	272	AN.13 Valuables		
	3,875	AN.2 Nonproduced assets		
	3,809	AN.21 Tangible nonproduced assets		
	66	AN.22 Intangible nonproduced assets		
618	**6,955**	**AF Financial assets/liabilities**	**6,446**	**357**
	770	AF.1 Monetary gold and SDRs		
105	1,482	AF.2 Currency and deposits	1,471	116
125	1,263	AF.3 Securities other than shares	1,311	77
70	1,384	AF.4 Loans	1,437	17
113	1,296	AF.5 Shares and other equity	1,406	3
26	370	AF.6 Insurance technical reserves	371	25
45	163	AF.7 Financial derivatives	148	60
134	227	AF.8 Other accounts receivable/payable	302	59
		B.90 Net worth	10,431	261

Note: Shaded areas indicate cells that are not applicable; codes from the *1993 SNA* balance sheets are shown in center column.

Data are derived from *1993 SNA*, Table 13.1: Balance sheets—a line for financial derivatives has been added to reflect the 1999 revision to the *1993 SNA*. Data differ slightly due to small errors in the *1993 SNA* table.

various balance sheets that shows nonfinancial as well as financial assets and liabilities by sector and instrument; for example, households hold fixed assets of 1,423 as well as shares and other equity of 411. For each financial asset/liability, the rows show total holdings and issues by sector, and the matching of asset and liability positions.[4] For each sector, the columns show financial assets owned or liabilities incurred, and also the net worth of the sector. The need for consistency among the rows and columns helps to minimize errors in the data.

10. The financial accounts in a simplified form can be derived from the second part of Figure A4.1 because financial assets and liabilities are shown for all institutional sectors involved. Net financial assets may be derived as the balancing item between financial assets and liabilities.

11. Figure A4.1 may be further simplified to show only the balance sheets of the total economy and the

rest of the world sector. In Figure A4.2, the net worth of the total economy—its national wealth—equals the sum of a country's nonfinancial assets (9,922) plus its net financial claims on the rest of the world (618 – 357). In the balance sheet for the total economy, all financial assets and liabilities between residents are netted out in the consolidation to leave only the net financial assets position (positive or negative) on the rest of the world. For the rest of the world balance sheet, only financial assets and liabilities are shown.

A More Detailed Version of Financial Account Balance Sheets

12. Financial accounts may be expanded into three dimensions to track each instrument category, the financial claims of each sector on each other sector. By indicating who has lent to whom and with what instrument, such a matrix lends considerable analytical power to financial accounts. As with the two-dimensional approach described above, the interlocking row and column constraints of the three-dimensional matrix provide an important check on the consistency of data. This is because for each sector, each transaction involves at least, and usually, two

---

[4]Total financial assets and liabilities do not match because monetary gold and SDRs are financial assets that have no counterparty liability.

balance sheet changes,[5] and similarly for each instrument, each transaction involves two balance sheet changes. For example, the issue of a new debt security by a nonfinancial corporation that is purchased by a nonresident results in the following entries: the nonfinancial corporation reports the increase in *securities other than shares* liabilities, and an increase in *currency and deposit* assets; while the nonresident reports an increase in *securities other than shares* assets, and a reduction in *currency and deposits*.

13. The full three-dimensional matrix is an important analytical tool but, because of the cost and/or the conceptual complexity, relatively few countries have full flow of funds data. Figure A4.3 provides the three-dimensional financial asset matrix taken from the *1993 SNA* (Table 13.3a, page 302). As can be seen, across the top of the matrix the columns show the financial assets owned by the five mutually exclusive institutional sectors, with subsector detail for the financial corporations sector. The rows show the type of claim disaggregated by institutional sector. While a detailed breakdown of the sector of debtor is shown for *securities other than shares*, for *loans*, and for *trade credit and advances*, only a resident/nonresident breakdown is shown for *shares and other equity* and for *currency and deposits*. The matrix on financial liabilities in the *1993 SNA* (Table 13.3b, page 303), not shown here, is similar to the financial assets matrix, although the columns show the institutional sector of debtor and the rows show the institutional sector of creditor. Using both matrixes, all asset, liability, and counterpart combinations can be found. Compilers can adjust the sectors and instrument classifications in either matrix, in order to reflect national conditions and needs of users.

14. Table A4.3 is derived from the matrix in Figure A4.3 but includes only the balance sheet of the rest of the world. In comparison to the approach in Figure A4.3, financial assets and liabilities of the rest of the world account are shown by counterpart institutional sector. Compared with the *1993 SNA*, Table A4.3 includes additional counterpart sector information on the following instruments: currency, transferable deposits, other deposits, quoted shares, and nonquoted shares. In some countries this additional sectoral information is available.

International Investment Position (IIP)

15. The IIP is described in Chapter 17, and so only a brief summary is provided here. The instrument classification required by the *BPM5* in respect of the IIP and the financial account of the balance of payments consists of equity instruments (which include equity securities, equity in unincorporated enterprises, and reinvested earnings), debt instruments (which include bonds and notes, money market instruments, trade credits, use of IMF credit and loans, other loans, currency and deposits, and other accounts such as arrears), and financial derivatives. Two other financial assets—monetary gold and SDRs—are identified as part of reserve assets.

16. The institutional sector of the resident creditor, for assets, and that of the resident debtor, for liabilities, is of analytical value. Accordingly, for portfolio investment, financial derivatives and other investment, the IIP distinguishes four sectors: general government, monetary authorities, banks, and other. For direct investment, however, the domestic sector is a less significant factor. For this reason, the IIP does not classify direct investment by sector. Also, because by definition reserve assets can be owned or controlled only by the monetary authorities, no sectoral classification is required for this item.

17. Classification of balance of payments transactions by institutional sector plays a significant role in linking balance of payments statistics with other statistical systems, such as the system of national accounts, money and banking statistics, and government finance statistics. While the institutional sector attribution in the IIP is not the same as in the *1993 SNA,* because of the differing analytical needs, there is a significant degree of concordance. This is described in more detail below.

Comparison Summary of the Rest of the World Balance Sheet Account and the IIP

Similarities Between the Rest of the World Balance Sheet Account and the IIP

18. As a consequence of an explicit decision by the drafters of the *1993 SNA* and *BPM5*, there is

---

[5]An example of the need for more than two entries is the settlement of a foreign currency financial derivative contract under which the currency and deposits exchanged do not equal each other in value, with the difference recorded as a redemption of a financial derivative contract.

Figure A4.3. Detailed Version of Balance Sheet Accounts

						Financial Assets						
								Financial corporations				
								Other depository corporations					
Type of Claim and Debtor	Total	Non-financial corporations	General govern-ment	NPISH	House-holds	Central bank	Deposit money corpo-rations	Other	Other financial inter-mediaries	Financial auxiliaries	Insurance corporations and pension funds	Rest of the world
1. Monetary gold and SDRs												
2. Currency and deposits a. Currency i. National –Residents –Nonresidents ii. Foreign –Residents b. Transferable deposits i. National currency –Residents –Nonresidents ii. Foreign currency –Residents –Nonresidents c. Other deposits i. National currency –Residents –Nonresidents ii. Foreign currency –Residents –Nonresidents												
3. Securities other than shares a. Short-term i. Nonfinancial corporations ii. Financial corporations iii. Central government iv. State and local governments v. Other resident sectors vi. Rest of the world b. Long-term i. Nonfinancial corporations ii. Financial corporations iii. Central government iv. State and local governments v. Other resident sectors vi. Rest of the world												
4. Loans a. Short-term i. Nonfinancial corporations ii. Financial corporations iii. Central government iv. State and local governments v. Other resident sectors vi. Rest of the world b. Long-term i. Nonfinancial corporations ii. Financial corporations iii. Central government iv. State and local governments v. Other resident sectors vi. Rest of the world												

Figure A4.3 *(concluded)*

Type of Claim and Debtor	Financial Assets												
	Total	Non-financial corporations	General govern-ment	NPISH	House-holds	Financial corporations						Rest of the world
						Central bank	Other depository corporations		Other financial inter-mediaries	Financial auxiliaries	Insurance corporations and pension funds	
							Deposit money corpo-rations	Other				
5. Shares and other equity												
a. Resident enterprises												
i. Quoted												
ii. Not quoted												
b. Nonresident enterprises												
i. Quoted												
ii. Not quoted												
6. Insurance technical reserves												
6.1 Net equity of households in life insurance reserves and in pension funds												
6.2 Prepayments of premiums and reserves against outstanding claims												
7. Financial Derivatives												
i. Nonfinancial corporations												
ii. Financial corporations												
iii. Central government												
iv. State and local governments												
v. Other resident sectors												
vi. Rest of the world												
8. Other accounts receivable and payable												
8.1 Trade credit and advances												
a. Nonfinancial corporations												
b. Households												
c. Central government												
d. State and local governments												
e. Other resident sectors												
f. Rest of the world												
8.2 Other												
a. Resident sectors												
b. Rest of the world												
Memorandum items												
Direct investment												
Equity												
Loans												
Other												

considerable homogeneity between the conceptual framework for the rest of the world balance sheet account and the IIP. The degree of homogeneity may be demonstrated by comparing their respective approaches to the coverage of financial instruments, and the application of principles such as residence, market valuation, accrual accounting, and maturity.

Coverage of Financial Instruments

19. The financial instruments recognized as financial assets and liabilities in the *1993 SNA* are identical with those recognized in *BPM5* and included in the IIP. However, the presentation of these financial assets and liabilities is not identical in the two accounts, primarily because for analytical

Table A4.3. Rest of the World Balance Sheet by Counterpart Sector

Financial Assets of Rest of World	Liabilities of Rest of World

2. Currency and deposits
  a. Currency
    i. National
    ii. Foreign
  b. Transferable deposits
    i. National currency
    ii. Foreign currency
  c. Other deposits
    i. National currency
    ii. Foreign currency
	2. Currency and deposits
	  a. Currency
	    i. National currency
	      i. Nonfinancial corporations
	      ii. Financial corporations
	      iii. Central government
	      iv. State and local governments
	      v. Other resident sectors
	    ii. Foreign currency
	      i. Nonfinancial corporations
	      ii. Financial corporations
	      iii. Central government
	      iv. State and local governments
	      v. Other resident sectors
	  b. Transferable deposits
	    i. National currency
	      i. Nonfinancial corporations
	      ii. Financial corporations
	      iii. Central government
	      iv. State and local governments
	      v. Other resident sectors
	    ii. Foreign currency
	      i. Nonfinancial corporations
	      ii. Financial corporations
	      iii. Central government
	      iv. State and local governments
	      v. Other resident sectors
	  c. Other deposits
	    i. National currency
	      i. Nonfinancial corporations
	      ii. Financial corporations
	      iii. Central government
	      iv. State and local governments
	      v. Other resident sectors
	    ii. Foreign currency
	      i. Nonfinancial corporations
	      ii. Financial corporations
	      iii. Central government
	      iv. State and local governments
	      v. Other resident sectors

3. Securities other than shares
  a. Short-term
    i. Nonfinancial corporations
    ii. Financial corporations
    iii. Central government
    iv. State and local governments
    v. Other resident sectors
  b. Long-term
    i. Nonfinancial corporations
    ii. Financial corporations
    iii. Central government
    iv. State and local governments
    v. Other resident sectors
	3. Securities other than shares
	  a. Short-term
	    i. Nonfinancial corporations
	    ii. Financial corporations
	    iii. Central government
	    iv. State and local governments
	    v. Other resident sectors
	  b. Long-term
	    i. Nonfinancial corporations
	    ii. Financial corporations
	    iii. Central government
	    iv. State and local governments
	    v. Other resident sectors

purposes the IIP groups financial instruments into functional categories. This makes reconciliation between the two accounts difficult. Table A4.4 provides a concordance between the eight categories of financial instruments in the *1993 SNA* and their attribution in the IIP. The extent to which instruments are separately identified in the two accounts varies, as is evident from the table. However, the balance of payments transaction data provide a greater degree of detail than the

---

Table A4.3 *(concluded)*

Financial Assets of Rest of World	Liabilities of Rest of World

4. Loans
  a. Short-term
    i. Nonfinancial corporations
    ii. Financial corporations
    iii. Central government
    iv. State and local governments
    v. Other resident sectors
  b. Long-term
    i. Nonfinancial corporations
    ii. Financial corporations
    iii. Central government
    iv. State and local governments
    v. Other resident sectors

5. Shares and other equity
  a. Resident enterprises
    i. Quoted
    ii. Not quoted

6. Insurance technical reserves
  6.1 Net equity of nonresident households in life insurance reserves and in pension funds
  6.2 Prepayments of premiums and reserves against outstanding claims

7. Financial derivatives
    i. Nonfinancial corporations
    ii. Households
    iii. Central government
    iv. State and local governments
    v. Other resident sectors

8. Other accounts receivable
  8.1 Trade credit and advances
    a. Nonfinancial corporations
    b. Households
    c. Central government
    d. State and local governments
    e. Other resident sectors
  8.2 Other
    a. Resident sectors

4. Loans
  a. Short-term
    i. Nonfinancial corporations
    ii. Financial corporations
    iii. Central government
    iv. State and local governments
    v. Other resident sectors
  b. Long-term
    i. Nonfinancial corporations
    ii. Financial corporations
    iii. Central government
    iv. State and local governments
    v. Other resident sectors

5. Shares and other equity
  i. Quoted
    i. Nonfinancial corporations
    ii. Financial corporations
    iii. Central government
    iv. State and local governments
    v. Other resident sectors
  ii. Not quoted
    i. Nonfinancial corporations
    ii. Financial corporations
    iii. Central government
    iv. State and local governments
    v. Other resident sectors

6. Insurance technical reserves
  6.1 Net equity of resident households in life insurance reserves and in pension funds
  6.2 Prepayments of premiums and reserves against outstanding claims

7. Financial derivatives
    i. Nonfinancial corporations
    ii. Households
    iii. Central government
    iv. State and local governments
    v. Other resident sectors

8. Other accounts payable
  8.1 Trade credit and advances
    a. Nonfinancial corporations
    b. Households
    c. Central government
    d. State and local governments
    e. Other resident sectors
  8.2 Other
    a. Nonresident sectors

IIP and so greater subdetail concordance with the *1993 SNA* flow accounts than there is between the stock measures. (See Table A4.5 of this appendix. The detailed presentation of balance of payments transactions is provided on pages 132–40 of *BPM5*.)

Monetary gold and SDRs

20. The *1993 SNA* does not separately identify monetary gold from SDRs (see Table A4.4), unlike the IIP, which separately identifies these financial assets within *reserve assets*. Gold is a component of

Table A4.4. Comparison of Breakdowns by Financial Instrument

1993 SNA Classification of Financial Instruments	1993 SNA Code	BPM5 Classification of Financial Instruments	IIP Code[1]
Monetary gold and special drawing rights	**AF.1**		
		Monetary gold	5.1 (RA)
		Special drawing rights (SDRs)	5.2 (RA)
Currency and deposits	**AF.2**	**Currency and deposits**	4.3 (OI)
Currency	AF.21		5.4.1 (RA, foreign exchange)
Transferable deposits	AF.22		5.3. (RA, RPF)
Other deposits	AF.29		5.5 (part of RA, other claims)
Securities other than shares	**AF.3**	**Debt securities**	1.2 (part of DI, other capital)
Securities other than shares		Money market instruments	2.2.1 (PI, debt securities)
Short-term	AF.31	Bonds and notes	2.2.2 (PI, debt securities)
Long-term	AF.32		5.4.2.2 (RA, foreign exch.)
			5.4.2.3 (RA, foreign exch.)
			5.5 (part of RA, other claims)
Loans	**AF.4**	**Loans**	4.2.1.2 (OI)
Short-term	AF.41	Short-term loans	4.2.2.2 (OI)
Long-term	AF.42		4.2.3.2 (OI)
			<u>4.2.4.2 (OI)</u>
		Long-term loans	4.2.1.1 (OI)
			4.2.2.1 (OI
			4.2.3.1 (OI)
			<u>4.2.4.1 (OI)</u>
			5.3 (part of RA, RPF)
Shares and other equity	**AF.5**		
		Reinvested earnings	1.1 (part of DI)
		Equity capital	1.1 (part of DI)
		Equity securities	2.1 (PI)
		Equities	5.4.2.1 (RA, for. exchange)
			5.5 (part of RA, other claims)
Insurance technical reserves	**AF.6**		4.4.1.1 (part of OI, other assets/liabilities, long term)
Net equity of households in life insurance reserves and in pension funds reserves	AF.61	Net equity of households in life insurance reserves and in pension funds	4.4.2.1 (part of OI, other assets/liabilities, long term)
Net equity of households in life insurance reserves	AF.611	Prepayments of premiums and reserves against outstanding claims	4.4.3.1 (part of OI, other assets/liabilities, long term)
Net equity of households in pension funds reserves	AF.612		4.4.4.1 (part of OI, other assets/liabilities, long term)
Prepayments of insurance premiums and reserves for outstanding claims	F.62		
Financial derivatives	**AF.7**	**Financial derivatives**	3 (FD)
			5.4.3 (RA)
Other accounts receivable/payable	**AF.8**		
Trade credits and advances	AF.81	Other claims on affiliated enterprises/other liabilities to affiliated enterprises	1.2 (part of DI other capital)
Other	AF.89	Other claims on direct investors/other liabilities to direct investors	1.2 (part of DI other capital)
		Trade credits (short- and long-term)	4.1 (OI)
		Other	4.4 (part of OI, other assets/liabilities)
		Short-term	
		Long-term	
Memorandum item			
Direct investment	**AF.m**		

Note: DI, direct investment; PI, portfolio investment; FD, financial derivatives; OI, other investment; RA, reserve assets; RPF, reserve position in the Fund.
[1]In the 1999 revision to the IIP, the financial derivatives functional category is included between the portfolio and other investment functional categories. This affects the numbering of other investment and reserve assets as compared with the published *BPM5*.

reserve assets if owned by the authorities (or by others who are subject to the effective control of the authorities) and held as a reserve asset. SDRs are international reserve assets created by the IMF to supplement other reserve assets. In the rest of the world balance sheet, monetary gold and SDRs are not regarded as liabilities of the rest of the world sector, although they are regarded as external assets of the domestic economy.

Currency and deposits

21. In the *1993 SNA* category, the *currency and deposits* category is subcategorized into *currency*, *transferable deposits*, and *other deposits* (see Table A4.4). Such a subcategorization is not provided in the IIP. However, for all sectors except the monetary authorities, for whom currency and deposit data are in reserve assets, the *1993 SNA* category may be derived from 4.3 in *other investment*.

Securities other than shares

22. The *1993 SNA* subcategorizes *securities other than shares* into short- and long-term (see Table A4.4). The same principle applies to the subcategorization in the IIP, although the subcategories are entitled *money market instruments*, and *bonds and notes*. However, the IIP allocates *securities other than shares* to direct investment and reserve assets if they meet the criteria to be included in those functional categories. For direct investment, a breakdown of *securities other than shares* by subcategories is not available.

Loans

23. In both accounts, data on loans are subcategorized into short- and long-term on the basis of original maturity (see Table A4.4). Within reserve assets, loans to the IMF are included.

Shares and other equity

24. The *1993 SNA* does not subcategorize *shares and other equity*, while the IIP provides information on *reinvested earnings*, *equity capital*, *equity securities*, and *equities* (see Table A4.4). As elsewhere, the IIP attribution is primarily on a functional category basis, so if shares and other equity meet the definition of direct investment or reserve assets they are included in these functional categories. Otherwise these instruments are included in portfolio investment.

Insurance technical reserves

25. In the *1993 SNA* the *insurance technical reserves* category is subcategorized into *net equity of households in life insurance reserves and in pension funds* and *prepayments of insurance premiums and reserves for outstanding claims* (see Table A4.4). There is no subcategorization included in the IIP, and indeed the whole category is indistinguishably included in the *other assets, other investment* category in the IIP. The different approach in the two accounts reflects the relative analytical importance of this category to the domestic sectors compared with the rest of the world sector: much insurance and pension fund activity is within an economy.

Financial derivatives

26. Following the 1999 revisions, both the *1993 SNA* and the IIP show separate categories for *financial derivatives* (see Table A4.4). However, the IIP also allocates *financial derivatives* to reserve assets if they meet the criteria to be included in this functional category.

Other accounts receivable/payable

27. In the *1993 SNA*, the category *other accounts receivable or payable* has two subcategories—*trade credits and advances* and *other* (see Table A4.4). In the IIP, *trade credit* is separately identified within *other investment*, with a breakdown between short- and long-term trade credits, on an original maturity basis. The *other* subcategory from the *1993 SNA* is included within the *other assets* subcategory of *other investment*, which has a breakdown between short- and long-term. Trade credit and other assets that meet the criteria are included within direct investment.

Core Principles

28. The core principles of the *1993 SNA*, the IIP, and this *Guide* are the same. The concepts of **residence** and **valuation** are identical. A resident is an institutional unit that has its center of economic interest in the economic territory of a country, while valuation of the position data is to be at prices current on the day to which the balance sheet refers—that is, the market price.[6] Both the *1993 SNA* and

---

[6]The *Guide* also defines nominal value (Chapter 2) and regards this method of valuation as central to debt analysis.

BPM5 provide specific as well as general guidance on valuation.[7]

29. The *1993 SNA* and IIP, as well as this *Guide*, follow the principle of **accrual accounting** in that transactions are recorded when economic value is created, transformed, exchanged, transferred, or extinguished. Claims and liabilities are deemed to arise when there is a change in ownership (that is, when both the creditor and debtor enter the claim and liability, respectively, on their books). By contrast, under the *cash basis* of recording, transactions are recorded only when payment is made or received. Under the *due-for-payment basis* of recording, a variation of the cash basis, transactions are recorded when receipts or payments arising from the transactions fall due.

30. The *1993 SNA* and *BPM5* recommend the same method for **converting** positions denominated in **foreign currencies** into the national currency or a single foreign currency, such as U.S. dollars: the use of the market exchange rates prevailing on the date to which the balance sheet relates—the midpoint between buying and selling spot rates—is recommended. The **maturity** concept used in both the *1993 SNA* and for the IIP is that of original maturity breakdown, albeit as a secondary classification criterion. Short-term financial assets are usually defined as those with an original maturity of one year or less, and in exceptional cases two years at maximum. Long-term financial assets are defined as having an original maturity of normally more than one year and in exceptional cases more than two years at maximum.

Discrepancies Between the Rest of the World Balance Sheet Account and the IIP

31. The main discrepancies between the rest of the world balance sheet in the *1993 SNA* and the IIP are in presentation, reflecting different analytical needs. As mentioned above, the IIP gives primacy in presentation to functional categories—such as direct investment—whereas the *1993 SNA* gives primacy to

Figure A4.4. Sectoral Breakdown in *1993 SNA* and in IIP

1993 SNA	IIP
Nonfinancial corporations (S.11)	Other sectors
Central bank (S.121)	Monetary authorities
Other depository corporations (S.122)	Banks
Other financial intermediaries (except insurance corporations and pension funds) (S.123) Financial auxiliaries (S.124) Insurance corporations and pension funds (S.125)	Other sectors
General government (S.13) • Central government (S.1311) • State government (S.1312) • Local government (S.1313) • Social security funds (S.1314)	General government
Households (including noncorporations) (S.14)	Other sectors
Nonprofit institutions serving households (S.15)	Other sectors

instrument and sector. In addition, the *1993 SNA* recommends the presentation of a broader range of institutional sectors than is recommended by *BPM5* for the IIP. Whereas the IIP presents data for up to four institutional sectors—monetary authorities, general government, banks, and other—the *1993 SNA* recommends that data be presented for five institutional sectors in the economy. In addition, the *1993 SNA* recommends the collection of subsector detail, unlike *BPM5*. The broad reconciliation between the *1993 SNA* and *BPM5* institutional sectors is presented in Figure A4.4.

32. As shown in the figure, two subsectors of *financial corporations* (central bank (S.121) and other depository corporations (S.122)) are related to the *BPM5* sectors *monetary authorities* and *banks*. However, the *monetary authorities* sector in the IIP includes not only the central bank but also the operations of other government institutions or commercial banks when these operations are usually attributed to the central bank. As a consequence, the delimitation of the sector *general government* in the IIP is not necessarily identical to the *1993 SNA* definition, which recommends a further breakdown into the subsectors central, state, and local government, and social security funds.[8] The other sector in the IIP comprises non-

---

[7]For instance, see paragraphs 14.48–14.52 of the *1993 SNA*. Chapter V of *BPM5* notes the need to apply market price proxies or equivalents in situations in which a market price in its literal sense cannot be determined (for example, the possible case of transfer pricing that significantly distorts measurement in resource transfers between affiliated enterprises).

[8]Although, as noted above, the *1993 SNA* also recommends an alternative presentation of the subcategories of general government.

**Table A4.5. Correspondence of *1993 SNA* Tables with *BPM5* and IIP Components:[1]
Account V—Rest of the World Account, V.III—External Accumulation Accounts**

V.III.1: Capital Account

1993 SNA categories	Correspondence to balance of payments standard components [items], additional details and aggregates
Changes in assets	***Transactions in liabilities***
K.2 Acquisitions less disposals of nonproduced nonfinancial assets	Item 2.A.2 acquisition/disposal of nonproduced nonfinancial assets
B.9 Net lending (+)/net borrowing (−)	Sum of items 1. Current account balance; and 2.A. Capital account balance
Changes in liabilities and net worth	***Transactions in assets***
B.12 Current external balance	Item 1. Current account
D.9 Capital transfers receivable	Item 2.A.1 Capital transfers
D.9 Capital transfers payable	Item 2.A.1 Capital transfers
B.10.1 Changes in net worth due to saving and net capital transfers	Sum of items 1. Current account balance; and 2.A.1 Net capital transfers

V.III.2: Financial Account[2]

Changes in assets	***Transactions in liabilities***
F.1 Monetary gold and SDRs	Sum of items 2.B.5.1 monetary gold; and 2.B.5.2 special drawing rights (with sign reversed[3])
F.2 Currency and deposits	Item 2.B.4.2.3 currency and deposits
F.3 Securities other than shares	Sum of items 2.B.1.1.3.2.1 debt securities issued by direct investor; 2.B.1.2.3.2.1 debt securities issued by affiliated enterprises; 2.B.2.2.2 debt securities (part of portfolio investment)
F.4 Loans	Item 2.B.4.2.2 loans
F.5 Shares and other equity	Sum of items 2.B.1.1.1.2 equity capital: liabilities to affiliated enterprises (part of direct investment abroad); 2.B.1.2.1.2 equity capital: liabilities to direct investors (part of direct investment in the reporting economy); 2.B.1.2.2 reinvested earnings (part of direct investment in the reporting economy); and 2.B.2.2.1 equity securities (part of portfolio investment)
F.6 Insurance technical reserves	Sum of items 2.B.4.2.4.4.1.1 net equity of households in life insurance reserves and in pension funds; and 2.B.4.2.4.1.1.2 prepayments of premiums and reserves against outstanding claims
F.7 Financial derivatives	2.B.3.2 liabilities (financial derivatives)
F.8 Other accounts receivable	Sum of items 2.B.1.1.3.2.2 other liabilities of direct investors (part of direct investment abroad); 2.B.1.2.3.2.2 other liabilities to direct investors (part of direct investment in the reporting economy); 2.B.4.2.1 trade credits (part of other investment); 2.B.4.2.4 other liabilities; Minus items 2.B.4.2.4.4.1.1 net equity of households in life insurance reserves and in pension funds; and 2.B.4.2.4.4.1.2 prepayments of premiums and reserves against outstanding claims (all part of other investment)

Table A4.5 *(continued)*

V.III.2: Financial Account *(continued)*	
1993 SNA categories	Correspondence to balance of payments standard components [items], additional details and aggregates
Changes in liabilities and net worth	***Transactions in assets***
F.2 Currency and deposits	Sum of items 2.B.4.1.3 currency and deposits (part of other investment); 2.B.5.3.1 deposits (part of reserve position in the Fund); 2.B.5.4.1 currency and deposits (part of foreign exchange); and 2.B.5.5.1 currency and deposits (part of other reserve claims)

F.3 Securities other than shares	Sum of items
	2.B.1.1.3.1.1 debt securities issued by affiliated enterprises
	    (part of direct investment abroad);
	2.B.1.2.3.1.1 debt securities issued by direct investors
	    (part of direct investment in the reporting economy);
	2.B.2.1.2 debt securities (part of portfolio investment);
	2.B.5.4.2.2 bonds and notes (part of foreign exchange);
	2.B.5.4.2.3 money market instruments and financial derivatives
	    (part of foreign exchange); and
	2.B.5.5.2.2 debt securities (part of other reserve claims)

F.4 Loans	Sum of items 2.B.4.1.2 loans (part of other investment); and 2.B.5.3.2 loans (part of reserve position in the Fund)

F.5 Shares and other equity	Sum of items
	2.B.1.1.1.1 equity capital: claims on affiliated enterprises
	    (part of direct investment abroad);
	2.B.1.1.2 reinvested earnings (part of direct investment abroad);
	2.B.1.2.1.1 equity capital: claims on direct investors
	    (part of direct investment in the reporting economy);
	2.B.2.1.1 equity securities (part of portfolio investment); and
	2.B.5.4.2.1 and 2.B.5.5.2.1 equities
	    (part of reserve assets, foreign exchange, and other claims)

F.6 Insurance technical reserves	Sum of items
	2.B.4.1.4.4.1.1 net equity of households in life insurance reserves and in pension
	    funds;
	2.B.4.1.4.1.1.1; 2.B.4.1.4.2.1.1; 2.B.4.1.4.3.1.1; and
	2.B.4.1.4.4.1.2 prepayments of premiums and reserves against outstanding claims
	    (all part of other investment)

F.7 Financial derivatives	Sum of items 2.B.3.1 assets (financial derivatives), and 2.B.5.4.3 financial derivatives (part of foreign exchange)

F.8 Other accounts payable	Sum of items
	2.B.1.1.3.1.2 other claims on affiliated enterprises (part of direct investment abroad);
	2.B.1.2.3.1.2 other claims on direct investors
	    (part of direct investment in the reporting economy);
	2.B.4.1.1 trade credits (part of other investment);
	2.B.4.1.4 other assets;
	
	Minus tems
	2.B.4.1.4.4.1.1 net equity of households in life insurance reserves and in pension
	    funds;
	2.B.4.1.4.1.1.1; 2.B.4.1.4.2.1.1; 2.B.4.1.4.3.1.1; and
	2.B.4.1.4.4.1.2 prepayments of premiums and reserves against outstanding claims
	    (all part of other investment)

B.9 Net lending (+)/net borrowing (−)	

Table A4.5 (concluded)

V.III.3: Other Changes in Assets Accounts, V.III.3.1: Other Changes in Volume of Assets Account

1993 SNA categories	Correspondence to balance of payments standard components [items], additional details and aggregates
Changes in assets	***Changes in liabilities***
K.7 Catastrophic losses	Catastrophic losses (part of other adjustments)
K.8 Uncompensated seizures	Uncompensated seizures (part of other adjustments)
K.10 Other volume changes in financial assets and liabilities, n.e.c.	Other volume changes (part of other adjustments)
K.12 Changes in classifications and structure	Change in classifications and structure (part of other adjustments)
Changes in liabilities and net worth	***Changes in assets***
K.7 Catastrophic losses	Catastrophic losses (part of other adjustments)
K.8 Uncompensated seizures	Uncompensated seizures (part of other adjustments)
K.10 Other volume changes in financial assets and liabilities, n.e.c.	Other volume changes (part of other adjustments)
K.12 Changes in classifications and structure	Change in classifications and structure (part of other adjustments)
B.10.2 Changes in net worth due to other changes in volume of assets	
Changes in assets	***Changes in liabilities***
K.11 Nominal holding gains/losses in financial assets	Sum of entries in the columns for price and exchange rate changes
K.11.1 Neutral holding gains/losses in financial assets	Sum of entries in the columns for neutral holding gains/losses
K.11.2 Real holding gains/losses in financial assets	Sum of entries in the columns for real holding gains/losses
Changes in liabilities and net worth	***Changes in assets***
K.11 Nominal holding gains/losses in liabilities	Sum of entries in the columns for price and exchange rate changes
K.11.1 Neutral holding gains/losses in liabilities	Sum of entries in the columns for neutral holding gains/losses
K.11.2 Real holding gains/losses in liabilities	Sum of entries in the columns for real holding gains/losses
B.10.3 Changes in net worth due to nominal holding gains/losses	Price and exchange rate changes in assets less price and exchange rate changes in liabilities
B.10.31 Changes in net worth due to neutral holding gains/losses	Neutral holding gains/losses in assets less neutral holding gains/losses in liabilities
B.10.32 Changes in net worth due to real holding gains/losses	Real holding gains/losses in assets less real holding gains/losses in liabilities

[1] The assets of the rest of the world sector in the *1993 SNA* correspond with the liabilities in the balance of payments and the IIP, and vice versa.

[2] The detailed presentation of balance of payments transactions that is used for this comparison with the *1993 SNA* financial instrument categories is provided on pp. 132–40 of *BPM5*. Due to the introduction of financial derivatives as a separate category in the *1993 SNA* and a separate functional category in *BPM5*, some series have been renumbered since the publication of these manuals.

[3] The domestic sector has a "claim" on the rest of the world sector.

financial corporations (S.11), some subsectors of financial corporations such as other financial intermediaries (S.123), financial auxiliaries (S.124), as well as insurance corporations and pension funds (S.125), households (S.14), and NPISH (S.15).

Detailed Examination of the Classification Linkages Among the Rest of the World Account, the Balance of Payments Accounts, and the IIP

33. Although harmonization in concepts has been attained between both systems, differences in presentation reflect differences in analytical require-

ments, the relative quantitative significance of some items in international transactions, and constraints imposed by the internal structures of the respective accounts. Nonetheless, bridges can be constructed to derive relevant national accounting flows and stocks from balance of payments accounts and the international investment position.

34. In terms of transactions, the *1993 SNA* distinguishes the following accounts in respect of the rest of the world account of goods and services:
- Account V.I: External account of goods and services (page 316 of the *1993 SNA*);
- Account V.II: External account of primary incomes and current transfers (page 316);

Table A4.6. Correspondence of *1993 SNA* Tables with *BPM5* and IIP Components:
Account V—Rest of the World Account, V.IV—External Assets and Liabilities Account

---

V.IV.1: Opening Balance Sheet

1993 SNA categories	Correspondence to international investment position standard components and additional details
AF Financial assets	Sum of items B.1.1.2 liabilities (equity capital and reinvested earnings) to direct investors (part of direct investment in the reporting economy); B.1.2.2 liabilities (other capital) to direct investors (part of direct investment in the reporting economy); A.1.1.2 liabilities (equity capital and reinvested earnings) to affiliated enterprises (part of direct investment abroad); A.1.2.2 liabilities (other capital) to affiliated enterprises (part of direct investment abroad); B.2 portfolio investment; and B.3 financial derivatives; and B.4 other investment.
AF Liabilities	Sum of items A.1.1.1 claims (equity capital and reinvested earnings) on affiliated enterprises (part of direct investment abroad); A.1.2.1 claims (other capital) on affiliated enterprises (part of direct investment abroad); B.1.1.1 claims (equity capital and reinvested earnings) (part of direct investment in the reporting economy); B.1.2.1 claims (other capital) on direct investors (part of direct investment in the reporting economy); A.2 portfolio investment; A.3 financial derivatives; and A.4 other investment; and A.5 reserve assets.[1]
B.90 Net worth	

V.IV.2: Changes in Balance Sheet

AF Total changes in financial assets	Sum of transactions, price and exchange rate changes, and other adjustments in respect of the corresponding international investment position items identified in account V.IV.1.
AF Total changes in liabilities	Sum of transactions, price and exchange rate changes, and other adjustments in respect of the corresponding international investment position items identified in account V.IV.1.
B.10 Changes in net worth, total	Total changes in assets – total changes in liabilities.

V.IV.3: Closing Balance Sheet

AF Financial assets	Sum of end of period values of corresponding items in the international investment position and identified in Account V.IV.1.
AF Liabilities	Sum of end of period values of corresponding items in the international investment position and identified in Account V.IV.1.
B.90 Net worth	

[1]Monetary gold and SDRs are components of reserve assets that have no counterpart liability in the rest of the world sector of the national accounts.

- Account V.III.1: Capital account (page 316) and V.III.2: Financial account (page 317), which are components of V.III: External accumulation accounts (page 316).

In *BPM5*, the transactions reflected in Accounts V.I and V.II are those in the current account component of the balance of payments accounts, while those reflected in Account V.III.1 are contained in the capital account component of the capital and finan-cial account of the balance of payments. The flows reflected in V.III.2 are shown in the financial account component of the capital and financial account. Account V.III.3.1: Other changes in volume of assets (page 317) and Account V.III.3.2: Revaluation account (page 317) are included within the IIP statement in *BPM5*, in order to reconcile the transactions between reporting dates with the change in positions. Thus, Account V.III.3.1 corre-sponds to the column for "other adjustments" in the IIP statement, while Account V.III.3.2 corresponds to the columns for "price changes" and "exchange rate changes" in the IIP statement. Account V.IV: External assets and liabilities account (page 318) is equivalent to the IIP statement in *BPM5*.

35. Tables A4.5 and A4.6 (on preceeding page) provide reconciliation between the categories shown in the relevant capital and financial accounts for the external sector of the *1993 SNA* and corresponding items in balance of payments accounts and the IIP. The major elements of the *1993 SNA* capital account of the external accumulation accounts (Table A4.5, Account V.III.1) are identical with the capital account component of the capital and financial account of the balance of payments. Although the balancing item, net lending/net borrowing, in the capital account of the *1993 SNA* is not explicitly identified in the balance of payments, it nonetheless can be derived by adding the current account balance and the balance of transactions reflected in the capital account of *BPM5*.

36. Coverage of the *1993 SNA* financial account (Table A4.5, Account V.III.2) is identical with the coverage of the financial account of the capital and financial account in the balance of payments, although the level of detail is different. As noted above, in the *1993 SNA* the primary focus is on financial instruments, whereas in the balance of payments the primary focus is on functional categorization (that is, direct investment, portfolio investment, financial derivatives, other investment, and reserve assets). In addition to identifying types of financial instruments (insurance technical reserves being an exception), the balance of payments includes an abbreviated sector breakdown (that is, monetary authorities, general government, banks, and other). Furthermore, to conform with the *1993 SNA*, *BPM5* states that entries in the credit and debit sides of the financial account of the balance of payments are recorded, in principle, on a net basis (that is, increases less decreases in assets or liabilities). However, gross recording is recommended as supplementary information, such as in the case of drawings and repayments on long-term loans.

Appendix V. Heavily Indebted Poor Countries (HIPC) Initiative and Debt Sustainability Analysis

1. The Heavily Indebted Poor Countries (HIPC) Initiative is a major initiative of consequence to the monitoring of external debt position. The objective of this Initiative is to reduce external debt positions of some low-income countries to sustainable levels—that is, to levels that enable them to meet their current and future external debt-service obligations in full, without recourse to debt rescheduling or accumulation of arrears, and without compromising growth. Among other things, this requires accurate measurement of the external debt position. In this appendix, the HIPC Initiative is described, along with Debt Sustainability Analysis (DSA), a building block of the HIPC Initiative.

HIPC Initiative

Origin and Description of the HIPC Initiative

2. For a number of low-income countries, it was recognized in the second half of the 1990s, by official creditors in particular, that the external debt situation was becoming extremely difficult. For such countries, even full use of traditional mechanisms of rescheduling and debt reduction—together with continued provision of concessional financing and pursuit of sound economic policies—would not be sufficient to attain sustainable external debt levels within a reasonable period of time and without additional external support. The HIPC Initiative is a comprehensive, integrated, and coordinated framework developed jointly by the IMF and the World Bank to address these external debt problems of the HIPCs. The framework was adopted in September 1996, through its endorsement by the Interim and Development Committees of the IMF and World Bank. Following a comprehensive review launched in early 1999, the Initiative was enhanced in September 1999 to provide faster, deeper, and broader debt relief, and to strengthen the links between debt relief, poverty reduction, and social policies.

3. The Initiative is designed to enable HIPCs that have a strong track record of economic adjustment and reform to achieve a sustainable debt position over the medium term. Central to the Initiative are the country's continued efforts toward macroeconomic and structural adjustment and social reforms, with an emphasis on poverty reduction. Thus, all countries requesting HIPC Initiative assistance must (1) have adopted a Poverty Reduction Strategy Paper (PRSP) through a broad-based participatory process, by the decision point (see below), and (2) have made progress in implementing this strategy for at least one year by the completion point (see below).[1] These efforts are complemented by a commitment from the international financial community to tackle the country's external debt problem in a comprehensive and coordinated fashion. Indeed, the Initiative requires the participation of all creditors—bilateral, multilateral, and commercial.

Eligibility Criteria and the Structure of the HIPC Initiative

4. To receive assistance under the HIPC Initiative, countries need to be both eligible and face unsustainable external debt positions. To be eligible, a country needs to have satisfied a set of criteria. Specifically, it must:
- Be eligible for concessional assistance from the IMF and World Bank;
- Face an unsustainable debt burden, beyond existing, traditional debt-relief mechanisms;[2] and

---

[1]On a transitional basis, given the time country authorities need to prepare a participatory PRSP, countries can reach their decision points based on an interim PRSP (I-PRSP), which sets out the government's commitment to and plans for developing a PRSP.

[2]Such as a Paris Club stock-of-debt operation on a Naples terms 67 percent present value reduction with at least comparable action from bilateral creditors. Table 8.2 in Chapter 8 sets out the evolution of Paris Club rescheduling terms.

• Establish a track record of reform and sound policies through IMF- and World Bank-supported programs.

5. The sustainability of the external debt position is determined by comparing the outcome of a comprehensive loan-by-loan DSA, agreed both with the authorities and creditors, with the HIPC targets. At the time of writing, these targets are set at 150 percent for the present value of the ratio of debt to exports, and 15 percent for the ratio of debt service to exports. For very open economies (with an exports-to-GDP ratio of at least 30 percent) that have a heavy fiscal burden of debt despite strong efforts to generate revenue (indicated by a ratio of fiscal revenue to GDP of at least 15 percent), the present value of debt-to-exports target can be lower than 150 percent and is set so as to achieve a 250 percent ratio of the present value of debt to fiscal revenue at the decision point.[3]

6. The IMF and World Bank Executive Boards determine need, and commit assistance, at the decision point. Those institutions and some other creditors also start delivering part of their assistance between the decision and completion points (interim relief).[4] Assistance is provided, irrevocably by all creditors, at (or before) the completion point—subject, as mentioned above, to the country implementing a set of key, predefined structural reforms.[5] Thus, there is an incentive for countries to implement reforms quickly, and so develop ownership over the timetable. Figure A5.1 sets out the process in diagrammatical form.

Calculations of Overall Assistance

7. Assistance under the HIPC Initiative is defined as the present value reduction required to lower external debt at the decision point to the Initiative's targets.

---

[3]The export denominator is derived as the "backward-looking" three-year average of exports of goods and services (*BPM5* definition) over the latest actual data that will be available at the decision point. The fiscal revenue denominator, if used, is the latest actual end-of-period figure, and is defined as central government revenue (excluding grants).

[4]Bilateral and commercial creditors are generally expected to reschedule obligations coming due. There are limits to the maximum assistance that the IMF and World Bank can provide during the interim period.

[5]A number of key elements or triggers are identified that would adequately represent overall progress in macroeconomic, structural, and social areas, and that would eventually translate into durable growth, debt sustainability, and poverty reduction.

Total assistance is defined as assistance at the completion point plus the action provided during the interim period. The external debt position calculation under the HIPC Initiative (or net present value, NPV, calculation of external debt as it is described in HIPC terminology)[6] is the sum of all future debt-service obligations (interest and principal) on existing debt on a loan-by-loan basis, discounted at the market interest rate (the Commercial Interest Reference Rate, CIRR, from the OECD). So for concessional lending, the calculation results in a present value of debt less than its nominal value, because the interest rate on the loan is less than the market rate. The calculation of the external debt position at the decision point uses the latest actual end-of-period data available, measured after assuming a hypothetical Paris Club stock-of-debt operation on Naples terms (67 percent reduction on eligible debt) and comparable treatment on other official bilateral and commercial claims.

Burden-Sharing Among Creditors and Delivery of Assistance

8. One of the Initiative's guiding principles is broad and equitable participation of all creditors (multilateral, official bilateral, and commercial) in providing assistance sufficient for the country to achieve debt sustainability. For the Paris Club, this generally involves a stock-of-debt operation with a reduction of up to 90 percent in the present value of eligible claims. The country is required to seek at least comparable treatment from its other official bilateral and commercial creditors.

9. Multilateral creditors take action proportional to bilateral creditors to reduce the present value of their claims on the country. Each multilateral institution chooses the vehicle to deliver its share of assistance (derived in proportion to its share in the present value of multilateral claims at the decision point). The IMF's contribution is made in the form of grants financed from Poverty Reduction and Growth Facility (PRGF) resources[7] and is used only to meet debt-

---

[6]While the term NPV is commonly used, frequently it would be more accurate to describe the calculation as present value—discounting future interest and principal payments by an interest rate—and this is the approach taken in the *Guide*.

[7]The PRGF is available to those countries that are facing protracted balance of payments problems and are eligible to borrow on concessional terms under the International Development Association (IDA). Previous to November 1999, the PRGF was known as the Enhanced Structural Adjustment Facility (ESAF).

Figure A5.1. Enhanced HIPC Initiative Flow Chart

First Stage

- Country establishes three-year track record of good performance and develops together with civil society a Poverty Reduction Strategy Paper (PRSP); in early cases, an Interim PRSP may be sufficient to reach the decision point.
- Paris Club provides flow rescheduling on Naples terms, i.e., rescheduling of debt service on eligible debt falling due (up to 67 percent reduction on a net present value (NPV) basis).
- Other bilateral and commercial creditors provide at least comparable treatment.[1]
- Multilateral institutions continue to provide adjustment support in the framework of World Bank- and IMF-supported adjustment programs.

Either ← **Decision Point** → *Or*

Paris Club stock-of-debt operation under Naples terms and comparable treatment by other bilateral and commercial creditors **is adequate** for the country to reach external debt sustainability. ========> **Exit** (Country does not qualify for HIPC Initiative assistance.)	Paris Club stock-of-debt operation under Naples terms and comparable treatment by other bilateral and commercial creditors **is not sufficient** for the country to reach external debt sustainability. ========> **World Bank and IMF Boards** determine eligibility for assistance.

All creditors (multilateral, bilateral, and commercial) commit debt relief to be delivered at the floating completion point. The amount of assistance depends on the need to bring the debt to a sustainable level. This is calculated based on latest available data at the decision point.

Second Stage

- Country establishes a second track record by implementing the policies determined at the decision point (which are triggers to reaching the floating completion point) and linked to the (Interim) PRSP.
- World Bank and IMF provide interim assistance.
- Paris Club provides flow rescheduling on Cologne Terms (90 percent debt reduction on NPV basis or higher if needed).
- Other bilateral and commercial creditors provide debt relief on comparable terms.[1]
- Other multilateral creditors provide interim debt relief at their discretion.
- All creditors and donors continue to provide support within the framework of a comprehensive poverty reduction strategy designed by governments, with broad participation of civil society and donor community.

"Floating Completion Point"

- Timing of completion point for nonretroactive HIPCs (i.e., those countries that did not qualify for treatment under the original HIPC Initiative) is tied to at least one full year of implementation of a comprehensive poverty reduction strategy, including macroeconomic stabilization policies and structural adjustment. For retroactive HIPCs (those countries that did qualify under the original HIPC Initiative), the timing of the completion point is tied to the adoption of a comprehensive PRSP.
- All creditors provide the assistance determined at the decision point; interim debt relief provided between decision and completion points counts toward this assistance.
- All groups of creditors provide equal reduction (in NPV terms) on their claims as determined by the sustainability target. This debt relief is provided with no further policy conditionality.
    - Paris Club provides stock-of-debt reduction on Cologne terms (90 percent NPV reduction or higher if needed) on eligible debt.
    - Other bilateral and commercial creditors provide at least comparable treatment on stock of debt.[1]
    - Multilateral institutions provide debt relief, each choosing from a menu of options, and ensuring broad and equitable participation by all creditors involved.

---

[1]Recognizing the need for flexibility in exceptional cases.

service obligations to the IMF. The European Union provides grants.

10. The World Bank is committed to take action after the decision point—through the selective use of IDA grants and allocations—and at the completion point. The principal vehicle for the Bank's participation, together with some other multilateral creditors, is the HIPC Trust Fund. This Trust Fund provides relief to eligible countries on debt owed to participating multilaterals and is administered by IDA, with contributions from participating multilateral creditors and bilateral donors. To provide relief on debt owed to IDA, the Bank made transfers from its IBRD net income and surplus to the HIPC Trust Fund.

11. The debt contracted with multilateral and bilateral creditors, covered by the HIPC Initiative, is limited to public and publicly guaranteed debt—that is, external obligations of a public debtor including national government and autonomous public bodies and external obligations of a private debtor that are guaranteed for repayment by a public entity. The debt comprises:

- All medium- and long-term government and government-guaranteed external debt;
- Short-term debt[8] only if it has long been in arrears;
- Debt of public enterprises defined as "at least 50 percent owned by the government"; and
- Debt of public enterprises being privatized, if the debt remains with the government.

Treatment of Arrears

12. Countries seeking assistance under the HIPC Initiative need to work toward elimination or reduction of existing arrears and the nonaccumulation of new external payments arrears. All arrears to multilateral creditors are expected to be cleared, or included in an agreement on a schedule for their clearance before the decision point is reached. However, clearance of such arrears needs to be consistent with a country's financing constraint. In addition, concessionality that is granted in arrears-clearance operations by multilateral banks can count toward assistance required under the Initiative, on a case-by-case basis.

Debt Sustainability Analysis (DSA)

13. DSAs are central to the work of the HIPC Initiative. DSAs are prepared, on a tripartite basis, jointly by the country authorities, the World Bank, and the IMF and, where appropriate, by the relevant regional development banks, such as the African Development Bank and the Inter-American Development Bank. Figure A5.2 sets out the DSA process in diagrammatical form.

DSA Process

14. In preparation for the decision point discussion, a DSA is carried out to determine the current external debt situation of the country. This is essentially a medium-term balance of payments projection that assesses the debt burden of the country and its capacity to service those obligations. If external debt ratios for that country fall above applicable targets after application of traditional debt-relief mechanisms, HIPC Initiative assistance is considered.

15. The DSA is undertaken on the basis of debt stock and flow projections. All the information needs to be obtained on a loan-by-loan basis, disaggregated by creditor and currency. The stock of debt is the amount outstanding at the end of the latest available fiscal or calendar year, depending on whether the country operated on a fiscal or calendar year basis. Projections of financial flows consist of expected amortization payments, disbursements on existing debt, and new loans.

16. Countries seeking assistance under the HIPC Initiative are expected to fully reconcile all debt data on a loan-by-loan basis with the creditor billing records before the decision point.[9] The reconciliation process refers to the position and flows. If a loan is amortized according to its original schedule (if there are no adjustments such as rescheduling, forgiveness, cancellations, supplemental commitments, arrears, or prepayments), the periodic flows depend mainly on the original terms of the loan. Any adjustments to the loan amount, such as write-offs or rescheduling, have to be taken into account, so that a reconciled debt service is agreed (and, by extension, the present value of the debt). The information needed by a HIPC country compiler is set out in Table A5.1.

---

[8]Debt that has an original maturity of one year or less.

[9]The preliminary HIPC document data might be on the basis of partially reconciled data.

Figure A5.2. Steps Toward a Debt Sustainability Analysis (DSA)

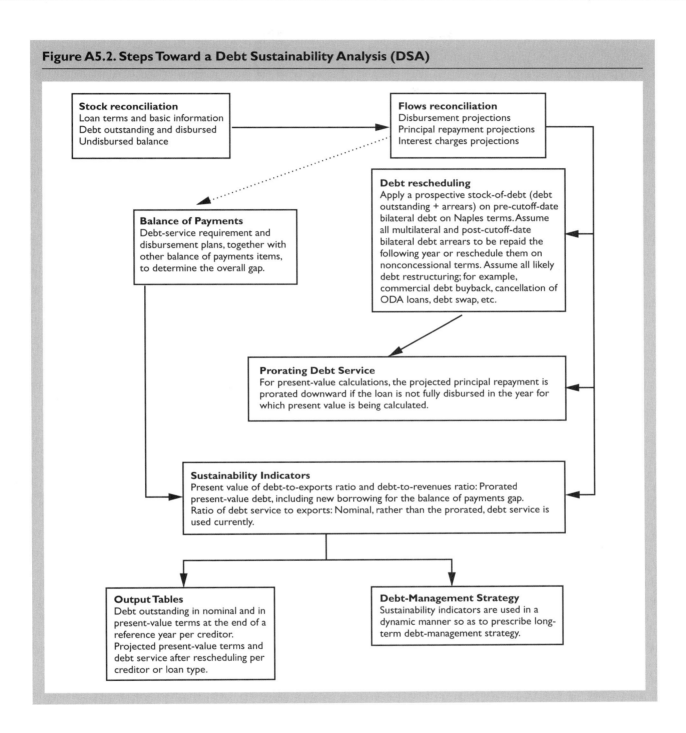

Stock reconciliation
Loan terms and basic information
Debt outstanding and disbursed
Undisbursed balance

Flows reconciliation
Disbursement projections
Principal repayment projections
Interest charges projections

Balance of Payments
Debt-service requirement and disbursement plans, together with other balance of payments items, to determine the overall gap.

Debt rescheduling
Apply a prospective stock-of-debt (debt outstanding + arrears) on pre-cutoff-date bilateral debt on Naples terms. Assume all multilateral and post-cutoff-date bilateral debt arrears to be repaid the following year or reschedule them on nonconcessional terms. Assume all likely debt restructuring; for example, commercial debt buyback, cancellation of ODA loans, debt swap, etc.

Prorating Debt Service
For present-value calculations, the projected principal repayment is prorated downward if the loan is not fully disbursed in the year for which present value is being calculated.

Sustainability Indicators
Present value of debt-to-exports ratio and debt-to-revenues ratio: Prorated present-value debt, including new borrowing for the balance of payments gap. Ratio of debt service to exports: Nominal, rather than the prorated, debt service is used currently.

Output Tables
Debt outstanding in nominal and in present-value terms at the end of a reference year per creditor. Projected present-value terms and debt service after rescheduling per creditor or loan type.

Debt-Management Strategy
Sustainability indicators are used in a dynamic manner so as to prescribe long-term debt-management strategy.

17. The consistency of stock and flow data on existing debt needs to be assessed. Simple equations can help the data compiler to complete this task, such as:

• The sum of future repayments of loan principal equals the outstanding debt (assuming no accrual of interest costs);

• The sum of future disbursements of loan principal equals the undisbursed balance; and

• For interest projections, egregious errors could be checked by calculating the implied interest rate (interest t/stock of debt $t - 1$) for a reference year and comparing it to the interest rate recorded in the original terms. For each loan there is a declining

---

Table A5.1. Data Needed by a HIPC Country Compiler

General information
— Debtor
— Debtor type (central bank, public enterprises, etc.)
— Creditor
— Creditor type (official, bilateral, commercial banks)
— Debtor loan identification
— Creditor loan identification
— Project title
— Loan type (supplier's credit, export credit, etc.)
— Date of signature
— Committed amount and currency of the loan
— Disbursed amount
— First and last date of amortization
— Grace period
— Maturity
— Interest rate and other charges (fixed or variable interest rate)
— Penalty on arrears
— Repayment schedule (equal installments, annuity, etc.)
— Cutoff date
— Grant element
— Identification of ODA loans

At the end of a period
— Stock of debt
— Arrears on principal (on a loan-by-loan basis)
— Arrears on interest
— Exchange rates at the end-of-period and average exchange rate of the year
— Average six-month CIRR rates

Disbursements
— On "pipeline" debt
— New debt

Macroeconomic data
— Gross domestic product
— Balance of payments
— Government finance statistics

Note: ODA, official development assistance; CIRR, Commercial Interest Reference Rate (OECD).

---

interest charge as the years progress and the debt stock is being reduced with each amortization.

18. Regarding new loans, given certain underlying assumptions, the expected financing gap on the balance of payments is projected. This is the baseline scenario. Assumptions have to be made about how the gap is to be filled—by grants, concessional loans, or commercial borrowing. The terms of any gap-filling loans can be assumed to be the same as the assumptions on new disbursement terms, or they can vary according to the assessment of willingness to fill the financing gap—if this is possible to assess. For instance, new borrowing to finance the gap can be

introduced into the DSA framework as two separate loans for each year. The first might be assumed to be available on IDA terms, while the remainder is secured at less concessional terms, but still at a concessional rate.

19. Interest charges on new borrowing enter the debt-service stream six months to one year after they are assumed to be committed, and the repayments of the principal become due after the grace period ended. So, for each year, the balance of payments financing gap is established, with any resultant new borrowing being fed back into DSA as a new loan. Hence, the balance of payments and the DSA data are obtained interactively over the projection period, and the new debt-service flows taken into account in calculating the present value[10] and debt-service indicators that are presented in the decision point document. This document is the basis for the Bank and IMF Boards' decisions on the eligibility and amount of assistance for the country.

20. Furthermore, sensitivity analysis is undertaken— the decision point document includes the results of alternative macroeconomic scenarios, thus providing a quantitative assessment of the impact of downside risks of the baseline balance of payments scenario. Modified assumptions are applied to external sector variables, such as international prices and trade volumes, and availability and terms of the financing items in the balance of payments. A modification to an assumption may have numerous direct and secondary effects on the balance of payments projections and the whole macroframework. In principle there are two ways for reflecting the impact of the envisaged shock. The first would be to capture only the immediate direct effect of any adverse shock on the balance of payments, which is reflected in lower credit entries or higher debit entries along with a higher additional financing gap. The additional financing gap would then be covered by new borrowing, which in turn would raise the debt ratios. This is normally the preferred approach for HIPC alternative scenarios.

21. The alternative approach takes into account secondary effects, such as slower economic growth, which would typically dampen the initial increase in the financing gap. For example, a significant short-

---

[10]Debt service on new borrowing did not affect the external debt position in the reference year used for decision point calculation of assistance.

fall in coffee exports would, in the first instance, cause a higher balance of payments financing gap. In addition, however, it would also lead to slower GDP growth and lower import demand, which would partially compensate for the initial increase in the financing gap. However, this approach is applied only in cases where the first approach implies highly unrealistic outcomes.

Interest Rate and Currency Assumptions Under the DSA

22. The currency-specific CIRR discount rates used in DSAs to calculate the present value of external debt are averages over the six-month period up to the reference date. For those currencies for which no CIRR rates are available but that are pegged to another currency, such as the U.S. dollar, the CIRR for the latter is used. In the absence of an exchange rate arrangement, as well as for the units of account used by various multilateral institutions, the SDR rate should be applied.

23. The present value of external debt is converted from its currency components into U.S. dollars using the actual end-of-period exchange rates—the same date as the reference date for the gross external debt position. These rates are applied to base-year calculations, as well as to projections. The conversion of debt-service payments in the numerator of the debt-service ratio is performed on the basis of average exchange rates using actual rates for the past and projections for the future taken from the IMF's *World Economic Outlook*.

24. For the purpose of determining a country's eligibility for the fiscal/openness criteria, central government revenue and GDP used in the revenue-to-GDP ratio (the three-year average) at the decision point are converted into U.S. dollars on the basis of actual average exchange rates in each of the three years. Projected central government revenue used to determine the NPV of the debt-to-revenue ratio at the completion point are converted by applying the latest end-of-period exchange rate available at the decision point.

Bibliography

Andrews, David, Anthony R. Boote, Syed S. Rizavi, and Sukhwinder Singh, 1999, *Debt Relief for Low-Income Countries: The Enhanced HIPC Initiative,* IMF Pamphlet Series, No. 51 (Washington: International Monetary Fund, 1999).

Australia, Department of Finance, Australian National Audit Office, annual, *Aggregate Financial Statement Prepared by the Minister of Finance* (Canberra: Australian Government Publishing Service).

Avramovic, Dragoslav and others, 1964, *Economic Growth and External Debt* (Baltimore, Maryland: Johns Hopkins University Press for the World Bank).

Bank of England, 1998, *Financial Terminology Database* (London).

Bank for International Settlements, quarterly, *International Banking and Financial Market Developments: Quarterly Review.*

———, 2000a, *Guide to the International Banking Statistics,* 7th ed. (Basel, Switzerland: BIS).

———, 2000b, *Report of the Working Group on the BIS International Banking Statistics.*

———, 2002, *Comparison of Creditor and Debtor Data on Short-Term External Debt* (Basel, Switzerland).

———, International Monetary Fund, Organisation for Economic Co-operation and Development, and World Bank, 1988, *External Debt: Definition, Statistical Coverage and Methodology* (Paris: OECD); the "Grey Book."

———, 1994, *Debt Stocks, Debt Flows and the Balance of Payments* (Paris: OECD).

Basel Committee on Banking Supervision, 1982, *Management of Banks' International Lending: Country Risk Analysis and Country Exposure—Measurement and Control* (Basel, Switzerland: Bank for International Settlements).

Berg, Andrew, Eduardo Borensztein, Gian-Maria Melesi-Ferretti, and Catherine Pattillo, 1999, *Anticipating Balance of Payments Crises: The Role of Early Warning Systems,* IMF Occasional Paper No. 186 (Washington: International Monetary Fund).

Blejer, Mario I., and Liliana Shumacher, 2000, "Central Banks Use of Derivatives and Other Contingent Liabilities: Analytical Issues and Policy Implications," IMF Working Paper 00/66 (Washington: International Monetary Fund).

Borensztein, Eduardo, and G. Pennacchi, 1990, "Valuation of Interest Payment Guarantees on Developing Country Debt," *IMF Staff Papers,* Vol. 37 (December), pp. 806–24.

Bussière, Matthieu, and Christian Mulder, 1999, "External Vulnerability in Emerging Market Economies: How High Liquidity Can Offset Weak Fundamentals and the Effects of Contagion," IMF Working Paper 99/88 (Washington: International Monetary Fund).

Calvo, Guillermo A., 1996, "Capital Flows and Macroeconomic Management: Tequila Lessons," *International Journal of Finance and Economics,* Vol. 1 (July), pp. 207–23.

———, and Pablo E. Guidotti, 1992, "Optimal Maturity of Nominal Government Debt: An Infinite Horizon Mode," *International Economic Review,* Vol. 33 (November), pp. 895–919.

Commission of the European Communities—Eurostat, International Monetary Fund, Organisation for Economic Co-operation and Development, United Nations, and World Bank, 1993, *System of National Accounts 1993* (Brussels/Luxembourg, New York, Paris, and Washington).

Committeri, Marco, 2000, "Effects of Volatile Asset Prices on Balance of Payments and International Investment Position Data," IMF Working Paper 00/191 (Washington: International Monetary Fund).

Cosio-Pascal, Enrique, 1997, *Debt Sustainability and Social and Human Development,* UNCTAD Discussion Paper No. 128 (Geneva: United Nations Conference on Trade and Development).

Davis, E.P., Robert Hamilton, Robert Heath, Fiona Mackie, and Aditya Narain, 1999, *Financial Market Data for International Financial Stability* (London: Centre for Central Banking Studies, Bank of England).

Efford, Don, 1996, "The Case for Accrual Recording in the IMF's Government Finance Statistics System," IMF Working Paper 96/73 (Washington: International Monetary Fund).

European Central Bank, 1999, *European Union Balance of Payments/International Investment Position Statistical Methods* (Frankfurt am Main).

Eurostat, 1996, *European System of Accounts: ESA 1995* (Luxembourg: Office for Official Publications of the European Communities).

————, 2000, *ESA95 Manual on Government Deficit and Debt* (Luxembourg: Office for Official Publications of the European Communities).

Forum for International Development Economics, 1998, *Measuring External Capital Flows to the Private Sector*, report prepared for the Macroeconomic and Financial Management Institute for Eastern and Southern Africa (Harare, Zimbabwe: FIDE International).

Furman, Jason, and Joseph E. Stiglitz, 1998, "Economic Crises: Evidence and Insights from East Asia," *Brookings Papers on Economic Activity: 2*, pp. 1–114.

Group of Twenty-Two Countries, 1998, *Report of the Working Group on Transparency and Accountability* (Basel, Switzerland: Bank for International Settlements).

India, Ministry of Finance, annual, *India's External Debt: A Status Report* (New Delhi).

Institute of International Finance, 1999, *Report of the Working Group on Transparency in Emerging Market Finance* (Washington).

International Monetary Fund, annual, *Balance of Payments Statistics Yearbook* (Washington).

————, monthly, *International Financial Statistics* (Washington).

————, 1986, *A Manual on Government Finance Statistics* (Washington).

————, 1992, *Report on the Measurement of International Capital Flows* (Washington).

————, 1993, *Balance of Payments Manual,* 5th ed. (Washington).

————, 1995, *Balance of Payments Compilation Guide* (Washington).

————, 1996a, *Balance of Payments Textbook* (Washington).

————, 1996b, *Coordinated Portfolio Investment Survey Guide* (Washington).

————, 1999, *Results of the 1997 Coordinated Portfolio Investment Survey* (Washington).

————, 2000a, *Analysis of the 1997 Coordinated Portfolio Investment Survey Results and Plans for the 2001 Survey* (Washington).

————, 2000b, *Debt- and Reserve-Related Indicators of External Vulnerability* (Washington, March 23); available on the Internet at http://www.imf.org/external/np/pdr/debtres/index.htm.

————, 2000c, *Financial Derivatives: A Supplement to the Fifth Edition (1993) of the Balance of Payments Manual* (Washington).

————, 2000d, *Monetary and Financial Statistics Manual* (Washington).

————, 2001, *Government Finance Statistics Manual 2001* (Washington).

————, 2002, *Coordinated Portfolio Investment Survey Guide,* 2nd ed. (Washington).

————, and Organisation for Economic Co-operation and Development, 2000, *Report on the Survey of Implementation of Methodological Standards for Direct Investment* (Washington).

International Monetary Fund, and World Bank, 2001, *Guidelines for Public Debt Management* (Washington).

Irwin, Timothy, M. Klein, G. Perry, and M. Thobani, eds., 1997, *Dealing with Public Risk in Private Infrastructure* (Washington: World Bank).

Kester, Anne Y., 2001, *International Reserves and Foreign Currency Liquidity: Guidelines for a Data Template* (Washington: International Monetary Fund).

Kiguel, Miguel, 1999, "Monitoring Financial Vulnerability" (unpublished; Buenos Aires: Argentina, Ministry of Finance and Public Works, June).

Kindleberger C.P., 1978, *Manias, Panics, and Crashes: A History of Financial Crises* (New York: Basic Books).

Klein, Thomas M., 1994, *External Debt Management: An Introduction,* World Bank Technical Paper No. 245 (Washington: World Bank).

Kumar, Raj, 1999, "Framework for Monitoring External Debt of Corporates Under Capital Account Liberalization," in *Corporate External Debt Management*, proceedings of a seminar held at Kathmandu, Nepal, compiled by The Credit Rating Information Services of India, Limited.

Krugman, Paul R., 1996, "Are Currency Crises Self-Fulfilling?" *NBER Macroeconomics Annual.*

Laliberté, Lucie, and Réjean Tremblay, 1996, "Measurement of Foreign Portfolio Investment in Canadian Bonds" (Ottawa: Statistics Canada).

Lucas, Robert E., and Nancy L. Stokey, 1983, "Optimal Fiscal and Monetary Policy in an Economy Without Capital," *Journal of Monetary Economics*, Vol. 106 (July), pp. 911–24.

Merton, Robert C., 1977, "An Analytical Derivation of the Cost of Deposit Insurance and Loan Guarantees," *Journal of Banking and Finance*, Vol. 1 (Suppl.), pp. 3–11.

Mody, Ashoka, and Dilip Patro, 1996, "Valuing and Accounting for Loan Guarantees," *World Bank Research Observer*, Vol. 11 (February), pp. 119–42.

New Zealand, Department of Finance, annual, *Budget Economic and Fiscal Update* (Wellington).

Obstfeld, Maurice, 1994, "The Logic of Currency Crises," *Cahiers Economiques et Monetaires* (Banque de France), No. 43, pp. 189–213; available also as NBER Working Paper No. 4640 (Cambridge, Massachusetts: National Bureau of Economic Research).

Oesterreichische Nationalbank, 1995, *Reports and Summaries, 1/1995* (Vienna).

————, 1999, *Focus on Austria, 1/1999* (Vienna).

————, 2000, *Balance of Payments Book of Austria* (Vienna).

Organisation for Economic Co-operation and Development, annual, *Development Co-operation Report* (Paris: OECD, Development Assistance Committee).

————, annual, *External Debt Statistics: Main Aggregates* (Paris).

————, annual, *Geographical Distribution of Financial Flows to Aid Recipients* (Paris).

———, 1996, *OECD Benchmark Definition of Foreign Direct Investment,* 3rd ed. (Paris).

———, 1999, *Handbook for Reporting Debt Reorganization on the DAC Questionnaire* (Paris).

Polackova Brixi, Hana, 1999, *Contemporary Approaches to the Analysis and Management of Government Risks* (Washington: World Bank).

Stephens, Malcolm, 1999, *The Changing Role of Export Credit Agencies* (Washington: International Monetary Fund).

Sundaresan, Suresh M., 2002, "Institutional and Analytical Framework for Measuring and Managing Government's Contingent Liabilities," in *Government at Risk*, pp. 99–122, ed. by Hana Polackova Brixi and Allen Schick (New York: Oxford University Press for the World Bank).

Towe, Christopher M., 1990, "Government Contingent Liabilities and the Measurement of Fiscal Impact," IMF Working Paper 90/57 (Washington: International Monetary Fund).

United Nations Conference on Trade and Development (UNCTAD), 1993, *Effective Debt Management,* UNCTAD/GID/DMS/15 (Geneva: UNCTAD, DMFAS Program).

———, 1998, *DMFAS Glossary,* UNCTAD/GID/DMFAS/Misc.3/Rev.2 (Geneva: UNCTAD, DMFAS Program).

———, 1999, *Proceedings of the Inter-Regional Debt Management Conference, December 1997,* UNCTAD/GDS/DMFAS/Misc.12 (Geneva: UNCTAD, DMFAS Program).

———, 2000, *DMFAS 5.2 Software, Hardware and Training Requirements,* UNCTAD/GID/DMFAS/MISC.6/Rev.5 (Geneva: UNCTAD, DMFAS Program).

World Bank, annual, *Global Development Finance* (Washington).

World Bank, annual, *World Development Report* (New York: Oxford University Press for the World Bank).

World Bank, 2000, *Debtor Reporting System Manual* (Washington).

Index

Numbers in references refer to paragraphs in chapters, boxes, or appendices.

Development Co-operation Report (OECD), 17.17
Direct investment, 3.14–3.18, 12.33
Direct reporting companies, 12.21
Disbursed and outstanding debt, 1.3–1.5
Disbursed loans, defined, App. III
Disbursements, defined, App. III
Discount bonds, App. I (Part 1)
Discounted instruments, interest cost accrual,
    2.74–2.76
Discounted principal, interest cost accrual, 2.64–2.65
DMFAS, *See* Debt Management and Financial Analysis
    System (UNCTAD)
DOD. *See* Disbursed and outstanding debt
Domestic currency
    defined, 6.12, App. III
    external debt composition, 6.12, 7.19–7.21
Domestic currency debt, 6.12
Domestic-currency-linked debt, 6.13
Domestic currency unit, 2.51
Domestically issued securities
    classification of, 6.21
    nonresident investment, 13.10–13.25
DRCs. *See* Direct reporting companies
DRS. *See* Debtor Reporting System
DSA. *See* Debt sustainability analysis
Dual-currency bonds, classification of, App. I (Part 1)
Due-for-payment recording, Box 2.1
Duration, defined, App. III

Early repayment provisions, projected payments, 6.33
ECB. *See* European Central Bank
Economic territory, defined, 2.14
EFF. *See* Extended fund facility
Eligible debt, defined, App. III
Eligible debt service, defined, App. III
Embedded derivatives, instruments with, 2.89
Enhanced concessions, defined, App. III
Enhanced Structural Adjustment Facility, defined,
    App. III
Enhanced Toronto terms, defined, App. III
Enterprise surveys
    agency coordination, 12.13
    census data, 12.14
    confirming data reliability, 12.20
    cross-border activity, 12.12
    debt statistics compilation, 12.11
    encouraging participation, 12.19
    form testing, 12.18
    group level approach, 12.15
    partial coverage collections, 12.14
    random samples, 12.14
    stratified random samples, 12.14
    survey development, 12.16–12.18
Equity, classification of, App. I (Part 1)
Equity capital
    defined, 3.16
    valuation, 2.49

Equity liabilities
    and external debt, 1.7
    memorandum tables, 4.12–4.13
Equity-linked bonds, classification of, App. I (Part 1)
Equity-linked derivatives, classification of, App. I (Part 1)
Equity securities
    defined, 3.23
    valuation, 2.48
Equity-warrant bonds, classification of, App. I (Part 1)
ESA95. See European System of Accounts: ESA 1995
ESAF. *See* Enhanced Structural Adjustment Facility
ESAF-HIPC Trust, defined, App. III
ESCB. *See* European System of Central Banks
Escrow accounts, defined, App. III
EU. *See* European Union
Eurobonds, restructuring, Box 8.1
European Central Bank, 19.5–19.8
European Commission, Box 14.1
European System of Accounts: ESA 1995, Box 14.1
European System of Central Banks, 19.5
European Union, statistics on the excessive deficit
    procedure, Box 14.1
Eurostat. *See* European Commission
Eurosystem, 19.5
Exceptional financing, defined, App. III
Exchange rate conversion, 2.52
Exchange rates, data collection, 11.14
Executive debt management, 11.20–11.21
Explicit contingent liabilities
    credit availability guarantees, 9.7–9.8
    credit guarantees, 9.6
    defined, 9.4
    loan guarantees, 9.5
    payment guarantees, 9.5
Export credit, defined, App. III
Export credit agencies
    defined, App. III
    reinsurance by, App. III
Exports
    debt-service-to-exports ratio, 15.21–15.25
    debt-to-exports ratio, 15.14–15.16
    present value of debt-to-exports ratio, App. III
Extended Fund Facility, defined, App. III
External debt
    accounting principles, 2.12–2.53, 6.1–6.36
    analysis of, 1.6–1.8, 16.1–16.39
    compatibility of data, 2.2
    composition of, 16.1–16.19
    creditor information, 16.37–16.39
    by creditor sectors, 7.40–7.43
    current liabilities, 2.10
    defined, 2.1, 2.3, App. III
    financial derivatives, 16.30–16.34
    foreign currency composition, 1.10
    gross external debt, 2.3, 4.1–4.15
    interest rate composition, 7.35–7.37
    loan drawings, 2.23